Writing Posthumanism, Posthuman Writing

NEW MEDIA THEORY
Series Editor, Byron Hawk

The New Media Theory series investigates both media and new media as complex rhetorical ecologies. The merger of media and new media creates a global public sphere that is changing the ways we work, play, write, teach, think, and connect. Because these ecologies operate through evolving arrangements, theories of new media have yet to establish a rhetorical and theoretical paradigm that fully articulates this emerging digital life.

The series includes books that deploy rhetorical, social, cultural, political, textual, aesthetic, and material theories in order to articulate moments of mediation that compose these contemporary media ecologies. Such works typically bring rhetorical and critical theories to bear on media and new media in ways that elaborate on a burgeoning post-disciplinary "material turn" as one further development of the linguistic and social turns that have already influenced scholarly work across the humanities.

BOOKS IN THE SERIES

Writing Posthumanism, Posthuman Writing, edited by Sidney I. Dobrin (2015)

Ready to Wear: A Rhetoric of Wearable Computers and Reality-Shifting Media by Isabel Pedersen (2013)

Mics, Cameras, Symbolic Action: Audio-Visual Rhetoric for Writing Teachers, by Bump Halbritter (2013). Computers and Composition Best Book Award 2014.

The Available Means of Persuasion: Mapping a Theory and Pedagogy of Multimodal Public Rhetoric, by David M. Sheridan, Jim Ridolfo, and Anthony J. Michel (2012)

Avatar Emergency by Gregory L. Ulmer (2012)

New Media/New Methods: The Academic Turn from Literacy to Electracy, edited by Jeff Rice and Marcel O'Gorman (2008)

The Two Virtuals: New Media and Composition, by Alexander Reid (2007). Honorable Mention, W. Ross Winterowd/*JAC* Award for Best Book in Composition Theory, 2007.

WRITING POSTHUMANISM, POSTHUMAN WRITING

Edited by Sidney I. Dobrin

Parlor Press
Anderson, South Carolina
www.parlorpress.com

Parlor Press LLC, Anderson, South Carolina, USA
© 2015 by Parlor Press
All rights reserved.
Printed in the United States of America on acid-free paper.

S A N: 2 5 4 - 8 8 7 9

Cataloging-in-Publication Data

Writing posthumanism, posthuman writing / edited by Sidney I. Dobrin.
   pages cm. -- (New Media Theory)
 Includes bibliographical references and index.
   ISBN 978-1-60235-429-6 (pbk. : acid-free paper) -- ISBN 978-1-60235-430-2 (cloth : acid-free paper) -- ISBN 978-1-60235-431-9 (adobe ebook) -- ISBN 978-1-60235-432-6 (epub) -- ISBN 978-1-60235-589-7 (kindle) -- ISBN 978-1-60235-590-3 (ibook)
 1. English language--Rhetoric--Study and teaching (Higher) 2. Human body and technology. 3. Authorship. 4. Human beings--Philosophy. 5. Postmodernism and education. I. Dobrin, Sidney I., 1967- editor.
 PE1404.W7294 2014
 808'.0420711--dc23
                        2014030387

1 2 3 4 5

New Media Theory
Series Editor: Byron Hawk

Cover image: "Red Spot" © 2013 by Gregory Glau. http://gglau.zenfolio.com. Used by permission.

Cover design by Jason Crider. "The difficulty with designing a cover for a book of this subject is that posthumanism covers such an enormous range of focuses. From theoretical discussions of nature and ecology, to the conceptualization of hybrid human technologies and digital identities, to remapping of literacy with procedural rhetorics, posthumanism isn't easy to put in a neat little box. It ranges from the cell to the cyborg and questions the traditional liberal humanist ideology of what it means to be "human." This cover works because of its abstract quality and because of its fluidity. Lines, colors, shapes and depth all blur and are difficult to define, much like traditional humanist classifications of reality. A common question in the posthuman imaginary is 'how do I define x?' and that is precisely the question I wanted to raise (or at the very least toy with) with this cover design."

Parlor Press, LLC is an independent publisher of scholarly and trade titles in print and multimedia formats. This book is available in paper, cloth and eBook formats from Parlor Press on the World Wide Web at http://www.parlorpress.com or through online and brick-and-mortar bookstores. For submission information or to find out about Parlor Press publications, write to Parlor Press, 3015 Brackenberry Drive, Anderson, South Carolina, 29621, or email editor@parlorpress.com.

Contents

1 Introduction   3
   Sidney I. Dobrin

2 Moving Beyond the Logic of Sacrifice: Animal Studies, Trauma Studies, and the Path to Posthumanism   19
   Lynn Worsham

3 Writing-Being: Another Look at the "Symbol-Using Animal"   56
   Diane Davis

4 Zombies / Writing: Awaiting Our Posthumous, Monstrous (Be)Coming   79
   Michelle Ballif

5 Wanting Ourselves: Writing (And) The Postsexual Subject   99
   Kate Birdsall and Julie Drew

6 Becoming T@iled   133
   Sean Morey

7 Inscriptions of the Possible; or, A Pedagogy of Posthumanist Style   155
   J. A. Rice

8 Rethinking Human and Non-Human Actors as a Strategy for Rhetorical Delivery   174
   Jim Ridolfo

9 Utopian Laptop Initiatives: From Technological Deism to Object-Oriented Rhetoric 192
    Byron Hawk, Chris Lindgren, and Andrew Mara

10 From Handwriting to 'Brain' Writing: Graphology and the Neuroscientific Turn 214
    Melissa M. Littlefield

11 I Am Spam; A Posthuman Approach to Writer's Block 234
    Kyle Jensen

12 Cyborg Vision for Cyborg Writing 254
    Kristie S. Fleckenstien

13 Evolutionary Equality: Neocybernetic Posthumanism and Margulis and Sagan's Writing Practice 275
    Bruce Clarke

Contributors 298

Index 303

Writing Posthumanism, Posthuman Writing

1 Introduction

Sidney I. Dobrin

Writing *Writing Posthumanism, Posthuman Writing*'s posthumanism identifies a moment of inquiry in which the human subject is called into question via its imbrications with technologies such as cybernetics, informatics, artificial intelligence, genetic manipulation, psychotropic and other pharmaceuticals, and other bio-technologies, as well as species interactions (as ventures in Animal Studies have begun to make evident). *Writing Posthumanism, Posthuman Writing* considers the non-human subject, the prosthetic subject, the technologically augmented subject, the psychic-altered subject, and the (becoming) animal subject in relation to writing. That is to say, the particular avenue of entrance into posthumanist inquiry is of less importance in this project than is that avenue's projection upon writing and writing studies. Ultimately, this collection asks as to the relationship between posthumanisms and writing toward the end of developing posthumanist theories of writing. Of course, some posthumanist theorists might argue that the very idea of posthumanist writing theories is a redundant concept as any writing theory is always already a posthumanist theory given that human interaction with technologies like writing are precisely the kinds of convergences that allow the becoming of the posthuman. Others—like Andy Clark in his book *Natural-Born Cyborgs: Minds, Technologies, and the Future of Human Intelligence*—might argue that technologies like writing are, in fact, what make us uniquely human. In any case—or any other case—it is within the theoretical possibilities of what the reciprocity between posthumanism and writing might reveal that this collection unfolds.

Toward this end, *Writing Posthumanism, Posthuman Writing* inevitably runs headlong into complications of definition and complexity, as any theoretical intervention is bound to do. Yet, within these complications lies the occasion for the emergence of this collection. Posthumanism and the posthuman are inextricably problematic concepts given both the breadth of approaches historically provided to describe them and the territories into which they intervene. Fundamentally, they function as amorphous umbrella terms for a variety of theories and critiques regarding human subjectivity. While some might find their shapelessness problematic, this collection embraces the complexities and nascence of the very idea of posthumanism and the posthuman as indicative of the rich potential of inquiry under the posthuman umbrella. In fact, within these pages, contributors provide more incentive to fragment the umbrella than to coalesce its subsumptions.

Traditionally, posthumanist inquiry has employed a number of classifications as an attempt to both explain its complexities and to control—or at least provide taxonomies of—its lines of inquiry. Most fundamentally, posthumanist inquiry can be divided between what Bart Simon has characterized as an unproductive division between a "popular and a more critical posthumanism" (2) or, as N. Katherine Hayles calls it, a "complacent posthumanism" and a more critical posthumanism. According to Simon, the popular approach to posthumanism is exemplified in Francis Fukuyama's 2002 book *Our Posthuman Future: Consequences of the Biotechnology Revolution*. There, Fukuyama argues that "the most significant threat posed by contemporary biotechnology is the possibility that it will alter human nature and thereby move us into a 'posthuman' stage of history" (7). For Fukuyama, this is important because "human nature exists, is a meaningful concept, and has provided a stable continuity to our experiences as a species" (7). *Our Posthuman Future* is, as Simon has characterized it "an impassioned defense of liberal humanism against contemporary cultures of laissez-faire individualism and unregulated corporate technoscience" (1). Citing Christopher Dewdney's *Last Flesh: Life in the Transhuman Era*, Simon summarizes popular posthumanism: "[W]e are on the verge of the next stage in life's evolution, the stage where, by human agency, life takes control of itself and guides its own destiny. Never before has human life been able to change itself, to reach into its own genetic structure and rearrange its molecular basis; now it can (qtd. in Simon 2). As Simon explains, "This popular posthumanist (sometimes transhumanist) discourse structures the research agendas of much of corporate biotechnology and informatics as well as serving as a legitimating narrative for new social entities (cyborgs, artificial intelligence, and virtual societies) composed of fundamentally fluid, flexible, and changeable identities. For popular posthumanism, the future is a space for the realization of individuality, the transcendence of biological limits, and the creation of a new social order" (2).[1]

On the other hand, as Jill Didur's "Re-embodying Technoscientific Fantasies: Posthumanism, Genetically Modified Foods, and the Colonization of Life" explains a more critical posthumanism: "a more radical notion of posthumanism can serve as a basis for critiquing what is essentially a disembodied colonial attitude toward the theory/practice of biotech research today" (100). Didur's more critical, more radical posthumanism calls into question not only various humanisms, but popular approaches to posthumanism, as well. Simon, for instance, critiques *Our Posthuman Future* as being a popular humanist text, noting its important engagement with posthuman concerns, but lacking the critical engagement to provide any serious intervention. The kind of critical intervention into posthumanism Simon and Didur initiate has been described by Catherine Waldby as "a general critical space in which the techno-cultural forces which both produce and undermine the stability of the categories of 'human' and 'nonhuman,' can be investigated" (qtd. in Simon 3).

Within this distinction between popular posthumanism and critical posthumanism, we witness another taxonomic convenience emerge: the distinction between posthumanism as addressing alterations in subject and body by way of technological interaction and the distinctions between human subject and non-human subjects. That is, traditional posthumanist inquiry often reduces its scope to following one of two paths: the technological or the biological. These divisions are, of course, not only problematic but down right fallacious. In the simplest cases, we can see this division dissolve within the realm of biotechnologies. More importantly, however, we can acknowledge the essentialism of these kinds of divisions once we recognize the biologic as technologic. Likewise, posthumanist definitions used to distinguish various approaches to posthumanism are inherently anthropocentric taxonomies. Evolution, which undergirds the very notion that posthumanism is something that can be addressed, is a technology; its status as such not called to question by transhumanist or posthumanist thinking, but emphasized. Such an acknowledgement allows, then, further recognition of all that might be categorized as operating outside of human subjectivity and human control as technological. The importance here is twofold: first, as posthumanism argues that technologies like evolution might now be controlled to influence evolutionary teleologies (the posthuman becoming/the transhuman), we should recognize that what have been assumed to be "natural" events and processes can equally be deemed technological. Second (and imbricated within the first), is that within writing studies the inextricably bound and nebulous relationship between subject and technology a) renders subjectivity inseparable from technology, thus rendering the writing subject indistinguishable from writing and b) exposes writing (and circulation) as saturating not just the intellectual inquiry surrounding posthumanism, but the very phenomenological encounters all subjects, human and non-human, posthuman and transhuman, have with the world, not to mention the very idea that there can even be something called "subjectivity." Such an understanding of technology lends to a rethinking of all technologies from the writing of genetic code and evolutionary circulation to the high-techne cyborg construction.

Within composition and rhetoric, discussions regarding posthumanism and the posthuman are by no means new. The figure of the cyborg, for example, has been taken up since the mid-1980s to the extent that it is an accepted and familiar referent throughout the field regarding the interaction between self and technology. Likewise, to some degree, the posthuman has been visible in the field's attention to identity and concepts of the Other. Despite its presence, though limited, posthumanism and the posthuman have appeared in our professional dialogue primarily in connection with conversations about writers and readers, not about writing. That is to say, the figure of the posthuman has been most useful to the field as a way of talking about subjects, bodies, and identity. In 2000, *JAC: A Journal of Rhetoric, Culture, and Politics,* published a special cluster devoted to "Posthuman Rhetorics." In their introduction to the cluster of five articles, guest editors John Muckelbauer and Debra Hawhee explain "posthumanism poses intriguing questions to many longstanding, 'self-evident' assumptions about rhetoric and communication, broadly conceived" (768) and ask as to the implications of these emerging questions for composition and rhetoric. The five essays that comprise the special cluster then attend to possibilities for engaging and producing posthuman rhetorics. Collin Gifford Brooke, for example, poses a dual question akin to one asked in *Writing Posthumanism, Posthuman Writ-*

ing: how does posthumanism affect discourse production and how/what does rhetoric contribute to the understanding of posthumanism? Brooke's inquiry demands that we reconsider the relationships between nature, culture, and subjectivity and suggests that posthumanism offers a "return to embodied information" and an increased attention to kairos (791). David J. Gunkle uses the model of the parasitic hacker to explore hacking as a way of thinking about teaching and discourse production. He "proposes a method of investigation that infiltrates, re-evaluates, and reprograms the systems that have shaped and delimited cyberspace" (798). Jeffery T. Nealon's contribution to the cluster turns to Nietzsche as a way of proposing a posthuman ethic for encountering third-wave capital. His inquiry turns not toward familiar questions regarding representation and capital, but to questions of power. He provides, then, a posthuman ethic for engaging capital. Richard Doyle's contribution to the cluster examines emerging technologies and their entanglement with the self as well as the role of science fiction and science in inquiries of intersections between organism and machine. Christina L. Harold argues that "humanist critiques of both oppressive and subversive rhetorics often assume an a priori unity, or sameness, that oppressive discourse conceals and subversive discourse reveals" (865) and that "if we conceive of bodies as unstable, fragmented, or even dispersed across a field of discourses—in other words, as posthuman . . . then we require a very different critical framework through which to account for their rhetorical force" (865).

In his award-winning 2007 book *A Counter-History of Composition: Toward Methodologies of Complexity,* Byron Hawk takes up posthumanism as a central part of his a method for establishing what he calls "complex vitalism" (158). Noting a distinction between theories of human action which "operate from an opposition between human intention as active and material context as static and passive, thus privileging human action" and a humanist model in which human action functions as part of the feedback loop, Hawk proposes a posthumanist model that "sees humans as functioning parts of life, and any theory of action or change must take this larger, more complex situatedness into account" (158). Hawk ties this posthumanist model to Deleuze and Guattari's desire to see any body "organic or inorganic, not as a whole but as a constellation of parts that participate in multiple systems" (158). Turning to the opening section of *Anti-Oedipus: Capitalism and Schizophrenia* called "The Desiring-Machines," Hawk brings

Deleuze and Guattari's notion of machines into the posthumanist perspectives as a means of showing not just the interaction between human and machine, but between the machines themselves, machines that are neither objects to be used by subjects nor objects that suppress subjects. Instead each machine is connected and is part. "Everything is Machine," Deleuze and Guattari explain (2). The human (though they use the word "man"), they continue, "does not live as nature, but as a process of production. There is no such thing as either man or nature now, only a process that produces one within the other and couples machines together. Producing-machines, desiring-machines everywhere, schizophrenic machines, all of species of life: the self and the non-self, outside and inside, no longer have any meaning whatsoever" (2). This is the basis for Deleuze and Guattari's posthumanism (though they don't employ the term), and tied with N. Katherine Hayles address of cognitive distribution and feedback loops, is the place from which Hawk establishes a posthumanist theory for Composition Studies. Through Deleuze and Guattari's posthumanism, Hawk is able to reposition the subject not as individual, but as part of the whole: "The subject is not a person, a whole, but a part of the whole that is made up of parts: it is part of the machine and also itself divided into cuts from the continuous material flow and parts of the detached signifying chain" (160). This kind of relationship between subjects and whole systems/networks is also taken up by others attending to complexity theories in Composition Studies, such as Edith Wyschogrod in "Newtorking the Unpredictable: The Lure of Complexity" in which she cites Jean-Pierre Dupuy's "subjectless processes in which 'the subject is not a ghost in the cerebral machine but the machine itself'" (871).

Hawk's objective in turning to posthumanism is to more fully develop a theory of complexity and as part of this task to develop a posthuman pedagogy for composition and rhetoric. Yet, embedded in his objective is a sophisticated theory of the subject that radically disrupts composition's traditional consideration of—and, I would argue, encumbrance with—the subject. He writes, "The subject, then, becomes a side effect of the pedagogical-machine that cannot be completely determined" (255). For Hawk, subjects are more akin to Geregory Ulmer's notion of the conductor; Hawk explains: "As conductors we are active initiators of movement and organization, passive conduits that allow discourses and forces to pass through and reconnect to other circuits and function in new machines, and participants in constellations that are co-responsible for our conduct. We are our accidents and our connections as much as our choices" (155). Hawk's posthumanism embarks on a Foucauldian recast of the subject not as anti-human, but as a collapse of seeing the subject as an individual and rather as an intricate complexity inseparable from technology and language.

While these kinds of discussions have situated posthumanist issues within composition studies, the conversations have been minimal despite what many see as their importance. Likewise, posthumanism enters composition and rhetoric with a substantial gaze directed toward subjects and identities, not with much attention to writing. The taxonomies used in such discussions are inevitably problematic and require concentrated theoretical dismantling. Admittedly, though, they do provide a convenient rhetorical structure for organizing the contributions to this collection. I acknowledge the convenience of making such editorial decisions and will claim I do so also to emphasize the problematics of such distinctions in light of my claims throughout this introduction regarding distinctions between various kinds of technologies, including biologies. Thus, *Writing Posthumanism, Posthuman Writing* begins its consideration of posthuman theories of writing with two pioneering interventions that bring Animal Studies and Writing Studies into conversation.

Lynn Worsham, in a ground-breaking contribution, situates animal studies within a question of violence and the powerful call to "relinquish, once and for all, the habit and the hubris of anthropocentrism and humanism and to broaden the sense of 'our time' to include the catastrophe that is the systematic and relentless and ongoing exploitation, abuse, and killing of nonhuman animals." For Worsham, animal studies "calls on us to see the deep and abiding connection between how we treat each other and how we treat nonhuman others." Worsham's treatment of the animal and posthumanism asks us to grapple with the often mind-boggling issue of violence. For Worsham, language, rhetoric, and writing stand at the center of the human/animal/violence convergence. As she explains, "the theory and practice of effective argumentation must be understood as forms of conceptual or symbolic violence—in other words, as part of the problem of human violence and not simply or simplistically as the antidote or alternative to violence, as classical rhetorical theorists proposed." More provocatively, then, Worsham also claims that "A posthuman perspective on language, rhetoric, and writing makes available the possibility that language may have arisen in human evolution as an adaptive response to a persistent and persistently overwhelming experience of the difficulty of reality: the struggle to survive in a dangerous and threatening environment."

Worsham's previous, extensive work in trauma theory informs an intervening theory of "deflection" in her contribution to this collection. *False witness* and *deflection*, concepts Worsham adapts from Robert Jay Lifton, allow humans to deflect their own fears of death onto others through violent acts. Posthumanist sensibility, Worsham suggests, might be a productive avenue for making sense of the often "difficult realities" of extreme acts of violence, including those that result from deflection and result in trauma. Worsham traces the history of such traumas in order to suggest that "many of our human ways of being bear the traces of what [Judith] Herman calls 'complex post-traumatic stress disorder,' which is a spectrum of conditions, rather than a single disorder, arising from prolonged, repeated trauma" and that "what we mean by 'human being' or 'human nature' might be understood as post-traumatic symptoms that have endured for thousands of generations, symptoms that are the legacy of our traumatic encounter with nonhuman animals." She challenges us, then, to move beyond anthropocentric humanism by way of a posthuman sensibility to counter the acts of deflection and violence with "arts of connection."

Working within Animal Studies, as well, D. Diane Davis, in her thought-provoking contribution, "Writing-Being: Another Look at the 'Symbol-Using Animal,'" establishes that "the posthuman scene of writing is not simply about the communication of a message; it is like any scene of writing, irreducible to humanist notions of 'authorship.'" Davis dismantles common perceptions of both writing and animal, and in the wake of the disassembly, she asks as to whether animal—any animal—is capable of writing. Such an inquiry is no simple task as what is at stake, Davis shows, is "the protection and continued promotion of the metaphysical distinction between language and life (or, if you prefer, between the symbolic and the real), and therefore between 'the human' and 'the animal.'" For Davis there can be no irreducible duality between life and language without defining "the latter as speech, sign or signifier" or more specifically, language as human language. Her agenda in such claims is not to mitigate difference, but to "expose a wild plurality of differences by zooming in on the metaphysical prejudice" that exists when, as Derrida puts it, we take up position between the human subject and the nonsubject: the animal. Life, that is, cannot be opposed to language. Davis unfolds her claims within two provocative situations of animal communication: communicative tool use among bonobos in the Congo and the collective communication of bees.

As noted, the categories we use to (over)simplify distinctions within posthumanism are inherently problematic. Michelle Ballif's "Zombies / Writing: Awaiting Our Posthumous, Monstrous (Be)Coming" straddles categories, considering the place between life and death which zombies occupy: not human, not animal, not alive, not dead, but monstrous—quite literally, post-human. The zombie, lacking consciousness, without mind, is subhuman; it lacks subjectivity, belonging instead to the horde, to the category of not-human. The zombie embodies the question "what does it mean to be human?" Ballif, brings the zombie figure to bear upon writing studies, even identifying writing studies' precursor rhetoric and composition as "disciplines of the dead." Ballif uses the figure of the zombie to rethink—by way of Derrida—the very idea of the human and the animal in order to provide an additional option to the accommodating or appropriate choices traditionally seen as the only viable responses to the monstrous other. For Ballif this other option is grave speech/writing. Ballif theorizes writing a la Plato as a type of living dead pressed into servitude, a domesticated zombie. Noting that zombies eat people, and that consumptive practices contribute to the distinctions between the human and the animal, Ballif argues "Posing the consumptive practices of the Zombie as an analogue to monstrous rhetorical possibilities, we can investigate the difference between eating well and eating poorly." Ballif gives us an incredible opportunity to rethink writing within the uncertainty of "writing's monstrous (be)coming." She also provides this collection a transitional move from Animal Studies by way of the zombie toward questions of what it means to be human.

Turning the posthuman gaze toward the cyborg, Kate Birdsall and Julie Drew's "Wanting Ourselves: Writing (And) the Postsexual Subject" examines how mid-twentieth century cybernetics and systems theory shifted the ways we think about human embodiment and boundaries in technological contexts. Reflexivity, they show, became "a spiral rather than a circle, resulting in dynamic hierarchies of emergent behaviors" (Hayles 241). Birdsall and Drew consider ways in which this spiral might reveal how new dimensions of subjectivity, paired with the kinds of self-objectification that prevail in the new media society, result in a dynamic conception of the "entanglement of language and code." This entanglement, they argue, results in the loss of the borders that allow a subject to define the Other or, as the authors suggest, the Self. In this way, they show, posthumanist thinking—like that of Hayles—is generative and offers exciting opportunities to reconfigure the corporeal human, (sexual) desire, and writing in/with technological interfaces. Where posthumanisms provides other ways of imagining subjects without recourse to the categories of Enlightenment/modernity, Birdsall and Drew contend that the postsexual challenges the traditional binary between the discrete categories of information and human, thereby challenging the boundaries between writing and being, text and self. Drawing, in part, on feminist film theory and queer theory to imagine how the postsexual might both limit and expand possibilities for (textual) production and agency, "Wanting Ourselves" explores the ways in which contemporary consumer and visual culture and the new media environments we currently inhabit create space for a reworking of Foucault's care/technologies of the self, Judith Butler's performance of the self, Derrida's consideration of the slippage between present self and future self-as-Other, and what used to be called, pejoratively, ludic feminism.

Sean Morey's "Becoming T@iled" examines the prosthetic function that we often assume of computers and in doing so, considers questions as to where the human begins and ends. The prosthetic function, he explains, is one of calculations, of performing mathematical-based utilities which augments the processing speed of the human brain, making a posthuman mind. Morey explains that perhaps because of this preoccupation with the cerebral, the "brain" or "mind" becomes an iconic idea of where the prosthetic connection occurs. One only has to think of the science-fiction fantasy motif of uploading one's consciousness into a machine and leaving the body behind, or such films as *The Matrix* where the "mind" is inserted into a virtual environment—a prosthetic space—and the manipulation of such an environment is one of manipulating codes: the savviest posthuman is one that never loses her ability to compute. Instead of leaving the body behind, Morey asks, how should posthuman thinking consider the body's "behind"? Instead of focusing on the head of the posthuman, Morey focuses on the "post" of the posthuman—the tail.

In a savvy deliberation, Morey turns his attention to a tail that we have already begun to embrace: the @, sometimes referred to as "the monkey's tail." The @ appears nearly ubiquitously in online environments, and provides one kind of code that we commonly write with. However, because of its ubiquity, we often overlook its function as a code, that it instructs our "intelligent" computers to enact a certain command, or that it changes the way that we write/think in other kinds of environments. Morey argues we write everyday with the @, yet it remains transparent even to our thinking prosthetics. The @ as a monkey's tail, however, does more than just instruct our posthuman parts toward some specific function: it becomes prosthetic as a posthuman tail, and serves a different kind of prosthetic function than one of "thinking." As such, Morey theorizes the @ both inside and outside current conversations of how posthuman bodies and codes interact. He shows what it means to both "write" a prosthetic such as a t@il, as well as what that t@il looks like once written, and how it performs a function of/through writing at the level of code.

J.A. Rice, in "Inscriptions of the Possible; or, A Pedagogy of Posthumanist Style," contends that "A posthumanist writing cannot express content or concepts because it only outlines a vague direction; it only marks difference. A posthumanist writing, then, acts almost like a series of random inscriptive events—it is an irreconcilable accident that connects a rhetor's choices and the nomadic moments of style's specific, iterable capacity." Rice rethinks posthumanism and style's enjoining logic so that it better reflects the possibilities of a disruptive grammar. Within this examination, Rice claims that one of the salient features of posthumanist disruption is how well it foregrounds writing and writing style as rhetoric's first premises. For Rice, posthuman writing style should be "the horizon by which we think, and not the object of our thought."

Jim Ridolfo argues in "Rethinking Human and Non-Human Actors as a Strategy for Rhetorical Delivery" that the next phase in delivery studies will not only need to encompass oral, print, and digital delivery simultaneously, but will also need to frame these posthuman activities as embedded in a material world of great complexity." By looking at interrelated human and non-human actors, Ridolfo uses three case studies to push theories of delivery into the posthuman era. He asks us not to settle for traditional understandings of delivery as singular in their approaches; instead, he argues, delivery is multimodal and complex. Delivery brings the human and non-human together; it brings the digital and print together.

Contending that a posthuman rhetoric must consider ways to compose nonhuman agents, Byron Hawk, Chris Lindgren, and Andrew Mara show how creating complex technological movements require a more nuanced notion of rhetoric that focuses on a diverse array of agents, including everything "from digital code to material objects, groups of actions to constellations of things." By way of Nicholas Negroponte's constructivism in the One Laptop Per Child (OLPC) project Hawk, Lindgren, and Mara examine the ways in which language and writing stand as socially constructed knowledge. The OLPC project, they argue, foregrounds rhetoric on the transformative power of education and formulates education as a type of technological deism, with the laptop acting as a proxy for a now-absent organizing presence. The authors show that Negroponte portrays writing as a naturally occurring process (education) and casts it as the victim of ideological, political, and historical processes. Hawk, Lindgren, and Mara compare early promises made at a TED conference about OLCP with the eventual rollout and deployment of the laptops. They look specifically at how laptop distribution in Rwanda constructs a specific set of relations between the OLPC project and notions of writing and language as enabling and limiting systems. They trace the gaps between Negroponte's deist rhetoric and the latent posthumanism in the deployment of technological objects into the networks that they co-produce. The deployment of these laptops as networks with an incipient, object-oriented philosophy on writing, they show, remakes the systemic role of writing in relation to learning, knowledge, and globalism.

Turning to graphology and expanding upon her work (with Jenell Johnson) about neurosciences and writing, Melissa M. Littlefield considers the idea that "handwriting is brainwriting" and asks "Why do neuroscience and graphology ostensibly share the brain as a common locus of self? How have both diagnostic technologies constructed the self as stable and knowable via a transparent human body?" Graphology, or the study of handwriting for clues about character and identity, has been a popular American pastime—and (pseudo)science —for nearly two centuries. Littlefield shows how even though the practice of seeking the self in/of script has fallen out of favor in the past few decades, another—related—practice has come to prominence: the neuroscientific study of writing and its relationship to emotion, health, and state of mind. For Littlefield, this turn to neuroscience as a better arbiter of tried philosophical question(s) is neither novel, nor unique to graphology; the phenomenon, she shows, has become so prevalent, in disciplines from economics to English, that she and Jenell Johnson have termed it a *neuroscientific turn* (Johnson and Littlefield forthcoming 2011). In her contribution to *Writing Posthumanism, Posthuman Writing*, Littlefield considers the postmodern, the poststructural, and the posthuman era in order to evaluate the "remains" of humanism that inform neuroscientific studies of writing. Littlefield argues that instead of breaking with traditions of graphology's search for the self, medical imaging technologies's studies of writing are shifting the locus of self from hand to brain, a shift she shows that, not coincidentally, was already happening in the early twentieth century.

Kyle Jensen, in "I am Spam: A Posthuman Approach to Writer's Block" works to reimagine writer's block from a posthuman perspective. To do so, Jensen identifies the importance in demonstrating how humanism's "aspirations are undercut by the philosophical and ethical frameworks used to conceptualize them." Only then, he argues, can writing scholars begin to envision writer's block in terms that confront the complexities of both human and non-human writing. For Jensen, the study and practice of writing has become considerably more complex in the posthuman era as a consequence of proliferating digital technologies that blur the distinction between human and machine. As numerous posthuman theorists have demonstrated, digital technologies blur such distinctions by transforming life into a set of data that can be described, transformed, replicated and transmitted through wires. Jensen examines how such blurring occurs in and through writing by theorizing the contemporary phenomenon of SPAM, which has fostered a range of technological innovations that effectively informationalize the "author" identification process and thereby facilitate new forms of bot-based writing. According to Jensen, Writing Studies has yet to take up SPAM in any serious manner because it is considered a morally abject approach to writing that threatens the safety of online interactions. While this may be true, he argues, the widespread abjection of SPAM-based writing conceals a major shift in our understanding of a central concept to Writing Studies: writer's block. Whereas before, writers block identified the phenomenon in which a writer experienced an acute struggle to produce a written document, now the term announces the pressing need to stop the proliferation of "inauthentic" and potential dangerous forms of writing. In order to theorize SPAM along this axis, Jensen introduces a new concept to writing studies: the authenticity function. A posthuman revision of Foucault's author function, this concept addresses how the authentication of identity has become predominantly informational insofar as information itself tests the veracity of disseminated identity information. The deeper implications of this concept cannot be addressed, however, until scholars and Internet security specialists come to terms with the rhetorical work of abjection that stigmatizes this writing practice. Such abjection, Jensen shows, affectively masks the complexity of this writing practice by insisting upon Humanist imperatives for singular authors, secure identity, and biological unity. To pursue this line of inquiry, Jensen turns to systems maintenance and second-order systems theories to analyze SPAM and the role of spam-bots as a representative anecdote of the complexities of non-human writing. Jensen brings this investigation to bear on the future of Writing Studies in order to test the field's humanistic underpinnings.

Kristie S. Fleckenstein, in "Cyborg Vision for Cyborg Writing," examines the reciprocity between discourses on vision and discourses on writing. She focuses, in particular, on the ways in which the epistemology undergirding a theory of vision reinforces the epistemology undergirding a theory of writing. In what is perhaps one of the most theoretically rich texts to examine the relationship between seeing and writing beyond the superficial ways in which such relationships are most often addressed in writing studies, Fleckenstein examines the historical intersection between Renaissance perspectivalism and Ramist rhetoric, a union of vision and writing central to the Enlightenment agenda that Donna Haraway seeks to dismantle. Likewise, she examines the intersection between ecological approaches to vision and composing. Fleckenstein's powerful essay contends that the qualities of embodiment, embeddedness, and transactivity that characterize discourses on vision and writing as ecologies support Haraway's cyborgian agenda by privileging the dynamic relationship among individual bodies, material-social environments, and coding systems as a strategy and site for change. "When we see and write ecologically," she says, "we see and write through the partiality and particularity of sited bodies, in-corporating the cyborg writing and vision that Haraway advocates."

Bruce Clarke's "Evolutionary Equality: Neocybernetic Posthumanism and Margulis and Sagan's Writing Practice" starts to unfold and clarify distinctions of definitions within posthumanism and the posthuman. By way of systems theory and deconstruction, Clarke considers the scriptive and rhetorical strategies employed in evolutionist Lynn Margulis and writer Dorion Sagan's writing. Clarke asks—and looks to answer—a number of questions about the relationship between posthumanism and writing: "How does one write about science for non-scientists in a way that challenges and ultimately subverts the verities of scientific humanism? How does one present posthumanist science to a general audience?" Through the works of microbiologist Lynn Margulis and her son, science-journalist Dorion Sagan, Clarke poses these questions with particular attention to how Margulis and Sagan's scriptive and rhetorical strategies play against their posthumanist constructions.

In sum, these essays galvanize a convergence of Writing Studies and Posthumanism toward the possibility of theoretical generation. By no means should this collection be considered an attempt to press posthuman writing theories into the archive. Instead, *Writing Posthumanism, Posthuman Writing* should be read as a jailbreak, as a public act of defiance, as noted at the beginning of this introduction, an attempt to incite and disrupt Writing Studies from the constraints of humanist thought. The essays gathered here examine the relationship between posthumanism and writing in the theoretically demanding space of Writing Studies.

Note

1. The term *transhuman* derives from thinking that in order to achieve a condition of the posthuman, a figure must have at one time been human. In this thinking, because the posthuman is yet to come, or by some accounts only hypothetically may become posthuman, the condition of the transhuman is the state between being human and being posthuman. For those who see the posthuman as either inevitable or hypothetical, the transhuman represents a current condition in which we have moved beyond humanity but not yet achieved posthumanity. In the case of this collection, it would seem that transhumanism provides a convenient appeal to the nascence of posthumanism. Yet, to extract the transhuman from the posthuman—or vice versa—would be to further contribute to the taxonomic impulse.

Works Cited

Brooke, Collin Gifford. "Forgetting the be (Post)Human: Media and Memory in a Kairotic Age." *JAC: A Journal of Rhetoric, Culture, and Politics.* 20.4. (2000). 775–95. Print.

Clark, Andy. *Natural Born Cyborgs: Minds, Technologies, and the Future of Human Intelligence.* New York: Oxford UP, 2003. Print.

Deleuze, Gilles and Félix Guattari. *A Thousand Plateaus: Capitalism and Schizophrenia.* Minneapolis: U of Minneapolis P, 1987. Print.

Didur, Jill. "Re-embodying Technoscientific Fantasies: Posthumanism, Genetically Modified Foods, and the Colonization of Life." *Cultural Critique* 53 (2003) 98–115. Print.

Doyle, Richard. "Uploading Anticipation, Becoming-Silicon." *JAC: A Journal of Rhetoric, Culture, and Politics.* 20.4 (2000). 840–64. Print.

Fukuyama, Francis. *Our Posthuman Future: Consequences of the Biotechnology Revolution.* New York: Picador, 2003. Print.

Gunkel, David J. "Hacking Cyberspace." *JAC: A Journal of Rhetoric, Culture, and Politics.* 20.4 (2000). 797–823. Print.

Harold, Christine L. "The Rhetorical Function of the Abject Body: Transgressive Corporeality in Trainspotting." *JAC: A Journal of Rhetoric, Culture, and Politics.* 20.4 (2000). 865–87. Print.

Hawk, Byron. *A Counter-History of Composition: Toward Methodologies of Complexity.* Pittsburgh. U Pittsburgh P, 2007. Print.

Hayles, N. Katherine. *How We Became Posthuman: Virtual Bodies in Cybernetics, Literature, and Informatics.* Chicago: u of Chicago P, 1999. Print. 19.

Mucklebauer, John and Debra Hawhee. "Posthuman Rhetorics: 'It's the Future, Pikul.'" *JAC: A Journal of Rhetoric, Culture, and Politics.* 20.4 (2000). 767–74. Print.

Nealon, Jeffrey T. "Nietzsche's Money!" *JAC: A Journal of Rhetoric, Culture, and Politics.* 20.4 (2000). 825–37. Print.

Simon, Bart. "Introduction: Toward a Critique of Posthuman Futures." *Cultural Critique* 53 (2003): 1–9. Print.

Ulmer, Gregory. "Foreword: Becoming Electrate." *Inter/vention: Free Play in the Age of Electracy.* Jan Rune Holmevik. Cambridge, MA: The MIT Press, 2012. Print. ix-xvi.

Wyschogrod, Edith. "Newtorking the Unpredictable: The Lure of Complexity." *JAC: A Journal of Rhetoric, Culture, and Politics.* 24.4 (2004). 871–79. Print.

2 Moving Beyond the Logic of Sacrifice: Animal Studies, Trauma Studies, and the Path to Posthumanism

Lynn Worsham

> *No, no, my cat, the cat that looks back at me in my bedroom or in the bathroom, this cat . . . does not appear here as a representative. . . . If I say "it is a real cat" that sees me naked, it is in order to mark its unsubstitutable singularity. . . . When it responds in its name . . . it doesn't do so as the exemplar of a species called cat, even less so of an animal genus or realm. . . . I see it as this irreplaceable living being that one day enters my space, enters this place where it can encounter me, see me, even see me naked. Nothing can ever take away from me the certainty that what we have here is an existence that refuses to be conceptualized. And a mortal existence. . . .*
>
> —Jacques Derrida

On January 3, 2012, with the new year still tottering on its new legs, the *New York Times* featured an article announcing the emergence of the new interdisciplinary field of animal studies, which, we learn, is spreading across college campuses in new course offerings, new majors, and new undergraduate and graduate programs. This new field, the *Times* reported, grows out of, on the one hand, a long history of scientific research on animals whose cumulative results (animal cognition, animal emotions, animal communication, animal morality) have now decisively blurred the "once-sharp distinction" between human and nonhuman animals, and, on the other hand, the field of cultural studies, which has been focused on "ignored and marginalized humans"—for example, women and minorities who were once considered "outsiders," not quite fully human, and often closer to animals (Gorman D2). The article explained to a general reader that the field of animal studies—not yet a tightly focused academic discipline, more nearly an "emergent scholarly community," to quote one scholar who was interviewed for the story—is wide open in its investigation of how humans interact with and use animals and what animals have meant to humans in human history. The article suggested that inasmuch as animal studies has successfully blurred the boundaries between human and animal and has pressed for recognition of the "animality" of the human, the human as one species among other species, animal studies may be ushering the humanities out of the academy and replacing the traditional disciplines of the liberal arts with the "post-humanities." How this news will play in Peoria is anyone's guess.

Just three years earlier, in 2009, the Modern Language Association, through a special cluster of articles in its flagship publication, *PMLA*, announced to an academic audience the emergence of the new interdisciplinary field of animal studies. Writing for "The Changing Profession" section of this issue, Cary Wolfe made a potentially decisive intervention in the field of animal studies with his observation that animal studies has two possible routes of development. It may develop according to the logic of "the cultural studies template," in which case animal studies is "only the latest permutation of a socially and ethically responsive cultural studies working to stay abreast of new social movements" and is "itself an academic expression of a larger democratic impulse toward greater inclusiveness." Or it may develop as part of the larger "problematic of posthumanism," in which case animal studies will destabilize and question the "schema of the human" and as a consequence pose a fundamental challenge to "the disciplinarity of the humanities and cultural studies" (568). For Wolfe, the problem with cultural studies, at least as it is practiced in North America, is that in spite of itself—in spite of its effort to be oppositional, multicultural, and materialist—cultural studies "ends up reproducing an ideologically familiar mode of subjectivity based, philosophically and politically, on the canons of liberal humanism" (569). He wrote, "Just because a historian or literary critic devotes attention to the topic or theme of nonhuman animals doesn't mean that a familiar form of humanism isn't being maintained through the internal disciplinary practices that rely on a specific schema of the knowing subject and of the kind of knowledge he or she can have" (572). He argued that if "the animal" is taken "seriously," "not just as another topic or object of study among many," then animal studies "would not so much extend or refine a certain mode of cultural studies as bring it to an end" (568).

One problem, then, with a certain dominant mode of cultural studies is that it remains blind to its own commitment to humanism and to the anthropocentrism and human exceptionalism characteristic of humanism. A related problem is that the dominant mode of cultural studies reproduces a knowing subject that is deemed capable of critical consciousness through introspection and self-reflection—that is, the autonomous knowing subject of liberal humanism. Still another problem is that cultural studies has been appropriated to do the ideological work of the neoliberal order, "in which capitalist globalization gets repackaged as pluralism and attention to difference" (568).[1] For Wolfe, the promise of posthumanism—as a mode of being, knowing, and engaging with the world—comes in its resolute nonanthropocentrism and nonspeciesism. Posthumanism makes explicit the fact that historically what has counted as knowledge and as a knowing subject has been decisively limited by our species-being. Posthumanism, as a questioning of humanism and the schema of the human that humanism installs, does not seek to transcend or eclipse the human; nor does it deny the uniqueness and difference of human beings from other species, which are themselves unique and different from one another. Posthumanism starts from the fact that humanism has denied human finitude—specifically, the fact of human embodiment and human evolution as a "specific form of animality" (Wolfe 572).[2] Posthumanism's focus on human embodiment trains attention on the fact of physical vulnerability and mortality, which are conditions of existence we share with all living beings.[3]

My own engagement, first, with cultural studies, and, more recently, with animal studies has also been motivated by the theme of human vulnerability and mortality—specifically, by a longstanding preoccupation (obsession might be a better word) with violence, with how we human animals treat one another (see, for example, Worsham, "Composing"; "Going Postal"). For a quarter of a century, I have been driven to understand precisely that which I have not yet been able to get my mind around in all these years of concentrated study: those extravagant forms of violence that almost everyone would recognize as atrocities (genocide, ethnic cleansing, suicide bombings, mass rape as a weapon of war, torture) as well as those forms of violence that have become almost routine in the U.S. (rape, domestic abuse, child sexual abuse and murder, spree serial killings, rampage murders, workplace and school killings, family annihilation).[4] Likewise, I have been determined to understand the relation between these forms of what might be called extravagant violence and the more invisible forms of structural and symbolic violence that organize everyday life for the vast majority of people throughout the world (sexism, sexual exploitation and slavery, racism, social and economic disenfranchisement, heteronormativity). I have been especially keen to understand the reciprocal relation between violence and emotion: the role that emotion plays in creating situations in which violence occurs and the role that violence and its representation play in shaping, even producing, our affective lives.

I have no doubt that this preoccupation with violence and its affective economy results from having lived through the aftermath of World War II, the cold war and its omnipresent threat of nuclear war, the violence of the 1960s and early 70s, and the violence that this world has seen in the last forty years. Indeed, I have felt a sense of having lived through what psychologist Robert Jay Lifton describes as a death-saturated age, an age in which all of us are in some sense survivors of catastrophe, our experience inescapably and profoundly marked by death and the violence of our time ("Survivor" 479). Although Steven Pinker has argued recently that violence has been in decline for millennia and that we are living in the most peaceful time in human existence, from the perspective of many more scholars, the twentieth century, was marked by unprecedented violence, so much so that it has been called a "post-traumatic age" and a "catastrophic age" (Farrell 3–7; Caruth 3–12).[5] The violence that has consumed the first decade of the twenty-first century portends an even more deadly and traumatizing future.

In this context of violence and trauma, the field of animal studies emerges in recent years not as the latest academic curiosity to be reported, somewhat smugly, in the *New York Times* or as the most recent challenge from within the university to business-as-usual in the crisis-prone humanities. The interdisciplinary field of animal studies emerges as a call to all of us to relinquish, once and for all, the habit and the hubris of anthropocentrism and humanism and to broaden the sense of "our time" to include the catastrophe that is the systematic and relentless and ongoing exploitation, abuse, and killing of nonhuman animals. More to the point that I want to make here, animal studies calls on us to see the deep and abiding connection between how we interact with and treat each other and how we interact with and treat nonhuman others. (Is it surprising to anyone that the period marked by unspeakable forms of interhuman violence is also marked by what Derrida calls "unprecedented" violence against animals?)[6] The field of animal studies calls on us to understand and appreciate, as David Wood puts it (following Derrida), "the importance of the logic of sacrifice in understanding why we [humans] act as we do": human history as the relentless and enduring "age of sacrifice" ("Thinking" 129). Death, catastrophe, trauma, sacrifice—there is more than enough in this history to rivet attention and sustain reflection on the use and abuse of animals as a proving ground for human violence. As a result of my own engagement with the interdisciplinary field of animal studies, the problem of human violence seems to me to be paradoxically clearer yet more utterly mind-boggling today than it has ever been.

Tracking a Line of Thought

The problem of human violence is not mind-boggling in the sense of being entirely inexplicable. Many theories have been advanced over the years to account for the origin and dynamics of violence; I want to pursue only one here, the one I find most compelling.

In his response to Derrida's essay "The Animal That Therefore I am (More to Follow)," Wood outlines an explanation of human violence toward both human and nonhuman others and its function in the life of the being we call "human." He begins with the connection between language and violence—language, that tool, that medium through which we humans have claimed our difference from and superiority over nonhuman animals. Wood points out that "the use of the word 'animal' or 'the animal' to refer to any and all living creatures is a conceptual violence that expeditiously legitimates our actual violence" ("Thinking" 133). In two different essays, Wood takes Derrida to task for his use of the words "animal" or "the animal"—"as if this were not already a form of deadening shorthand" ("*Comment*" 29). Wood explains:

> Categories are gross ways in which we (humans) carve up the world. Violence arises at two levels. First, these categorial distinctions (man/animal, man/woman) are affirmations of the very kinds of distinctions that would block the extension of consideration (for example, from man to animal). For it is no accident that these categorial distinctions are actually wielded by only one of each pair. . . . Second, these categories can be deployed *nominally* and *descriptively* so that such violence can be applied to this or that specific animal. "Animal," in other words, is one of the ways we say "Other." ("Thinking" 133; emphasis added)

Humans, then, are creatures who habitually wield conceptual categories as if they were descriptions of reality when in fact they are deeply interested interpretations of reality. Humans are the creatures who use those conceptual categories to exclude others (human and nonhuman others) from moral consideration and to rationalize and justify actual violence against those we consign to the category "animal." Humans, in short, are the creatures who historically have wielded conceptual categories to deny the "unsubstitutable singularity" and irreplaceability of individual living beings, both human and nonhuman.[7] We claim the "life of the mind" as the crowning achievement of evolution, yet ours is the kind of mind that urgently performs its tricks to dazzle the only beings we deem worthy of dazzling: ourselves.[8]

"Animal," clearly, is not just one conceptual category among others; it is the foundation, if not the origin, of all practices of othering—of claiming and justifying, first, human exceptionalism and, then, of claiming the superiority of particular groups who are seen as belonging legitimately in the category "human." As Wood puts it, "The other animal is the Other *par excellence,* the being who or which exceeds my concepts, my grasp, etc." ("*Comment*" 32). Wolfe puts the matter somewhat more pointedly: "Violence against human others (and particularly racially marked others) has often operated by means of a double movement that *animalizes* them for the purposes of domination, oppression, or even genocide—a maneuver that is effective because we take for granted the prior assumption that violence against the animal is ethically permissible" (567; emphasis added).[9] True though it may be, Wolfe's observation, with its focus on "racially marked others" as the exemplary case, also obscures the more enduring history in which the category of gender has been used across racial, class, and ethnic lines to animalize, dominate, and oppress women and girls.[10]

But why? Why do we humans use the category "animal" in this way, and why do we use those beings we assign to this category in the ways that we do? In his study of the history of slavery in the Americas, *Inhuman Bondage,* David Brion Davis argues that historically the human freedom to animalize human others and thereby "degrade, dishonor, enslave, and even kill and eat" them has the social and symbolic purpose of creating solidarity and a sense of superiority within a human tribe or group (28–29). Wood says something similar in the context of our treatment of animals: "The way we treat animals is deeply caught up with the ongoing need for symbolic reaffirmation of our own humanity" ("Thinking" 133). In the way we treat nonhuman animals and human others, we symbolically create and recreate the meaning of "human being" as our separation from and transcendence of animal life. Wood makes the same point more forcefully when he states that the way we treat nonhuman animals is a "ritual reenactment of a problematic internal relation to our own 'animality'" (132). Perhaps the phrase, "a problematic internal relation to our own animality," offers some insight into what accounts for the deeply contradictory ways in which we live with, think with, and use nonhuman animals—for example, as beloved companions and family members who are given names and sometimes birthday celebrations, funerals, and even trust funds, on the one hand, and on the other, as mere source material for food, clothing, and knowledge (see Fudge).

What is it about our animality that is so problematic as to inspire or necessitate the violent reaffirmation of our humanity? Let me just suggest one direction for thought. In *Hiding from Humanity,* Martha Nussbaum writes, "What we are anxious about is a type of vulnerability that we share with other animals, the propensity to decay and to become waste products ourselves" (92). In "The Difficulty of Reality," Cora Diamond makes the same observation but goes a bit further:

> The awareness we each have of being a living body, being "alive to the world," carries with it exposure to the bodily sense of vulnerability to death, sheer animal vulnerability, the vulnerability we share with them. This vulnerability is capable of panicking us. To be able to acknowledge it at all, let alone as shared, is wounding; but acknowledging it as shared with other animals, in the presence of what we do to them, is capable not only of panicking one but also of isolating one. . . . (74)

In "Thinking with Cats," Wood glosses Derrida's comments on human vulnerability and finitude: "Man is distinctive in knowing he is naked, needing to be clothed, supplemented with technics (like fire, and, we might add, writing and even philosophy), aware of his lack" (139). Naked and therefore vulnerable, seeking to overcome our own naked vulnerability through tools and technologies (including writing and, more recently, digital technology and new media), humiliated (indeed, mortified) by the awareness of our animal vulnerability and mortality, wounded and panicked by this difficult knowledge, and isolated by the shame of knowing what we do to our fellow creatures, we engage in both symbolic and material practices that are essentially violent in a vain and futile attempt to deny vulnerability and reassert our distinctiveness, our separateness from and superiority over animal life.[11]

Central to Diamond's discussion of vulnerability is a focus on the experience of what she calls "a difficulty of reality." To experience a difficulty of reality is to experience something I cannot conceptualize, an experience that is resistant to my thinking it, one that is astonishing in its incomprehensibility, or one that is "painful in its inexplicability" (45–46). In Diamond's words, "The difficulty lies in the apparent resistance by reality to one's ordinary mode of life, including one's ordinary modes of thinking" (58). An encounter with a difficulty of reality marks the limit of our concepts and categories, renders them inadequate in the face of reality, renders us vulnerable to their inadequacy, and renders us vulnerable to something we cannot get our minds around. As suggested above, an experience of a difficulty of reality may be wounding, panicking, and isolating. What's more, the exposure to a difficulty of reality "shoulders us from a familiar sense of moral life, from a sense of being able to take in and think a moral world" (64). Diamond points out that these sorts of experiences can be highly individual. In other words, what I take to be resistant to my thinking it—what may be astonishing or painful to me in its inexplicability (violence toward others, for example)—may not present the same difficulty to others, may even be seen by others as "unsurprising" (62).

In her exploration of the experience of a difficulty of reality, Diamond employs a number of examples, among them J.M. Coetzee's novella, *The Lives of Animals*. She includes as part of her example the four essays, included in the volume, that follow the novella, essays written by a diverse group of scholars. The novella, *The Lives of Animals*, is Coetzee's Tanner Lectures, which were presented in 1997 and 1998 at Princeton University. His lectures take the form of a story that is principally comprised of two lectures given by his main character, Elizabeth Costello, an elderly Australian novelist and professor of literature who, like Coetzee, has travelled to the United States on the invitation of an American university. This mirroring at the level of structure—two lectures that take the form of a story, a story (with minimal narrative frame) that is comprised almost entirely of two lectures and a portrayal of an academic debate between Costello and a fictional philosophy professor—is itself an important theme of the novella. In her remarkable essay, "The Difficulty of Reality," Diamond presents two different ways of reading the volume (that is, the novella and the commentators' responses to it).

She reads Coetzee's novella as "presenting a kind of woundedness or hauntedness." For her, the novella is "centrally concerned with the presenting of a wounded woman," Elizabeth Costello (47). The commentators, Diamond points out, view the novella quite differently: as Coetzee's "device" for presenting "a position on the issue [of] how we should treat animals" (49). For Diamond, Elizabeth Costello is "haunted by the horror of what we do to animals. We see her as wounded by this knowledge, this horror, and by the knowledge of how unhaunted others are" (46). Diamond continues: "What wounds this woman, what haunts her mind . . . is what we do to animals. This, in all its horror, is there, in our world. How is it possible to live in the face of it? How is it possible to live in the face of the fact that, for nearly everyone, it is as nothing, as the mere accepted background of life?" (47). In Diamond's reading, Costello encounters a difficulty of reality in the way we treat animals and also in the callous indifference that most people exhibit over our treatment of them. Diamond observes that woundedness—the wounded life of the animal at the center of the narrative, Elizabeth Costello—is not seen or appreciated by the commentators who view the central character as Coetzee's mouthpiece for putting forward abstract ethical ideas for debate. For them, her suffering is "as nothing, as the mere accepted background" of the life of the minds that are only interested in the argument that Costello (Coetzee) gives—or, more accurately, fails to give—in support of the ethical position she (he) is seen to be taking. Diamond writes, "For none of the commentators does the title of the story have any particular significance in relation to the wounded animal that the story has as its central character. For none of the commentators does the title of the story have any significance in how we might understand the story in relation to our own lives, the lives of the animals we are" (49). For none of the commentators does the central character of the story provide a mirror onto what they (we) share with every living being, human and nonhuman alike.

In the context of these two readings, Diamond introduces the concept of deflection, which she draws from the work of Stanley Cavell. Deflection, Diamond proposes, is a conceptual strategy for dealing with an experience of a difficulty of reality. Deflection occurs "when we are moved from the appreciation, or attempt at appreciation, of a difficulty of reality to a philosophical or moral problem apparently in the vicinity" (57). In other words, deflection converts a difficulty of reality into a purely intellectual difficulty "*apparently* in the vicinity" and treats it as an intellectual problem through abstraction—that is, through the distancing practices of conceptual categorization, representation, analysis, and argumentation. The commentators whose essays are included in *The Lives of Animals* engage in deflection when they do not see Elizabeth Costello's woundedness—do not even see her at all—or the significance of her woundedness. Through deflection, they distance themselves from her woundedness, from any possibility of identification with her vulnerability, from any possibility of bridging the distance between self and other. They treat the novella as Coetzee's rather too obvious and (in their view) clumsy device for positing a philosophical position on animal rights. One commentator—notably, the animal rights philosopher Peter Singer—suggests that Coetzee frames his lectures as fiction in order to maintain a safe distance from the position he is seen to be taking so as to avoid having to take responsibility for it by defending it. Singer, and to various degrees all the commentators, convert the difficult reality of Elizabeth Costello's woundedness, which they do not see as such, into an intellectual position on the rights of animals. Implied in Diamond's reading, but in no way made explicit, is the insight that the commentators take Coetzee to be engaging in the same distancing act of deflection that they engage in and that his posture precisely mirrors their own. Most important, deflection, Diamond observes, represents the "capacity to miss the suffering of others"—for example, Costello's woundedness, our own woundedness—and "the possibility of our own suffering being unknown and uncared about" (68). The operation of deflection, I must emphasize, offers an important insight into the phenomenon of indifference as the human capacity to not know or care about the suffering of others. The earlier mentioned "categorial distinctions" that we take to be nominal and descriptive—such as "man" or "the animal"—are products of and part of the operation of deflection, in that such distinctions move us from attention to the unsubstitutable singularity and irreplaceability of the individual living being before us to the category, or "kind," that that being is taken to represent. There is sacrifice happening in this move and the logic of substitution.

In her reading of the novella, Diamond thematizes something else the commentators miss: Costello's reluctance, if not her outright refusal, to engage in academic debate with various members of her audience who are keen to press her to defend the position she is seen to be taking with regard to animals and animal rights. Diamond explains Costello's reluctance in this way:

> Our reliance on argumentation is a way we make unavailable to ourselves our own sense of what it is to be a living animal. . . . To think of Coetzee's lectures as contributing to the "debate" on how to treat animals is to fail to see how "debate" as we understand it may have built into it a distancing of ourselves from our sense of our own bodily life and our capacity to respond to and to imagine the bodily life of others. (53)

Debate and argumentation are forms and practices of deflection that take us out of our vulnerable and mortal animal bodies; they are practices of deflection that move attention away from exposure to the difficult reality of bodily life and death. Whereas exposure to a difficulty of reality exceeds our conceptual repertoire and is experienced and known only in the body as a form of embodied knowledge, debate and argumentation move attention to a kind of thinking done with concepts and categories and positions taken and defended—that is, to a kind of thinking identified as abstract and deemed exclusively human. Our habitual recourse to argumentation (both oral and written) in response to exposure to a difficulty of reality serves effectively as an assertion of the superior value of the life of the (human) mind and knowledge that is abstract. If, as Costello says, "there is no limit to the extent to which we can think ourselves into the being of another," if "[t]here are no bounds to the sympathetic imagination," then Diamond would counter that debate and argumentation have served historically as the limits imposed by a certain kind of thinking on our capacity to imagine and respond to the lives of others, including the suffering of both human and nonhuman animals (Coetzee 35).

In this way, rhetoric understood as the theory and practice of persuasion, of effective argumentation, must be viewed as the art of deflection *par excellence*. From this perspective, the theory and practice of effective argumentation (both oral and written) must be understood as forms of conceptual or symbolic violence—in other words, as part of the problem of human violence and not simply or simplistically as the antidote or alternative to violence, as classical rhetorical theorists proposed. Modern rhetorical theorists have also pursued an understanding of rhetoric as an alternative to violence; however, because they have felt compelled to address an urgent social and historical milieu characterized by massive violence (our "catastrophic" age), they have also broadened the scope of rhetoric to include rhetoric as a crucial antecedent to and instrument of violence. Kenneth Burke is the obvious and preeminent example here. He developed a view of language as a form of symbolic action; he was interested in what we can *do* with language, with language as instrument and agency. He shifted attention from persuasion and argumentation to the ways in which we employ language and complex symbol systems to create identity and identification. He was especially concerned with the way we employ language to identify particular individuals or groups as scapegoats whose subordination, marginalization, and expulsion from society is accomplished, first, through a choice (nonconscious or conscious) of words, through a developed way of conceiving of individuals or groups as threatening. He called the symbolic practice of scapegoating "the sacrificial principle of victimage," which is essentially a rhetorical strategy for creating social solidarity and identification through the symbolic creation of the "Other" (see "Definition" and *Permanence*). While classical theorists viewed rhetoric as an alternative to violence, Burke reconceived rhetoric as both the disease and the cure, to use his terms, by which he meant that violence or victimage—the disease—arises from the same source as the cure: from the very terms in which we categorize and frame a given situation as a problem, terms that train us to look in one direction rather than another for possible solutions.

Burke was keenly aware of the way deflection is built into language and language use and thus the way it is built into our habitual response to the phenomena of experience. In "Terministic Screens," he famously wrote, "Even if any given terminology is a *reflection* of reality, by its very nature as a terminology it must be a *selection* of reality; and to this extent it must function as a *deflection* of reality" (45). For Burke, then, deflection is an inevitable feature of our habitual and ordinary mode of thinking and responding to the world through language. Only when our concepts, categories, and terms fail us in the experience of a difficulty of reality do we have the potential opening to appreciate that difficulty of reality for what it is, just as it is: an experience that will not be put into words and thus one that confronts us with our isolation and helplessness—that is, with human finitude. In *Permanence and Change,* Burke commented on the "Eternal Enigma" of existence and nothingness, which, he said, are equally "unthinkable"—that is, both are, equally, beyond our concepts and categories to grasp them. He wrote, "And in this staggering disproportion between man and no-man, there is no place for purely human boasts of grandeur, or for forgetting that men build their cultures by huddling together, nervously loquacious, at the edge of an abyss" (272). Julia Kristeva makes a related observation about the role of fear, death anxiety, and language in the formation of human subjectivity. She writes, "when death brushes us by, depriving us of the assurance . . . of being ourselves, that is, untouchable, unchangeable, immortal," we turn to "metaphorizing to keep from being frightened to death" (38). In these passages, Burke and Kristeva point to the decisive fact of vulnerability and a corresponding fear and anxiety about vulnerability and mortality that move us into language as a deflection of and a defense mechanism against reality, a reality we share with all living beings. While language and culture are distinguishing features of *homo sapiens sapiens,* the species that describes and categorizes itself as "doubly wise," human language and culture are also the principal means by which we separate and disconnect ourselves from each other and all living beings. Through what trick with words and categories does the desire not to know become the hallmark of wisdom?

CLOSING IN ON THE PROBLEM: THE TRAUMATIC ORIGINS OF VIOLENCE

I now want to link the notions of *deflection* and *victimage* to what Robert Lifton calls "false witness." I want to suggest the ways in which *deflection*, *victimage*, and *false witness* are intimately related in an effort to bring into sharper focus the logic of sacrifice that is at work in a particular mode of being and knowing that is distinctively human.

False witness, as Lifton explains it, refers to both a subject position one takes up (one becomes a *false witness*) and an action one engages in (one engages in *false witnessing*) as a way of dealing with an experience that is traumatizing (Lifton, 1991). An event is traumatizing, as both Judith Herman and Lifton point out, by virtue of its perceived power to threaten real or symbolic annihilation. At its most literal level, trauma results from an overwhelming and terrifying confrontation with death and the utter helpless to prevent or avoid it. Yet trauma may also result from experiences that are routine and part of everyday life, such as the daily degradation of poverty or the routine shaming practices of sexism and racism. Whether the threat is real or symbolic, extravagant or routine, a traumatic experience is one that exceeds the mind's ability to grasp it fully, to take it in and assimilate it to existing frameworks of meaning and value.[12] A traumatic experience is by definition an experience of a difficulty of reality. Shattered by this kind of traumatic encounter with one's own real or psychological death, terrified and utterly helpless and vulnerable, an individual may react to the death encounter by violently striking out at others and thereby engage in violent actions that make one a false witness. False witness is a defense mechanism, a form of "acting out" in response to a threatening and terrifying experience; it displaces one's own death anxiety onto others.

False witness, Lifton observes, is central to most victimization:

> Groups victimize others, they create what I now call "designated victims," the Jews in Europe, the Blacks in this country. They are people off whom we live not only economically, as is often the case, but psychologically. That is, we reassert our own vitality and symbolic immortality by denying them their right to life and by identifying them with the death taint, by designating them as victims. So we live off them. *That's* what false witness is. It's deriving one's solution to one's death anxiety from extreme trauma . . by exploiting a group of people and rendering them

victims, designated victims for that psychological work. (qtd. in Caruth 139)

What Lifton describes here is a nonconscious, psychosocial process of scapegoating in which we transfer or displace or *deflect* onto a victim or victim-group our own death anxiety, a victim whose injury or death (real or psychological) becomes the substitute for our own vulnerability to death.[13] When we engage in false witness, we deny the unsubstitutable singularity and irreplaceability of the bodily life before us and make the bodily, psychological, or symbolic death of that victim a symbol of our power, superiority, and transcendence of the constraints of mortal existence.[14] The reassertion of vitality and symbolic immortality in the face of the threat of death is simultaneously a denial of vulnerability and potential death. This denial of death is itself numbing—that is, psychic numbing further traumatizes the individual who engages in the denial of death through false witness.

False witness is "false" in the sense of being a self-deceptive practice in relation to our own vulnerability and mortality; it is a deflection from an awareness of that difficulty of reality. It is a form of witnessing in the sense that victimizing others as a response to overwhelming trauma becomes a way of making known, or indirectly testifying, that a prior traumatic encounter with death has occurred. Having survived a traumatizing event, one has a need to bear witness and take on what Lifton calls "the survivor mission" (Lifton, 1991); instead of taking up the survivor mission, however, the individual blocks out the death encounter by scapegoating others. Lifton calls *false witness* "a perverse quest for meaning": "What is perverse is that one must impose death on others in order to reassert one's own life as an individual and a group. . . . So my view is that you cannot kill large numbers of people except with a claim to virtue, so that killing on a large scale is always an attempt at affirming the life power of one's own group" (qtd. in Caruth 140). In a similar vein, René Girard suggests that there is always an element of delusion in scapegoating: we do not consciously know that the claim to virtue is a rationalization and that we are engaging in the kind of *deflection* enacted in *scapegoating* or *false witness*.

The concept of *false witness* is useful in my pursuit of an understanding of violence because it suggests that some (perhaps all) forms of violence cannot be readily traced to an innately murderous disposition (the legacy of the alleged "killer-ape" within; see Cartmill 1–14). The concept of *false witness* suggests that an alternative view is available to us: at least some forms of violence arise from a prior experience that is traumatizing, an experience or a history of experiences that is overwhelming in its power to expose vulnerability and helplessness. Especially heinous acts of violence may require a long history of experiences of trauma to form the context for and solicitation of violent actions that are perversely meant to shore up potency and self-respect.[15] In his extensive research on extremely violent, sadistic murderers, forensic psychiatrist James Gilligan finds a common experience among them that, in his view, provoked their violent acts: a history of childhood experiences of crushing shame and humiliation that can only be described as profoundly traumatizing. "Soul-murder" is the term Gilligan uses to describe what these violent criminals underwent before turning to homicide (43). While Gilligan's research is focused on individual criminals with a view toward articulating a theory of criminal violence as a public health issue, his insights can be extended, for example, to understanding what many regard as the criminal history of colonialism—aided and abetted by the intersecting forces of racism, sexism, class (or caste) privilege, heterosexism, and often theism—and its traumatizing effects on colonized subjects and cultures, perhaps explaining why these cultures, once colonialism nominally ends, are too often highly unstable and prone to violence of various kinds.[16]

What needs to be emphasized at this point of the discussion is that situations that elicit the kind of response that might be described as *false witness* are not always world historical events, such as colonialism or the Holocaust, or those extreme events that everyone would agree are atrocities. In *Payback: Why We Retaliate, Redirect Aggression, and Take Revenge,* David Barash and Judith Lipton develop a theory of violence as a response to prior trauma. They are especially concerned with the phenomenon of redirected aggression, which they define as "the targeting of an innocent bystander in response to one's own pain and injury" (5). They write, redirected aggression "isn't so much payback as 'pay-forward' or—more precisely—'pay sideways'" (4). They present an account of redirected aggression in which we are to understand not only overt acts of violence but also those everyday occurrences in which one person verbally or symbolically lashes out, for no apparent reason, at another. In Barash and Lipton's account, redirected aggression is explained as an effort to "pass the pain along" (3-24), an effort to unburden oneself of the stress of carrying the pain one has suffered. Redirected aggression, as one form of "passing the pain along," is another way of approaching what Lifton means by *false witness.*

Consider this example of the everyday violence of *false witness* and *redirected aggression* that is especially relevant to animal studies as a posthumanist practice: in the U.S., and increasingly in developing countries, ordinary life has been founded on, as Elizabeth Costello puts it, "an enterprise of degradation, cruelty, and killing which rivals anything that the Third Reich was capable of, indeed dwarfs it, in that ours is an enterprise without end, self-regenerating, bringing rabbits, rats, poultry, livestock ceaselessly into the world for the purpose of killing them" (21). The living beings we call animals are humanity's *designated victims* who are brought into being to be abused and slaughtered in the interest of what we see as our superior form of life. We live off of animals in every sense available. They are, as Costello observes, our slaves (59). Derrida makes a similar observation, arguing that for the last two centuries "we who call ourselves men or humans, we who recognize ourselves in that name, have been involved in an unprecedented transformation" in the "traditional forms of treatment of the animal" (392–94). He is referring, of course, to the same enterprise Costello points to: the industrialization of farming and meat production, animal experimentation including genetic experimentation and transformation, the artificial insemination of animals on a massive scale, and the international smuggling of wild animals. To this list we might add sport hunting and fishing; the keeping of exotic "pets;" and the use of animals as entertainment in film and television, zoos, wildlife theme parks, circuses, fighting contests, and sexual gratification (for example, "crush" films). Derrida offers this searing appraisal of the situation:

> . . . no one can deny this event any more, no one can deny the *unprecedented* proportions of this subjection of the animal. Such a subjection . . . can be called violence in the most morally neutral sense of the term. . . . Neither can one seriously deny the disavowal that this involves. No one can deny seriously, or for very long, that men do all they can in order to dissimulate this cruelty or to hide it from themselves, in order to organize on a global scale the forgetting or misunderstanding of this violence that some would compare to the worst cases of genocide. . . . (394)

In this passage, with the repetition and use of terms such as "deny," "disavowal," and "dissimulate," Derrida confronts us with our habitual condition of *deflection* and indifference.

Coetzee's and Derrida's strategic use of the analogy between genocide and animal abuse and killing—indeed, any use of this analogy—has been viewed as controversial and even highly offensive to some who see it as an egregious category mistake, an unacceptable "trick with words" (Coetzee 49).[17] The reasoning goes something like this: "Genocide" cannot apply to animals because humans and animals are of different kinds; what is permissible to do to the latter is unacceptable and unethical to do to the former. For reasons that I hope are obvious at this point in this discussion, I will forgo entering the debate about this analogy, its factual claim of similarity or its ethical implications. Instead, I simply want to suggest that the analogy might be usefully understood as a figure of thought—indeed, a trick with words—that captures attention and stops thought of an abstract kind. It attempts to bring a difficulty of reality into view in an effort to convey the pain and anguish that that difficulty causes to some of us. The problem is this: how to convey the experience of a difficulty of reality, an experience that is highly individual, one that too few people experience and appreciate as such. One strategy might be to compare that difficult reality to another difficult reality (genocide, the Holocaust) that more people appreciate as mind-boggling, as beyond the limit of ethical acceptability—indeed, as an atrocity. Perhaps the analogy is meant to make its appeal not to reason, but to emotion and to a posthuman (nonanthropocentric) ethical sensibility. Perhaps the analogy offers a way of moving us into the vicinity of a difficulty of reality, a way of bridging the distance that *deflection* creates through its recourse to concepts and categories. If so, then the controversy over this analogy—whether it is factually accurate or ethically appropriate—may be yet another instance of *deflection*, another instance of the refusal to see or care about the suffering of those for whom the subjection of animals is an atrocity of genocidal proportions. Of course, while we debate the accuracy or appropriateness of the analogy, individual animals continue to suffer the cruelty and indifference of the vast majority of their human animal kin.

The violent subjection of nonhuman animals has certainly become, through *deflection*, denial, and disavowal, "as nothing, as the mere accepted background of life." We do not even see that their violent subjection serves our vain attempt to deny our own vulnerability and mortality, our vain attempt to claim symbolic immortality and transcendence from animal vulnerability and animal life. Wood makes an important point in his formulation of the following rhetorical question: "Might not the *legitimacy* of meat-eating rest, albeit precariously, not on our clear superiority to 'the animal,' but on our need to demonstrate this over and over again?" ("Thinking" 138; emphasis added).[18] Meat-eating and the whole "enterprise of degradation, cruelty, and killing" of animals, in this view, has become in the last two centuries an everyday instance of *false witness* and redirected aggression and a *deflection* from knowing and appreciating the difficult reality of our shared vulnerability with nonhuman animals.

THE PREHISTORY OF DEFLECTION

Thus far, I have been tracking a line of thinking that makes plausible my deeply felt sense that the human-animal relation, however it has varied over time and whatever forms it has taken, is also in some meaningful way a fundamentally traumatized relation, a relation deeply wounded by the history of the kind of animal we humans are, and especially so in the last two centuries. It is traumatized by the history of our problematic internal relation to our own animality, by our refusal to seek solidarity in a community of the living. It is as if we humans cannot accept our own failed transcendence of animal life.

Yet, the human-animal relation is also traumatized by the so-called animal side of the relation. For all of our prehistory and early history, the animal-hominin relation was one of predator to prey. Evidence suggests that our transition from prey to predator was only accomplished some 25,000 years ago, and the victory was decisively ours only since the invention of the gun. The greatest challenge, then, for the earliest ancestors and early humans was to avoid, through skill or luck, becoming dinner for large and practiced predators. This primordial experience of predation is, in Barbara Ehrenreich's view, the ur-trauma in our evolutionary history: the terror of being caught unaware and suddenly felled; of being hunted, stalked, and chased; the terror and humiliation of being captured and quickly killed or ripped apart while still alive—that is, the humiliation (indeed, the mortification) of being *taken to be mere meat* to feed another animal whose struggle for survival was precisely mirrored in our own ancestors' struggle for survival (70, 91). This experience of being prey, this embodied experience of trauma, was surely hard-wired into our ancestors' brains and represents an evolutionary legacy to which we have no direct access.[19] In *Thought in a Hostile World*, Kim Sterelny argues that human cognitive abilities and cognitive architecture, including our capacity for language, evolved in a dangerous and threatening world, a world in which forms of physical, social, and environmental predation were the most consequential threats.[20] Today, we meet the predator beast in nightmares, myths, fairytales, literature (especially children's literature), and popular culture. We also meet the predator beast in the mirror: in those predatory structures, institutions, and practices that organize life as an agonizingly slow depredation of the many in the interests of the few.

In Ehrenreich's view, the original trauma of predation and the long and arduous transformation from prey to predator is restaged again and again in the collective trauma of war, which makes immediate and vividly felt the anxiety of vulnerability and the elation of potency through defensive solidarity that, she argues, "evolved in combat with a deadly, nonhuman 'other'" (96). Apart from any "reasons" we give ourselves for going to war, war serves as an effective psychosocial drama that restages primordial emotions, and it has the function of producing the social solidarity—what Arjun Appadurai calls "full attachment"—that configures an "enemy" against which one human group identifies itself and moves in solidarity against another group.[21] As Appadurai argues, "Full attachment, rather than coming from an authentic prior sense of shared community (whether based on language, history, soil or some other primordium), might actually be produced by various forms of violence . . ." ("Grounds" 132). Our longstanding undeclared war on animals, especially as it has taken shape in the last two centuries, arguably serves the same function as forms of interhuman violence, including war. Through various permissible and prohibited forms of violence against nonhuman animals, we have created social solidarity among humans over and against "the animal," and we have claimed for human beings what Appadurai, in a different context, calls "predatory identities"—that is, "large-scale group identities that seem to require . . . the restriction, degradation or outright elimination of other identities"—in the case at hand, nonhuman animals and human "others" (133).[22] Furthermore, the original trauma of being prey rather than predator, and the long struggle to reverse this relation, is, in my view, the prehistory to which the human penchant for violence as the ultimate conflict resolution can be traced (if only speculatively and suggestively). This original trauma may also be the evolutionary origin of our traumatized relation to our own animality, to vulnerability and mortality, and thus to our deeply invested cultural practice of false witness, of seeking transcendence through animalizing and sacrificing those living beings we designate "animal" and "Other." It is as if we cannot tolerate awareness of the difficult reality of our own failed transcendence and we seek revenge on those beings we call "animal" for having the arrogance to remind us of this failure.

Several things need to be said at this point in my effort to track a line of thinking that leads to an appreciation of the difficult reality of the woundedness of the human-nonhuman animal relation, to an appreciation of the prehistory and history of trauma that we share with other animals. After spending so much time on this trail, I am convinced that we must appreciate the difficult reality of this wounded relation if we are to escape or move beyond what is by now the reflex of anthropocentric practices and the arrogant claim of human exceptionalism.

Among the many things that need to be said here, the first is that the quest for meaning in life (at least for human animals) must occur, as Lifton notes, in the context of an awareness and appreciation of the difficult reality of our vulnerability and eventual death. "Full life power, or genuine life power," he observes, "depends upon some degree of confrontation with the idea of death, some degree of death being part of one's life, and artists have always known this" (qtd. in Caruth 141). This awareness of finitude is difficult to maintain because, as Diamond observes, it wounds and panics and isolates us (43-89). Yet, the way forward, beyond anthropocentrism and humanism to posthumanism, consists in our collective efforts to appreciate this difficulty of reality, to keep in focus this history of shared woundedness and finitude. Contrary to the longstanding view that nonhuman animals are insensate automatons and have no awareness or appreciation of death, ethologists and other observers of animal behavior have documented that a number of nonhuman animals demonstrate an awareness of vulnerability and death, to the point of burying or attempting to bury their dead.[23] Second, the history and prehistory of traumatic exposure is insufficiently thematized in much of the research and scholarship in the field of animal studies. When Jeremy Bentham changed the question from "Can animals reason?" and "Can they talk?" to "Can they suffer?" he placed on the horizon of the human conversation about nonhuman animal life an awareness of the trauma that nonhuman animals suffer, though until very recently it has not been discussed specifically as "trauma"—again, in large part because of the human denial that animals experience their own vulnerability and impending death. Third, the interdisciplinary research and scholarship on human trauma is now beginning to be employed in understanding the traumatic effects on nonhuman animals of our violent subjection of them.[24] A 2006 *New York Times Magazine* article on post-traumatic stress disorder among elephant populations brought this news to the attention of the general public (Siebert; see also Bradshaw). Of particular relevance to this discussion are the documented instances in which elephants in the wild have not only attacked and killed humans but also raped and killed rhinoceroses. Researchers argue that elephants are suffering a kind of social trauma as a result of decades of poaching, culling, and habitat loss that have disrupted the network of familial and social relations that historically have provided stability to elephant culture (Siebert 44; see also Gowdy). Finally, there is too little recognition of the fact that our human ways of being offer indirect testimony to the legacy of the trauma of predation.

An obvious example of this legacy of predation is the "fight or flight" response, which means it should be reinterpreted as a residual form of hyperarousal, one of the symptoms of post-traumatic stress disorder (see Herman 35–36). Citing recent neurobiological research, Ehrenreich suggests that "the pathologies of paranoia—for example, chronic anxiety and the fear of abandonment—may all have evolutionary roots in the perpetual vigilance of potential prey" (56; see also 54). And she points to the psychiatric evidence that "panic disorders, phobias, and chronic anxiety all represent evolutionary adaptations to a dangerous environment, replete with predators and nonliving things such as lightning and heights" (90). Along these same lines, we might usefully redescribe *false witness* and *scapegoating* as forms of traumatic displacement, and *deflection* as a form of traumatic dissociation, as an out-of-body experience of thought occasioned by exposure to a difficulty of reality—perhaps originally, the trauma of predation, which is perhaps indirectly restaged in any death encounter, regardless of whether the threat is to physical or psychological existence. As Derrida remarks, "the animal looks at us, and we are naked before it. Thinking perhaps begins there" (397). In this view, *deflection* and the "deadening shorthand" of conceptual categories are forms of dissociated thinking that produce abstract knowledge, which takes us out of the body, deflects awareness away from the fact of bodily vulnerability and death, and thereby sacrifices bodies, including embodied knowledge, for the illusory promise of symbolic immortality offered in the life of the mind.[25] The "war on pity" that, according to Derrida, has been waged against animals for the last two hundred years surely has had its casualties. The violation of animal life, he suggests, also violates the "sentiment of compassion"—that is, it damages, diminishes, and perhaps, in some individuals and groups, destroys the human capacity for empathy and sympathetic imagination (397). Indifference to the suffering of others (both human and nonhuman), then, is not in any simplistic sense mere "hard-heartedness" or a lack of pity and compassion. It is certainly that, but indifference might also be more complexly understood as an effect of traumatic exposure. Accordingly, indifference might be redescribed as a form of "constriction" (Herman) and "psychic numbing" or "reinforced invulnerability" (Lifton)—that is, as a profound narrowing and numbing of consciousness and perception to the point that one simply does not *see* the difficulty of the reality of another animal's suffering, does not see one's connection to that suffering, just as the commentators in *The Lives of Animals* do not see Costello's woundedness and therefore do not feel any connection to it or responsibility for it (Herman 42–50; Lifton, "Survivor" 500–10).

The denial, disavowal, and dissimulation to which Derrida refers in his indictment of our violent subjection of animals can only be achieved and maintained at a high cost to us—in particular, a diminution in, even the loss of, what Lifton calls "full life power" and what Coetzee (through Costello) calls "fullness of being." Perhaps human subjectivity, and our deep investment in a sense of individual autonomy, are an effect of traumatic repression—specifically, the repression of our dependency on and vulnerability to others. Millennia of employing *deflection* as a way of avoiding awareness of the difficulties of reality to which our ancestors were undoubtedly exposed (especially the trauma of predation) might be sufficient to evolve human subjectivity as a residue and effect of trauma.[26] If acknowledging our shared vulnerability with animals is, as Diamond observes, wounding and isolating, perhaps over time the trauma of isolation was symbolically refigured (and masked) as a sense of and commitment to autonomy, superiority, and exceptionalism (see Herman 121). Our enduring need to demonstrate our transcendence of animal life—our need to deny human vulnerability and mortality—leads to something that looks much like repetition compulsion, which is one of the symptoms of post-traumatic stress disorder: we compulsively repeat an act (*deflection, false witness*) in a futile effort to achieve a different outcome. In this light, anthropocentrism and humanism appear to be instances of collective reaction-formation that have served rather successfully to *deflect* awareness from the truth of what human and nonhuman animals share.

Following Wolfe's proposal that animal studies join with the problematic of posthumanism and return us to human embodiment and human evolution as "a specific form of animality," I have pursued a recognition that the human psyche has evolved in the context of a history of traumatic experiences, especially with nonhuman animals, a history that, even though it has not been the focus of evolutionary psychology, cannot reasonably be doubted (572). Much of what we mean by "human being" or "human nature" surely must be understood in terms of a long history of trauma, a history that produces post-traumatic symptoms that have endured for thousands of generations, symptoms that are in some part the legacy of our traumatic encounter with nonhuman animals.

IN THE END, A WAY FORWARD

The modern human mind did not evolve in the context of modern industrial life. The modern human mind evolved to meet the challenges that our ancient ancestors faced in a world in which their greatest survival strategy was their intensely social nature. In *The Stone Age Present: How Evolution Has Shaped Modern Life,* William Allman draws on recent evolutionary science to argue that "the behaviors that make up our modern everyday lives . . . all have deep-seated evolutionary roots that stretch back to the times when or ancient ancestors were struggling to meet the challenges of the world around them. These mental mechanisms are part of an ancient, Stone Age legacy that is still very much a part of the human psyche today . . ." (19). Allman devotes a chapter to violence and its causes, arguing that "violence is not the result of some sort of predestined emergence of a beast within" but is rather the ultimate strategy for conflict resolution for the social creatures our human ancestors were. Yet he does not consider the prehistory and history of trauma that surely shaped the modern human mind (144).

Certainly, the highly consequential legacy of this prehistory and history of traumatic exposure is the disconnection, alienation, and isolation from the community of the living (see Herman 51–73). In my view, this insight motivates Wood's suggestion that we need a "moral evolution beyond a species tribalism," one that proceeds from a recognition that "dependency—and inter-dependency—is the name of the game" ("Thinking" 143). In response to the undeclared war on animals, Wood calls for "a war on 'deception,' on 'self-deception,' and, yes, on the ignorance that knows many things but does not connect them" (141). He calls for "a war on the culpable blindness that hides from us the sites at which compassion is pathologically suppressed" and "a war on the environmental destruction that is multiplying the occasions calling for such pity as we may still possess" (144). In 2010, the massive oil spill in the Gulf of Mexico, larger and more destructive than anything we humans have seen, was a deep-sounding bell tolling for each and every one of us.[27]

If war has the social function of restaging primordial emotions and creating solidarity—this time between and among human and nonhuman animals—then a war on deception and self-deception, on disconnection and isolation, is long overdue. What will be sacrificed are not bodies and lives but our use of concepts and categories and practices that historically have been employed in driving each one of us apart from others, all others, making impossible a community of the living. What will be lost in this war is the logic of sacrifice itself, of *false witness* and *scapegoating*, which, as Girard argues about *scapegoating* in its most brutal form, is the logic of the mob (85). This war will be comprised of sundry efforts to make conscious and explicit what Girard calls the "scapegoat mechanism"—in other words, efforts that make explicit *scapegoating*, *victimage*, and *false witness* for what they are—which actually weakens the operation of these mechanisms, for they must remain nonconscious in order to function (Girard 115).

Yet, in my view of this pivotal moment in human history, war must not be the metaphor we choose to keep from being frightened to death while we attempt to chart a way forward out of the morass of a human-centered history. My preference would be a metaphor drawn from the healing arts, those arts that develop our capacity for sympathetic imagination and identification with and empathy for others, those arts that are resolutely nonanthropocentric and nonspeciesist, those arts that have the potential to create and foster solidarity among the living.[28] We human animals need a metaphor that looks human finitude in the face while at the same time fostering kinship and connection, humility and acceptance, (self)forgiveness and rapprochement. While the interdisciplinary field of animal studies may present a formidable, if not fatal, challenge to the future of the humanities, including cultural studies, the humanities nevertheless offer a rich repository of metaphors that may lead us forward, beyond the reactionary and self-serving appeal of anthropocentrism and humanism. Under the pressure of a posthuman sensibility, the humanities might finally move toward becoming truly "doubly wise" by remaking themselves from the ground up as the "posthumanities" so as to counter, or at least balance, the arts of *deflection* with the arts of connection and responsive cohabitation.[29]

Notes

1. See Harvey and Giroux for especially useful discussions of neoliberalism.

2. Wolfe's *PMLA* article appears, in revised form, in his book, *What is Posthumanism?*, which offers a wide-ranging exploration of several paths to the posthuman, which, Wolfe cautions, is not about transcending the human and human embodiment. In both the *PMLA* article and the book chapter, Wolfe focuses on two kinds of finitude: the finitude that arises from the fact of human embodiment (physical vulnerability and mortality); and the finitude we experience in our subjection to and constitution in language. For additional treatments of posthumanism, see Hayles; Badmington.

3. In *Straw Dogs*, Gray offers a trenchant analysis of the tradition of humanism and its commitment to human exceptionalism, especially the idea that humans can transcend animal life.

4. Writing about the soaring increase in violence in post-apartheid South Africa, Farred coins the term "mundanacity of violence" to suggest that the phenomenon of violence has become so routine that it is now mundane and part of the accepted fabric of everyday life. I think this term can be usefully exported to several locations across the globe, including the U.S., to call into question the processes and practices that make violence seem tolerable and acceptable.

5. Pinker's book on violence has created something of a firestorm of controversy. See, for example, Gray's "Delusions of Peace," an incisive review of Pinker's book in which Gray identifies Pinker as an "evangelist" for humanism. (Pinker himself suggests that violence has declined because of the success of Enlightenment humanism.) See also Daly and Wilson's 1988 study of homicide, which concludes with an observation Pinker could agree with: "Twentieth-century, industrial man may well have a better chance of dying peacefully in his bed than any of his predecessors" (291). For a view quite different from Pinker's, see Lifton, *Witness*. Pinker, Lifton, and other readers discuss Pinker's book and violence in human history in "Sunday Dialogue."

6. It is important to note that at the same time that we see unprecedented forms and frequencies of interhuman violence and violence against animals we also see the development of a multitude of industries associated with pet-keeping—not only a vast array of pet products and services as well as books and films about pets but also the professionalization of the industry of veterinary medicine. The development of these industries goes hand-in-hand with the intensification of the sentimentalization of pet-keeping. As Fudge points out, "A pet is a pet first, an animal second" (32). (On the topic of pet-keeping, see also

Garber; Grier; Shell; Tuan.) These developments—violence (against humans and against animals), on the one hand, and on the other, the sentimentalization of pet-keeping—are not unrelated. The idea that a pet is a pet first and an animal second is a deflection (in the sense discussed in this essay) of the reality of its animality, which makes the use, abuse, and killing of animals that are not pets permissible and acceptable and largely invisible—in other words, the idea that a pet is a pet first and an animal second makes possible the differential treatment of animals, some of whom are pets and some of whom are not. We sit at the dinner table and enjoy a steak while Kitty is curled up at our feet; we make no connection between our use of one animal and our different use of the other. We deflect attention from the sacrifice of the "other" animals—factory-farmed animals and animals used in scientific research, for example—through an often intensely sentimentalized attachment to our pets. See Fudge for more on our contradictory relation to animals.

7. The way of thinking that automatically moves from the individual to the group is the essence of speciesist logic. As Kappeler argues in a brilliant analysis of speciesism, we tolerate or allow a moderate, acceptable, or lawful amount of killing as long as the species survives, not through individuals but through group reproduction. When the group's survival is threatened, we call it "genocide," but only in the case that the group is identified as "human."

8. An extensive literature is available on the existence of "animal minds"—that is, on animal cognition, emotion, and moral sensibility. See, for example, Griffin; Bekoff; and Haraway. See Kennedy for a discussion of nonhuman animals' use of rhetoric (understood traditionally as persuasion, eloquence, deception, deliberation, and judgment).

9. See also Kappeler and Roberts. For different treatments of the relationship between animalization and dehumanization, see Haslam and Smith. Of particular interest is Smith's view that animalization is necessary for dehumanization to occur. He argues that because women and girls are not animalized, but only objectified, they are not dehumanized. Smith's claim flies in the face of the extensive feminist literature on sexual objectification as a form of dehumanization. Haslam's treatment is more sensitive to the realities and experiences of dehumanization because he admits two forms: dehumanization through objectification and dehumanization through animalization.

10. In her analysis of the interconnections (or interanimations) among sexism, racism, class privilege, ethnicism, speciesism, nationalism, and capitalism, Kappeler argues that sexism is at the center of, and is the anchor for, speciesist logic. She argues that "reproduction, the sexist instrumentalization of women as reproducers of their 'kind,' is the pivot of all speciesism, racism, ethnicism, and nationalism—the construction of collective entities at the cost of the rights and interests of individuals" (348). Kappeler's analysis suggests that sexism is intrinsic to all these systems of oppression, including and especially

speciesism. Thus, sexism and systems of oppression based on gender must be a focus of posthumanist critique.

11. Nussbaum, Diamond, Derrida, and Wood are among many scholars who have recently developed a focus on vulnerability. See also, for example, Butler and Cavarero. For a classic study of the denial of death in human history, see Becker. See Gray, *Immortalization*, for a recent historical perspective on the human effort to cheat death.

12. Traumatic experience also rewires the autonomic nervous system and creates long-term physiological changes in the individual, such as a heightened startle response or a tendency to the kind of explosive anger that might lead to false witness. Trauma produces memories that are not stored in the same way as ordinary memories, which are narrativized and are easily retrieved under normal circumstances. Traumatic memories, Herman explains, lack context and a place in a coherent narrative. They are encoded in the body through vivid sensations and images and are typically elicited involuntarily in nightmares and in flashbacks (38).

13. Girard insists that scapegoating is and must be "nonconscious," a state that he differentiates from the Freudian notion of the "unconscious." In describing false witness as a process of scapegoating, I do not intend to conflate Lifton's notion of false witness with Girard's notion of psychosocial scapegoating or Burke's notion of victimage. Lifton's notion of false witness operates within a psychological discourse on human trauma; Girard's notion of psychosocial scapegoating operates within a broad theory of religious ritual and myth; Burke's notion of victimage derives from his view of language as symbolic action. What Lifton's notion of false witness brings to the discussion of scapegoating and victimage is a recognition that these practices may have their roots in prior traumatic experiences.

14. Slavery is an exemplary case of the kind of victimization that Lifton describes as false witness. In his highly influential comparative study of slavery, Orlando Patterson describes slavery as a form of "human parasitism" and details the many ways the slaveholder lives off of those who are enslaved—not only physically and economically but also psychologically and symbolically. Patterson defines slavery as "the permanent, violent domination of natally alienated and generally dishonored persons," a condition that he defines as "social death" (13). Through the institution of slavery, the slaveholding group asserts its vitality and symbolic immortality by denying slaves their right to life and by identifying them with death. Social death is accomplished by denying to each slave his or her individuality, his or her unsubstitutable singularity and irreplaceability.

15. Criminologist Lonnie Athens has identified a four-stage process of social development, which he calls "violentization," that, he argues, all violent people have undergone: a stage of *brutalization* in which a young person is forced, through real or threatened violence, to submit to an aggressive author-

ity; a stage of *belligerency* in which the young person, in an attempt to prevent further violent subjugation, resolves to engage in violent acts; a stage of *violent performances* in which the individual learns that violent actions produce respect and fear in others; and, last, a stage of *virulency* in which violence becomes the preferred means of dealing with others. See Rhodes for a discussion of Athens' theory of violence. See DeMause for a related discussion of how styles of leadership, on the world stage, derive from how those leaders undergo violent socialization.

16. See, for example, Kincaid's *A Small Place*, an essay that delivers a scorching indictment of the history of colonialism in the Caribbean (in particular, Antigua, her home island) and its enduring legacy of traumatic effects, especially crime, corruption, abuse, and tourism as a form of secondary colonialism.

17. Coetzee and Derrida are not the only writers who make the comparison between the massive abuse and killing of animals and genocide and the Holocaust. See, for example, Charles Patterson's *Eternal Treblinka*, which takes its title from "The Letter Writer," by Nobel Laureate Isaac Bashevis Singer: "In relation to them [the animals], all people are Nazis; for the animals it is an eternal Treblinka" (qtd. in C. Patterson). See also Buettner. While the analogy may be controversial or even offensive to some, the analogy is misleading and even erroneous, as Wolfe points out, "since ten *billion* land animals are killed each year in the United States alone for food, the vast majority of them—about eighty percent—under the deplorable conditions of factory farming" (567).

18. Wood's point about meat-eating as a form of what I would call repetition compulsion occurs in the context of a discussion of the symbolic role of animals in human life and history. His point is not about the role of hunting and meat-eating in evolution—that is, whether meat-eating contributed to the possibility of the emergence of a larger brain in humans, a topic of some controversy among scientists. It is perhaps worth noting in this context that the earliest direct ancestors of modern humans, the *australopithecines* (who lived 4.2 to 1 million years ago), were not hunters but were specialized vegetarians. Similarly, *Homo habilis* (emergence around 2.5 million years ago) also were not hunters, but had a diet consisting of vegetable material and leftover meat scavenged from dead animal carcasses abandoned by large predators. It is likely, in other words, that meat made up only a tiny part of the diet of *Homo habilis*. Neanderthals hunted and scavenged on dead carcasses. By 500,000 years ago, early humans were hunting animals for meat (see Mithen 119–20). I present this information to make the point that, contrary to popular, "meat-centric" opinion in the West, humans are not carnivores in the same way as, say, big cats. Our earliest ancestors were vegetarians; and for most of our prehistory and history, we have been omnivores, with meat occupying a very small part of our diet. This kind of diet continues to sustain traditional and non-western cultures. Developing countries that are in the process of shifting to a meat-based

western diet are experiencing an increase in health issues related to meat-eating and a diet high in animal protein, animal fat, and processed sugars.

19. The neurobiological memory of this original trauma of predation may well be the source, as Steeves suggests, of our fear of being eaten and, in many cultures, the prohibition on cannibalism ("They Say" 168; see also Ehrenreich 77–96).

20. To balance Sterelny's view that thought evolves in response to threat, I should mention that the consensus among evolutionary scientists is that most of what we view as distinctively human (eg., the big brain, language) evolved as a result of the fact that our early hominin ancestors and early humans were especially social and cooperative and their success as a species must be attributed to their ability to form and sustain social bonds, even in the context of predation. As Dunbar argues, "primates live in groups as a mutual defence against predation. Indeed, sociality is at the very core of primate existence; it is their principal evolutionary strategy, the thing that marks them out as different from all other species" (18).

21. See Appadurai, *Fear*, "Full Attachment," and "Grounds" for more on the concept of *full attachment*, which is a term he coins to account for the affective side of social solidarity and which often is, in his view, inadequately understood through the familiar (and more cerebral) concepts of loyalty or patriotism. With the concept of *full attachment*, Appadurai attempts to account for "an order of attachment" or "a surplus of attachment" to others in one's group, nation, or territory that allows them "to kill and die in its name" ("Full" 445; "Grounds" 130). I think Appadurai mines the metaphor of attachment, as it is developed in psychological research on individual identity (Bowlby, for example), to account for another order of identity and identification that links the individual to the collective.

22. As a long-term vegan, I have been more than a little perplexed by the often strongly negative reactions to these dietary practices, reactions that, at times, have seemed wildly out of proportion and creepily personal and vicious. I now see that these dietary practices are more than simply a personal "lifestyle choice"; they also represent a radical repudiation of the social solidarity created by patriarchy, misogyny and sexism, and speciesism (see Adams on the sexual politics of meat). A vegan commits (intentionally or unintentionally) the ultimate betrayal: a repudiation of the social compact that constructs "human" (especially the human male) as the preeminent predatory identity. Perhaps this explains why some individuals feel so threatened by these dietary practices that they are compelled to lash out by "othering" vegans and vegetarians. See Coetzee for an insightful treatment of vegetarianism. Elizabeth Costello explains that her own vegetarianism does not arise from "moral conviction" but comes out of a desire to save her soul, which suggests that her decision is not about following or attaining an abstract ethical ideal but arises from a more personal and intimate sense of endangerment (43).

23. Pliny the Elder's "Combats of Elephants" offers a graphic description of elephants' awareness of their own vulnerability and potential death and their capacity to appeal to human empathy. Gowdy's novel, *The White Bone*, is an especially moving fictional account of the trauma and suffering of several individual elephants and their clans, suffering caused by human rapaciousness and predation. See also Bradshaw; and Bekoff.

24. In the context of the recent turn to trauma studies to understand animal suffering, it might be useful to note that the term *post-traumatic stress disorder* was coined and the diagnosis formally recognized in 1980, which opened the way for the contemporary study of human trauma (see Herman). Our understanding of traumatic experience has been developed in part through the interdisciplinary field of trauma studies, which began to consolidate itself as a field in the 1990s with the recording and study of the oral testimony of Holocaust survivors (see Caruth). In my view, it is unsurprising, given the present argument, that this extensive body of interdisciplinary knowledge is only beginning to be employed in an understanding of animals and the nature of their suffering. While some may object that the extension of this knowledge of human trauma to create an understanding of animal suffering is but another instance of anthropomorphism and is therefore anthropocentric, I would propose that anthropomorphism in this instance is defensible, for it increases the likelihood that this understanding will lead to greater justice for nonhuman animals. For very different arguments in defense of anthropomorphism, see Diamond, "Eating Meat"; Oerlemans; and Daston and Mitman.

25. In "Losing Your Concepts," which was published before "The Difficulty of Reality," Diamond employs the phrase "that great arena of dissociated thought" to describe the debate on animal rights (276). She does not link what she means by "dissociated thought" to the experience or legacy of trauma, nor does she discuss deflection as dissociated thought in the later essay. Nonetheless, the phrase, "dissociated thought," led me to think of deflection as dissociated thought, as a style of thinking that bears the legacy of traumatic exposure in dissociating the mind from the body and thereby sacrificing the body and its knowledge (including its knowledge of vulnerability and mortality) for an investment in the symbolic immortality offered in the life of the mind.

26. In "*Comment*" Wood suggests that Derrida writes "as though he is on the brink" of developing a "historico-psycho-anthropology" that "would reveal human subjectivity as something like surplus repression . . ." (33). Inasmuch as repression results from trauma (in Freudian theory, childhood trauma), I am indebted to Wood for the insight that human subjectivity might be an effect of a history of traumatic experience. But see also Kristeva's remark, cited above, which suggests that human subjectivity is an effect of repression.

27. A "spill" is easily and quickly cleaned up, and recovery from a spill is also easy and relatively effortless. As in "spilled milk," a spill has no serious or lasting consequences. In addition, when we are admonished "not to cry over

spilled milk," we are admonished not to cry over things we cannot change. In the context of the BP disaster, the use of the term, "spill," especially in the initial weeks after the disaster, represents a deflection of the difficulty of the reality of this disaster and its horrific consequences for habitats and their inhabitants. This choice of words also lends a kind of inevitability to this disaster and perhaps others in the future, since our remorse cannot change the outcome. The phrase, "deep-sounding bell," is a recurring motif in Roy's novel, *The God of Small Things*, which presents a powerful critique of Western colonialism and neocolonialism, a critique that in part arises from an equally powerful environmental ethic. In her novel, the phrase alludes to the well-known poem by John Donne, "No Man is An Island," and also to Ernest Hemingway's *For Whom the Bell Tolls*, which focuses on the Spanish Civil War and the threat of fascism. Donne's poem, and Roy's repeated allusion to it, memorialize our interconnectedness and interdependency and therefore our responsibility to one another, to all life, including the earth.

28. The healing arts to which I refer will have help from neuroscientists, who have discovered the neurobiological basis for empathy in mirror neurons found in the brain. These neurons fire when an individual is engaged in an action and also when the individual is simply watching another engage in the same action. They were originally discovered in the laboratory in macaque monkeys in the 1990s (see, for example, Rizzolatti and Sinigaglia; Iacoboni). Mirror neurons have also been found in other species of animals and are thought to be the neurobiological basis for empathy in some nonhuman animal species (see Bekoff). Baron-Cohen describes the mirror neuron system and the neural circuits involved in human empathy, and he argues that when the empathy circuit fails to develop properly the result is "zero-degrees of empathy," which he describes as an inability to read other people's feelings and thoughts, an inability to respond appropriately to social cues, and a deep-seated self-centeredness. He differentiates between "positive" and "negative" forms of *zero-degrees of empathy*. Autism is, in his view, the positive side of zero-degrees of empathy, because people on the autism spectrum, while they do not have normal empathy, show various talents and capabilities that are not harmful to self or others. On the negative side of zero-degrees of empathy, he argues, one of three different personality types occurs: narcissistic personality, psychopathic personality, and borderline personality. Because empathy is a deep and ancient genetic endowment that may be developed or damaged by an individual's environment, Baron-Cohen wonders how modern life shapes our natural resources for empathy. In an award-winning study of emotions linked to moral sensibility, such as compassion, Damasio et al. find that social emotions require "a level of persistent, emotional attention" (Marziali). The study raises questions "about the emotional cost—particularly for the developing brain—of heavy reliance on a rapid stream of news snippets" provided by digital media (Marziali). As Manuel Castells observes, "In a media culture in which violence and suffering

becomes an endless show, be it in fiction or in infotainment, indifference to the vision of human suffering gradually sets in" (qtd. in Marzali). What we are learning about the neurological and social basis of empathy presses us to assume our specifically human obligation to develop and extend empathy and social justice to all living beings, including nonhuman animals.

    29. This article is a substantially revised and expanded version of my article, "Thinking with Cats (More, to Follow)," which appeared in a special issue of *JAC* on the human-animal relation.

WORKS CITED

Adams, Carol J. *The Sexual Politics of Meat: A Feminist-Vegetarian Critical Theory.* New York: Continuum, 1990. Print.

Allman, William F. *The Stone Age Present: How Evolution Has Shaped Modern Life.* New York: Simon, 1994. Print.

Appadurai, Arjun. *Fear of Small Numbers: An Essay on the Geography of Anger.* Durham: Duke UP, 2006. Print.

—. "Full Attachment." *Public Culture* 10 (1998): 443–49. Web. 2 Apr. 2009.

—. "The Grounds of the Nation-State: Identity, Violence, and Territory." *Nationalism and Internationalism in the Post-Cold War Era.* London: Routledge, 2000. 129–42. Print.

Badmington, Neil. "Theorizing Posthumanism." *Cultural Critique* 53 (2003): 10–27. Print.

Barash, David P., and Judith E. Lipton. *Payback: Why We Retaliate, Redirect Aggression, and Take Revenge.* New York: Oxford UP, 2011. Print.

Baron-Cohen, Simon. *The Science of Evil: On Empathy and the Origins of Cruelty.* New York: Basic, 2011. Print.

Bekoff, Marc. *The Emotional Lives of Animals.* Novato, CA: New World, 2007. Print.

Becker, Ernest. *The Denial of Death.* New York: Free P, 1973. Print.

Bradshaw, Isabel Gay A. *Elephants on the Edge: What Animals Teach Us about Humanity.* New Haven: Yale UP, 2009. Print.

—. "Not by Bread Alone: Symbolic Loss, Trauma, and Recovery in Elephant Communities." *Society and Animals* 12 (2004):143–58. Print.

Buettner, Angi. "Animal Holocausts." *Cultural Studies Review* 8 (2002): 28–44. Print.

Burke, Kenneth. "Definition of Man." *Language as Symbolic Action: Essays on Life, Literature, and Method.* Berkeley: U of California P, 1966. 3–24. Print.

—. *Permanence and Change: An Anatomy of Purpose.* Berkeley: U of California P, 1954. Print.

—. "Terministic Screens." *Language as Symbolic Action: Essays on Life, Literature, and Method.* Berkeley: U of California P, 1966. 43–62. Print.

Butler, Judith. *Precarious Life: The Powers of Mourning and Violence*. London: Verso, 2006. Print.

Cartmill, Matt. *A View to a Death in the Morning: Hunting and Nature through History*. Cambridge: Harvard UP, 1993. Print.

Caruth, Cathy. "An Interview with Robert Jay Lifton." *Trauma: Explorations in Memory*. Ed. Cathy Caruth. Baltimore: Johns Hopkins UP, 1995. 128–47. Print.

Cavarero, Adriana. *Horrorism: Naming Contemporary Violence*. Trans. William McCuaig. New York: Columbia UP, 2008. Print.

Cavell, Stanley, et al. *Philosophy and Animal Life*. New York: Columbia UP, 2008. Print.

Coetzee, J.M. *The Lives of Animals*. Princeton UP, 1999. Print.

Daly, Martin, and Margo Wilson. *Homicide*. New York: De Gruyter, 1988. Print.

Daston, Lorraine, and Gregg Mitman. *Thinking With Animals: New Perspectives on Anthropomorphism*. New York: Columbia UP, 2004. Print.

Davis, David Brion. *Inhuman Bondage: The Rise and Fall of Slavery in the New World*. New York: Oxford UP, 2006. Print.

DeMause, Lloyd. *The Emotional Life of Nations*. New York: Karnac, 2002. Print.

Derrida, Jacques. "The Animal that Therefore I Am (More to Follow)." Trans. David Wills. *Critical Inquiry* 28 (2002): 369–418. Print.

Diamond, Cora. "The Difficulty of Reality and the Difficulty of Philosophy." Cavell et al. 43–89. Print.

—. "Eating Meat and Eating People." *The Realistic Spirit: Wittgenstein, Philosophy, and the Mind*. Cambridge: MIT P, 1991. 319–34. Print.

—. "Injustice and Animals." *Slow Cures and Bad Philosophers: Essays on Wittgenstein, Medicine, and Bioethics*. Ed. Carl Elliott. Durham: Duke UP, 2001. 118–48. Print.

—. "Losing Your Concepts." *Ethics* 98 (1988): 255–77. Print.

Dunbar, Robin. *Grooming, Gossip, and the Evolution of Language*. Cambridge: Harvard UP, 1996. Print.

Ehrenreich, Barbara. *Blood Rites: Origins and History of the Passions of War*. New York: Holt, 1997. Print.

Farred, Grant. "The Mundanacity of Violence: Living in a State of Disgrace." *Interventions* 4.3 (2002): 352–62. Print.

Farrell, Kirby. *Post-traumatic Culture: Injury and Interpretation in the Nineties*. Baltimore: Johns Hopkins UP, 1998. Print.

Fudge, Erica. *Animal*. London: Reaktion, 2002. Print.

Garber, Marjorie. *Dog Love*. New York: Simon, 1996. Print.

Gilligan, James. *Violence: Reflections on a National Epidemic*. New York: Vintage, 1997. Print.

Girard, René. "Generative Scapegoating." *Violent Origins: Ritual Killing and Cultural Formation.* Ed. Robert G. Hamerton-Kelly. Stanford: Stanford UP, 1987. Print.
Giroux, Henry A. *Against the Terror of Neoliberalism: Politics Beyond the Age of Greed.* Boulder: Paradigm, 2008. Print.
Gorman, James. "Animal Studies Cross Campus to Lecture Hall." *New York Times* 3 Jan. 2012. D1+. Print.
Gowdy, Barbara. *The White Bone.* New York: Picador, 1998. Print.
Gray, John. "Delusions of Peace." *Prospect* 21 Sept. 2011. Web. 26 Dec. 2011.
—. *The Immortalization Commission: Science and the Strange Quest to Cheat Death.* New York: Farrar, 2011. Print.
—. *Straw Dogs: Thoughts on Humans and Other Animals.* New York: Farrar, 2007. Print.
Grier, Katherine C. *Pets in America: A History.* Orlando: Harcourt, 2006. Print.
Griffin, Donald R. *Animal Minds.* Chicago: U of Chicago P, 1992. Print.
Haslam, Nick. "Dehumanization: An Integrative Review." *Personality and Social Psychology Review* 10.3 (2006): 252–64. Print.
Haraway, Donna. *The Companion Species Manifesto: Dogs, People, and Significant Otherness.* Chicago: Prickly Paradigm, 2003. Print.
Harvey, David. *A Brief History of Neoliberalism.* Oxford: Oxford UP, 2005. Print.
Hayles, N. Katherine. *How We Became Posthuman: Virtual Bodies in Cybernetics, Literature, and Informatics.* Chicago: U of Chicago P, 1999. Print.
Herman, Judith. *Trauma and Recovery.* New York: Basic, 1992. Print.
Iacoboni, Marco. *Mirroring People: The New Science of How We Connect with Others.* New York: Farrar, 2008. Print.
Kalof, Linda, and Amy Fitzgerald, eds. *The Animals Reader: The Essential Classic and Contemporary Writings.* Oxford: Berg, 2007. Print.
Kappeler, Susanne. "Speciesism, Racism, Nationalism . . . or the Power of Scientific Subjectivity." *Animals and Women: Feminist Theoretical Explorations.* Ed. Carol J. Adams and Josephine Donovan. Durham: Duke UP, 1995. 320–52. Print.
Kennedy, George A. "Rhetoric Among Social Animals." *Comparative Rhetoric: An Historical and Cross-Cultural Introduction.* New York: Oxford UP, 1998. 11–28. Print.
Kincaid, Jamaica. *A Small Place.* New York: Farrar, 1988. Print.
Kristeva, Julia. *Powers of Horror: An Essay on Abjection.* New York: Columbia UP, 1982. Print.
Lifton, Robert Jay. "The Survivor." *Death in Life: Survivors of Hiroshima.* Chapel Hill: U of North Carolina P, 1991. 479–541. Print.
—. *Witness to an Extreme Century: A Memoir.* New York: Free, 2011.
Marziali, Carl. "Nobler Instincts Take Time." *USC News* 14 Apr. 2009. Web. 19 Jan. 2012.

Mithen, Steven. "The Hunter-Gatherer Prehistory of Human-Animal Interactions." Kalof and Fitzgerald. 117–28. Print.

Nussbaum, Martha C. *Hiding from Humanity: Disgust, Shame, and the Law*. Princeton, NJ: Princeton UP, 2004. Print.

Oerlemans, Onno. "A Defense of Anthropomorphism: Comparing Coetzee and Gowdy." *Mosaic* 40 (2007): 181–96. Print.

Patterson, Charles. *Eternal Treblinka: Our Treatment of Animals and the Holocaust*. New York: Lantern, 2002. Print.

Patterson, Orlando. *Slavery and Social Death: A Comparative Study*. Cambridge: Harvard UP, 1982. Print.

Pinker, Stephen. *The Better Angels of Our Nature: Why Violence Has Declined*. New York: Viking, 2011. Print.

Pliny the Elder. "Combats of Elephants." Kalof and Fitzgerald. 195–96. Print.

Rhodes, Richard. *Why They Kill: The Discoveries of a Maverick Criminologist*. New York: Knopf, 1999. Print.

Rizzolatti, Giacomo, and Corrado Sinigaglia. *Mirrors in the Brain: How Our Minds Share Actions and Emotions*. Trans. Frances Anderson. London: Oxford UP, 2008. Print.

Roberts, Mark S. *The Mark of the Beast: Animality and Human Oppression*. West Lafayette, IN: Purdue UP, 2008. Print.

Roy, Arundhati. *The God of Small Things*. New York: Harper, 1998. Print.

Shell, Marc. "The Family Pet." *Representations* 15 (1986): 121–53. Print.

Siebert, Charles. "An Elephant Crackup?" *New York Times Magazine* 8 Oct. 2006. 42+. Print.

Smith, David Livingstone. *Less Than Human: Why We Demean, Enslave, and Exterminate Others*. New York: St. Martin's, 2011. Print.

Spiegel, Marjorie. *The Dreaded Comparison: Human and Animal Slavery*. New York: Mirror, 1996. Print.

Steeves, H. Peter, ed. *Animal Others: On Ethics, Ontology, and Animal Life*. New York: State U of New York P, 1999. Print.

Steeves, H. Peter. "They Say Animals Can Smell Fear." Steeves 133–78. Print.

Sterelny, Kim. *Thought in a Hostile World: The Evolution of Human Cognition*. Malden, MA: Blackwell, 2003. Print.

"Sunday Dialogue: Do We Live in a Less Deadly Time, or Not?" *New York Times* 8 Jan. 2012. Web. 9 Jan. 2012.

Tuan, Yi-Fu. *Dominance and Affection: The Making of Pets*. New Haven: Yale UP, 1984. Print.

Wolfe, Cary. "Human, All Too Human: 'Animal Studies' and the Humanities." *PMLA* 124 (2009): 564–75. Print.

Wood, David. "*Comment ne pas manger*—Deconstruction and Humanism." Steeves 15–35. Print.

—. "Thinking with Cats." *Animal Philosophy: Ethics and Identity*. Ed. Peter Atterton and Matthew Calarco. London: Continuum, 2004. 129–44. Print.

Worsham, Lynn. "Composing (Identities) in a Post-Traumatic Age." *Identity Papers: Literacy and Power in Higher Education*. Ed. Bronwyn T. Williams. Utah State UP, 2006. 170–81. Print.

—. "Going Postal: Pedagogic Violence and the Schooling of Emotion." *JAC* 18.2 (1998): 213–45. Print.

—. "Thinking with Cats (More, to Follow). *JAC* 30.3–4 (2010): 405–33. Print.

3 Writing-Being: Another Look at the "Symbol-Using Animal"

Diane Davis

In 2008, world renowned primatologist Frans de Waal appeared on *The Colbert Report* to discuss his new book *Our Inner Ape*. The interview was conducted in typical *Colbert Report* fashion, with Colbert performing antic resistance to the narcissistic wound that is unceremoniously re-opened in de Waal's study:

> Colbert: "I thought all you scientist types say we *descended from* apes. Aren't we different?"
> De Waal: "No, you're a large primate without a tail—I hope, for you."
> Colbert: "It's none of your damn business. But go on. A large primate without a tail . . ."
> De Waal: "Yes, so you're an ape."
> Colbert: "Wait, wait, wait!"

In response to the many familiar objections Colbert comically mimes ("but I have a soul! etc.), de Waal notes that "the only reason we biologists don't call humans apes is to protect the fragile human ego." But "our DNA is basically the same," he says. "It's very hard to distinguish. It is 98.5 % identical to an ape's DNA." And though a human's brain is roughly three times larger than an ape's brain, they "share all the same parts," de Waal tells Colbert, "all the parts of an ape brain are present in your brain." Colbert then poses the obvious question, pleading one last time for some sliver of human exceptionalism: "Is there *anything* about human beings that apes don't have?" Given both his distinguished oeuvre and the discussion so far, de Waal's recuperative and thoroughly humanist response to this question is somewhat surprising: "Language would probably be one," he says, flatly. Colbert: "Language? Do apes write?" De Wahl: "No."

The disappointing lapse into metaphysical prejudices leaves the celebrated primatologist in full agreement with a long line of anthropocentric philosophers from Descartes and Kant to Heidegger, Lacan, and Levinas. The difference between the apes who call themselves human and the apes we humans call apes, he echoes—and echoes and echoes—is that the latter do not have language and (so) they do not write. Given the casual manner in which the question is asked and answered, I assume Colbert and de Waal are talking about language in the representational sense, as that which refers to a full-presence that precedes it, and about writing as an author's harnessing of language for the making-manifest of reality. You couldn't pay Heidegger, Lacan, or Levinas to take you into these conceptual neighborhoods or their surrounding areas. And yet, these thinkers remain in basic agreement that "having" language and writing is what separates the specifically human being from all the other beings.

I'd like to challenge this proposition, but not in order to dialogue with de Waal, per se, nor to grant a certain "humanity" or even specific human rights to apes, rights that other animals less "like us" might more obviously be denied—as if rights discourse were not already implicated in precisely the questions we have before us. I have no desire to confront this metaphysical separationism with an equally problematic notion of biological continuism. My goal is simply to call into question, once again, longstanding and robust humanist convictions about language and about writing, and to do it by attending to what Jean-Luc Nancy describes as the ethico-political *task* or *practice* of writing: to expose the not-simply-human threshold or limit that both shares and divides "us," the limit on which writing is given, and without which there would be no writing and no reading (*Inoperable Community*, 69, 135, 152n4).

DRAWING IT OUT

In his foreword to the English translation of Nancy's *La communauté désoeuvrée* (*The Inoperative Community*), Christopher Fynsk notes that Nancy uses the term *writing* in a double sense: as "the original tracing out of a differential articulation" and as an ethical and political practice that draws out (rearticulates) this articulation (155n39). Writing, for Nancy, is always the writing *of* community, which is to say that it is, first of all, the inscription of the differential relation that constitutes singular beings. So on the one hand, *writing* indicates the gesture through which community is inscribed: wherever the singular being communicates—that is, wherever it says or articulates difference—"it communicates *itself* as an opening to alterity," as Fynsk puts it (xxiii, my emphasis). Community exists only *as* this communication, which takes place on the limit that separates what it also joins, "you" and "me." Communication is a *writing* in Nancy's first sense of the term; it's the inscribing or articulation of community, of a being-together on the limit in a way that resists fusional impulses. But this original inscription, Nancy insists, also issues a prescription: "The communication that takes place on this limit, and that, in truth, constitutes it, demands a way of destining ourselves in common that we call politics, that way of opening community to itself, rather than to a destiny or to a future" (80).

So, on the other hand, there is the ethico-political *practice* of writing that devotes itself to retracing its own inscription, exposing the unexposable limit or threshold—not *of* communication but—*on* which communication takes place. Its only aim is to open community to itself. "What is at stake" in this writing practice, Nancy writes, "is the articulation of community. . . . an articulation according to which there is no singularity but that exposed in common, and no community but that offered to the limit of singularities" (80). So the two senses of writing, neither of which is reducible to representation, are indissociable: the one needs the other "in order to occur" (155n39). The prescription demands the practice, but it is only in the practice that the prescription is drawn out and taken up. What writing says, in either case, is that writing is given on/at this limit, which is inscribed (constituted) by communication and which both separates and shares "us." Nancy:

> The call that convokes us, as well as the one we address to one another at this limit (this call from one to the other is no doubt the same call, and yet not the same) can be named, for want of a better term, writing, or literature. (71)

Two indissociable senses of writing, then, both convoked, tracing and retracing the limit that "we" are. "We would not write if our being were not shared," Nancy writes. "And consequently this truth: if we write (which might also be a way of speaking), we share being-in-common, or else we are shared, and exposed, by it" (69).

Obviously, what Nancy is calling "the writer" here is not what the humanist tradition calls "the author," and we'll have to shake off that metaphysical connotation to be able to hear him at all. The practice of writing *interrupts* this myth of the author. Nancy:

> The writer neither gives nor addresses anything to the others; he does not envisage his project as one that involves communicating something to them, be it a message or himself. Of course, there are always messages, and there are always persons, and it is important that both of these—if I may for a moment treat them as identical—be communicated. But writing is the act that obeys the sole necessity of exposing the limit: not the limit of communication, but the limit upon which communication takes place. (67)

The limit that writing aims to expose takes place in the between of the "I" and the "you," where, as Nancy puts it, " 'you (are/and/is) (entirely other than) I' ('*toi [e(s)t] [tout autre que] moi*'). Or again, more simply: [where] *you shares me* ('*toi partage moi*')" (29; his emphasis). Again, a limit both divides and shares: to be up against a limit is to be exposed to and continually affected by—constituted through—a dynamic relation with that which the limit also sets apart from "you." Writing aims to point to the limit that simultaneously shares and divides "you," exposing "your" exposedness and so sharing out an originary sharing that has nothing to do with appropriation or fusion—with a bond or with communion. Writing aims simply (!) to (re)trace the limit "upon which communication takes place."

Being-in-common, as Nancy insists everywhere, is not common being; the "community" drawn out in writing is "inaugural—not final. It is not finished; on the contrary, it is made up of the interruption of mythic communion and communal myth" (68). Writing is an event "and an advent" in which being-in-common *comes about,* in which a writing shares "us" (69). Again, the writer, who becomes thinkable only when myth is interrupted,

> is not the author, nor is he the hero, and perhaps he is no longer what has been called the poet or what has been called the thinker; rather he is a singular voice (a writing: which might also be a way of speaking). He is this singular voice, this resolutely and irreducibly singular (mortal) voice, *in common:* just as one can never be "a voice" ("a writing") but *in common.* (70)

According to Nancy, the writer *is* a writing and writing *is* the writing of community, of being-in-common; writing is the exposition of exposedness, the sharing of sharedness. And the writer (who could also, by the way, be a "she") is the singular voice, in-common, giving voice to this exposition, this sharing.

The writer has nothing to do with the sovereignty of a subject, which "thwarts a thinking of community" (23). When we talk about the writer, we are talking about "the being communicating" and not "the subject representing" (24). And when we talk about writing, we are talking about an exposition and not a representation, an inscription that involves an interruption in anthropological appropriations of this practice, so that, as Nancy writes,

> a certain [humanist] scene, an attitude, and a creativity pertaining to the writer are no longer possible. The task of what has been designated as écriture (writing) and the thinking of écriture has been, precisely, to render them impossible—and consequently to render impossible a certain type of foundation, utterance, and literary and communitarian fulfillment: in short, a politics. (69)

The ethico-political task of this writing is to render impossible writing's *metaphysical* politics, its politics of fulfillment. The task of the writer after the death of the author, as Avital Ronell has put it, has been to "write for writing because it died" (*Finitude's* xiii). Once writing's teleological goals and its foundational and transcendental claims "can be safely said to have perished. . . . once its more church and state-like responsibilities have been suspended," she writes, "there is something that, despite it all, liberates writing to another realm" ("Confessions" 253). To write after the death of writing is to deal precisely with writing's remains, which are powerful, haunting, "difficult and demanding"—that is to say: lively (253).[1]

Gutted of its author, its representational message, and its telic purpose, writing—which precedes and exceeds all of that—engages its own spirited remains, retracing its own tracings in order to expose what it will never be able to appropriate or represent: the limit upon which it takes place. We might call this writing that deals with writing's remains a posthuman writing, a writing no longer at the service of church or state, of author or telos, a convoked writing devoted only to a tracing out of this limit—only to the inscription of community. What that suggests, provocatively, is that posthuman writing is the *condition* for humanist writing practices, which of course never *stop* dying. The fusional impulse is a panicked response to the experience of the limit. Whether or not it communicates a message, writing is irreducible to that message; it involves a saying that is irreducible to what gets said. What its saying says is *that* there is the saying, that there is exposedness, finitude, vulnerability, sharing—that there is community. What its saying says is that "we" are, that "we" share precisely the limit that divides "us."

Ek-Sistence

The question driving our inquiry is whether human beings are being's only writers, the only beings called to the limit to write the limit, the only beings who *share* being. According to Nancy, again, "We would not write if our being were not shared. And consequently this truth: *if* we write . . . we share being-in-common, or else we are shared, and exposed, by it" (69, my emphasis). Only a singularity whose being is shared, who experiences the limit where s/he is both divided and shared, writes; and so the flipside, if a singularity writes, s/he is sharing being-in-common. Though he would be put off by the biological appropriation, Heidegger would agree with de Waal that human dasein are being's *only* writers because, as he famously insists, human dasein are the only beings who share being. Whereas nonhuman animals exist in the sense that they *are*, in the sense that they *have* being, they do not *share* being, nor do they *concern* themselves with being. Nonhuman animals exist but they do not ek-sist, as Heidegger puts it. But human dasien exist in another manner entirely: "Man is rather 'thrown' from Being itself into the truth of Being, so that ek-sisting in this fashion he might guard the truth of Being, in order that beings might appear in the light of Being as the beings they are" ("Letter" 234). To ek-sist, as only human dasein does, is to exist in such a way that one stands "out into the truth of Being," letting being be, as he says. Dasein is da-sein, being-*there*, or *there*, where it has been thrown into the world. The transcendence marked by this "into" makes all the difference; it *is* the ontological difference. There is no being-there at all that is not already being-with-others-*in*-the-world. "World," for Heidegger, is always a shared world; it takes place *through* dasein's being-together. Human dasein, then, ek-sist *in*-the-world-with-others, but no animal at all ek-sists and therefore no animal at all would write, no matter how adeptly it might be trained to manipulate signs.

Having no "as-structure," and so no understanding of this *as* that, "the animal" lives but has no relation to that life: it lives but it does not exist in Heidegger's sense of the term. In *The Fundamental Concepts of Metaphysics,* Heidegger famously proposes that, "[w]hen we say that the lizard is lying on the rock, we ought to cross out the word 'rock' in order to indicate that whatever the lizard is lying on is certainly given *in some way* for the lizard, and yet is not known to the lizard as a rock" (198). The lizard does not understand the rock *as* a rock, in other words. It doesn't and can't inquire into the rock's elemental makeup or history. Indeed, according to Heidegger it is "the *essence* of animality" to lack precisely this understanding: the essence of animality is to live *sans* this all-important "as-structure."[2] And by that, he means that every single animal, no exceptions—from a sea urchin to a great ape—is *captivated* by its environment (which is not a world) in a way that leaves it without any real access to this captor. The "as" structure, a gift of language, is what grants dasein's irruption into being as ek-sistent. The animal is "poor in world," Heidegger avers throughout Part II of the *Fundamental Concepts*, because it is merely *in* its life without being granted what he calls a "clearing" (language ["Letter" 249]) by which to step back (transcend) and reflect on any aspect of it, to "let it be," to use one of his favorite phrases.

The honeybee, Heidegger notes, is instinctively drawn toward its food, but this relation demonstrates no recognition of honey *as* honey. The bee is driven toward its hive, as well, toward "home," and it is captivated by the sun, given over to the sun without being able to reflect on it as something grasped. It doesn't comport itself toward particular entities, in other words, but behaves in a *driven* way in relation to them; it is driven to produce a direction or to gather nectar, for example. Animals—all of them, according to Heidegger—relate to other entities (sun, nectar, hive), but not to entities "as such." The relation between an animal and its others is not a comportment toward or a being-with but a captivation. This is why animals, he says, don't really exist but merely live, reserving "existence"—and therefore language and writing—for human dasein alone (*Fundamental Concepts*, 241-48).

Whereas Sartre suggested in *Being and Nothingness* that Heidegger's philosophy sought to expose the priority of existence over essence (the existentialist mantra: existence precedes essence), Heidegger corrected the misreading by reiterating that the essence of existence is "ek-sistence." Ek-sistence, which can only occur in language (the "clearing-concealing advent of being itself"), is a being-outside-oneself that is unique to human dasein ("Letter" 249). Existence is uncanny, ek-static, and this ecstasis grants a space for self-gathering that no animal at all can approximate. And dasein, he insists, is *not* an animal—that would be a biological appropriation of an essence irreducible to biology: "the human body is something essentially other than an animal organism" (247). No matter what sort of missing link might one day be discovered, according to Heidegger, there will remain an uncrossable gap separating "the animal" from human dasein: whereas the former is forever trapped within itself (its cosmology, its "encircling ring"), the latter is "free," ek-sisting outside-itself, with-others, in-the-world, and able by that very self-distance to understand beings *as* beings, and so to inquire into its own being. Dasein: the being for whom being is an issue.

In very different terminology and to very different ends, Jacques Lacan proposes something similar: "the animal"—trapped in the imaginary (the presymbolic) and forever denied access to the symbolic—communicates via a pre-wired code that permits fixed reactions to stimuli but has no access to the shared articulations of linguistic subjects capable of genuine responses to questions or situations. Animals communicate through a complex code of signs, Lacan explains, but a code is not a language: "it is distinguished from language precisely by the fixed correlation of its signs to the reality that they signify" (*Ecrits: A Selection* 85). Interestingly his primary example of the difference is the honeybee's dance. When a bee finds nectar and returns to its hive to spread the word, Lacan notes, it dances in such a way that informs the others of, on the one hand, "exactly the direction to be followed, determined in relation to the inclination of the sun . . . and, on the other hand, the distance, up to several miles, at which the nectar is to be found. And the other bees respond to this message by setting off immediately for the place thus designated." Successful communication. However, whereas "in a language signs take on their value from their relations to each other," Lacan insists, the bee's "system of signaling" is, again, fixed by each sign's strict correlation to "the reality it signifies" (84–84).

A linguistic sign has no positive identity; its identity is purely relational. The letter "e" retains its identity even when it's written or pronounced in vastly different ways, so long as it remains distinct from "b," "d," "a," "f," and so on. Wildly different styles of waving hello (from Queen Elizabeth's to George W. Bush's) retain their identity as greetings only so long as they remain distinct from other hand gestures, such as a shaking fist, a peace sign, or an extended middle finger. The meaning of any linguistic sign, whether alphabetical or gestural, is the function of a differential relation; that is, it's drawn from a series of "nots": blue is "not green," "not red," "not orange." But the prewired code, according to Lacan, involves no difference or *différance,* no distance between the sign and "the reality it signifies"; inasmuch as that relation is rigidly fixed, it transmits its meaning to others immediately, transparently, mechanically, and therefore sans any interpretation, any reflection or reflexivity.

Furthermore, Lacan continues, though the message transmitted by the bee "determines the action of the *socius* . . . it is never retransmitted by it." That is, "the message remains fixed in its function as a relay of the action, from which no subject detaches it as a symbol of communication itself" (85). The code amounts to a fixed form of signaling that involves no touching of the limit, and so no inscription of community and no reflexivity at all, neither on the part of the "sender" nor the "receiver;" the extent of its function is to transmit the fixed message. But language is completely different, says Lacan; its function "is not to inform but to evoke." I speak not so much to pass on information as to be recognized by the other. What the bee seeks through its "system of signaling"—if it seeks anything at all—is simply the appropriate re-action to the information it transmits; but what one seeks in speech, whatever the message, is "the response of the other." And "a reaction is not a response," he insists. Indeed, nothing imaginable "can make a reaction out of what the response is" (86). A response first of all requires language, ecstatic existence, shared being, and the self-distancing necessary for reflection and reflexivity, the very auto-deictic capacity that reaction by definition lacks. No ecstatic sharing, no reflexivity; no reflexivity, no response.

In his famous 1960 essay "The Subversion of the Subject and the Dialectic of Desire in the Freudian Unconscious," Lacan builds on this distinction, suggesting now that an animal is certainly capable of strategic pretense, for example in "physical combat or sexual display" (305); however, it is not capable of true deception, which requires, as Jacques Derrida puts it, a "second-degree reflexive power, a power that is *conscious* of deceiving by pretending to pretend" (*Animal* 128). An animal can pretend, but it cannot "pretend to pretend," says Lacan; it cannot lie by telling the truth, in other words, which requires a level of reflexivity available only to linguistic existents, to "subjects of the signifier"—that is, to human beings alone. Whereas the "subject of the signifier" emerges as a subject through this reflexive power (auto-deixis, the power of the

"I"), "the animal" in general is defined precisely by its deprivation of it. "Without the dimension that it constitutes," Lacan writes, "the deception practiced by Speech would be indistinguishable from the very different pretense to be found in physical combat or sexual display. Pretense of this kind is deployed in imaginary capture.... Indeed, animals, too, show that they are capable of such behaviour when they are being hunted.... But an animal does not pretend to pretend" (305). Both response and pretense to pretense require, Lacan insists, that of which "the animal" is deprived: the ecstatic sharing that writing requires, and that a writing *practice* devotes itself to exposing.

Life, Language, and the Question of "the Animal"

If not one nonhuman animal has language, then not one nonhuman animal shares being or touches the limit on which communication takes place; if all nonhuman animals simply transmit fixed messages, in other words, then there are no nonhuman animals who communicate at all, and so no nonhuman animals who write. "The animal"—code for the animal *in general*, as opposed to "the human" *in general*—does not have language or world and does not write. Period. It is "the essence of animality," as Heidegger puts it, to be without language and so without writing. But Derrida notes that "any code, animal or human," is surely a function of the very differential relations Lacan would like to reserve for human language alone. He points out that Lacan himself, in "The Subversion of the Subject" and referring to information technology rather than to animals, argues that "one can speak of a code only if it's already the code of the Other" ("Subversion" 305; Derrida 126). Here's Derrida, quoting Lacan:

> He refers to that Other as the one from whom "the subject receives even the message that he emits." This axiom should complicate the simple distinction between *responsibility* and *reaction*, and all that follows from it. It would therefore be a matter of reinscribing this *différance* between reaction and response and hence this historicity of ethical, juridical, or political responsibility, within another thinking of life, of the living, within another relation of the living to their ipseity, to their *autos*, to their own autokinesis and reactional automaticity, to death, to technics, or to the mechanical. (126)

That is, it's not only that the bee's "system of signaling" would necessarily involve some measure of the differential relations Lacan had explicitly denied them and so *some* measure of communication and the sharing of the limit that communication implies. It is also, maybe more importantly, that this responsivity reserved for "the human" alone cannot be simply or dichotomously distinguished from the "reactional automaticity" reserved for "the animal" (the animal-machine) alone. The difference between response and reaction is *differential,* already a function of *différance.*

So on the one hand, it seems necessary to admit that in order to communicate a specific direction to others, an interlocutor—human or nonhuman—would at the very least have to have *some* sense of the direction *as* a direction and the destination *as* a destination, and perhaps some understanding of symbols as indications of direction and destination. That is to say, honeybees and every other being that communicates with others surely must have—by *some* differential measure—the very "as-structure" that Heidegger denies "the animal" *as such.*[3] This indicates that the "captivation" of "the animal" may not be as definitive as Heidegger, Lacan, and other major thinkers (from Descartes to Kant and Levinas) have insisted: "existence," which always means *linguistic* ek-sistence, is not cleanly and clearly distinguishable from whatever one might mean by "merely living." On the other hand, it's also necessary to admit that human dasein is surely not as free from "captivation" as Heidegger insists, nor is the "subject of the signifier" as free from mechanical reaction as Lacan insists.[4]

The "symptomatic disavowal" of the differential relation between response and reaction amounts today, as Derrida puts it, to something like "a general topology and even, in a somewhat new sense for this term, a worldwide anthropology, a way for today's man to position himself in the face of what he calls 'the animal' within what he calls 'the world'—so many motifs (man, animal, and especially world) that I would like, as it were, to reproblematize" (*Animal* 54). This positioning, in all its glorious sovereignty, depends, from top to bottom, upon "the animal's" inability to respond and "the human's" full capacity to do so. It depends, that is, upon the presumption of an indivisible border between response and reaction, between linguistic existence and merely living: between the letter "as such" and the trace (or the mark).

The trace, in Derrida's terminology, names the complication of nonpresence in any instance of presence, the entwinement of the other-in-the-same (the presence of an absence or the absence of a presence) which is the condition for the same itself. Derrida describes the basic unit of communication not as the word or signifier but as the trace, which cannot, he insists everywhere, be restricted to human communication. The trace is the heart of *any* sign, which could be a word but also, for example, a deictic gesture, any inscription of difference and so of meaning. A letter, a color, a gesture—any sign—retains its identity when articulated in any number of ways, as I noted previously, because it is already a function of the trace: its identity consists not in any positive presence but in this differential relation. Nancy describes singular being, "the writer" him or herself, *as* a trace, as the inscription of a differential relation.

It is because Derrida begins with the trace, and not with the signifier, that he can suggest that "auto-deicticity" is surely "at work, in various forms . . . in every genetic system in general, where each element of the genetic writing has to identify itself, mark itself according to a certain reflexivity, in order to signify in the genetic chain" (*Animal* 95). What is foreclosed by the anthropological definition of language—as speech, sign, or signifier—is the recognition that auto-deicticity is already involved at the level of the trace, an arche-writing that is the condition for both life and the letter. So yes, there is the real; but no, strictly speaking there is no outside the text (*"il n'ya pas de hors-texte"*).

The point, of course, is not to homogenize everything, to cover up a multitude of significant "ruptures and heterogeneities" in order to erase any distinction between those beings who call themselves human and those beings that human beings call animals, between linguistic existence and "merely living," response and reaction. On the contrary, the point would be to expose a wild *plurality* of differences by zooming in on the metaphysical prejudices grounding the assertion of a "single linear, indivisible, oppositional limit . . . a binary opposition between the human and the infra-human" ("Eating Well" 116). Or, as Derrida puts it elsewhere, it's not a matter of

> erasing the difference—a nonoppositional and infinitely differentiated, qualitative, and intensive difference between reaction and response—it is a matter, on the contrary, of taking that difference into account within the differentiated field of experience and of a world of life forms, and of doing that without reducing this differentiated and multiple difference, in a conversely massive and homogenizing manner, to one between the human

subject, on the one hand, and the nonsubject, that is the animal in general, on the other. (*Animal* 126)

Life can no more be simply *opposed* to language in the broadest (non-anthropological) sense than the organic can be simply opposed to the inorganic or the mechanical: "Mark, gramma, trace, and *différance* refer differentially to all living things," Derrida notes, "all the relations between living and nonliving" (*Animal* 104). Acknowledging that, he continues, "should allow us to take into account scientific knowledge about the complexity of 'animal languages,' genetic coding, all forms of marking within which so-called human language, as original as it might be, does not allow us to 'cut' once and for all where we would in general like to cut" ("Eating Well" 116–117). What we are faced with as soon as we drop the anthropological definition of language and its attendant humanist baggage is that "[w]e know less than ever where to cut—either at birth or at death. And this also means that we never know, and never have known, how to *cut up* a subject" ("Eating Well" 117). How to determine—precisely, definitively—where the animal transmitting messages ends and the "subject of the signifier" begins?

Writing Apes

In the face of de Waal's casual "No" to Colbert's question, "do they write?" I give you the three generations of bonobos at the Great Ape Trust in Des Moines, IA, who routinely engage in what can only be described as a kind of electronic writing. These apes have reportedly demonstrated a grasp of spoken English that is at least equivalent to the capacities of a 2 ½ to 3 year old human child, perhaps higher.[5] One of the many ways they indicate this extensive comprehension is by responding to specific questions put to them, either by physically moving or by writing with a lexigram keyboard system. They also initiate conversations with researchers through the same keyboard, mostly to request food or initiate a game (like "chase" or "keep away") but also occasionally to communicate about many other things—including, for example, blabbing about other apes at the facility: in other words, they gossip (Johnson).

The lexigram keyboard system includes over 400 lexigrams or abstract symbols representing words, each one connected to a speech synthesizer so that when any individual lexigram is pushed, the word it represents is spoken by the computer. These include lexigrams for highly abstract concepts, such as "good" and "bad," "quiet," "now," "later," "think," "easy," "hard," "scare," etc. (Great Ape, "Interactive"). According to the head primatologist, Dr. Sue Savage-Rumbaugh, the first time Panbanisha, the most linguistically competent bonobo so far, used the word "quiet" was when she (Savage-Rumbaugh) was disciplining Panbanisha in a raised voice ("Bonobos Learning"). She used it again to shush Pär Segerdahl, a visiting associate professor of philosophy from Sweden who had agreed to "sit quietly and just observe the apes" in a chair outside Panbanisha's enclosure; he forgot and spoke. She went to the keyboard and wrote "quiet" (Segerdahl 9–10). According to Savage-Rambaugh, the bonobos at the Great Ape Trust know not only the lexigram keyboard but many other words; indeed, they are estimated to have grasped "several thousand words" (Great Ape, "2011 Bonobo"). Each of the writing apes involved in Savage-Rumabugh's language study is, by definition, a "symbol-using animal," but their writing is irreducible to the messages those symbols convey.

Kanzi, the first bonobo in the mature study, which began at the Georgia State University Language Research Center in the early 1980s, elected to learn and use the lexigram on his own and, in a sense, behind the backs of the scientists who were trying without much luck to train his mother, Matada, to use it. Kanzi was an infant when Matada's training started, and he hung around the lab (mostly making trouble) during her training sessions. After a few years, the Center temporarily sent Matada off to another facility to mate again with Kanzi's father, leaving Kanzi behind. The next day, the scientists set up the keyboard hoping to begin the same sort of language training with Kanzi. However, according to Savage-Rumbaugh, Kanzi was way ahead of them and "began at once to make it evident by using [the keyboard] on more than 120 occasions during that first day. Not only was Kanzi using the keyboard as a means of communicating," she explains, "but he also knew what the symbols meant—in spite of the fact that his mother had never learned them" (135). He had picked it up on his own, according to his own interests, without training, without vocabulary drills or rewards for correct answers. That was the beginning of a new approach to ape language research,[6] and Savage-Rumbaugh's work has been highly successful if also extremely controversial—so successful, in fact, that Savage-Rumbaugh made *Time* magazine's list of the one hundred most influential people in the world in 2011.

Her bonobos have not stuck exclusively to the lexigram keyboard system; at least one, anyway, has found another writing instrument or two.

According to the TED Talk Savage-Rumbaugh gave in 2004, "Panbanisha began writing the lexigrams on the forest floor," presumably with a stick. She then began writing them on the lab's tile floor with chalk. For example, when prevented from strolling in the forest to her favorite places for several days, she picked up a piece of chalk and began drawing the lexigrams associated with those places. She wrote the symbols for the A-frame and Flatrock destinations, as well as the symbol for the collar she is by law required to wear on these forest outings. Impressive. But again, what interests me here is that she "would not write if [her] being were not shared," and *that* she writes indicates that she "share[s] being-in-common" (Nancy 69). What Panbanisha and the other bonobos at the Great Ape Trust are writing, what they are called to write, above and beyond the message, is the communication of a community, a community that includes the human beings with whom they communicate. Now, I concede that even Panbanisha's freehanded lexigrams are the product of a human invention devised to help apes communicate with human beings, and that according to Lacan, "domestics" are a special category of "homme-sick animals" sick with the lack reserved for Man.[7] So let's go back out, out of the lab and into to the so-called wild.

Inscribing Branch

During a two month sample period in 1990, Ellen J. Ingmanson, a member of the bonobo research team at the Wamba forest site in the Democratic Republic of Congo, observed 604 occurrences of an intriguing form of tool use among (mostly) adult male apes that she named "branch dragging."[8] Branch dragging consists, first, in carefully selecting a branch, "often a small tree, approximately 2 m in length." Selection might take a while, she notes, with several possibilities considered and eventually rejected before the ape finally commits to "the 'right' one." "Length and leafiness at the top" appeared to Ingmanson to be the most desired characteristics in a branch. Once an ape makes his selection, "a delay of up to 30 minutes might occur before use," she writes, during which he just sort of sits with his branch, maybe snacking or grooming someone. "Finally, the individual [runs] through the forest dragging the branch behind him. This result[s] in considerable noise as the leafy end of the branch move[s] through the underbrush." Ingmanson determines that this behavior is used as a "communicative gesture" and that it is associated most frequently with "group movement promoting social cohesiveness rather than accenting an aggressive display." Branch dragging, she surmises, is typically used to "initiate group movement, to initiate direction of movement, to signal directional changes once movement is underway, and to keep straggling group members together" (201–203).

> In order to initiate group movement, one of the central, high-ranking males would begin branch dragging from the current location of the group, off into the forest for 20—30 m. He would then return to the group along the same route, continuing to branch drag. This process would be repeated several times. The rest of the group would slowly begin to move off, following the same direction the male had used while branch dragging. Frequently, more than one male would branch drag simultaneously, sometimes in conflicting directions. It was then necessary for the group to make a choice as to whom they would follow. The basis of this decision is still unclear, but may be related to the rank of the branch dragger, the intensity of the activity, or his persistence. (203)

The basis of the group's decision, then, is perhaps related to ethos, pathos, or the sheer ability to wear down resistance.

Ingmanson determined that branch dragging is a reliable predictor of the direction the group will eventually take and that the individuals engaging in the branch dragging behavior have specific destinations in mind, as she was very often "able to identify a single, discrete goal at the end of the movement." The destination goals included "a large fruit tree, a road that bisected the group's range, a stream where they foraged, the location of a neighboring group or small party of the same group, and a provisioning site." Once the group heads off in a specific direction, she notes, the branch dragging behavior decreases and often stops completely. However, it starts up again to initiate a change in direction, and occasionally adult males will drop to the rear of the group and branch drag in semi-circles behind the stragglers, presumably in an attempt to keep the group together (203–204).

Though typically used to initiate group movement, Ingmanson recorded one instance in 1989 in which branch dragging was used to motivate movement in a single ape. In the wee hours of the morning, an adult male (Mon) climbed out of his nest and sat under his nesting tree, "alternately gazing up at another nest and towards a fruit tree that was about 8 m. off to the side." He selected a small sapling, broke it off, and began branch dragging between the nesting tree and the fruit tree. Within ten minutes, Ika, another adult male, peered out of his nest to investigate the clamor. Mon stopped dragging and let out a few excited "squeaks and bounces," staring up at Ika. When "Ika disappeared back into his nest," Mon started the branch dragging racket again and kept it up for five more minutes until Ika reappeared and climbed down. Mon stopped dragging, let out more excited squeaks and bounces, and then darted off for the fruit tree, with Ika (an older male) following behind more slowly. "Mon had succeeded," Ingmanson muses, "in getting a friend to join him for breakfast" (204).

Savage-Rumbaugh has noted that bonobo branch dragging "has elements of symbolism to it, much like the honeybees' dance;" it's concerned with "controlling and manipulating social activity" and involves "complex communication of a kind not thought possible in nonhuman primates" (210). A means of communicating a specific request or claim or desire through the manipulation of signs, branch dragging is a rather intense form of non-alphabetic writing, one means through which wild bonobos communicate information that is significant to the group's cohesiveness and survival. It may also be a means through which—as in the case of Mon and Ika—individual desires are articulated and interpersonal relations are initiated and sustained. It is simultaneously a form of rhetorical practice, then, a scene either of public debate concerning the community's immediate future or of private appeal concerning the imminent actions of the interlocutors. But this writing practice is irreducible to the messages and appeals it communicates, and to the intentions of the writer, who is not simply an "author." This is also the writing of community, a tracing and retracing of the limit upon which communication takes place.

Ingmanson highlights the care involved in selecting the writing instrument, the tool by which to trace out a differential articulation—that is, a "direction," a "destination," but also and first of all the limit on which this writing is given, at which "you" shares "me." The would-be writer appears to labor over this task, considering and then rejecting several options before settling on one. And then: the inexplicable waiting period. Perhaps it's a time to clarify aim or style, to mentally or emotionally prepare, to build anticipation in the target audience, or maybe it's a procrastination ritual (when faced with a new writing project, I snack, too, and clean the house).[9] Branch dragging is intense and emotional, and it clearly aims both to communicate information and to persuade others to act. But it would not take place at all among "merely living," self-sufficient creatures; it would not take place at all among beings who did not share being, among beings uninterested in "the response of the other." Writing, alphabetic or nonalphabetic, is already a response to the call of "community," a tracing out of the limit and an inscription of the sharing that community *is*.

Despite their obvious affinities, one of the many differences between the honeybee's "wagging" dance and the bonobo's branch dragging is that bees do not appear (but, seriously, who knows?) to challenge each other through their writing practices. If a worker bee finds nectar and begins the dance that communicates to her audience its distance and direction from the hive, she is not, as far as we currently know, contradicted by another bee who is eager to take another route or to head toward another destination. According to Ingmanson's observations, however, bonobos do sometimes challenge each other. When one dominant male begins branch dragging, others may join in, proposing different directions and destinations, forcing the group to choose. The course of action is not fixed in advance, then; there is a decision to be made that will require presentation and interpretation. The branch draggers must make a persuasive case in order to move the group to a particular action, if not attitude.

What most interests me here, however, is their *desire* to do so, especially since—unlike their chimp cousins—bonobos enjoy a bountiful food source in the Congo. They do not need to fight over or work together to capture food; they do not need to worry about going hungry. It would be easy, especially for a strong high-ranking male, simply to take off on his own to satisfy his hunger or thirst, or even his sudden hankering for a certain sort of fruit, just as Mon could easily have gotten and enjoyed breakfast without the company of Ika. Instead, however, the branch dragger turns to the group, expending considerable energy inscribing his appeal, attempting to convince the others to join him. The group itself responds by making a collective decision, deliberately staying together—so deliberately, in fact, that once a decision is made, other dominant males in the group hang back to *retrace the inscription of the other* in order to motivate the stragglers (the message transmitted by the branch dragger is, then, "retransmitted" by the "*socius*"). The debate, in other words, does not continue beyond the group's decision: the group moves off *together* in the direction proposed and accepted. This seems less about the tyranny of consensus, however, than the responsiveness of bonobo singularities to their writing practices, to the exposition of their exposedness.

Bonobos are incredibly peaceful and peaceable beings, so much so that de Waal has coined them the hippie chimp, the chimp who makes love not war. But they do disagree and debate, they fight and then, as de Waal explains to Colbert, they have makeup sex. Their peaceable rapport is not fusional but suggests "the unity of plurality," in Levinas's terms, rather than "the coherence of the elements that constitute plurality" (306). The bonobos Ingmanson describes appear to share a kind of being-together, a togetherness of otherness that can take place only on or at the limit. Like any other mode of inscription, branch dragging amounts, before anything else, to a saying of this limit, to its reinscription. The writer, called to the limit by an *experience* of it, calls others to it. Branch dragging—even *branch dragging*—involves an address through which the writer draws out the sharing of a limit that also separates, a limit in which or at which a relation takes place, a differential relation, an exposedness, which a practice of writing exposes [to "us"].

Writing, Nancy explains, "inscribes the sharing: the limit marks the advent of singularity, and its withdrawal (that is, it never advenes as indivisible: it does not make a work)" (78)—writing does not dissolve the limit, in other words, but exposes the limit. The limit that "we" share or that shares "us" is not an indivisible limit; it is infinitely divided (infinitely shared). It does not make a "work," as Nancy puts it, because it "does not complete a figure, or a figuration, and consequently does not propose one, or does not impose the content or the exemplary (which also means legendary, hence, mythic) message of the figure" (79). Writing unworks or interrupts the work of the figure/myth. No matter what its content, it involves "the inscription of a meaning whose transcendence or presence is indefinitely and constitutively deferred" (80). Branch dragging offers a specific message, makes a specific appeal. But this writing practice is not reducible to its representational dimension. In the articulation of the message, it says something beyond its content; it says the communication of community.

Notes

1. For a more elaborate discussion of how one might best deal with the hauntingly animated remains of writing, see Michelle Ballif's chapter in this volume.

2. Heidegger argues that a being must be in possession of language to inquire into anything. When a dog enthusiastically sniffs another dog or cat or human—or a previously "marked" tree, for example—Heidegger would not grant that this dog is inquiring into any aspect of that other entity. It is the essence of animality *not* to question, according to him. This is why he also says apes don't have hands but "prehensile organs" for grasping. Only a being who can reflect on itself and on being *as such* has "hands," which are for more than grasping. Only human dasein questions because only human dasein has language. Ronell has questioned Heidegger's insistence on this point about questioning, noting that "every living being is equipped for receiving information. Every living being is capable of investigation, looking for something, one doesn't always know what. Vegetal beings show curiosity: a plant or root probes" (*Finitude's* 3). There is the tracing of a limit, a communication involved in any act of probing. If Heidegger is correct that it takes language to inquire into anything (I do not disagree), then our notion of language will need to be expanded; every living being exists, at least at the level of the trace or the mark, as a sort of linguistic existent.

3. Studies in the early 1900s had already indicated that bees distinguish between colors, which involves engaging a differential relation. See, for example, chapter nine of Carew's *Behavioral Neurobiology*, "Associative Learning in Honeybees."

4. I am thinking here of the ways in which human responsivity is "captured" by the mechanicity of grammar, for example—something Paul de Man eloquently illustrates—but also by Derrida's notion of iterability, the *structural* repeatability of the sign: for a sign to be a sign, it must be repeat*able*, whether or not it is ever empirically repeated. Iterability therefore names the originary contamination of the sign. There is no authentic articulation of meaning that does not involve contamination-by-repetition, or by simulation, or dissimulation. This means that there is something automatic in *any* utterance—yours and mine no less than the parrot's. In the so-called authentic response there is already something of its presumed opposite: reaction. The "iterability that is essential to every response," Derrida writes, "and to the ideality of every response, can and cannot fail to introduce nonresponse, automatic reaction, mechanical reaction into the most alive, most 'authentic,' and most responsible response" (*The Animal* 112).

5. In *Language Comprehension in Ape and Child*, Savage-Rumbaugh, et. al, describe a comparative study they ran in the late 1980s in which they tested the language comprehension of Kanzi, the bonobo, and a human child named Alia. Alia was about two years old by the end of the study; Kanzi was eight. Kanzi slightly outscored her in every category. Savage-Rumbaugh, however, proposes elsewhere that the subjective impression one has in working with the bonobos at the Trust is that "their comprehension is at least between that of a five-to-seven-year-old [human child]; that may be higher in some cases." Ac-

cording to her, "they can comprehend entire dialogues, they can comprehend extensive narratives, they can understand stories about things that happened elsewhere, or stories about something that happened the previous day—*if they're interested*" ("Bonobos Learning").

6. Earlier efforts to teach chimps to sign with American Sign Language were only minimally successful: after years of laborious training, the chimps learned a relatively small number of signs, and even then much of the signing was determined to be simple mimicry without much comprehension. Bonobos at The Great Ape Trust, however, have learned—without drills or training—hundreds, perhaps thousands of words, and they are not mimicking; they use their vocabulary in highly original and context appropriate ways that are readily discernible on any number of videos posted to YouTube and the Trust's website. Kanzi demonstrates an understanding of the difference between the ball that is sitting right beside him and the ball that is outside and out of sight, which he retrieves when asked. Panbanisha demonstrates a remarkably nuanced understanding of spoken English when she is asked to give a bite of her hotdog to the dog (canine) sitting on the floor beside her. As Savage-Rumbaugh notes in that video, Panbanisha has to distinguish between the hotdog in her hand and the dog on the floor, as well as between a hotdog and a hot *dog* (canine) and a hot or cold hotdog, etc. ("Bonobos"). Apparently, approach is everything when it comes to teaching apes to communicate with human beings. Savage-Rumbaugh's approach doesn't involve drilling the apes in a vocabulary of interest to the scientists but exposing the apes very early to a means of interacting about what interests *them*—again, in much the way children first pick up words and phrases that are of interest to them.

7. Here's Lacan:

> There is no unconscious except for the speaking being. The others, who possess being only through being named—even though they impose themselves from within the real—have instinct, namely the knowledge needed for their survival. Yet this is so only for our thought, which might be inadequate here.
>
> This still leaves the category of homme-sick animals, thereby called domestics [d'hommestiques], who for that reason are shaken, however briefly, by unconscious, seismic tremors. ("Television" 9)

8. Though branch-dragging appears to Ingmanson to be mostly the activity of high-ranking males, it seems worth noting that bonobo society is considered by primatologists to be matriarchal; females appear to enjoy a higher social status than males, who inherit their social rank from their mothers, and the group's social interactions appear to be female-centered and female-dominated.

9. If this seems to be morphing into a shameless display of anthropomorphism, let me counter that beginning with the trace or mark, and not with an anthropological description of language, which exposes what's at stake in insist-

ing that descriptions of animal behavior be restricted to the machinic language of stimulus-response: a *prior* belief in human exceptionalism.

Works Cited

"Bonobos Learning Language." Online video clip. *YouTube*. YouTube, 15 Dec. 2009. Web. 22 Sept. 2011

Carew, Thomas J. *Behavioral Neurobiology: The Cellular Organization of Natural Behavior*. Sunderland, MA: Sinauer Associates, Inc., 2000. Print.

Derrida, Jacques. *The Animal that Therefore I Am*. Ed. Marie-Louise Mallet. Trans. David Wills. New York: Fordham, 2008. Print.

—."'Eating Well,' or the Calculation of the Subject: An Interview with Jacques Derrida." *Who Comes After The Subject*. Ed. Eduardo Cadava, Peter Connor, and Jean-Luc Nancy. New York: Routledge, 1991. Print.

Freud, Sigmund. "A Difficulty in the Path of Psychoanalysis." *The Standard Edition of the Complete Psychological Works of Sigmund Freud*. Vol. 17. London: Hogarth P, 1953–74. Print.

Fynsk, Christopher. Foreword. *The Inoperative Community*. By Jean Luc Nancy, 1991. Minneapolis, MN: U of Minnesota P, 1991. viixxxv. Print

Great Ape Trust, The. "Interactive Lexigram." Web. September 22, 2011.

—. "2011 Bonobo Research Program at Great Ape Trust." Online video clip. *YouTube*. YouTube, 20 Dec. 2010. Web. 22 Sept. 2011.

Heidegger, Martin. *The Fundamental Concepts of Metaphysics: World, Finitude, Solitude*. Trans. William McNeill and Nicholas Walker. Bloomington: Indiana UP, 1995. Print.

—. "Letter on Humanism." *Pathmarks*. Ed. William McNeill. Cambridge: Cambridge UP, 1998. 239–76. Print.

Ingmanson, Ellen J. "Tool-Using Behavior in Wild *Pan Paniscus*: Social and Ecological Considerations." *Reaching Into Thought: The Minds of the Great Apes*. Ed. Anne E. Russon, Kim A. Bard, and Sue Taylor Parker. Cambridge: Cambridge UP, 1996. 190–210. Print.

Johnson, George. "Chimp Talk Debate: Is It Really Language?" *The New York Times*. 6 June 1995. Web. 22 Sept. 2011..

Lacan, Jacques. *Ecrits: A Selection*. Trans. Alan Sheridan. New York: Norton, 1977. Print.

—. "Television." Trans. Denis Hollier, Rosalind Krauss and Annette Michelson. *October* 40 (Spring, 1987): 6–50. Web.

Levinas, Emmanuel. *Totality and Infinity: An Essay on Exteriority*. Trans. Alphonso Lingis. Pittsburgh: Duquesne UP, 1969. Print.

Nancy, Jean-Luc. *The Inoperative Community*. Trans. Peter Connor, Lisa Garbus, Michael Holland, and Simona Sawhney. Minneapolis, MN: U of Minnesota P, 1991. Print.

Ronell, Avital. *Finitude's Score: Essays for the End of the Millennium*. Lincoln: U of Nebraska P, 1994. Print.

—. "Confessions of an Anacoluthon: Avital Ronell on Writing, Technology, Pedagogy, Politics." Interview with Diane Davis. *JAC* 20.2 (2000): 243–81. Print.

Savage-Rumbaugh, Sue E., et al. "Language Comprehension in Ape and Child." *Monographs of the Society for Research in Child Development* 58.34 (1993): 1–252. Print.

Savage-Rumbaugh, Sue, and Roger Lewin. *Kanzi: The Ape at the Brink of the Human Mind*. New York: John Wiley & Sons, 1994. Print.

Savage-Rumbaugh. "Susan Savage-Rumbaugh on Apes." TED. Feb., 2004. Lecture..

Segerdahl, Pär. *Undisciplined Animals: Invitations to Animal Studies*. Newcastle-upon-Tyne, United Kingdom: Cambridge Scholars Publishing, 2011. Print.

4 Zombies / Writing: Awaiting Our Posthumous, Monstrous (Be) Coming

Michelle Ballif

> *"The future is necessarily monstrous. . . .*
> *All experience open to the future is prepared or prepares itself*
> *to welcome the monstrous arrivant."*
>
> —Derrida, "Passages"

Jacques Derrida has claimed that "to learn to live, . . finally," is a lesson that cannot be learned from life, but only from "the other and by death. In any case from the other at the edge of life. At the internal border or the external border, it is a heterodidactics between life and death" (*Specters of Marx* xvii). Specifically, the lesson is learned *at the border* of life and death. Might not, then, we have much to learn from the figure of the Zombie, as one who "lives on"—"sur/vives"—this very border?[1] By posing this question, however, I am not suggesting that we know where the border begins and ends between the living and the dead, or—more to the (non)point of this essay—where the border begins and ends between the Zombie and ourselves.

Clearly, however, there is a rapid—one might say "viral"—proliferation of Zombies within our contemporary scene in popular films and television productions,[2] as well as within academic discourses of philosophy (e.g., Greene and Mohammad's *The Undead and Philosophy*), political science (e.g., Drezner's *Theories of International Politics and Zombies*), and cultural studies (e.g., Lauro's *The Modern Zombie: Living Death in the Technological Age*). This Zombie epidemic could be a manifestion of a growing fear that our posthuman future as the "end" of Man—presaged for centuries—is imminent, having been long prophesied in apocalyptic tones of certain destruction and demise—with or without four horsemen, contagious outbreaks, ecological disaster, nuclear desolation, marauding zombies, and arriving messiahs—as humans, "rotten with perfection,"[3] with transhuman hubris, seek their perfection as H+. Or, it could be a manifestation, on the contrary, of the *immanence*[4] of this posthuman future, as we inhabit a contemporary apocalyptic landscape of death and destruction. Or, still yet, it could be either-or, simultaneously, as an awaited future that is, paradoxically, now, always already, and yet, not-yet—neither, however, realizable as such, *precisely because of its monstrosity*. Derrida concludes his essay "Structure, Sign, and Play in the Human Sciences," by announcing that our posthuman future is "proclaiming itself . . . under the species of the non-species, the formless, mute, . . . and terrifying form of monstrosity" (293). I invoke the "posthuman" as such a (de)figuration of monstrosity. That is: I appropriate Jean-François Lyotard's notion of postmodernism as an "incredulity toward meta-narratives" (xxiv), so that posthumanism becomes an incredulity toward the meta-narrative of the so-called "human." Similarly, following Lyotard, the "post" in postmodernism or in posthumanism does not indicate a linear temporality (as in "after" modernism or "after" humanism), but rather points to an "ambiguous temporal frame of 'always already' and yet 'not yet'" (Ballif, *Seduction* 129). Posthumanism is thus monstrous because it exceeds and precedes any categorical imperative, any meta-narrative, any regime of knowledge—particulary, in this instantiation, of the "human" or of "writing."

In what follows are speculative—or spectral—notes toward imagining writing's now-but-not-yet future as *monstrous*, which—as do the (living) dead—defies our categorical ways and means of knowing and communicating. This future is anticipated, awaited, like an apocalyptic horizon, but that will never arrive as such. We take our first uncertain step [*pas*] (Derrida) toward this border (which is not one) by attempting to write (with) the Zombie in order to "learn to live," "finally."

Referring to the title of Maurice Blanchot's *Pas-au-delà* ["The Step Beyond"], which means both "step(s) beyond" and "not beyond," Derrida argues that Blanchot "approaches death" in "a step-by-step procedure of overstepping or of impossible transgression" (*The Ear of the Other* 19); similarly, Derrida cites a *passage* in *Ecce Homo*, wherein Nietzsche writes: "In order to understand anything at all of my Zarathustra, one must perhaps be similarly conditioned as I am—with one foot beyond life" (qtd.

in *The Ear of the Other* 19). In his fragmented comment, Derrida only writes: "A foot, and going beyond the opposition between life and/or death, a single step" (19). And, yet, this "step" is simultaneously a "not"[5] [*pas*], indicating a certain movement—but also a certain immobilization, "the *pas* of a recumbent corpse" (Derrida, *Aporias* 6), or more to our (non)point the *pas of* a shuffling corpse. We begin, then, with a certain uncertainty, a certain paradox, and an uncertainty regarding a border between the living and the dead. To cite Derrida, once again, learning to live, finally, learning from "the other at the edge of life" necessitates that we adopt a certain uncertainty regarding both "life" and "death." And a step, which is not. And a Zombie's foot.

I began with Derrida's claim that this step [*pas*] is a uniquely ethical move. And, as we will have noted, since the Zombie apparently has trouble speaking, it is a step taken, a move (im)mobilized in *writing*.

First Step [Pas]: But Zombies Aren't Conscious

Perhaps it goes without saying, or perhaps not, that the key, identifying feature of a Zombie is its mindlessness: its lack of consciousness, identity, subjectivity, and agency. Tracing the Zombie's historical origin, we find it born in the cradle of slavery and colonization of Haiti, where it still walks (and is still slavishly unemployed by the impovering consequences of imperialism and tyranny). The Haitian Zombie is/was a corpse reanimated through voodoo power to be used for slave labor, and the popularized Zombie of the film industry inherits this history, as the Zombie shuffles about as a slave of capitalist forces, as mindless consumer. Unlike the Vampire, another un/dead figure, the Zombie is a Zombie precisely because, although it retains its physical form, its "consciousness is permanently lost" (Lauro and Embry 89). And this, according to Sarah Juliet Lauro and Karen Embry, authors of "A Zombie Manifesto," is precisely what makes the threat of becoming a Zombie so terrifying: it denies us of our humanity. Lauro and Embry write: "Humanity defines itself by its individual consciousness and its personal agency: to be a body without a mind is to be subhuman, animal; to be a human without agency is to be a prisoner, a slave" (90).

The figure of the Zombie, then, foregrounds and destabilizes the central question: what does it mean to be human? Lauro and Embry extrapolate:

> The zombie is different from other monsters because the body is resurrected and retained: only consciousness is permanently lost. Like the vampire and the werewolf, the zombie threatens with its material form. Whereas the vampire and even the intangible ghost retain their mental faculties, and the werewolf may become irrational, bestial only part of time, only the zombie has completely lost its mind, becoming a blank—animate, but wholly devoid of consciousness. The terror that comes from an identification of oneself with the zombie is, therefore, primarily a fear of the loss of consciousness. As unconscious but animate flesh, the zombie emphasizes that humanity is defined by its cognizance. (89–90)

Lauro and Embry's discussion of the "real *live* zombie," Terri Schiavo, who the courts finally deemed lacked "consciousness," demonstrates that "the determining factor of what constitutes [human] life," as such, is consciousness (105). "Indeed," as they further point out, "it seems an eerie coincidence worthy of mention that *schiavo* means 'slave' in Italian, given the origins and continued characterization of the zombie as a slave" (105).

The Zombie, then, again, foregrounds and destabilizes the figure of "the human" by its similarity to an animated human body but yet a body that lacks the very qualities of "the human," as such: consciousness and agency. Defined as a supposedly "human" art of "communication," then, rhetoric—as Joshua Gunn and Shaun Treat argue—suffers from a "zombie complex" (146), manifest in the continuing "investment in the philosophy of absolute consciousness" (165) of the classical rhetorical agent, who—as Thomas Cole defines him—"self-consciously manipulat[es] his medium with a view to ensuring his message as favorable a reception as possible on the part of the particular audience being addressed" (ix). According to the discipline of rhetorical studies, rhetors are certainly not zombies (although—it may be argued—audiences may be figured as such, which only underscores the conscious power and will of the rhetor). And, according to the field of composition studies, writers are certainly not zombies. Indeed, as Sidney Dobrin compellingly argues in his *Postcomposition,* the field is overinvested in (student) *subjects,* their formation, and their management, which ironically, Dobrin points out, works to homogenize or zombify student writers.[6] The further irony, of course, is that the field of composition studies marks the 1960s as the "birth" of composition as a discipline—the very decade that Derrida heralded another birth, the one noted above, of "monstrosity" that would destabilize and deconstruct all claims to the identity of the writing subject and communicable prose—the very foundations upon which composition studies rested its new-born head. Rhetoric and composition: disciplines of the living dead.

Of course, the obituary for the death of man, the death of the author, the death of the subject, has long since been publicized. No need, here, to re/hearse the legitimatization crises that cast into doubt the grand narratives of the Enlightenment or the Transcendental Signified of consciousness, which gave life and legitimacy to the subject called Man. Yet, this death, as all deaths, has been greatly exaggerated, as even in the name of "posthumanism" or "transhumanism," a professed aim has been to jack in and jack up, consciousness to make it *more* human than human—or, more pointedly, to make it immortal. N. Katherine Hayles criticizes this attempt as "lethal," as a mere "grafting of the posthuman onto a liberal humanist view of the self" (286–87), a view that really only applies, she argues, "to that fraction of humanity who had the wealth, power, and leisure to conceptualize themselves as autonomous beings exercising their will through individual agency and choice" (286). Although I don't agree with all of her conclusions, I concur with her "posthuman view" that "conscious agency has never been 'in control.' In fact, the very illusion of control bespeaks a fundamental ignorance about the nature of the emergent processes through which consciousness, the organism, and the environment are constituted. Mastery through the exercise of autonomous will is merely the story consciousness tells itself to explain results that actually come about through chaotic dynamics and emergent structures" (288). We find ourselves, now, stepping into territory traversed by Dobrin in *Postcomposition,* where he posits the "obsolescence of subjectivity and subject formation as a central feature to theorizing and understanding writing" (4), as he explores posthuman writing in/as complexity theory. We do not need, that is, consciousness, the writing subject, to theorize Zombie/writing.

In any event, it is precisely the Zombie's ability to unsettle our conceptions of consciousness, identity, and self that is our first lesson in the heterodidactics between the living and the dead. Risking the instability of this conceptual border simultaneously invites us to risk the borders that sustain our ("human") self, as such. This is to risk the "abject," as we do when we encounter a corpse. Of this encounter, Julia Kristeva writes: "A massive and sudden emergence of uncanniness, which, familiar as it

might have been in an opaque and forgotten life, now harries me....
On the edge of non-existence and hallucination, of a reality that, if I
acknowledge it, annihilates me.... There, I am at the border of my condition as a living being" (3–4). We find ourselves, now, in the so-called
"Uncanny Valley," where the conceptual border of what we thought we
knew of "life"—and "the human"—dissolves, along with the distinction between subject and object, the distinction that renders knowledge
possible.

As you may know, the "Uncanny Valley" is a theory proposed by
Masahiro Mori, a robotics expert, to explain how humans respond to
robots—specifically to robots that take on a human resemblance. At
first, humans respond positively to the resemblance, but then at a certain
point, the resemblance causes an overwhelming sense of disgust. Below
you will find an image of the Uncanny Valley, and note that the figure
that effects this dissolution more strongly than the corpse is the Zombie (because the Zombie is animated; recall Freud's "TheW Uncanny"
and the "automaton" via Jentsch). That is, the Zombie appears more
"human" than a corpse.

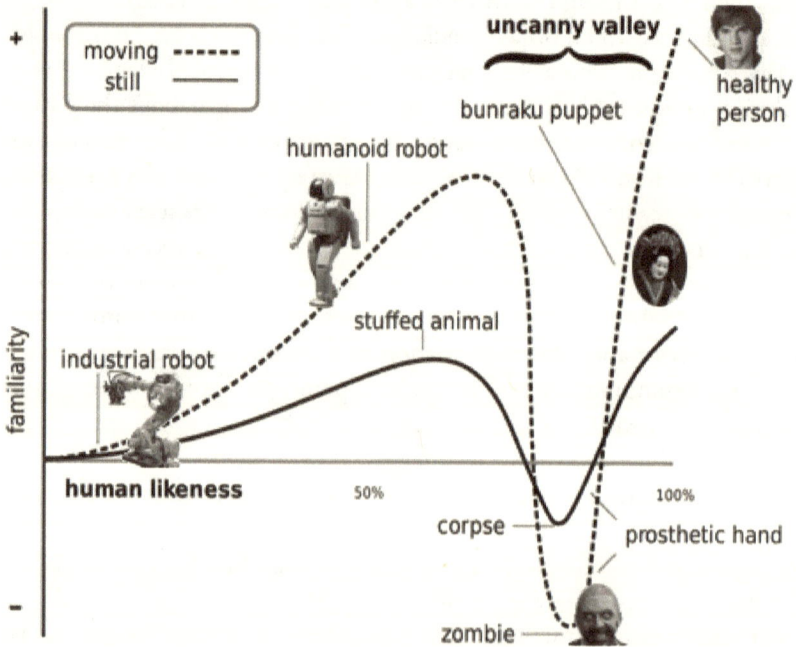

Figure 3.1. Adapted from Mori Uncanny Valley. http://spectrum.ieee.org/
automaton/robotics/humanoids/040210-who-is-afraid-of-the-uncanny-valley.

Jamais Cascio refigured the model of the Uncanny Valley to propose a second Uncanny Valley experienced when the human encounters the "transhuman" (see figure below). The transhuman, then, is equated with the Zombie, and generates the same abject disgust.

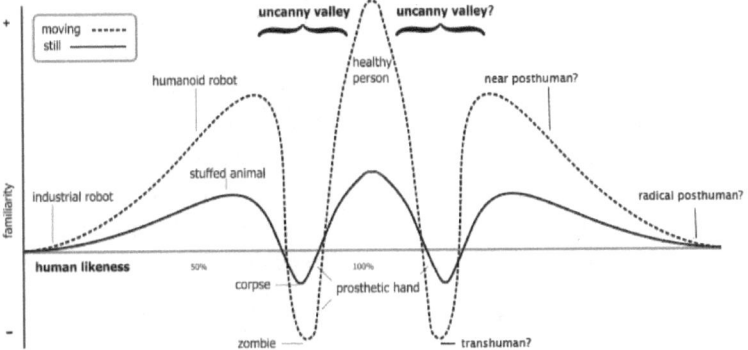

Caption: Figure 3.2. The Second Uncanny Valley; permissions: http://www.openthefuture.com/2007/10/the_second_uncanny_valley.html

Note in both figures, both instances, the exit out of the Uncanny Valley ultimately leads us to "the human," as a "healthy person" (that is, healthy, *living human*), where our abjection is mollified—or, more likely, disavowed. Our encounters with the nonhuman, specifically—the Zombie and the Transhuman—trouble us precisely because of their *human likeness*. This moment erupts precisely because it renders that which is familiar ("the human") unfamiliar ("the human").

In Freud's infamous essay on "The Uncanny," he tracks how the familiar (*heimlich*) and the unfamiliar (*unheimlich*) ultimately "coincide" (622). Coincidentally, it seems worth mentioning, that etymologically "coincide" comes from the Latin for "to fall upon each other." We have fallen into an aporia; we have descended into the Uncanny Valley, where that which is creepily familiar and yet creepily unfamiliar simultaneously haunt our very being. The exit, quickly sought, we look back and name the creepy stranger: as Zombie, as Transhuman. And in so doing, according to Kristeva, as explicated by Richard Kearney, we "externalize what is 'strange' within us onto an external 'stranger.' The result is a denial of the fact that we are strangers to ourselves" (73). Specifically, we are strangers to ourselves—as "the human" in the face of our own death, when we encounter the Other as Dead, and yet—even more to the (non) point—when we encounter ourselves in the *aporia*, the impossible border line between the living and the dead, between the human and the non human.

The "human" response is, then, to disavow the uncanny, to render canny—or familiar—that which is threateningly uncanny by naming it, as such, *as the nonhuman*—as the stranger, as the monster. What if, rather, we embrace the aporia, tarry within the Uncanny Valley, before rushing to domesticate the stranger, the monster, by naming it, as such. Derrida writes: "The monster is . . . that which appears for the first time and, consequently, is not yet recognized. . . . But as soon as one perceives a monster in a monster, one begins to domesticate it, one begins, because of the "as such"—it is a monster *as* monster—to compare it to the norms, to analyze it, consequently to master whatever could be terrifying in this figure of the monster" ("Passages" 386). Hence our desire to domesticate the Zombie—to enslave it for personal or military purposes. And, of course, if the monstrous cannot be domesticated, it must be killed.

The Zombie, then, *uncannily* confuses this—and all of the supposed binaries that he purportedly demarcates, most pointedly: living/dead. Indeed, the Zombie foregrounds the uncanny confusion of all binaries, most pointedly for our purposes: the (civilized, conscious) self and the (monstrous) other. As we know, via the logic of negation, any demonic/demonized figure can do the ideological work of demarcation, of "othering." But some figures—namely the Zombie—are "not *merely* outside of any single, given category, but situated exactly *between* [—*and yet, beyond*—] two categories that are otherwise considered to be mutually exclusive" (Johnston 171).

Second Step [Pas]: But Zombies Don't Speak

In *The Animal That Therefore I Am* and elsewhere, Derrida takes on a number of key philosophers' insistence that "the animal" is "the animal" vis a vis "the human," specifically because of "the animal's" inability to "respond" rather than to just "react" (32). It is not my purpose, here, to unpack Derrida's careful criticism of this foundational denial nor to engage the theoretical trajectory of the important work being done on this score contemporaneously, which asks further questions, such as can "the animal" deceive, play, or mourn, for example; I leave that work to others with only a glance in that direction with the prefatory discussion to follow (see for an exceptional example of such work, Diane Davis' entry in this same volume).

Of import is the use of scare quotes around "the human" and "the animal," which call attention to the status of the enunciation: *the* animal: "an appellation that men have instituted," Derrida writes, "a name they have given themselves the right and the authority to give to the living other" (*The Animal* 23); a presumption to "name in general but in the singular, *the animal*" (24). What this presumptive enunciation will have accomplished is nothing less than establishing the categorical construction of "the human" *as such*, as specifically the human-subject-who-speaks with its accompanying rights and privileges, accomplished via the epistemic violence that establishes any identity—*as such*. But, more to the (non)point, is the categorical construction of the animal-as-non-subject-who-does-not-speak, and therefore has no accompanying rights and privileges. This act of categorization of homogenization of the "immense multiplicity of living things," Derrida points out, can only be accomplished "by means of violence and willful ignorance" (*The Animal* 48).

Therefore, to answer to this violence and willful ignorance of constructing "the animal" and "the human" *as such* would not, Derrida argues, "be a matter of 'giving speech back' to animals but perhaps of acceding to a thinking, however fabulous or chimerical it might be" (*The Animal 48)* that would question not only "the animal," but "the human" as well—a thinking that would lead us to beyond "the edge of the *so-called* human" (*The Animal* 31), beyond the need to "always [seek] to draw the limit, the unique and indivisible limit held to separate human from animal" (*The Animal* 48).

Likewise, I would like to accede to such a thinking by further attending to the figure of the Zombie, however fabulous or chimerical he may be—a figure that can only be thought beyond "the edge of the so-called human," as a figure that con/fuses and effuses the categorical limits of "the human." As Derrida noted, the ethical gesture, here, is not simply a matter of "giving the voice" back to the Zombie (obviously lacking in oratorical skill), but straining an ear, listening at the limits, beyond "the edge of the so-called human," and learning what it means, finally, to live. This will have been our second lesson.

This is a lesson that hermeneutics cannot teach us.[8] Richard Kearney, in *Strangers, Gods, and Monsters*, suggests that when the monster speaks to us, we have two choices: we can either "try to understand and accommodate our experience of strangeness" or we can "repudiate it by projecting it exclusively onto outsiders" (4), which gives us the justification and the motivation to exclude and to even exterminate the monster. This leaves only two choices: accommodate (and thus appropriate as "non" stranger) or appropriate (as "stranger") and exterminate. I am suggesting that there is a third option—not a "choice," as such—but a third alternative that opens the *aporia*, or the impossible encounter with the monster—before the monster has been named, as such, and then either "understood" or killed.

In *The Infinite Conversation*, Maurice Blanchot addresses the impossible moment when one is approached by the stranger, by the radically other, and you find yourself with two impossible choices: "to speak or to kill" (61). But here is the radical difference: at this moment, at the "approach of the Other," you are both "utterly exposed to each other without so much as bread to share between you and certainly no common language as a middle ground" (Smock 131). So the "choice" is "not really a matter of such a simple either/or, for to choose speech over murder is not simply to opt for one of two opposed alternatives and against the other, but rather to enter the interval between—when, however, there is no in-between. It's to approach a limit one cannot encounter, a boundary one cannot reach" (Smock 131). This *impossible* speech is, Blanchot writes, "as grave, perhaps, as the death that it diverts" (62). This grave and impossible speech, diverting death, acknowledges "no common measure between" the other and "myself" (63), affirming the abyss that there is between 'myself'" and the Other. This is a speech vastly different from "legitimate" speech (dialectics), which aims at reducing difference in order to render knowledge, understanding, and communication possible (63).

I will call this "grave" speech *writing,* for writing is s/cryptic.[9] Like the Zombie, it is radically uncanny, "at home, yet not at home" in the Uncanny Valley, as Philippe Lacoue-Labarthe notes: "The *Unheimliche,* as estrangement, is the estrangement of the human.... It follows that the *Unheimliche* is essentially a matter of language, or that language is the site of the *Unheimliche*—if the latter can be said to have site" (qtd. in Royle, *Uncanny* 51). Writing is s/cryptic—but it is a simultaneously opened and closed crypt, and although the buried never remain buried, they exceed any communicational imperative; they walk amongst us, but only commune ekstatically.

As you'll recall, Plato had a veritable laundry list of complaints against writing. Without rehearsing all of his criticisms, I'll remind you that one of them was that writing—like painting—is dead:

> The painter's products stand before us as though they were alive, but if you question them, they maintain a most majestic silence. It is the same with written words; they seem to talk to you as though they were intelligent, but if you ask them anything about what they say . . . they keep on telling you the same thing forever. (*Phaedrus* 275d)

Plato, thus, condemns writing for being just a speaking corpse, as Derrida explains: In contrast to *logos*, which is a "living thing," as it "issues from a father," writing is orphaned, thus having no father, and thus not living, but not "completely dead: a living dead, a reprieved corpse, a deferred life, a semblance of breath" (*Dissemination* 143).

Although I would be hard pressed to agree with Plato on hardly anything, I will concur that writing is and has been traditionally conceived of as a type of living dead, a kind of Zombie that has been pressed into servitude, and I am, of course, once again, referencing the history of the Zombie and its relation to slavery and colonization. Writing has been pressed into servitude—to serve civic bodies and meaning-making enterprises, colonized by rhetoric's imperialistic drive. Accordingly, rhetoric is and has been theorized and employed as an art of knowing, doing, making, specifically as a *productive* art in order to serve communicative and exchange demands. One of the most enduring myths about the origin of rhetoric is that rhetoric, like Prometheus's stolen fire, is the civilizing *techné*, that rhetoric is, as Aristotle argues, not only the handmaiden of dialectic, but also of politics, which is the "*architechné* or master art of the good for man" (*Ethics* 1.1.1094b3–4). That is: rhetoric has been figured as that which binds communities together, that which allows a group of beings to identify with each other through practices of public discourse. This story gives rhetorical studies the unifying and edifying belief that rhetorical practices and pedagogies serve a political function: to prepare people to participate within a common community. This story, however, obscures another version of the story: that Corax and Tisias (who may have been *rhetoric's* invention) "invented rhetorical theory as a way of teaching citizens how to argue in the courts to regain their confiscated property" (Mailloux xii). That is: rhetorical practices played and continue to play a particular role in the exchange and circulation of property, and it is this rhetorical exchange—that is the "communication of property"—that maintains community. This communicational process then is the master art whereby we commodify language in order to ensure that the message has exchange value, that is, is communicable, just as we—by way of the same art—become commodities, so that we, too, can circulate as goods and participate in the restricted—that is, civilized—economy that produces us as such. This insistence that rhetoric serve the purposes of communication and exchange is, therefore, the zombification of language—or rather, the domestication of the living dead, of the monstrous in language, of excessive signification, and of the radical singularity of the event. As Nietzsche taught us: there is no singular "leaf." It has been co-opted by the concept of "the leaf," as such ("On Truth and Lying" 249), domesticating the monstrousness of the singular leaf, in all its radical difference.

There are monsters lurking in this forest, but our traditional theorization of rhetoric ensures that we can't see the monster for "the leaf." Blanchot suggests that "In literature, however, the word does not transform the negativity of language into the positivity of the concept" (Haase and Large 32). It "stubbornly" refuses to reduce language to a communicative and commodified use, which "conceals this absence"—this negation of the thing for the concept. This suspension of language's use-value, on the contrary, allows us to

> experience the absence as absence. . . . If the word links to another word, rather than to some idea outside the text, then what we have is not an item of information, but an infinite displacement of meaning that cannot be stabilized in a single interpretation. Blanchot describes this displacement as the power words have when they are not longer tied to the function of the concept, of destroying themselves. (Haase and Large 32–33)

The living dead, no longer pressed into communicative servitude, are impossible to inter(pret), and thus are doubly s/(en)crypted.[10]

It might be objected that Blanchot is speaking exclusively of "literature" or "literary language," and hence "out of bounds" for rhetoric, as such. As I have argued elsewhere,[11] however, there is philosophic rhetoric and there is sophistic rhetoric (which is not one); there is composition and there is de/composition. I presume that it is this "stubborn refusal to reduce language to a communicative and commodified use" that best characterizes sophistic rhetoric, or—as Paul de Man has written—rhetoric is that which "radically suspends logic and opens up vertiginous possibilities of referential *aberration*" (*Allegories of Reading* 10; emphasis added). Rhetoric, then, might be figured as an opening to the monstrous—and invitation, even, of "saying 'yes' or 'come' . . . to the future [of writing] that cannot be anticipated" (Derrida, *Specters* 168).

Third Step [Pas]: But Zombies Eat People

In an interview entitled "'Eating Well,' or the Calculation of the Subject," Derrida argues that the so-called "human" is constructed precisely by way of the logic of "*carno-phallogocentrism*" (113). We, no doubt, recognize the logics of logocentrism and phallocentrism operative in the construction of "the human," but Derrida further suggests that the discourses of Western humanism are founded on a "sacrificial structure" that allows for a "noncriminal putting to death" (112). He explains: "Such are the executions of ingestion, incorporation, or introjection of the corpse. An operation as real as it is symbolic when the corpse is 'animal'" and "a symbolic operation when the corpse is 'human'" (112). So, for Derrida, since we have been constructed, as such, through this structure of sacrifice (and insofar as sacrifice has yet to be sacrificed), the ethical question is not "should one eat or not eat, eat this and not that, the living or the nonliving, man or animal," but since "one must eat" (115), the ethical question then becomes "what is the best, most respectful, most grateful, and also most giving way of consuming—of relating to the other and of relating the other to the self," as such relations, Derrida further argues, are always at the "edge of the orifices," and always include appropriation and assimilation of the Other.[12] So, the ethical challenge becomes one of *eating well* (114).

Posing the consumptive practices of the Zombie as an analogue to monstrous rhetorical possibilities, we can investigate the difference between eating well and eating poorly. Eat we must, and—as the Zombie reminds us—there is a certain *cannibalistic* appetite that must be satisfied. As others before me have argued—from Freud to Hegel to Lacan—our relations with others exhibit this cannibalistic drive: we consume the other as a means to become one's self, one's human self. Writing also exhibits this cannibalistic drive: we consume, appropriate, accrete that which is other by making it our own, stamping it with our signature, mastering its difference. This is clearly a humanistic, disciplined, and systematized preference of "eating the other": to subject meaning and signification to a certain amount of identifiable rigor mortis by stabilizing it, to account for the remains of language, and to insist that those remains remain in identifiable crypts—as easily communicable and consumable prose.

Could there not be another way of "eating the other," eating as a Zombie? As we know, the Zombie does not, typically, respect the so-called niceties of dining; he does not sit atthe table or cut his food into little, chewable pieces. But he does eat slowly; not methodically, but he does eat brains, perhaps (un)mindfully. What would such an analogous writing practice be of "eating the other well?" Such a practice would challenge commodified rhetorical commonplaces and amount to allowing difference, radical—unconsummable—difference, to remain, undigested, as such.

Such a writing—a practice which is not one—would, according to Daniel Birnbaum and Anders Olsson, foreground the "*limits of eating*: not everything can be incorporated" (152). Acknowledging the *limits* of eating radically contrasts with a hermeneutic impulse and will to total appropriation:

> A register of oral and digestive terms leaves its mark on hermeneutic theory: assimilation, incorporation, *Verschmelzung*. There is no doubt that the modern theory of interpretation, like the Hegelian dialectic, has deep roots in Christian hermeneutics [, which is] governed by figures of incorporation; Western metaphysics of presence and phonocentrism come into contact here with the symbolism of ritual sacrifice and religious eating, even if at times in an extremely sublimated form. By incorporating and appropriating the flesh of the text [of the other], the interpretive subject assures itself of the presence of meaning. (Birnbaum and Olsson 150–51).

Adding to this, Birnbaum and Olsson further argue that such a totalizing appropriative gesture "demands the absolute sacrifice: a swallowing, a devouring, that leaves no traces of the sacrificial animal. No bones, no skin, no entrails can remain" (140), or if they do remain, the machine of "dialectical cannibalism" guarantees their eventual appropriation and assimilation (144). This totalizing move denies the "limits of eating" and/but struggles with the problem of excretion, as demonstrated by the event of a church mouse eating the "body of Christ," the sacramental Host, which is eventually excreted by the mouse. "A piece of mouse shit," Birnbaum and Olsson note (following Hamacher's commentary) foregrounds not only the limit of the edible, but also the limit of hermeneutics (140).

What to do with the remains? The remains that remain and that refuse to be incorporated? Eating—just as a textual encounter—always leaves traces (141)—so many tracks, so many mouse droppings. What to do with the remains of the dead? Just as hermeneutics struggles to incorporate remains, so do our cultural practices surrounding the remains of the dead. Derrida writes that mourning the dead "consists always in attempting to ontologize remains, to make them present, in the first place by *identifying* the bodily remains and by *localizing* the dead" to "make certain" that the remains *remain there*" (*"Fors"* 9). The remains must be made "present" *as the dead,* so that *the living* can be, likewise, made "present," as such. This is the border work between life and death. Birnbaum and Olsson write: "All of the categories of Western thought are based on a totalizing notion of life. What has meaning is that which can be incorporated into the great organism of life, that which resists this appropriation must be devoured in a violent appropriative act" (153). We have upended the tables, now: why do we fear being eaten by the (un) dead Zombie, when the living are constantly eating the dead and their remains?

In the early 1990s, Derrida gave a seminar entitled the "Rhetoric of Cannibalism"; David Farrell Krell, in his published remembrances of the course, provided the additive title: "All You Can't Eat." Eating well, then, acknowledges the limits of eating, and that "[s]omething remains inaccessible to hermeneutic exegesis: a remainder, a dead hieroglyph, an inaccessible encryption" (Birnbaum and Olsson 153), which cannot be made present (like meaning) nor localised (like a corpse). And so we have returned to the grounds of the crypt—or, rather, the groundlessness of the crypt, to the aporia of the boundary between the living and the dead, to the boundary between a human-all-too human and a monstrous, posthuman writing. Such an "eating," or relation to the radically other, Derrida notes, would be more like a "hermetics" than a "hermeneutics" (*"Fors"* xiv-xv). Perhaps the Zombie has much to teach us about "eating well." This will have been our third lesson.

An/Other Step [Pas]: But Zombies Have No Conscience

It may be objected/abjected that Zombies don't seem to manifest any sense of conscience: they'll eat their own mothers, perhaps eating her well, but certainly with no regrets nor remorse. However, it is precisely their lack of a "good" conscience that has much to teach us about learning to live, finally, as postmortem, posthumous, posthumans. Derrida argues compellingly in *Aporias* that we must resist any smug sense of good conscience. He writes:

> one must avoid good conscience at all costs. Not only good conscience as the grimace of an indulgent vulgarity, but quite simply the assured form of self-consciousness: good conscience as subjective certainty is incompatible with the absolute risk that every promise, every engagement, and every responsbile decision—if there are such—must run. To protect the decision or the responsibility by knowledge, by some theoretical assurance, or by the certainty of being right, of being on the side of science, of consciousness or of reason, is to transform this experience into the deployment of a program, into a technical application of a rule or a norm, or into the subsumption of a determined "case." (19)

This is why Derrida says that the "law" and "justice" can never be the same thing. Justice would only be justice when one acknowledges that *tout autre est tout autre* (*The Gift of Death* 82), something that the law—of the law—could never allow. In any event, to have a good conscience (or consciousness), as Derrida notes, is assured by *knowledge,* and one can never *know* whether one is eating (the other) well because such an ethics is irreducible to rules or norms.

According to Simon Critchley, reading Derrida, "[s]uch an ethics would not be based upon the recognition of the other, which is always self-recognition, but would rather begin with the expropriation of the self in the face of the other's approach. Ethics would begin with the recognition that the other is not an object of cognition or comprehension, but precisely that which exceeds my grasp and powers" (14).[12]

This is a future—like the *arrivant,* which is "summoned," but is "the very thing that will never present itself in the form of full presence," the very thing that will *never arrive* as such, and yet—this "not yet" future is to be summoned, just as *the arrivant* is to be summoned (Derrida, *Spec-*

ters 81; 82). This, as Derrida has argued, is an impossible apocalypse, a messianism without a messiah. To await writing's monstrous (be)coming, then, is to await a zombie-ism without a zombie. A monstrous writing lives on border lines—not only the border of the living and the dead as the "undead," but also the border of the past and the present as the "not-yet future."

We began with a certain uncertainty, a certain paradox, and an uncertain step toward a border that is impossible to cross—or to know: Where does the border begin and end between the living and the dead? To re-cite Derrida, once again, learning to live, finally, learning from "the other at the edge of life" necessitates that we adopt a particular uncertainty regarding both "life" and "death." To put it simply, as if such a thing were possible: we will have to acknowledge that we have no idea where the border is to be drawn between life and death, and that we will have to disavow our understanding of either, *as such*. It is precisely this uncertainty—this un/knowledge that will be our first step [*pas*] toward writing's monstrous (be)coming.

Notes

1. I am, of course, referring to Derrida's "Living On/Border Lines." This exordium on the zombie, on the heterodidactics between the living and the dead, is part of a greater book project in process, *Paranormal Investigations into the History of Rhetoric*. See Ballif, "Introduction" and "Historiography as Hauntology."

2. For an exceptional review of the literature on Zombies with/in popular culture, please consult Lauro and Embry's "A Zombie Manifesto."

3. Burke's characterization of "the human" in *Language as Symbolic Action*.

4. Kermode, *The Sense of an Ending*, but also see Gunn and Beard who play with this distinction in "On the Apocalyptic Sublime."

5. For more on "nots," see Taylor.

6. Dobrin writes: "Composition studies' attention to student subjects and its eagerness for normalized intellectual activity, FYC curriculum, and managerial oversight indicts composition studies as partner in larger political and institutional actions that actually deny subjectivity in favor of a normalized collective" (74).

7. See Davis's repudiation of hermeneutics in her *Inessential Solidarity*.

8. I render this from Zlomislic's "scryptal subject" (11).

9. Yes, I am referring to cryptology and Abraham and Torok's work on incorporation and mourning. See also Castricano.

10. See Ballif, *Seduction*.

11. See Guyer, as well as Calarco, for further discussion of the ethics of carnophallogocentrism. Also: Birnbaum and Olsson's interview with Derrida on the limits of eating.

12. Vitanza has always already had "some more" on this score: to know is always to no.

Works Cited

Abraham, Nicolas, and Maria Torok. *The Wolf Man's Magic Word*. Trans Nicholas Rand. Minneapolis: U of Minnesota P, 1986. Print.

Aristotle. *Ethics: The Nicomachean Ethics*. Trans. J.A.K. Thomson. New York: Penguin, 1988. Print.

Ballif, Michelle. "Historiography as Hauntology: Paranormal Investigations into the History of Rhetoric." *Theorizing Histories of Rhetoric*. Ed. Michelle Ballif. Carbondale: Southern Illinois UP, 2013. Print.

—. Introduction. *Theorizing Histories of Rhetoric*. Ed. Michelle Ballif. Carbondale: Southern Illinois UP, 2013. Print.

—. *Seduction, Sophistry, and the Woman with the Rhetorical Figure*. Carbondale: Southern Illinois UP, 2001. Print.

Birnbaum, Daniel, and Anders Olsson. "An Interview with Jacques Derrida on the Limits of Digestion." *E-flux Journal* 2 (2009). Web. 4 Aug. 2014.

—. *As a Weasel Sucks Eggs: An Essay on Melancholy and Cannibalism*. New York: Sternberg P, 2009. Print.

Blanchot, Maurice. *The Infinite Conversation*. Trans. Susan Hanson. Minneapolis: U of Minnesota P, 1993. Print.

Burke, Kennth. *Language as Symbolic Action*. Berkley: U of California P, 1966. Print.

Calarco, Matthew. "Deconstruction is not Vegetarianism: Humanism, Subjectivity, and Animal Ethics." *Continental Philosophy Review* 37 (2004): 175–201. Print.

Castricano, Jodey. *Cryptomimesis: The Gothic and Jacques Derrida's Ghost Writing*. Montreal: McGill-Queen's UP, 2001. Print.

Cole, Thomas. *The Origins of Rhetoric in Ancient Greece*. Baltimore: Johns Hopkins UP, 1991. Print.

Critchley, Simon. *Ethics, Politics. Subjectivity*. New York: Verso, 1999. Print.

Davis, Diane. *Inessential Solidarity*. Pittsburgh, PA: U of Pittsburgh P, 2010. Print.

de Man, Paul. *Allegories of Reading*. New Haven: Yale UP, 1979. Print.

Derrida, Jacques. *The Animal That Therefore I Am*. Trans. David Wills. New York: Fordham UP, 2008. Print.

—. *Aporias*. Trans. Thomas Dutoit. Stanford: Stanford UP, 1993. Print.

—. *Dissemination*. Trans. Barbara Johnson. Chicago: U of Chicago P, 1981. Print.

—. *The Ear of the Other*. Trans. Peggy Kamuf. Lincoln: U of Nebraska P, 1985. Print.
—. "'Eating Well' or the Calculation of the Subject: An Interview with Jacques Derrida." *Who Comes After the Subject?* Ed. Eduardo Cadava et al. New York: Routledge, 1991. 96–119. Print.
—. Foreward. "*Fors*." Trans. Barbara Johnson. *The Wolf Man's Magic Word*. Nicolas Abraham and Maria Torok. Trans. Nicholas Rand. Minneapolis: U of Minnesota P, 1986. xi–xlviii. Print.
—. *The Gift of Death* and *Literature in Secret*. Trans. David Wills. 2nd ed. Chicago: U of Chicago P, 2008. Print.
—. "Living On/Border Lines." Trans. James Hulbert. *Deconstructionism and Criticism*. Ed. Harold Bloom et al. New York: Seabury P, 1979. 75–176.
—. "Passages—from Traumatism to Promise." Trans. Peggy Kamuf. *Points . . . : interviews, 1974–1994*. Ed. Elisabeth Weber. Stanford: Stanford UP, 1995. 372–98. Print.
—. *Specters of Marx*. Trans. Peggy Kamuf. New York: Routledge, 2006. Print.
—. "Structure, Sign, and Play in the Discourse of the Human Sciences." *Writing and Difference*. Trans. Alan Bass. Chicago: U of Chicago P, 1978. 278–93. Print.
Dobrin, Sidney I. *Postcomposition*. Carbondale: Southern Illinois UP, 2011. Print.
Drezner, Daniel W. *Theories of International Politics and Zombies*. Princeton, NJ: Princeton UP, 2011. Print.
Freud, Sigmund. "The 'Uncanny.'" *New Literary History* 7.3 (1976). Print.
Greene, Richard, and K. Silem Mohammad, eds. *The Undead and Philosophy*. Chicago: Open Court, 2006. Print.
Gunn, Joshua, and David E. Beard. "On the Apocalyptic Sublime." *Southern Communication Journal* 65.4 (Summer 2000): 269–86. Print.
Gunn, Joshua, and Shaun Treat. "Zombie Trouble: A Propaedeutic on Ideological Subjectification and the Unconscious." *Quarterly Journal of Speech* 91.2 (May 2005): 144–74. Print.
Guyer, Sara. "Bucal Reading." *CR: The New Centennial Review* 7.2 (2007): 71–87. Print.
Haase, Ullrich, and William Large. *Maurice Blanchot*. London: Routledge, 2001. Print.
Hayles, N. Katherine. *How We Became Posthuman*. Chicago: U of Chicago P, 1999. Print.
Johnston, Sarah Iles. *Restless Dead: Encounters Between the Living and the Dead in Ancient Greece*. Berkeley: U of California P, 1999. Print.
Kearney, Richard. *Strangers, Gods, and Monsters*. London: Routledge, 2003. Print.
Kermode, Frank. *The Sense of an Ending*. Oxford: Oxford UP, 2000. Print.

Krell, David Farrell. "All You Can't Eat: Derrida's Course, *"Rhétorique du Cannibalisme"* (1990–1991)." *Research in Phenomenology* 36: 130–80. Print.

Kristeva, Julia. *Powers of Horror*. New York: Columbia UP, 1982. Print.

Lauro, Sarah Juliet. "The Modern Zombie: Living Death in the Technological Age." Diss. University of California, Davis. 2011. Print.

Lauro, Sarah, and Karen Embry. "A Zombie Manifesto." *Boundary 2* 35.1 (Spring 2008): 85–108. Print.

Lyotard, Jean-François. *The Postmodern Condition: A Report on Knowledge*. Trans. Geoff Benington and Brian Massumi. Minneapolis: U of Minnesota P, 1988. Print.

Mailloux, Steven. *Reception Histories*. Ithaca: Cornell UP, 1998. Print.

Nietzsche, Friedrich. "On Truth and Lying in an Extra-Moral Sense." Trans. David J. Parent. *Friedrich Nietzsche on Rhetoric and Language*. Ed. Sander L. Gilman, Carole Blair, and David J. Parent. Oxford: Oxford UP, 1989. 246–57. Print.

Plato. *Phaedrus*. Trans. and ed, R. Hackforth, Cambridge: Cambridge UP, 1972

Royle, Nicholas. *The Uncanny*. Manchester: Manchester UP, 2003. Print.

Taylor, Mark C. *Nots*. Chicago: Chicago UP, 1993. Print.

Vitanza, Victor J. *Negation, Subjectivity, and the History of Rhetoric*. Albany: State U of New York P, 1997. Print.

Zlomislic, Marko. *Jacques Derrida's Aporetic Ethics*. New York: Lexington, 2007. Print.

5 Wanting Ourselves: Writing (And) The Postsexual Subject

Kate Birdsall and Julie Drew

> "Representatives of a posthuman direction of thought . . . favor the amorphic state as the expression of a posthuman stage of development. This differs in many respects from the modern version of humans, in particular with regard to language and sexual difference and its associated desire."
>
> —Marie-Luise Angerer

> "In my computer-mediated worlds, the self is multiple, fluid, and constituted in interaction with machine connections; it is made and transformed by language; sexual congress is an exchange of signifiers. . . . And in the machine-generated world . . . I meet characters who put me in a new relationship with my own identity."
>
> —Sherry Turkle

> "The locus of agency is always a human-nonhuman working group."
>
> —Jane Bennett

> "Do I contradict myself? Very well, then I contradict myself. I am large, I contain multitudes."
>
> —Walt Whitman

Introduction

One hallmark of a computer age, in which our connections with others are increasingly mediated by machines, is the erasure of embodiment. Early work in cybernetics focused on mediated interactions in which differentiating between human and machine—based on "intelligence" as the primary criterion—became at once more difficult and more urgent.[1] As a related project, and in order to explore both new and expanded opportunities for agency, we wish to think the desiring subject and the desired object as entities distinct from the human bodies and the texts that purport to produce and circulate desire.

For our purposes here, we take *posthumanism* to be

- a theoretical and interpretive method that attempts to avoid the classical humanist binaries of self/other, mind/body, society/nature, human/animal, and organic/technological; locatable—but without a fixed location—on a continuum that includes the technological, the cultural, and the biological;

- concerned with the centrality of ethics and justice to all epistemological projects, whether or not that centrality is explicitly articulated.

The relevance and possibility we find in a postsexual rethinking of the subject is built upon this notion of posthumanism, and the work of a variety of scholars across disciplines, including cultural studies (Stuart Hall, Raymond Williams), auto/biographical theory (Sidonie Smith, Julia Watson, Gillian Whitlock), materialist feminism (Judith Butler, Monique Wittig, Judith Halberstam), and, to a degree, ecocriticism (here we are thinking, in particular, of Jane Bennett's *Vibrant Matter* and Timothy Morton's *Ecology without Nature*). We also see the possibilities inherent within a *critical* posthumanism, which Whitlock suggests "uses the 'post' as an opportunity to open up critical spaces for productive engagement with humanist ethics, epistemology, and ontology in worlds that we occupy in real time and space" (x). In what follows, we combine this with our chaotic vision of a postsexual subject who has the power to subvert the subject/object distinction in ways that echo the poststructuralism of the late 1980s and 1990s, updated for the twenty-first century. Whitlock posits, in her introduction to a recent special issue of *Biography*, that this kind of thinking promises to disrupt "the social history of [the] sovereign self," and we agree with her assertion (vi).[2]

N. Katherine Hayles, whose transdisciplinary work allows for this kind of rethinking, argues that the liberal subject has metamorphosed into the posthuman subject, where intelligence is realized as "a much broader cognitive function depending for its specificities on the embodied form enacting it" (*How We Became Posthuman* 1–5). We build upon this to suggest that the posthuman subject is already the postsexual subject, and we will attempt to think through this claim throughout this essay. In a nutshell, the desiring subject and the desired object are realized as a complex-systems function depending for its specificities on the interactions of the embodied subject, the represented subject, and the object—both sel(f)ves and other(s), desiring and desired, no longer distinguishable from one another and co-constitutive. This idea seems rife with possibilities.

Hayles reminds us that Lacan's and Derrida's "floating signifiers" have become, in the digital age, "flickering signifiers." When human will, desire, and perception are "spliced into a cybernetic circuit within a distributed cognitive system in which represented bodies are joined with enacted bodies through mutating and flexible machine interfaces—when we gaze at the flickering signifiers scrolling down the computer screens," we have already become posthuman (*How We Became Posthuman* xiv). We would add that we have also become postsexual. Perhaps writing transformed us into postsexual beings, since language is always already inadequate for constructing, recording, and experiencing the self or other without fixing them in place like pins in butterflies. Once they are fixed, they are no longer butterflies, or at least not those butterflies. Thus the discursive turn, announced by Stuart Hall and others, may also be understood as the postsexual turn.

In this essay we consider what might happen if, following the work of Jacques Derrida in "The Animal that Therefore I Am (More to Follow)," we were to carefully interrogate the rhetorical effects and ethical implications of allowing a boundary that seems to distinguish so clearly, so finally, and so permanently, the machine from the human, as he does with the animal and the human; both projects are fundamentally rooted in what such interrogations mean for subjectivity. Derrida works through the idea of "surrendering" to the animal other, by which, he posits, he's actually surrendering to the other-within-himself, comprehending himself via that other: "[The animal] surrounds me. . . . It has its point of view regarding me. The point of view of the absolute other, and nothing will ever have done more to make me think through this absolute alterity of the neighbor than these moments when I see myself seen naked under the gaze of a cat" (380). Comprehending the other-within-the self is a fundamentally performative act, one that echoes the ways in which Derrida has challenged other kinds of binary oppositions. The "entanglement of language and code" that Hayles describes leads to the loss of borders that allows a subject to define an other; at the same time, however, the loss of the other leads to the loss of the self, and therefore to the end of a relational subjectivity—but, importantly, potentially *to* the radical possibilities for agency suggested by the postsexual.

The performativity once inherent only in the corporeal, linguistic self—logically extended to include the concept of self-as-object-of-the-other's-gaze—may now be purely discursive, as Judith Butler helps us to imagine. The enacted self, understood corporeally, has become the enacting self, an always-becoming hybrid that suggests at once both less control and more, given the lie of an "interior essence" and the possibilities inherent in our ever-evolving digital identities. Hayles notes that "the analog subject implies a depth model of interiority," but postmodernism has made clear that this model is unattainable.[3] Digital subjectivity, however, and the ever-becoming, enacting self, open up a space for agency that is in part made salient only through language and the narratives that language enables.

From Freud to Lacan to Derrida to Delueze, there is always something outside the subject. Émile Benveniste notes that

> Language is possible only because each speaker sets himself up as a subject by referring to himself as I in his discourse. Because of this, I posits another person, the one who, being, as he is, completely exterior to 'me,' becomes my echo to whom I say you and who says you to me. (225)

Language is possible because of the self/other divide that exists in language. The other is my echo, and I the echo of the other. Our interest in this idea is twofold: first, in how the I/echo functions and perhaps is changed by thinking the self-as-code; second, in how the I/echo is operated on, and operates within, desire. Is the binary "I" (digital) the same as the analog "I" (language)? How might any difference in the "I" function allow for or limit a conception of self—and, importantly, how might it lead to individual and collective agency? How might *desire* re-thought afford some intellectual room to skirt some of the problems for agency that the postmodern subject has thus far unfailingly presented?

We construct our histories—and our selves—in narrative, and the self is fragmented, fractured, constantly in flux, and like the code on our screens and on the server. In that way, they're mutually illuminating. Again, we cannot escape the code any more than we can escape language. We might, however, briefly escape the linguistic conventions of our discipline in order to think otherwise, an exercise in creativity that may offer up some future yield. In this essay, we begin to examine some of the ways in which the theoretical shift from classical physics to quantum physics—specifically, the move from space/time to space-time via general relativity theory—offers a potential route to reimagining subjectivity.

Ultimately, we are drawn to these questions and hope to encounter additional questions as we go, because the issue of subjectivity for us is always grounded in the ethical pursuit of human agency in its material, textual, and contextual manifestations. Posthumanism is another way of talking about subjects without recourse to the categories of Enlightenment/modernity, and since Horkheimer and Adorno we have understood that destabilizing those categories is a political and ethical project. We are hopeful that the postsexual may offer similar possibilities.

We acknowledge the futility of definition. In fact, we embrace it; our postsexual selves desire—even require—such linguistic chaos. For all of this talk about moving past logocentrism, we find ourselves limited to a discursive space that reminds us of the past several hundred years of Western philosophy: What defines subjectivity? How does a subject construct herself? Does she have identity and agency? Do the flickering signifiers represent a different kind of embodiment, or, at the end of the day, are we rehashing old arguments, updated for the digital age?

Yes.

Hence the feeling of chaos, which we insist is a hallmark of the hybridity inherent in a postsexual world, where space and time, self and other, atom and bit all merge together into a simmering soup of confusion and play—but with very real ethical implications.

THE MACHINE THAT THEREFORE I AM: THE (D)EVOLVING POSTMODERN

What we posit as the postsexual is part of an evolution of a variety of other "posts," namely postmodernism, posthumanism, and poststructuralism. In his 1995 *Being Digital*, a work that startles us with its then-prescience, Nicholas Negroponte uses the term "digitality" to identify the condition(s) of living in a post-analog digital culture. His primary metaphor, one that drives some of our claims here, is that "the change from atoms to bits is irrevocable and unstoppable" (4). What Negroponte means is that *physical* matter—atoms, made of molecules—will be replaced, at least partially, by *digital* matter—binary code, made of ones and zeroes. Although Negroponte is careful to explain these differences, what we see from our vantage point in the twenty-first century is the emergence of a kind of subjectivity that combines both. Although we live(d) in a purely analog world, where time and space feel continuous and fluid, at the microscopic level even matter itself is in constant flux. This is true even in the hybrid world in which we now find ourselves: the atoms that make up our bodies, for instance, can almost fully merge with the binary code contained within the digital world—and we're getting closer to singularity every day. (At the time of this writing, we're still waiting for the public rollout of Google Glasses). In Negroponte's words, "[in 1990], most people did not believe you could reduce the 45 million bits per second of raw digital video to 1.2 million bits per second" (17). This was back when dialup modems screeched and crackled to connect; in 2013, data is routinely compressed far beyond what was imaginable in 1995. In the world of cable modems and fiber-optic connections, the transfer rate of *high-definition* video exceeds 28 million bits per second. This is an astounding amount of data.

It is these conditions that give rise to the postsexual subject, whose traces of modernity and postmodernity, no longer static liabilities, are continuously at work forming recombinations of pattern and randomness, simultaneously strategic and ethical. Beyond relegating it to any one of these theoretical schools, however, we define it as a fundamentally epistemological construction of self-as-other, and the resulting feedback loop of desire turned back on itself. In Hayles's terms, reflexivity itself becomes a "spiral rather than a circle, resulting in dynamic hierarchies of emergent behaviors" (*My Mother Was a Computer*, 241), and we build upon that notion to suggest that by viewing a constructed and constructing self through the spiral of reflexivity that Hayles describes, the postsexual subject becomes an object of her own gaze, embedded within an infinite feedback loop that may have far-reaching implications, both theoretical and practical. As members of a highly technological society, we approach the real possibility of singularity (an alterity that is not alterity) between human and digital machine as both an intellectual and a creative process. At the very least, this singularity may disrupt the conventional binary of self/other, interrupting its seemingly fixed outcome with an endless, Pong-like back-and-forth. As a part of the transdisciplinary project of considering the ethics of cybernetics and artificial intelligence, combined with an attempt to decipher digital code as another form of language, we attempt here to re-imagine the binary of self/other as a multi-dimensional helix—a feedback loop rather than a coupling—which erases the inevitability of privileging one side of the self/other binary. In this way, we might reconstitute the relationship between speaker and listener, between writer, reader, and meaning. In contemporary, Western media-mediated societies, the other is a version of the self, and the self a form of the other. The digital self, existing only in code, gazes back at the analog self, creating a mash-up that is well-adapted to the twenty-first century: a ghost of Lacan's mirror-image simultaneously generates an updated version of the postmodern schizoid.[4]

Such rhizomatic becomings are composed of bits *and* atoms; they are neither analog nor digital. They are both. The discursive self via postmodernism was constructed only in performative (analog) language; we may now understand such constructing as a product of the interstices between and among an organic being who sits in front of a screen filled with flickering signifiers that have been generated using a series of 0's and 1's, and the digital being that code engenders—and continues to construct. We wonder to what extent our now-adept deconstructions of analog language will be possible, and if various postmodern projects will suffice when the self/subject is (re)formed in digital code. The self/subject might be more unified than we have imagined—or, it just doesn't matter as much as we thought. Perhaps, by some act of radical hybridity, writing the self into digital contexts precludes us from continuing along the road of postmodern fragmentation in academic discussions of the self—we might have to include the embodied self and the embodied other, something long insisted upon by materialist feminism and various other theoretical and political critiques of postmodernism.[5]

This is, of course, rather tricky. As Judith Halberstam notes, following Andreas Huyssen and Jean-François Lyotard, "postmodernism does not simply follow after modernism: it arises out of modernism and indeed interrupts . . . modernism's grand narratives" (446). Similarly, we do not now merely exist in a state of posthumanism, as a next-evolutionary stage after postmodernism, where we might imagine our (re)assembled identities as no longer weighted down by the increasingly inadequate notion of a fragmented, unstable, and unknowable self. This becomes vaguely reminiscent of what Gilles Deleuze and Félix Guattari posit in *A Thousand Plateaus*: "[w]riting has nothing to do with signifying. It has to do with surveying, mapping, even realms that are yet to come" (5). We do not advocate letting go of the self as written—we are stuck with/in discourse, and traces of a postmodern, deconstructive project are necessarily embedded in and, at least in part, motoring our thinking now. Not unlike modernity, postmodernity is hanging on to our skirts, refusing to be left behind, and needing its nose wiped.

In her groundbreaking *Gender Trouble*, Judith Butler writes that "[d]iscourse becomes oppressive when it requires that the speaking subject, in order to speak, participate in the very terms of that opposition—that is, take for granted the speaking subject's own impossibility or unintelligibility" (157). Butler is writing here about Monique Wittig's work on lesbianism (we might recall Wittig's famous last line: "lesbians are not women"), and this is relevant here for a couple of reasons.[6] Discourse is how we police one another—how we police our selves, and others' selves. Given the kinds of discursive environments and new media contexts within which we now operate (remember, Butler published *Gender Trouble* in 1990), including online social networking, blogs, and even Google, which has purportedly changed the way our brains work, we posit taking this a step further and conceiving of a "digitally-generated subject" who constructs herself via a combination of analog language and digital code.[7] Although her analog selfhood can be deconstructed—and she can perform subversively within language if she so desires—she might feel a greater sense of control over her digital self: she can masquerade, perform in drag, and even become someone else (someone other) or simultaneously multiple selves/others, acting and interacting in unlimited environments with a mere click of the mouse. The postsexual self is not wholly (or holy) human.

As is often the case, an instructive and illustrative example may be found in popular culture. In January of 2013, the media broke a story about popular college linebacker Manti Te'o, then playing for Notre Dame, who had won the hearts of fans with his unfailing support of his girlfriend, Lennay Kekua. Kekua's tragic narrative included a serious car accident that left her comatose, followed by a long and ultimately fatal bout with leukemia. In fact, prior to a major football game, the media announced that Te'o's grandmother *and* Kekua had died on the same day; Te'o was going to play anyway, to honor their memories, and went on to lead his team to victory. There was just one problem: no record of Kekua existed. The car accident left no police report or hospital record. Conventional Google searches revealed only a Twitter and Facebook account for her. Ultimately, the pictures accompanying these social media profiles turned out to be of an unrelated woman. Kekua existed only in the electrons.

Only much later was it revealed that the online persona called "Lennay Kekua" was actually an acquaintance of Te'o's, a musician by the name of Ronaiah Tuiasosopo. According to Timothy Burke and Jack Dickey's *Deadspin* article, it's unclear how the two young men knew one another, but several of Tuiasosopo's friends and relatives claim that they knew he "was the man behind Lennay," that he had created her in 2008, and that "Te'o wasn't the first person to have an online 'relationship' with her." Ultimately, it became clear that Lennay Kekua did not exist in atoms, at least not as Lennay Kekua, and that Manti Te'o had been either the victim of or a perpetrator of the hoax.

As media outlets such as *Deadspin, SportsIllustrated.com,* and *CNN.com* reported, we learned that 1) Lennay Kekua did not exist, at least not as Lennay Kekua, and 2) Manti Te'o is either the nicest, most gullible college athlete in the country, or he deliberately went along with the hoax. If the answer is the latter, it's difficult to discern *why* he would do such a thing, but speculations by various sports media range from "he wanted to do well in the NFL draft" (he was actually drafted 38th in the second round, not early in the first round, as was predicted) to "Notre Dame made him do it so that the team could win and (maybe) become more well-liked" to the more offensive "Te'o is gay and used Kekua to make people think he isn't." *The New York Times* called Kekua Te'o's "noncorporeal girlfriend," and Katie Couric grilled him with more rancor than is her custom on a special edition of *Katie*. She followed up with testimonials from others who had been "duped," and featured interviews with Nev Schulman, the creator of a documentary called *Catfish*, in which he traces his own victimhood at the hands of someone, off in webspace, pretending to be someone else. In Schulman's words, "It's a lot harder to prove that your feelings were true than to assume that they weren't," and he has been publically supportive of Te'o.

Te'o has attempted to prove that his feelings were true. In a statement released to the press on January 16, 2013, that he "developed an emotional relationship with a woman [he] met online. [They] maintained what [he] thought to be an authentic relationship by communicating frequently online and on the phone, and [he] grew to care deeply about her" before realizing that he was "the victim of what was apparently someone's sick joke and constant lies [which] was, and is, painful and humiliating" (qtd. in Burke and Dickey). These "painful and humiliating" truths have affected the *actual postsexual subject*. Te'o, who has been adamant in his claims of authenticity—even heroism—found himself duped by someone who did not exist—or did s/he? When Lennay Kekua revealed herself to be a hoax and Te'o found out, he did not step forward right away to correct the public perception that he was "the perfect guy." He couldn't bring himself to admit the ruse; he'd become famous in part because of the heartbreaking love story, not just because of his athletic success.

Here, the postsexual subject's desire and its material effects loudly present themselves: Te'o told the press, his family, and his teammates that he'd met Kekua in person, though the entire relationship took place online and, briefly, over the telephone. He was embarrassed to have been a victim of "catfishing," to be in love with someone whose corporeal form he had never experienced or even seen.

The performative inventions that were contained within different kinds of self—the corporeal self and the self textually constructed/represented—may now be, in a postsexual world, purely discursive. This leaves such selves and performances open to readings that force us to question subjective reality as what Butler describes as a "fabricated... interior essence," especially given the amount of control we (think we) have over our digital identities (Butler 185). If, as Foucault and Butler insist, we lost control of the corporeal subject long ago, it makes sense that we would cling furiously to any semblance of sovereignty, even simulated, that we might have over our digital selves.[8] Hayles posits that "the analog subject implies a depth model of interiority, relations of resemblance between the interior and the surface that guarantee the meaning of what is deep inside"; however, as postmodernity has evolved, it has become clear that this model is unattainable. On the other side of the spectrum, Hayles suggests that the "digital subject implies an emergent complexity that is related through hierarchical coding levels to simple underlying rules, a dynamic of fragmentation and recombination that gives way to emergent properties" (*My Mother Was a Computer*, 203). This description of the digital self operates, in part, as a description of the postsexual self: a blend of fragmentation and recombination that allows for the possibility of agency that is founded within desire-for-the-self and nestled within a feedback loop of satisfaction and deferral. We long for a kind of authority over identity-in-(con)text, over an assemblage of self that is not watched and policed by an exterior other. Foucault's self-surveillance becomes instructive here and, paradoxically, the kinds of digital self-surveillance to which we refer might further enable the subversion that Butler calls for in *Gender Trouble*.

That is, the ability to construct a self beyond corporeal existence—and outside of an easily deconstructed, purely analog narrative—might reassure the hybrid, postsexual, and always already-enacting subject that her subject-position is stable. We certainly do not claim an end to the postmodern maxim established long ago that a unified and stable subject position is a grand theoretical hallucination, and we fully acknowledge an entire branch of postmodern thinking that does allow for subjective, individual agency. Linda Hutcheon, for example, argues that the postmodern is "a questioning of what reality can mean and how we can come to know it," which implies that, on some level, we can know "reality," as long as we question how we acquire our knowledge of it (32). Patricia Waugh contends that we must rethink the self by acknowledging the fact that "[e]veryone agrees that [p]ostmodernism is much concerned with fragmentation" but without the "apocalyptic nihilism about the possibility of ethical and imaginative subjective experience" that she believes is a characteristic of "postmodernist writing" (190, 193). As feminist critics, we appreciate Waugh's argument that "the goals of agency, personal autonomy, self-expression, and self-determination . . . can neither be taken for granted nor written off as exhausted." We take issue, however, with Waugh's conception of "the postmodern" as a monolithic exploration of the loss of Enlightenment autonomy within late capitalism (194). Instead, we posit that, like most other "isms," postmodernism exists in a variety of ideological and theoretical forms. The very notion of treating it as a single entity—or as a single, albeit fragmented, state-of-being, rather than a conceptual and linguistic tool, contradicts its oeuvre.

Here, our focus is on the loss of a center locus of control and on the lamentation for the loss of a grand narrative that, at one point, suggested the possibility of a static Enlightenment ideal of self. In this respect, we turn to Deleuze and Guattari's notion of "multiplicity," which "has neither subject nor object, only determinations, magnitudes, and dimensions that cannot increase in number without the multiplicity changing in nature," and the subsequent creation of an "assemblage," which "is . . . [an] increase in the dimensions of a multiplicity that necessarily changes in nature as it expands its connections" (8). Deleuze and Guattari's subject is a universe-unto-itself, ever-expanding, and it is fundamentally schizophrenic and chaotic: "[the] body is defined only by a longitude and a latitude" (260). Their seeming insistence that spatial positioning, at least as it relates to corporeality, takes precedence over temporal positioning, as it relates to subjectivity, becomes twice removed from the fulcrum of our thinking here, given our explorations of subjectivity re-imagined through the narratives of general relativity and quantum physics.

Further, we suggest that we build upon Deleuze and Guattari's expanding subject to include the notion of affect. Longing for a stable self and the experience of feelings of stability function as a call-and-response that allows the postsexual subject to ignore, sometimes effortlessly, the question of whether the self is or can be stable. We experience anxiety. We might feel reassured when we quell this anxiety with the simulacrum of control that we experience as digital selves. We desire stability; we feel a degree of satisfaction as we satiate that desire (and agency may be one possible result), even if that satiation is a mirage. The "truth" of the stable self—whether it is possible or not—is beside the point in practice. This call-and-response works in two ways: hegemonically (the belief in the stability of self is fundamentally flawed, so she must do her best to write a stable self into code), and subversively (she can construct herself in code to be whomever she wants to be).[9]

Another instructive example from popular culture comes from the science fiction television drama *Caprica*, in which Zoe Greystone is the teenaged heroine of a fictional future world. Her wealthy parents are somewhat estranged from one another, and from Zoe. Within their (analog and embodied) family, there is little communication or intimacy, and a lot of arguing. On Caprica, however, everyone can recreate and escape to "V World," a complex virtual reality program that expands and changes, not unlike a wiki, by those who frequent and interact with/in it. Zoe is a programming prodigy, and she focuses her teenage angst (parents who don't understand her, a passionate, if somewhat off-the-rails commitment to a particular set of religious and ethical beliefs, the violent acts of the underground terrorist group with whom those beliefs are equated, the physical and emotional changes she struggles to understand as she matures) on creating a program to which she can upload so much biological, psychological, and narrative information about herself that she can create an autonomous self, an AI that is her, but not her. Virtual Zoe has no body—she is not a robot, though she can be uploaded into one in order to act with/in the material world. Virtual Zoe is code that nonetheless thinks, feels emotion, communicates, desires, acts and reacts. Human Zoe creates, via digital code, a singularity that is at once self, other, and the possibility of unlimited others. For characters and viewers, this raises significant questions about who the "real" Zoe is, and the emotional connection her parents wind up making with virtual Zoe are fascinating, as are the inevitable questions of power and ethics that are necessarily a part of such a narrative about the constructed self.[10]

In an interview, Foucault once said that "[p]ower . . . produces effects at the level of desire—and also at the level of knowledge. Far from preventing knowledge, power produces it" ("Body/Power" 59). As power controls the body, the postsexual subject strains against its fixity and containment. As power directs discourse and prescribes that the individual write herself into being, she responds—at least on the surface—by following the rules. Her desire for self might be a desire for the Enlightenment's unified, autonomous self, but it is simultaneously a fundamental desire for agency projected into the electrons, where binaries do not break down in the same way they do in the "real life" of postmodern textual deconstruction. We insist that if the self longs for stability, our very knowledge that a stable self is impossible or false may be irrelevant. With/in the postsexual, we suggest that we might embrace the paradox of wanting a stable, unified self, while consciously knowing—and accepting—that it is not possible in the "real." The temporary satisfaction found in writing the self into code might, we think, be a means of achieving agency-in-the-moment. In other words, that stability is not to be found in the spatial is irrelevant, if the effects of stability may be found in the temporal.[11]

Hayles insists that binary code—computer code controlling the electric impulses that drive the machines with which we may eventually (and in some ways already do) merge—cannot simply be deconstructed in the way that analog language can; her claims are vaguely reminiscent of Deleuze and Guattari's assertion that "[t]he world has lost its pivot; the subject can no longer even dichotomize. . . . The world has become chaos" (6). This chaos, particularly when combined with a common identity-politics-based argument against poststructuralism—loath to accept the fragmentation of subjects that had only just been allowed into the exclusive, mostly-White, mostly-male, mostly-Western, and mostly-heterosexual club of Whole Subjects—demands that we acknowledge and agree with those who would advocate a wariness of the postsexual and with our accompanying calls for pattern recognition and recombination. We are aware that language games with slipping (or flickering) signifiers and pure différance might invite a view of the postsexual as an attempt to undo the theoretical and political gains that queer theory, for example, has enabled. This is not our goal. We do, however, suggest that a recombinative reading of the self/other binary, as written in code, might be politically and practically fruitful, and we find some of the linguistic and conceptual moves found in quantum physics helpful To wit, much as space and time, which may be read as space/time, is now understood as spacetime, we propose that subjectivity be explored within the concept not of *self/other* but of ∞*self/other*∞, a notion we will address at length in the next section.

Halberstam explains why deconstruction and its evolution into recombination might be both useful and important in regards to digital subjects. She describes postmodern theory (from her vantage point in 1991) as "participat[ing] in a different perception of space and time, in the production of a fragmented subjectivity, and in the breakdown of a surface/depth model in the realm of representation" (446). We are attempting to identify and discuss the postsexual in similar ways, but without some of the constraints within which the postmodern deconstructive project operates, given its heavy reliance on the presence/absence binary that is itself largely steeped in modernism. Hayles's model of a helix-like discursive structure suggests that the postsexual project of exponential coupling among and between analog and digital selves-others may effectively address the epistemological and ethical concerns that postmodernism has found so difficult. This multi-dimensional helix demands an analysis that focuses on the aporia of a necessary combination of both patterns and randomness, which works with Deleuze and Guattari's rhizome in the sense that "any point of [it] can be connected to anything other, and must be" (7), and which might allow us to operate outside of the severely limiting Enlightenment (and androcentrically embodied) concepts of "truth" and "reality."

Indeed, Halberstam, in her analysis of Fredric Jameson's attempt to cogently articulate the potential rift—and possible connection—between postmodernity and "marginalized Others" notes that:

> [T]he vertigo that Jameson describes . . . is nothing new for women and people of color. . . . We begin to ask questions about what interests were served by the stability of these categories

and about who, in contrast, benefits from a recognition of radical instability within the postmodern. . . . [We might ask] why it is that subjecthood splinters when marginalized groups begin to speak. The answer is already embedded in [the] question; subjecthood becomes problematic, fragmented, and stratified because marginalized Others begin to speak. (447)

This fragmented subject and its corresponding object represent a kind of systems failure that goes beyond a mere "death of the subject," and thus echoes what Jameson characterizes as "the end of the autonomous bourgeois monad or ego or individual—and the accompanying stress . . . on the decentering of that formerly centered subject or psyche" (*Postmodernism* 15). The fragmentation of the subject—by now accepted as a given—calls, in our conception of the postsexual, for a fundamental recombination that might, paradoxically, allow for utopian cynicism, a reformation of notions of subject-position that allows for never-ending adaptation and expansion and thus avoids the potential for further creation of (hierarchical) binary differences.

As Jameson suggests, "the most interesting postmodernist works" consider a "new mode of relationship through difference" (*Postmodernism*, 31), not an erasure of difference, and in *The Political Unconscious: Narrative as a Socially Symbolic Act* he establishes, from the get go, the need to historicize every narrative. For our purposes here, we interpret this as a need to historicize the amorphous postsexual subject via the narratives she generates. Even embedded in the radical uncertainty and subsequent decentered universe that characterizes some forms of "postmodernism" as a discipline within English studies, Jameson is adamant that narrative is one of the only means by which to glimpse totality. His basic theoretical strategies are recuperation, restoration, and recovery; history, because it is always mediated by language, texts, and interpretations, becomes an "absent cause," though it still contains meaning. The positive hermeneutics that he outlines in *The Political Unconscious* informs our theoretical methodology for a simple reason: we are investigating an anticipatory view of technological culture that allows for the erasure of traditional, hierarchical binaries and boundaries, in favor of a multi-dimensional model that allows for some degree of agency, whether or not that agency grows out of the will to power and whether or not that agency is born of the temporal illusion of a stable self.

Perhaps, as Jameson might argue, our quest to identify and narrate the hybridity inherent in the postsexual subject is, at its root, a utopian one. Following his methodology, which suggests that all narratives embody the longing for utopia, we suggest that the postsexual subject, as she creates herself in both analog and digital code, desires to escape the hegemonic control of late capitalism, given Jameson's description of "multiple subject-positions" and their political implications:

> [A]lthough the theory and the rhetoric of multiple subject-positions is an attractive one, it should always be completed by an insistence on the way in which subject-positions do not come into being in a void but are themselves the interpellated roles offered by this or that already existing group. Whatever truce or alliance one wants to stage between one's various subject-positions, therefore (deliberately excluding the stigmatized possibility that one might try to unify them), what will ultimately be at stake is some more concrete truth or alliance between the various real social groups thereby entailed. (*Political Unconscious* 345)

This complicates things. On one hand, the quest for utopia that Jameson describes enables the postsexual subject to write herself—to subvert the death of the author's authority—because the illusion of autonomous, stable subjectivity enables agency. To write oneself is to act; the possibility of disruption and subversion of any discourse always already exists within the discourse, as Foucault has famously argued. On the other hand, interpellation is still possible (and maybe necessary and unavoidable) within the helix. As Jameson notes, what is really at stake within the illusion of a stable, unified self are the truces or alliances that may be made among and between those social groups represented within the fragments of the postmodern self. This suggests limited agency, at best, and more so at a subcultural-group level than at the individual level, which makes the hope of agency something less than the utopian vision Jameson puts forth. Foucault, too, argues that the speaker is more constrained by the power of domination than the listener, who knows but does not speak. This raises the notion that agency—at least a utopian agency, an unbridled and limitless agency—does not belong to the speaking subject, an interesting and potentially disruptive notion given our theoretical assumptions within postcolonial studies, feminist studies, and queer theory.[12]

Consider the system of power that Foucault outlined across his corpus. His description of sexuality as a representation of complex power structures might illustrate the potential for the postsexual subject, despite her necessary position within the system, to subvert some or all of these structures. Foucault writes in the first volume of *The History of Sexuality* that "[t]he agency of domination does not reside in the one who speaks (for he is constrained), but in the one who listens and says nothing" (62). If we read Foucault's claim that the speaker (self) and the listener (other) are constituent components of the postsexual self—self-as-other-as-self, ad infinitum—the power of domination, as well as the means to disrupt or subvert the power of domination, lies within the postsexual subject. The postsexual subject is a hybrid/cyborg singularity, that alterity that is not alterity. The speaker is constrained by power, but if the speaker is also always already the listener who knows, rather than the absolute other to the speaker/subject, the constraints are strategic. They are rhetorical, brought into focus/pattern by both the speaker-listener and hegemonic power, not by hegemony alone.

The subject-that-speaks is also, necessarily, the subject-that-listens-and-knows, prior to the speech act. She therefore participates in her own constrained speech, making rhetorical decisions that are always already contextual, political, and strategic. Rhetoric itself is not agency any more than language is a transparent conduit of meaning, although both agency and meaning may be constructed (making pattern of chaos, chaos of pattern) in any given context. Despite the common and reductive misconception that postmodern thinking allows for the dismissal of nearly any kind of system, we suggest that rereading Jameson alongside this notion of the postsexual provides the possibility of revisiting and revising the grand narratives of "truth" and "reality" that prevail in Cartesian thought, in order that we might rethink not only human, but what is possible to and for humanity.

In "The End of Temporality," Jameson argues that the category of time encompasses interiority, subjectivity, consciousness and desire, whereas space is where the "realm of exteriority," including people and nature, may be found (697). Einstein altered the binary of space/time, however, fusing and twisting them together as spacetime, thereby altering our conception of what each side of the former binary may hold. Interiority and exteriority, self and other, may no longer be possible as a binary system, but subjectivity is still crucially important, experientially as well as theoretically. As we dismantle one system, we create another. This results in an endless making and unmaking of pattern and chaos, neither of which is ever complete or unchanged.[13]

Where does this leave gender? The postsexual subject frequently "speaks" across analog and digital languages as the enacting subject. This is the root of her desire for self, and perhaps the best indication that her gendered (human) identity is fundamentally unstable. Her desire for power, her digital performances, the performativity inherent in both her language (analog and digital, to varying degrees) and her actions reveal her intrinsically slippery subjectivity. Her notions of selfhood vary. She is alternately masculine, feminine, the organic human, the digital self, the language-user, the writer, the self, the other, a veritable apotheosis (as *Caprica* at times brilliantly illustrates). Through all of this, however, the postsexual subject wants others (including her own *selvesothers*) to perceive her as a (masculine and therefore powerful) human being, though she necessarily reveals herself to also be a (feminine and therefore threatening) technological self. She responds to modern power's demand that she produce her own identity; whether or not she feels hegemonically constrained, however, this production threatens to subvert biopower/biopolitics. As analog language fails her, she writes herself into binary code and reveals the agential possibilities of her hybrid postsexual identity. The laws governing the body do not apply in a digital context, which gives way to the desire for a purely digital *other/self* who is free to function outside of those laws.

This reminds us of Donna Haraway's early work in cyborg theory, which provided the means for posthumanism to establish itself as a discipline. Haraway's descriptions of the human-hybrid cyborg question the *self/other* dichotomy in ways that reflect our call for radical hybridity in the world of the postsexual. In "The Cyborg Manifesto," Haraway muses at length about the "leaky distinctions" between "animal-human (organism) and machine." In the "pre-cybernetic" days, Haraway argues, machines could not be autonomous and, "could not achieve man's dream, only mock it.... To think they were otherwise was paranoid," whereas:

> Now we are not so sure. Late twentieth-century machines have made thoroughly ambiguous the difference between natural and artificial, mind and body, self-developing and externally designed, and many other distinctions that used to apply to organisms and machines. Our machines are disturbingly lively, and we ourselves frighteningly inert. (152)

Haraway's work, while challenging traditional dualistic notions of feminism, takes on new resonance in the early twenty-first century. If we are "not so sure" anymore about the ambiguities between human and animal, we suggest that we rigorously investigate the (artificial) dichotomy between human and machine: even machines, it would seem, cannot function as an absolute other to human conceptions of subjectivity. Is the postsexual subject as inert as the purely human, Enlightenment-driven one? We think not.

The pejorative understanding of an inert subject, however, must be addressed in that its opposite—a subject who acts, who has agency—is always, at least, potentially dangerous. Feminist identity politics from the 1990s had a lot to say about community and social action and counterhegemonic possibilities in temporary, strategic affiliations with Others for specific aims, thus bypassing the problem of fixed identity for the individual and community. Here we are thinking most specifically about Spivak's "strategic essentialism" (*Outside*), which allows for the deployment of temporary essentialism in order to bring to the fore a simplified group identity, in order to incite political or ethical change. We might also consider Judith Butler's *Precarious Life*, in which she writes: "I am not fully known to myself, because part of what I am is the enigmatic traces of others" (46). The enigmatic traces of others, selves, other selves, and *selvesothers*. The postsexual subject is confusing. She is confounding. She is dangerous. And she ought to be.

In "The Animal That Therefore I Am (More to Follow)," Derrida outlines the philosophical aporias present within metaphysical conceptions of the absolute other. He advocates a careful examination of borders and boundaries between the human and that other, a category that we have expanded to include "machine" in addition to "animal." Derrida suggests that boundaries constantly fail, everywhere, all of the time, between the human and the animal; Western philosophy, he argues, hasn't taken it up as a question. His key concepts in the piece, namely borders, nudity, the other, corporeal morals, responding vs. reacting, absolute alterity, naming-as-control, and the back-and-forth of call and response, are all significant to our exploration of the postsexual because of his subsequent description of "limitrophy," or "what abuts onto limits, but also what feeds, is fed, is cared for, raised, and trained, what is cultivated on the edges of a limit" (397). For Derrida, thinking can begin only when the absolute other looks at us; in his world, this occurs when a cat looks at him while he is naked. For the postsexual subject, we suggest that this begins when the digital self gazes back at the analog self and/or when the embodied self gazes at the digital self as if each were the other. The borders become blurry. This new subject can no longer clearly discern where her corporeal existence ends and her digital one begins, or if her desire for her digital self makes her other (perhaps mitigating the feeling of agency she gains as she becomes digital). She experiences the alterity that is anti-alterity; she becomes the other because she already is her own other.[14]

As cybernetics and systems theory grew throughout the mid-twentieth century, critics discussed and debated the potential for a human/machine merger; contemplated the limits of computer intelligence and whether those limits could ever surpass human intelligence; and wrote, often with dread, about the possibility of the machine-other taking over the human subject.[15] It is tempting to construct the divide between human and machine in this way; contemplating a computer that is as or more intelligent than the postsexual subject is disturbing, indeed. Derrida offers us a way to consider this idea of singularity via an analysis of limits: he proposes that "instead of asking whether or not there is a discontinuous limit, [one should attempt] to think what a limit becomes . . . once the frontier no longer forms a single indivisible line but more than one internally divided line" (399). When we combine this with Hayles's conception of cybernetics, systems theory, and the ensuing introduction of feedback loops which connect subject and object and change the way we think about human embodiment and boundaries in technological contexts, we see very real implications for the kinds of hybrid assemblages the postsexual subject necessarily contains. We see the need for a reconfiguration of the digital other, and we posit that the postsexual subject is always already her other. Hayles's reflexive spiral may reveal how new dimensions of subjectivity, paired with the kinds of self-objectification that prevail in the new media society, result in a dynamic conception of the "entanglement of language and code." This culminates in the loss of the borders that allow a subject to define the other or, as we suggest here, the self.

The analog self is put under erasure as the digitally-constructed other is written into code. The absence of the self's presence (and the simultaneous presence of its absence) causes a feeling of loss, which leads to the desire—even the need—to rediscover the missing body. The other, at least as it is traditionally conceived, becomes unnecessary in a world of radical alterity where actors and the acted-upon merge into one subject. As the postsexual subject writes herself into digital existence, she is automatically excluding everyone and everything else from subjectivity, including her analog, corporeal self. Everything outside of the binary code she generates becomes object, other. This creates another paradox: she becomes other to herself only as she rewrites herself into code.

Benveniste writes about subjectivity within analog language in ways that might illuminate these speculations about postsexual subjectivity:

> The "subjectivity" we are discussing here is the capacity of the speaker to posit himself as "subject." It is defined not by the feeling which everyone experiences of being himself (this feeling, to the degree that it can be taken note of, is only a reflection) but as the psychic unity that transcends the totality of the actual experience it assembles and that makes the permanence of the consciousness. (224)

We thus return to one of our fundamental questions about postsexual (inter)subjectivity: because we construct ourselves in narrative, what happens when (analog and therefore binary) pronouns such as "I" and "you" merge with (digital) binary code? If, as Hayles contends, we cannot deconstruct binary code, do "I" and "you" continue to exist in opposition, or does the postsexual subject merge with her digital other via a complicated web of analog and digital language? Perhaps we became postsexual as soon as we began to write; perhaps this only happens when analog and digital language converge. Benveniste suggests that "[L]anguage is possible only because each speaker sets himself up as subject by referring to himself as I in his discourse" (225), implying that analog language is only possible because of the *self/other* divide that exists only in language. Given her desire for wholeness and stability—which is to say, agency—the postsexual subject turns to digital code to make and unmake and remake her self. The postsexual subject has no other but herself. The postsexual subject desires only her self.

∞Selfother∞: Uncertainty & The Postsexual Subject

We certainly are experiencing the desire to offer a genius–theory-that-ties-all-of-this-together here. We figure the best we can do is to organize all of this meandering speculation a bit, and then only temporarily, to offer a brief glimpse of something resembling a pattern. Readers' questions and concerns—as well as our own—will certainly scatter to the winds any attempt to identify a pattern as soon as we think we've recognized one. Our experience writing this essay, however, has served to confirm our sense that proceeding as if coherence is possible can at least get you writing, even when you know you're totally kidding yourself. Besides, a unifying-theory-of-everything flies so assuredly in the face of everything acceptably postmodern that we can't help but enjoy the idea, however fleeting.

We want to stage one very specific theoretical move in this section, our attempt to get around the linear binary of *self/other* that language (analog) locks us into, and that textual deconstruction has not been able to escape. We're going to try to do this by following the theoretical lead of quantum physics.[16]

As Stephen Hawking explains, Aristotle taught us in the *Physics* that bodies are naturally at rest and are moved only by a force. Scientists therefore assumed that "a heavy body should fall faster than a light one, because it would have a greater pull toward the earth" (Brief 10). In the seventeenth century, however, Isaac Newton, building on Galileo's work in astronomy, challenged those ideas and began what was later deemed the era of classical mechanics. With classical mechanics, scientists are able to predict movement quite accurately, but only in instances where the observed bodies are large, and only if the speeds at which they move do not approach the speed of light. The discovery of the molecular and atomic nature of matter engendered quantum mechanics, which attempts to bring the broader laws of classical physics into line with the observable behavior of subatomic matter and to make sense of the contradictory notions of wave and particle functions.[17]

Throughout these centuries, matter was understood to exist in three-dimensional space, something altogether distinct from time. Space and time were thought to be two very different things, things we might write as a binary: space/time. Then, in 1916, Albert Einstein's General Theory of Relativity posited a fourth dimension, spacetime, which may be described as like a rubber sheet upon which the planets sit, with gravity the indentation made upon the rubber sheet because of the mass/weight of the planets. Smaller planets—less mass and less weight than the larger ones—that intersect with the lip or edge of the indentation, are pulled down toward the larger mass. Quite literally, mass bends spacetime, thereby creating a gravitational field; when something with less mass enters the gravitational field (the lip of the indentation in the rubber sheet), it falls toward the larger mass and rolls along the rubber sheet (spacetime) toward the heavier object (Mallett).

We stated earlier in this essay that the postsexual subject is, for us, essentially an epistemological project. General relativity and quantum physics are also epistemological projects, ways of thinking and observing and understanding the universe in new ways that actually give rise to the possibility of agency. Thinking spacetime, rather than space/time, is an epistemological move that creates the theoretical possibility, at some point, of actual time travel. (Bear with us, here.) Because of the inability to fully reconcile wave and particle functions, quantum physics uses the Heisenberg Uncertainty Principle to perform certain probability, or differential equations. The Uncertainty Principle "implies that certain pairs of quantities, such as the position and velocity of a particle, cannot both be predicted with complete accuracy" (Hawking Brief 93). In other words, we cannot know with certainty both the where and the when of an object or event; the more you know of one, the less you know of the other.

Very abstract, we know. So try this on: if we throw a ball at the side of a wall, we can calculate with certainty the location of the ball (the where), or we can calculate with certainty the speed of the ball (the when), but we cannot know both with any certainty. Mathematically, it is possible that the ball will hit the wall and bounce off; mathematically, it is also possible that the ball will go through the wall and end up on the other side of it. Mathematically, we can only calculate the probability of unlimited possibilities (Mallett).

This uncertainty principle, in concert with spacetime, with General Relativity, with light speed and black hole theory and the frame-dragging that creates gravitational wakes and wells, opens up the possibility of the multiverse: ever-expanding, infinite universes that veer off from each other, multiplying exponentially. In quantum physics, this gives rise to the idea of closed time loops, connected and coiled and stacked like a slinky, and wormholes that connect one point on a closed time loop to another part, a straight line that might allow us to move in time—in different directions, not just what we experientially think of as "forward" in time. Quantum physics understands that time will appear to slow near a massive body (like a planet, or a black hole) because that's what gravity does to waves: it slows down the frequency, the length of time between the crests of waves. This has been tested with clocks and their relative proximity to the Earth's surface, and it functions in every moment of modern day life. After all, it is general relativity that allows us to successfully calculate satellite positions for the signals we rely on for contemporary communications.

As Hawking explains, general relativity "gets rid of the idea of absolute position in space, and absolute time" (*Brief* 20). He offers the rather well-known example of the twin paradox. In this example, one twin spends her life on the top of a mountain while the other stays at sea level. The mountaintop twin would age faster than the sea-level twin; when they met again, one would be older than the other. Not by much, of course, but the difference in their ages "would be far greater if the first twin went on a long journey in a spaceship at nearly the speed of light. When she returned, she would be much younger than the twin who had stayed on earth" (*Brief* 20). And here's the important part: this is only a paradox if we insist on the idea of absolute time. General relativity allows for each individual her own measure of time, depending on location (where) and movement (when):

> With Einstein's Special Theory of Relativity, bodies moved, forces attracted and repelled, but time and space simply continued, unaffected. It was natural to think that space and time went on forever. The situation, however, is quite different in the later, General Theory of Relativity. Space and time are no dynamic quantities: when a body moves, or a force acts, it affects the curvature of space and time—and in turn the structure of spacetime affects the way in which bodies move and forces act. Space and time not only affect but also are affected by everything that happens in the universe. This new understanding of spacetime revolutionized our view of the universe. (Hawking, *Brief* 22)

Which is to say, this new understanding of spacetime revolutionized our view of the universe and thus what we might do within it.

Agency. Volition. The possibility of action. The possibility of change. What might happen if we rewrite the old binary *self/other* as *selfother*, and what if we put the mathematical symbol for infinity (∞) on either end of it? Maybe nothing. Still, maybe something. We cannot escape the linear nature of the written word, or how we read, but we can better suggest Hayles's helix by writing it in this way, no beginning and no end, the self-other-self circling endlessly back, moving in and out of pattern and randomness, and appearing at times (and thus experienced at times) as stable. We do not posit a stable subject, but we insist that when pattern is discernable—made up of the truces and alliances that Jameson describes—one might perceive and experience a stable subject, and the possibility for agency occurs. The postmodern fragmented, multiple subject is only fragmented, only random, but the postsexual subject slips in and out of pattern and randomness and will not be determined by (post) modernity. Nor will it be sated by the coupling—or the deconstructive uncoupling—of linguistic binaries.[18]

We've come not to the death of the author—the author is alive and well, and she rewrites herselves continuously. We've come to the death of the human. In its modern form it is distinct from animal and machine, as a sentient and unique and unified being; in its postmodern form it becomes fragmented, fractured, unknowable, and yet fixed in its instability. The posthuman, postsexual subject has no discernable, stable boundaries; but unlike the postmodern subject, the postsexual subject is its own other, its own object of desire, as well as a desiring self. A chimera, the postsexual subject is its own endlessly expanding digital universe, a rotating black hole that pulls everything into itself, assembling, disassembling and reassembling (deconstructing and recombining) pattern from chaos, chaos from pattern.

Conclusion: Event Horizon

Quantum physics is full of relationships—and math, of course, but much of the mathematical work is geared toward solving the differential equations for a host of potentials: finding the relationships—the patterns—in chaos. Determining probabilities is, in a sense, writing narrative, and as Jameson says, all narrative is utopian. We would add that all narrative is therefore ethical, or in search of the ethics of its particular narrativity. One cannot think utopia without thinking ethics. Ethics cannot exist even in the imagination without a context; the ethical is always already situational, and so not static. Ethics hovers outside of postmodernism, never fully entering the room, with one foot always in the realm of potential coherence and unity. And we are okay with that contradiction. Our political selves insist upon it, actually. The maxim "do no harm" is tricky, with unforeseen consequences, always, and meaningless as an abstraction, yet it is a maxim, and deservedly so, transcendent at least as intention. Perhaps we are attempting to describe a moment in which we do not have to resolve our contradictions, or relegate desire and its satisfaction to that stunted corner of our imaginations reserved for "reality."

Perhaps we are attempting here to fully occupy the stability of pattern and coherence when it appears, even when it appears as a Stable Subject that smacks of modernist longing, even when we know that "I" is not "real." Because that knowledge doesn't change our desire or our satisfaction and subsequent ability to act, it makes it—makes "I"—as real as it gets.

We construct ourselves in narrative, and all of this digitized, textual self is stored on some infinitely large server, the embodied self relegated to a dream, remembered but never fully articulatable. Deleuze and Guattari's body without organs, not unlike the postsexual subject, is "not a scene, a place, or even a support upon which something comes to pass" (153). The postsexual subject is not real, it is unlocatable, and yet "[t]here is desire whenever there is the constitution of a body without organs under one relation or another" (165). This enables agency; this is the site of agency, or at least of its potential, but agency may be realized as a fight against fascism or fascism itself. Agency is neither ethical nor unethical.

But ethics may not be ignored when self and other together comprise the subject, and exteriority is recognized as interior after all. In "The End of Temporality," Jameson argues that "time governs the realm of interiority, in which both subjectivity and logic, the private and the epistemological, self-consciousness and desire, are to be found. Space, as the realm of exteriority, includes cities and globalization, but also other people and nature" (697). Spacetime and *selfother* erase the distinctions between selfishness and altruism, between self-interest and philanthropy; they are mathematically possible, which is to say they are possible. The danger, of course, lies in misperceiving the erasure of those boundaries, missing the postsexual turn in which we understand the other as a part of self—the ∞selfother∞—where ethics becomes self preservation in its most fundamental form. The least of us is, in fact, us. Jameson notes that "perhaps, as space is mute and time loquacious, we are able to make an approach to spatiality only by way of what it does to time," and following his logic, we note that perhaps we are able to make an approach to the self only by way of what it does to the other ("The End of Temporality" 706). We must not, he goes on to argue, "link the positive political content of modern existentialism with . . . the slaughter of the world wars," but rather "in the movement of decolonization that followed them and that suddenly released an explosion of otherness unparalleled in human history" (709). Agency is born of subjectivity, and we cannot hide from the fact that violence is only possible within agency. Agency necessitates the possibilities of horror: the infliction of pain and suffering and death distributed. How might this alter our world if the other is me, if I am the other?

Foucault similarly creates a space to think of the shaping of subjectivity within a context where self and other are one and the same, both necessary in the ongoing project of subject formation and the hallmark of subjectivity itself: desire. He writes:

> The confession is a ritual of discourse in which the speaking subject is also the subject of the statement; it is also a ritual that unfolds within a power relationship, for one does not confess without the presence (or virtual presence) of a partner who is not simply the interlocutor but the authority who requires the confession, prescribes and appreciates it, and intervenes in order to judge, punish, forgive, console, and reconcile; . . . a ritual in which the expression alone, independently of its external consequences, produces intrinsic modifications in the person who articulates it. (62)

We may never get away from deconstruction, and our intention is not to attempt that futile task; but Derrida calls for absolute justice to the other as the root of his entire project (especially his later work). We hope that our speculations here in some way approximate a green shoot of that subtle beast that may strengthen and grow. Postmodernism's deconstructive project may indeed be our event horizon—our point of no return, from which there is no escape—but if the black hole we find ourselves in pulls everything into itself, if the I and Thou are always already in here together, if there is no end to this expansion, we cannot help but wonder, does it really matter?[19]

Notes

1. For an excellent, simple overview of cybernetics, from its "prehistory" in the 1920s-30s to "coalescence" in the 1940s and "proliferation" in the following decades, see the American Society for Cybernetics's website: http://www.asc-cybernetics.org/.

2. This 2012 special issue of *Biography,* a journal dedicated to life writing studies, surrounds the disruptive nature of the posthuman in one of the most traditionally humanistic literary fields.

3. Here, we are thinking of postmodernism as conceived by Fredric Jameson, Jean-François Lyotard and, to a lesser degree, Jean Baudrillard.

We are aware that theoretical convergence, particularly within the vast realm of postmodernity, is nearly impossible, and we are certainly not claiming that we've reached it in this exploration. What we are suggesting is that we might rethink, collectively, various forms of postmodern subjects as they have been conceived throughout the last 30–40 years.

4. In his psychoanalytic exploration of Nietzsche's thought and philosophy, E. Victor Wolfenstein explains how Foucault's "knowledge-as-surveillance" might be conceived as "the paranoid-schizoid position, in which the possibility of persecution is combined with impersonal coldness." Wolfenstein argues that, because panopticism creates a fracture between mind and body, "placing 'the body' at the center of the struggle [is] . . . a thingification of the self and the reduction of a whole (no matter how complex and multicentered) to a part. . . . Panopticism creates the body as its object; it cannot be resisted on that basis" (31).

5. Critiques of postmodernism are many and varied, of course, but we refer primarily to those specifically concerned with identity, subjectivity, and agency. For example, see cultural studies scholars Hebdige and Slack, and feminist scholars Bordo, Butler, Ebert, Fraser and Nicholson, and Slack and Whitt, among many others.

6. Wittig, in her deconstruction of categories of gender within compulsory heterosexuality, argues that "lesbians are not women" because they exist outside of these categories. She writes that "'[w]oman' has meaning only in heterosexual systems of thought and heterosexual economic systems" (32). We wonder what her take on the postsexual subject might be.

7. For an exploration of Google's effects on the brain, see Nicholas Carr's "Is Google Making Us Stupid?" in the July/August 2008 *Atlantic Magazine*. Carr describes the "uncomfortable sense that someone, or something, has been tinkering with [his] brain, remapping the neural circuitry, reprogramming the memory" (1), and goes on to cite a variety of clinical studies, ongoing at the time of his writing, that suggest that the "universal medium" of the internet is, in fact, altering the way our brains process information.

8. We might think for a moment about the uproar surrounding *Facebook* and its ever-changing privacy settings. Among our "friends," for example, we notice this trend: although one ostensibly creates a *Facebook* account to become visible and to "stay connected," as the site has evolved, privacy settings have become more complicated and maybe more important. This coincides with a dramatic rise in media reports of identity theft and hacking; though we are supposed to be ever-vigilant with our online identities, we also do not want to be left out of the metaphorical loop. Yet another paradox.

This echoes debates about the public/private divide that have persisted since the mid-eighteenth century. For example, we might think about Facebook as a 21st-century version of Habermas's public sphere. Habermas characterizes "the bourgeois public sphere . . . as the sphere of private people come together as a public" (27) and, though far outside the scope of our immediate exploration, it might be that online social networking has created a new kind of public sphere that is not just for the bourgeoisie; after all, "it's free and anyone can join." (This also might answer, at least partially, Habermas's famous declaration that the project of modernity is incomplete).

9. The encroaching worry that this is creating a mighty paradox is disturbing—but we insist on continuing, in part because we are trying to abjure the presence/absence binary of deconstructive postmodernism, and instead, as Hayles and others have written so persuasively, think the world in terms of randomness and pattern. It is the disruption, the interruption of randomness that makes possible the (re)organization of pattern, and we are committed to powering through the anxiety of paradox, of randomness, in order to eventually—and with other scholars—think ourselves into discernable pattern, if only (and necessarily) temporarily. Even so, we remain more than a little uncomfortable with this line of thinking and what could certainly appear to be a rather easy dismissal of the material consequences on the bodies of others that have historically been, and continue to be even as we write this, a result of universalizing and essentializing others, as well as selves.

10. While the science fiction melodrama that is *Caprica* is fun and interesting, make no mistake: these issues and concerns are with us now. For a fascinating glimpse into current work in autonomous AI, see, for example, the July 2010 *New York Times* article "Making Friends with a Robot named Bina48" (be sure to watch the accompanying video) at http://www.nytimes.com/2010/07/05/science/05robotside.html?pagewanted=all and the for-profit website, touted as a research project, which purports to allow us all to "back up" our consciousness in order to achieve immortality, at http://lifenaut.com/Mind-How.html.

11. If we are attempting to move beyond the boundaries imposed by postmodern deconstructions of the self, might we also move beyond the unexpressed-but-thoroughly-implicated Marxist prohibition to eschew anything that smacks of false consciousness? We find troubling the idea of throwing Truth and Falsity out with the dirty bathwater and refilling the tub with some sparkling, clear pragmatism. We acknowledge that it does matter, it can matter, and it has mattered, with material consequences for real people; however, we wonder to what extent allowing ourselves to feel the desire of subject-stability, and to find strategies to temporarily satisfy that longing, might prove to be a far more effective means of producing agency than attempting to (unsuccessfully) school ourselves not to want what we know we cannot have.

12. Foundational postcolonial texts include Edward Said's *Orientalism* (1979) and *Culture and Imperialism* (1994), Homi K. Bhabha's *The Location of Culture* (1994), and Gayatri Chakravorty Spivak's "Can the Subaltern Speak?" (1988). *Feminisms* (1997), a popular literary and cultural studies anthology, provides an excellent overview of feminisms through the early 1990s. We also

suggest, particularly in our context, returning to Luce Irigaray's seminal *The Sex Which is Not One* (1985). In addition to Butler, Foucault, and Wittig, for overviews of queer theory, see Eve Kosofsky Sedgwick's *Epistemology of the Closet* (1990), Michael Warner's *Fear of a Queer Planet* (1993), and Nikki Sullivan's excellent *A Critical Introduction to Queer Theory* (2003).

13. It strikes us that this kind of theorizing might lead us to reconsider Foucault's role in writing studies, in postcolonial discourse theory, and in feminist theory, if his notion of a speaking subject is of a subject that is more constrained by power than a non-speaking subject who "just listens." From composition theory to Spivak to Cixous, to speak is to have/create/perform/exemplify agency. We suggest that the postsexual *selfother* might be one way of exploring this kind of authority; if the other is already the self, in who does sovereign power reside? For a more in-depth discussion of Jameson's "The End of Temporality," see the final section of this essay.

14. We acknowledge that "The Animal that Therefore I Am (More to Follow)" is not the most intuitive choice for reading Derrida on technology. Because our work on the postsexual necessarily takes into account the presence of the absolute other, however, we find it to be the most prescient of our many choices.

For a compelling look into other implications that deconstruction might bring to our technological world, see Timothy Clark's cogent "Deconstruction and Technology" in Nicholas Royle's *Deconstructions: A User's Guide*. In his article, Clark explores Derrida's "subtle and complex . . . double strategy" for evaluating the connections between langue, parole, and computers. Deconstruction, like the postsexual, "upsets received concepts of the human and the technological by affirming their mutual constitutive relation or, paradoxically, their constitutive disjunction" (247). Although our discussion calls for recombination and pattern-seeking, we suggest that any contemporary argument for recombination and hybridity must root itself within deconstruction. One must start somewhere.

15. Several philosophers and theorists have investigated the ethical and ontological implications of cybernetics. Two works from the 1970s stand out; see Kenneth M. Sayre's *Cybernetics and the Philosophy of Mind* (1976) and/or Ervin Laszlo's *Introduction to Systems Philosophy: Toward a New Paradigm of Contemporary Thought* (1972), which also provides an overview of the evolution of systems theory, as it was understood in the early 1970s.

For examples of science fiction dealing with cybernetics, cyborg subjectivity, and identity politics, see Philip K. Dick's *Do Androids Dream of Electric Sheep?* (1968) and the 1984 Ridley Scott film *Blade Runner*, based upon Dick's novel. Also see William Gibson's *Neuromancer* and James Tiptree, Jr.'s "The Girl Who Was Plugged In."

16. We do, of course, feel more than a little insecure about delving into quantum physics; we certainly don't mean to suggest that we have any expertise

or in-depth understanding of the very complex and highly mathematical aspects of this burgeoning field. We do, however, claim some expertise in reading narrative descriptions of events and objects and their interactions, and in this sense we hope to draw some parallels between the narrative of general relativity, and how it has changed the fields of physics and cosmology, and the narrative of subjectivity, and how putting the narratives together might open up the possibility of changes in human agency, for the better.

17. This is obviously simplistic, but follows the explanations of these matters found in Stephen Hawking's *A Brief History of Time*, as well as several other publications, also written for the non-scientist, that have been well-received by the scientific community. For examples of these narratives, see, in addition to Hawking: Kaku, Mallett, and Ouellette.

18. We realized after drafting the essay that at this point we had switched from the her/she pronoun to it/its; this seemed to happen organically as we wrote—we never discussed the issue until after we realized we had made the shift from the feminine to the neutered, more distant "it." Upon reflection we decided to leave it as is, having a fondness for the slight weirdness of it all, the rupture and the discomfort of struggling with inadequate, imprecise language. Julie suggested using "s/he/it," simply for the amusement factor of saying it out loud (and perhaps also because of both her and Kate's love of *The Wire*), but in the end we decided not to shoot for comedy, lest we fall too short of the mark.

19. The event horizon of a black hole is the boundary between its so-called "outside" and "inside." If you fell into a black hole you would not experience any passage from outside to inside as you passed through the event horizon, because for you, there would be no boundary. The boundary between outside and inside exists only for the observer, never for the subject. For discussions of event horizon and black hole theory, see Hawking, Kaku, Mallett, and Oellette.

Works Cited

Angerer, Mary-Luise. "The Making of . . . Desire, Digital." *Media Art Net*. Trans. Rebecca van Dyck. 8 Sep 2011. Web. 9 Nov. 2011.

Bennett, Jane. *Vibrant Matter: A Political Ecology of Things*. Durham: Duke UP, 2010. Print.

Benveniste, Émile. *Problems in General Linguistics*. Oxford: U of Miami P, 1973. Print.

Bhabha, Homi K. *The Location of Culture*. New York: Routledge, 2004. Print.

Blade Runner. Dir. Ridley Scott. Perf. Harrison Ford, Rutger Hauer, Sean Young, and Edward James Olmos. Warner Brothers. 1982. DVD.

Bordo, Susan. "Feminism, Postmodernism, and Gender Skepticism." *Feminism/Postmodernism*. Ed. Linda J. Nicholson. London: Routledge, 1990. 133–56. Print.

Butler, Judith. *Gender Trouble: Feminism and the Subversion of Identity.* 2nd ed. New York: Routledge, 1999. Print.

—. *Precarious Life: the Powers of Mourning and Violence.* New York: Verso, 2004. Print.

Burke, Timothy and Jack Dickey. "Manti Te'o's Dead Girlfriend, The Most Heartbreaking and Inspirational Story of the College Football Season, Is a Hoax." *Deadspin.com.* Gawker Media. 16 Jan 2013. Web. 1 Nov. 2011.

Caprica. Dir. Jeffrey Reiner. . Perf. Eric Stoltz, Esai Morales, Alessandra Torresani, and Magda Apanowicz. The Syfy Channel. 2009. Web. 18 Oct. 2011.

Catfish. Dir. Nev Schulman. Universal Pictures, 2010. DVD.

Clark, Timothy. "Deconstruction and Technology." *Deconstructions: A User's Guide.* Ed. Nicholas Royle. New York: Palgrave, 2000. 238–257. Print.

Couric, Katie. "Online Love Traps: the Victims and Masterminds Speak Out." *KatieCouric.com.* 1 Jun 2013. Web. 9 July 2013.

Deleuze, Gilles, and Félix Guattari. *A Thousand Plateaus: Capitalism & Schizophrenia.* Trans. Brian Massumi. Minneapolis: U of Minnesota P, 1987. Print.

Derrida, Jacques. "The Animal That Therefore I Am (More to Follow)." *Critical Inquiry* 28.2 (2002): 369–418. Web. 24 Aug 2011

Dick, Philip K. *Do Androids Dream of Electric Sheep? Philip K. Dick: Four Novels of the 1960s.* New York: Library of America, 2007. 431–608. Print.

Ebert, Tesesa L. *Ludic Feminism and After: Postmodernism, Desire, and Labor in Late Capitalism.* Ann Arbor: U of Michigan P, 1996. Print.

Foucault, Michel. "Body/Power." *Power/Knowledge.* Ed. Colin Gordon. Trans. Colin Gordon et al. New York: Random House, 1980. Print.

—. *The History of Sexuality.* Vol. 1. Trans. Robert Hurley. New York: Vintage, 1990. Print.

Fraser, Nancy, and Linda J. Nicholson. "Social Criticism without Philosophy: An Encounter Between Feminism and Postmodernism." *Feminism/Postmodernism.* Ed. Linda J. Nicholson. London: Routledge, 1990. 19–38. Print.

Gibson, William. *Neuromancer.* New York: Ace Books. 1984. Print.

Habermas, Jürgen. *The Structural Transformation of the Public Sphere.* Trans. Thomas Burger and Frederick Lawrence. Cambridge: MIT UP, 1991. Print.

Halberstam, Judith. "Automating Gender: Postmodern Feminism in the Age of the Intelligent Machine." *Feminist Studies* 17.3 (Autumn 1991): 439–60. *JSTOR.* Web. 24 Aug. 2011.

Haraway, Donna J. "A Manifesto for Cyborgs, Science, Technology, and Socialist Feminism in the 1980s." *Feminism/Postmodernism.* Ed. Linda J. Nicholson. New York: Routledge, 1989. 190–233. Print.

Hawking, Stephen. *A Brief History of Time: From the Big Bang to Black Holes.* New York: Random House, 1998. Print.

Hawking, Stephen and Leonard Mlodinow. *A Briefer History of Time*. New York: Bantam Dell/Random House, 2005. Print.
Hayles, N. Katherine. *How We Became Posthuman*. Chicago: U of Chicago P, 1999. Print.
—. *My Mother Was a Computer*. Chicago: U of Chicago P, 2005. Print.
Hebdige, Dick. "Postmodernism and the Other Side." *Stuart Hall: Critical Dialogues in Cultural Studies*. Ed. Kuan-Hsing Chen and David Morley. 174–200.
Hutcheon, Linda. *The Politics of Postmodernism*. New York: Routledge, 2002. Print.
Hyussen, Andreas. *After the Great Divide: Modernism, Mass Culture, Postmodernism*. Bloomington: Indiana UP, 1986. Print.
Irigaray, Luce. *This Sex Which Is Not One*. New York: Cornell UP, 1985. Print.
Jameson, Fredric. "The End of Temporality." *Critical Inquiry* 29 (Summer 2003): 695–722. Print.
—. *The Political Unconscious: Narrative as a Socially Symbolic Act*. Ithaca: Cornell UP, 1981. Print.
—. *Postmodernism, or, the Cultural Logic of Late Capitalism*. Durham: Duke UP, 1991. Print.
Kaku, Michio. *Parallel Worlds: A Journey Through Creation, Higher Dimensions, and the Future of the Cosmos*. New York: Anchor/Random House, 2005. Print.
Laszlo, Ervin. *Introduction to Systems Philosophy: Toward a New Paradigm of Contemporary Thought*. Newark: Gordon & Breach, 1972. Print.
Mallett, Ronald L, with Bruce Henderson. *Time Traveler: A Scientist's Personal Mission To Make Time Travel A Reality*. New York: Thunder's Mouth Press, 2006. Print.
Morton, Timothy. *Ecology without Nature: Rethinking Environmental Aesthetics*. Cambridge: Harvard UP, 2007. Print.
Ouellette, Jennifer. *Black Bodies and Quantum Cats: Tales from The Annals of Physics*. New York: Penguin, 2005. Print.
Said, Edward. *Orientalism*. New York: Pantheon. 1978. Print.
Sayre, Kenneth M. *Cybernetics and the Philosophy of Mind*. New York: Routledge, 1976. Print.
Sedgwick, Eve Kosofsky. *Epistemology of the Closet*. Berkeley: U of California P, 2008. Print.
Slack, Jennifer Darryl, and Laurie Anne Whitt. "Ethics and Cultural Studies." *Cultural Studies Reader*. Ed. Lawrence Grossberg, Carrie Nelson, and Paula Treichler. New York: Routledge, 1992. 571–92. Print.
Spivak, Gayatri Chakravorty. "Can the Subaltern Speak?" *Marxism and the Interpretation of Culture*. Ed. C. Nelson and L. Grossberg. Macmillan Education: Basingstoke, 1988: 271–313. Print.
—. *Ouside in the Teaching Machine*. New York: Routledge, 1993.

Sullivan, Nikki. *An Introduction to Queer Theory.* New York: NYU P, 2003. Print.

Tiptree, James, Jr. "The Girl Who Was Plugged In." *Screwtop/The Girl Who Was Plugged In. Tor Double.* New York: Tor Books. 1989. Print.

Turkle, Sherry. *Life on the Screen: Identity in the Age of the Internet.* New York: Simon & Schuster, 1997. Print.

Warhol, Robyn and Diane Price Herndl eds.. *Feminisms: An Anthology of Literary Theory and Criticism.* Piscataway: Rutgers UP, 1997. Print.

Warner, Michael. *Fear of a Queer Planet.* Minneapolis: U of Minnesota P, 1993. Print.

Waugh, Patricia. "Modernism, Postmodernism, Feminism: Gender and Autonomy Theory." *Postmodernism: A Reader.* Ed. Patricia Waugh. London: Edward Arnold, 1992. 189–204. Print.

Whitlock, Gillian. "Post-ing Lives." *Biography* 35.1 (Winter 2012): i-xvi. *Project Muse.* Web. 15 May 2013

Whitman, Walt. "Song of Myself." *Leaves of Grass.* 1881 d. *Leaves of Grass and Other Writings.* Ed. Michael Moon. New York: Norton, 2002. 26–78. Print.

Wittig, Monique. "The Straight Mind." *The Straight Mind and Other Essays.* Boston: Beacon, 1992. 21–32. Print.

Wolfenstein, E. Victor. *Inside/Outside Nietzsche: Psychoanalytic Explorations.* Ithaca: Cornell UP, 2000. Print.

6 Becoming T@iled

Sean Morey

> *Any extension, whether of skin, hand, or foot, affects the whole psychic and social complex.*
>
> —Marshall McLuhan, *Understanding Media*, 3

> *A Monkey perched upon a lofty tree saw some Fishermen casting their nets into a river, and narrowly watched their proceedings. The Fishermen after a while gave up fishing, and on going home to dinner left their nets upon the bank. The Monkey, who is the most imitative of animals, descended from the treetop and endeavored to do as they had done. Having handled the net, he threw it into the river, but became tangled in the meshes and drowned. With his last breath he said to himself, "I am rightly served; for what business had I who had never handled a net to try and catch fish?"*
>
> —Aesop, "The Monkey and the Fishermen"

As N. Katherine Hayles explains in *My Mother Was a Computer*, 1930s and 1940s computers required human beings to do most of the "thinking" and that interpretations of *computer* "from World War II to the end of the twentieth century mark a shift from a society in which the intelligence required for calculations was primarily associated with humans to the increasing degradation of these labors to computational machines" (1). Before computers became "intelligent" so that they could think for us, humans had to do the thinking for them. While this example should not be construed as providing an etiological anecdote for a transition into posthumanism, it does highlight one attitude toward a particular relationship between posthumans and computers: the prosthetic function that we often assume of computers is one of calculations, of performing mathematical-based utilities which augment the processing speed of the human brain, making a posthuman mind. Perhaps because of this preoccupation with the cerebral, the "brain" or "mind" becomes an iconic location of where the prosthetic connection occurs. One only has to think of the science-fiction fantasy motif of uploading one's consciousness into a machine and leaving the body behind, which occurs in films such as *The Matrix* where the "mind" is inserted into a virtual environment—a prosthetic space—and the manipulation of such an environment is one of manipulating codes: the savviest posthuman is one that never loses her ability to compute. Instead of leaving the body behind, though, what about the body's "behind"? Instead of focusing on the head of the posthuman, we might focus on the "post" of the posthuman—the tail.[1]

In the womb, we all have tails. The human embryo continues to grow its tail until the fourth or fifth week, but around the seventh week of development the tail begins to disappear. The tail is never something that any animal gains, but a body part that humans, in particular, lose. The human embryo grows out of a tail, which disappears as the embryo continues to develop. However, although we lose most of its physical aspects, except for the few vertebrae that compose the coccyx, do we lose all of the psychological ones? What parts of our tail remain? Do we still try to use our latent tails, or unconsciously sense that we have phantom tails? For those animals with tails remaining, what functions do the tail allow for that become missing for us? We are all conceived with tails, but what kind of conceiving would tails permit?

Other animals have found many uses for their tails. Fish use tails for hydrodynamic propulsion, and the thresher shark also uses its tail to stun prey; alligators and crocodiles use their tails in similar ways. A lizard can use its tail to deceive, fooling a predator into attacking its detachable appendage so that it may escape. The rubber boa also deceives with its tail, using "short, blunt tails that look almost identical to the head. When threatened by a predator, this snake arranges its body in such a manner that the tail is exposed while the head is hidden safely beneath the snake" (Gibbons). Birds may use their tails as a rudder, but also ostentatiously to attract, such as the elaborate tail displays of peacocks. Squirrels use their tails for balance as they prance around trees limbs, to help regulate and store body heat, and, like the bird, as a rudder when jumping.[2] Horses and cows swat flies away from their rears; the hippopotamus swats dung. Larger tails store fat in addition to their other functions. One of the main points to take from the tail, then, is that they most often have multiple uses. Besides providing attunement for balance, motion, temperature, and hunting, tails provide a means of telling—tails can become tales. Such tales are most commonly observed in the dog or the cat.

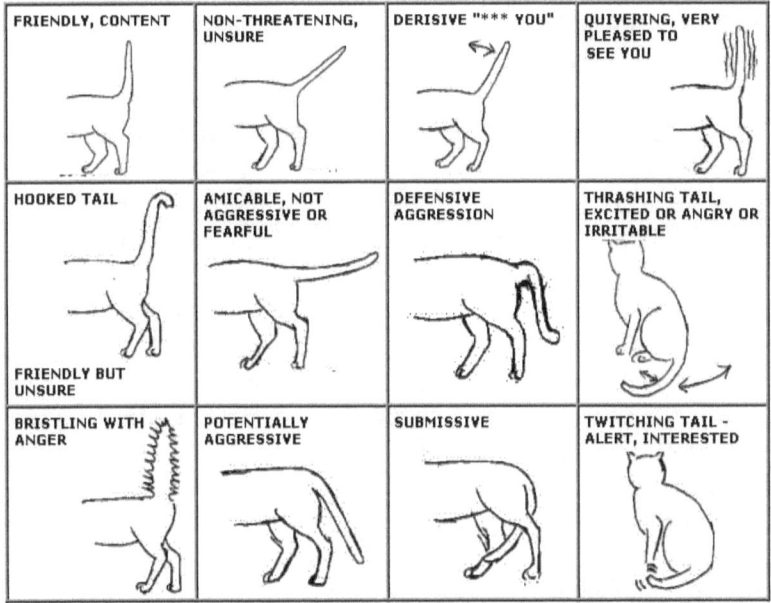

Figure 5.1 Cat communication through its tail from Sarah Hartwell; "Cat Communication—Body Language"; *Messybeast.com;* N.p., 2009; Web; 12 Feb. 2010.

Figure 5.1 depicts various tails/tales of the cat. While the cat can use its tail to communicate commands/requests, what the tail primarily delivers is mood. The cat tail is rhetorical and becomes a means to deliver, through a visible signal, what the animal cannot (or chooses not to) express audibly. The cat's tail gestures, and what it gestures is a state of mind. What a posthuman tail might afford is a way to account for affect and deliver emotion, which becomes an aesthetic action already apparent through Roland Barthes's image logic of the *punctum,* which injects an aesthetic experience like a scorpion's tail. We might consider the need to construct our own prosthetic tails to give us similar powers. We might consider what it would mean to re-tail ourselves.

One tail that we have already begun to adopt is the @, sometimes referred to as "the monkey's tail." The @ appears nearly ubiquitously in online environments, and provides one kind of code that we commonly write with. However, because of its ubiquity, we often overlook its function as a code, that it instructs our "intelligent" computers to enact a certain command, or that it changes the way that we write/think in other kinds of environments. The @ is so ubiquitously invisible that an internet search for @ does not return any documents.[3] We write everyday with the @, yet it remains transparent to our thinking prosthetics. The @ as a monkey's tail, however, does more than just instruct our posthuman parts toward some specific function: it becomes prosthetic as a posthuman tail, and serves a different kind of prosthetic function than one of "thinking." As such, the @ needs to be theorized both inside and outside current conversations of how posthuman bodies and codes interact. We need to theorize what it means to both "write" a prosthesis such as a t@il, what that t@il looks like once written, and how it performs as a function of/through writing at the level of code.[4]

Other digital appendices have already been tested for their integration with the posthuman. Dobromir G. Dotov, Lin Nie, and Anthony Chemero have demonstrated how easily the hand-mouse circuit becomes "natural" when using it to operate (assemble with) a computer. As Chemero states, "The person and the various parts of their brain and the mouse and the [computer] monitor are so tightly intertwined that they're just one thing . . . The tool isn't separate from you. It's part of you" (qtd. in Keim). Dotov, Nie, and Chemero sought to test Heidegger's "ready-to-hand" theory and determine if we normally overlook the mouse and monitor. By purposefully disrupting the hand-mouse circuit, the team noted a cognitive dissonance in the users, effectively creating Heidegger's "unreadiness-at-hand." The malfunction breaks the circuit, cuts the human from his or her cyborg infrastructure, but also from a prosthesis that aids in thinking. As Chemero further conjectures, "The thing that does the thinking is bigger than your biological body . . . You're so tightly coupled to the tools you use that they're literally part of you as a thinking, behaving thing" (qtd. in Keim). If we remove the hand-mouse and break this version of a posthuman machinic assemblage, then what occurs when we add (or cut off) the tail? What is the cognitive malfunction that would occur if one had (or no longer had) access to the @ and all that the @ affords? Is the @ already so "invisible" that we've incorporated it into our cognitive process? Or, another question: what does the @ give us access to in the first place?

What is the natural history of this m@rk? While many debate the origins of @, some competing theories are worth mentioning. Like proto-alphabetic writing in general, the @ begins in economics as a way to account for goods and currency. Berthold Louis Ullman claims that the @ might have been a ligature "which is really for *ad,* with an exaggerated uncial *d*" (187), perhaps used by medieval monks to save labor and space. Likewise, it may also represent an "a" inside of an "e" to signify "each," as in the accounting discourse, "each at $10," not unlike modern day accounting usage where @ means "at the rate of" (or short-hand for the Greek ἀνά which has the same meaning). Its evolution of design may have arisen from the Norman French by altering the grave-accentuated à—which is used similarly as "at" or "each" when referring to accounting—so that the writer can make the mark without raising the writing instrument. This practice is first documented in the writings of the Italian merchant Francesco Lapi, whose use of the @ within a letter is "the first recorded use of the 'at' sign outside a monastery" as discovered by Giorgio Stabile (Long, Stabile). Figure 5.2 renders this possible evolution.

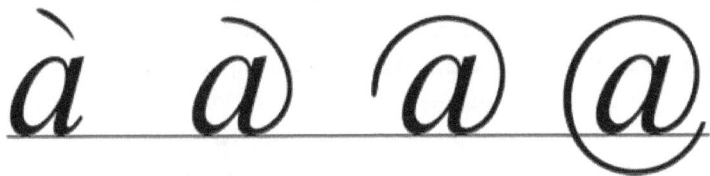

Figure 5.2. Possible evolution of the @ symbol (created by author).

For the Portuguese, the @ historically stood as a symbol for a unit of specific weight (16 liters of liquid), as in the weight of goods contained in an *arroba,* a kind of jar derived from the Greek *amphora.*⁵ Italians may also have adopted this usage as their @-term *anfora,* so that one @ equals one *anfora.* But besides a jar, an accounting symbol, or its other uses, the @ has a variety of epithets given by different cultures. For the Russians, the @ is a *sobachka,* or little dog. Koreans may refer to it as a snail (*dalphaengi*). The @ is sometimes referred to as an "ear" of a variety of species, from pigs to elephants. But in a variety of languages, the @ is referred to as a tail—sometimes a mouse's, pig's, or cat's—but most often a monkey's tail, where the tail section is that which wraps around the indefinite article. Many languages derive their tails from the German term, *Klammeraffe,* which refers specifically to the spider monkey and the prehensile use of its tale in New World arboreal habitats (Chung). The spider monkey, like many monkeys, uses its tail as another hand with which to grasp branches or other objects as it climbs about the rainforest. This tail becomes a tool for movement, for reaching places its other limbs might not find accessible, and for ascending into the arboreal habitat, leaving many of the dangers of the ground below. The tail of the spider monkey is transcendent.

The @ takes up a transcendent quality as well, in multiple ways. One way is through the lengthening of the tail—as shown in figure 2—which created a new typographical mark eventually transcending the symbol itself to that of art. As used in Twitter, the @ serves to gain one's attention—@seanmorey—as a peacock might spread its tail feathers and attract a mate: the @ becomes aesthetic, despite (or perhaps because of) its use as a functional code. In 2010, the Museum of Modern Art (MoMA) included the @ in its architecture and design collection; as Alice Rawsthorn notes, "That's as good as it gets in the design world, rather like bagging a Tony on Broadway or an Oscar in Hollywood." And what makes the @ aesthetic in MoMA's eyes? Rawsthorn points out that the acquisition committee determines each piece according to questions such as "Does it excel in terms of form and function? Does it embody the values of clarity, honesty and simplicity that MoMA considers essential to good design? Has it made an impact on our lives? Is it innovative?" Finally, "there's the clincher. 'If this object had never been designed or manufactured, would the world miss out?' said Paola Antonelli, senior curator of architecture and design at MoMA. 'Even just a bit?'" (Rawsthorn). And the @ met such criteria

> Brilliantly, according to Ms. Antonelli. By giving that once obscure accountancy symbol a new application without distorting its original meaning, Mr. Tomlinson was deemed to have checked all of MoMA's boxes in terms of form, function, values, cultural impact and innovation. She sees "snail," "pig's tail" and its other nicknames as proof of its importance, because we care so much about the @ that we've started to mythologize it. (Rawsthorn)

The @ develops so many pseudonyms/epithets but has never developed an official English name, and the Oxford English Dictionary simply includes it as the "at sign." And although the @ has not lost its "original" meaning, it takes on new ones. The @ symbol becomes a floating signifier, an open work of art, which can take on many meanings. The @ is an open sign, both figuratively and literally. Rawsthorn observes that the @ still looks the same after several hundred years despite not existing as "a physical object like the chairs, cars or architectural drawings that you'd expect to find in a design museum." This permanence, despite its lack of "physicality," is one reason that MoMA chose the @: "both the old and new @ fulfill the same function of simplifying and clarifying something that's fiendishly complicated to make and interpret: handwritten script and computer code respectively," which Antonelli views as "an act of design of extraordinary elegance and economy" (Rawsthorn).

The "new @" referred to by Rawsthorn and Antonelli is the @ "economically" borrowed by Raymond Tomlinson, historically noted to have sent the first email message. Tomlinson chose the @, a character not widely used for anything else but accounting (yet still on computer keyboards since it featured on the American Underwood typewriter in 1885), to serve as the bridge between the human and the computer. The user is located @ a particular computer server. The "elegance and economy" shown by this choice are qualities both "prized by MoMA, especially 'economy' in a time of recession and environmental crisis, when reinventing something that's under-used seems much smarter than designing something new" (Rawsthorn). So, we're back to economy after all. But its "under-use" within an economy of symbols is what allows it to function as a floating signifier, which is why Tomlinson was able to borrow it for email in the first place. So while the @ has only limited functions as a computer code, it's filled with many particular meanings, becoming many varieties of t@ils. Thus, the very character that we use in this transformational way, to create a variety of aesthetic designs via the programs that feature @, is itself an aesthetic glyph of writing ourselves a posthuman tail in order to further write our posthuman selves. Thus, in the economy of the @, its value is not (only) money, but how it might be used in multiple ways by a variety of desires. MoMA considered the potential variety of @s as well, which is why they "decided against adding a specific version of the @ to the collection in favor of using it in different typographic styles and sizes. Ms. Antonelli likens it to the museum's acquisition of 'The Kiss,' a performance art piece by

Tino Sehgal, in which a couple embrace for several hours. Just like the @, each performance can take a different form with new protagonists" (Rawsthorn). Each of the individual uses of @ takes on a unique performance as we t@il ourselves, eventually creating a long t@il that extends throughout the Internet.

Another aesthetic consideration (also in the MoMA collection): in *A Thousand Plateaus,* Gilles Deleuze and Félix Guattari begin the chapter "1837: Of the Refrain" with a plate of a painting by Paul Klee entitled *Twittering Machine* (figure 5.3). In the painting, four birds perch on a hand crank, perhaps chained to it. Birds sing for many reasons, such as to mark their territory, or to express their desire for a mate. These birds, in particular, have become territorialized and make up a twittering machine with the instrument on which they've become attached; and they don't sing, they twitter. At least, the integration with the hand crank creates a twittering machine, and not a singing machine. But what exactly is a twitter? Of a bird, to twitter is an intransitive verb that means "to utter a succession of light tremulous notes; to chirp continuously with a tremulous effect" ("Twitter, v.1"). It also means "to spin or twist unevenly, to make 'twitty'" ("Twitter, v.2"). As a noun, a twitter is implicated with desire, and so twittering delivers a performance of desire: "a condition of twittering or tremulous excitement (from eager desire, fear, etc.)" ("Twitter, n.1"). However, a twitter is also "an entanglement; a complication" ("Twitter, n.3.c"). And so, like the birds in Klee's painting, one cannot twitter without also becoming ensnared.

The microblogging site Twitter contains all of these definitional aspects of "twitter." The service prompts for spontaneous updates of excitement; the @ (which serves as a method of making responses to others public) and hyperlinks create a twitty, and even the nature of the short (140 characters or less), regular posts mimic the short, repeated "tweet tweet" of a bird's tune.[6] This rhythm is carried across by the @. Deleuze and Guattari indicate that the formal feature of language that best represents the way that their assemblages (desiring-machines) connect is the "and" and the indefinite article. The "and" and "a" provide a method toward linking machines together, to move from break to break in various flows. However, as an image these words may be quickly represented by the character @. In the digital internet, the @ provides one of the many points of connection for making assemblages, and integrating the post@ human via the t@il, of which the @ is always necessary for (email) posting in general. It is not just that the @ serves as the link between sender-receiver, between the sender, recipient, and the conduits (email address domains) making such a connection possible, but that it provides the conductor of desire itself, as if it were the indefinite article: "'A' stomach, 'an' eye, 'a' mouth: the indefinite article does not lack anything; it is not indeterminate or undifferentiated, but expresses the pure determination of intensity, intensive difference. The indefinite article is the conductor of desire" (Deleuze and Guattari 164).

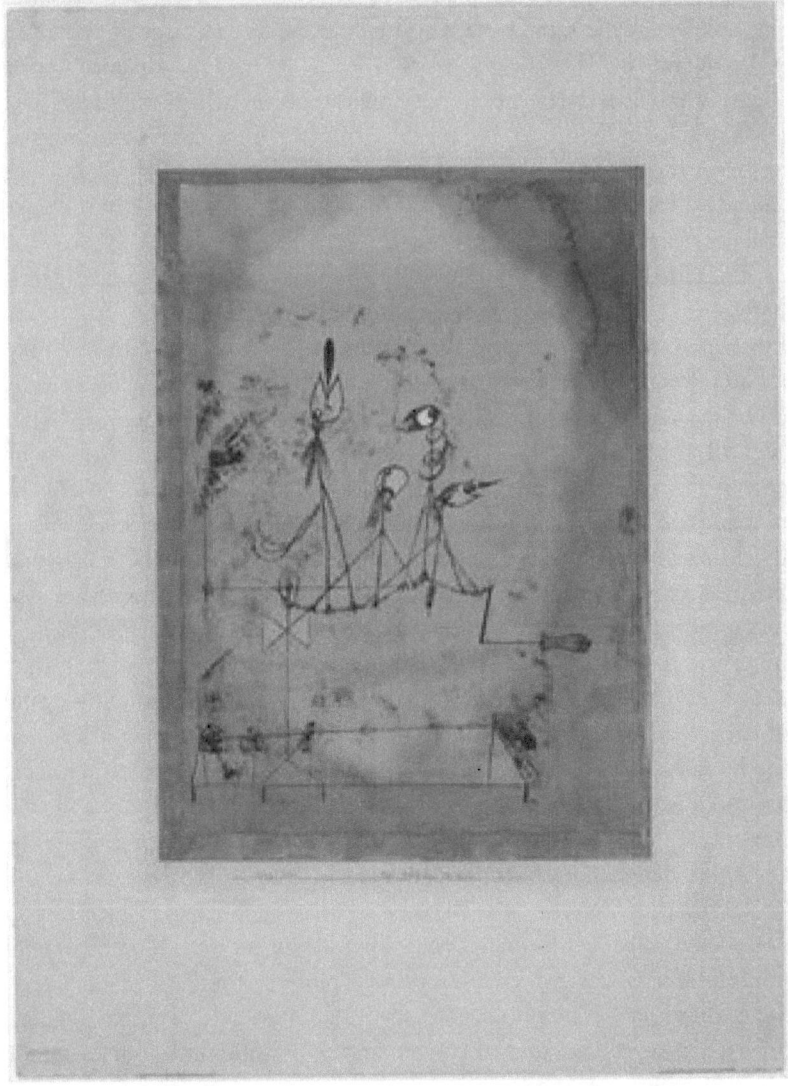

Figure 5.3. Paul Klee, *Twittering Machine* (*Die Zwitscher-Maschine*), 1922; *MoMA.org;* The Museum of Modern Art, New York. 2011. Web. 20 Sept. 2011.

This kind of linking, with the "@" as an "an" and as an "and," not only provides a way of connecting, but also one with a vector, projecting a line of flight. We might say the @ gives direction with purpose, if purpose can be taken to mean the striving toward a desire, Spinoza's *con@tus*. Lacan tells us that the desire expressed by the *objet petit a*, from where the theoretical functioning of the @ derives for Gregory L. Ulmer, can never be reached. Yet we strive for it. And we should also consider multiple @s at the same time, and include the @'s accounting meaning of "at the rate of." This origin refers to actual money, and fits nicely with Deleuze and Guattari's theories of how capitalism affects the socius and leads to schizophrenic coping mechanisms (the logic of and . . . and . . . and); for if capitalism requires the constant attainment of flow, puncept intended, then Lacan's *objet petit a* is indeed unreachable. A million @s will never be enough.

But rather than focus on the @s themselves, their function as the link between the human@post provides an aesthetic line of flight. Toward its function as art, as an image, the Portuguese's use of the @ to resemble an amphora lends credence to the potential of the @ image to serve as an image category for a means of connection, a way of gathering. While typically only two kinds of categories cluster about the current use of @—as the sender/receiver signifier and a signal of presence in the form of a domain address—is it possible that the @ could cluster many other machines around it as well, becoming a kind of Body without Organs, assembling different paths of desire, serving as a gathering place? Ulmer's chora—a new media collage space of gathering and invention—might be thought of as chor@, where @ is the non-place, a space that allows a gathering and sifting to occur. The @, then, becomes a point of departure (or arrival) for thinking about how to construct a t@il for the human@post of the posthuman, not in the limited sense that such a symbol is used to send emails or link usernames on Twitter, but as an important linking component that might be expanded upon, opening the @ further than even its current uses.

Ulmer theorizes the @ as the *objet petit a* for electracy, which might potentially foster posthuman group identity formation: "The object @, joining letter and signifier, preserving a piece of the Real in the Symbolic (discourse). The implication for individual and collective identity formation, in the context of the apparatus, is profound. The electrate category emerges at the opposite pole of the literate one. It is not universal, but is a sinthome, a non-sense letter sported by a particular body"

("Letter l'etre"). The @ is performed by the posthuman, twitched about like the cat's tail, and as a non-sense letter is a remainder that requires a body to which it desires, or creates desire, for the assemblage with a body. Toward this, the space at the center of the @ provides the hole of the unconscious, a black hole that spirals into the singularity.[7] However, Deleuze and Guattari read a black hole as "sometimes chaos . . . sometimes . . . a home . . . sometimes one grafts onto that pace a breakaway from the black hole" (312) and not always a collapse into the singularity. They offer that Klee provides the figure of the black hole (what Klee calls a "gray point") in which these three "sometimes" might be found:

> The gray point starts out as nonlocalizable, nondimensional chaos, the force of chaos, a tangled bundle of aberrant lines. Then the point "jumps over itself" and radiates a dimensional space with horizontal layers, vertical cross sections, unwritten customary lines, a whole terrestrial interior force. . . . The gray point (black hole) has thus jumped from one state to another, and no longer represents chaos but the abode or home. Finally, the point launches out of itself, impelled by the wandering centrifugal forces that fan out to the sphere of the cosmos. (312)

The @ is not only an unconscious that spirals inward, but outward, producing gr@y spots throughout. These gr@y spots works toward creating an unconscious state to unify desire/body/machine, spiraling outward and gathering parts, and while not universal for every body, the @ is also Lacan's empty universal, joined to particular bodies and filled with particular desires. The @ contains its own remainder, subverting its simple use as code: "the @ marks the object (a), the expressible standing in for the inexpressible" (Ulmer, "Corridor Window @ Shands Hospital").

In the movie *Avatar,* the Na'vi people network with the ecology of their planet Pandora through their ponytails, which might inform how we consider our own t@ils as a means to connect with our own networked ecologies and gain access to our own avatars.[8] As Ulmer explains, the term avatar was "adapted to cyberspace to name one's online persona" from the original Sanskrit *avatara,* for which the "original usage referred to the incarnation or human appearance of a deity, particularly Vishnu, in Hindu mythology" (Ulmer, "Avatar"). The avatar does not represent any single element of the online persona, but "has come to include every aspect of one's online representation, from the icon on a blog, or an email signature to the figure one plays in Second Life. 'Avatar,' then, is a practical point of entry for theorizing the emergence of the new identity experience of electracy, that is supplementing and displacing 'selfhood,' the identity formation of literacy" (Ulmer, "Avatar"). We constructs t@ils and link to others via the @, either through email, Twitter, or other platforms, and create online presences becoming avatars. As Ulmer further explains, the etymology of *avatara* includes "*ava,* down + *tarati,* he crosses over." The avatar via the @ provides a crossing down, a descendent movement, a movement opposite of the traditional ascendant direction of transcendence, not into the cloud, into a heaven, but down into the machine, a movement toward the tail. And, punningly enough, the *ava* (down) in Sanskrit and the ává (rate) in Greek can both be expressed by the @, which, through the avatar also links the individual with the collective through the process of identity formation: "The third dimension of a language apparatus (after technology and institutional practices) is identity formation, individual and collective. The term covering the site of new identity experience in electracy is avatar" (Ulmer, "Avatar"). As in the film, one's avatar joins the individual and collective in a group connected by a new kind of economy of t@ils.

The avatar, to the extent that it contains all the components of one's online persona, might be better stated here as @v@t@r, since unlike the t@il in Twitter alone, the @v@t@r necessarily contains many t@ils.[9] The @v@t@r contains multiple t@ils, multiple lines of flight. However, each t@il of the @v@t@r, or the total number of t@ils it contains can be long or short, many or few. In *The Long Tail,* Chris Anderson describes a new and developing business model for internet retail sales that entails selling less of any particular good and instead offering more types of products. As Anderson differentiates between "old" media and new media, the former "can bring one show to millions of people with unmatched efficiency. But it can't do the opposite—bring a million shows to one person each. Yet that is exactly what the internet can do so well" (5). The internet can deliver the "everything else," the non-hits that typical broadcast media and brick-and-mortar stores can't because of economics: "The simple picture of the few hits that mattered and the everything else that didn't is now becoming a confusing mosaic of a million mini-markets and micro-stars. Increasingly, the mass market is turning into a mass of niches" (5).

Micromolarities are becoming the norm. And these micromolarities cluster together to form what Anderson calls the "Long Tail" (see figure 4), which, although they don't sell as many quantities as the "hits" that make up the head, in aggregate can potentially add up to a greater mass: "The onesies and twosies were still only selling in small numbers, but there were so *many* of them that in aggregate they added up to a big business" (9). The Long Tail, by adding the prosthesis to the head, allows a way to make the invisible visible: "Many of these kinds of products have always been there, just not visible or easy to find. They are the movies that didn't make it to your local theater, the music not played on the local rock radio station, the sports equipment not sold at Wal-Mart. Now they're available, via Netflix, iTunes, Amazon, or just some random place Google turned up. The invisible market has turned visible" (6). The Long Tail aggregates, for it is an aggregate, and in doing so makes the formerly microscopic noticeable.

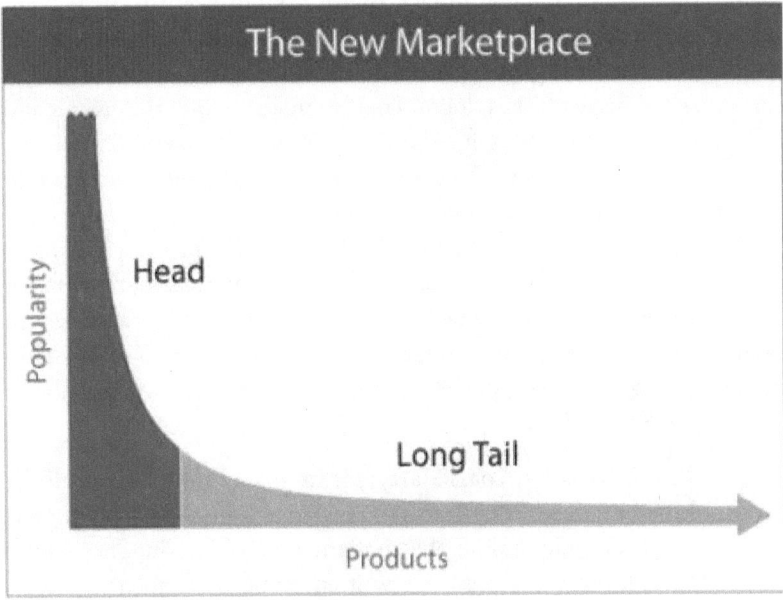

Figure 5.4. Diagram of the "Long Tail" from Chris Anderson; *The Long Tail: Why the Future of Business Is Selling Less of More;* New York: Hyperion, 2006; Print.

Connecting to the market/economic implications of the Long Tail, the form of "tail" in words such as "detail" and "retail" refers to its meaning of "cut," specifically to cut up into pieces. In contrast to wholesale, mass produced goods become cut up and distributed to smaller retail outlets. With schizophrenic logic, we often construct our avatars like Deleuze and Guattari's schizo, building an overall avatar through assemblages of multiple @'s, cutting off pieces from one flow and directing them into another. The avatar engineer schizzes them and assembles those cut pieces into his t@il, or creates a long t@il that grants access to an @v@t@r. One delivers herself, crosses over into the Internet in small quantities, re-tails herself, not (always) as a whole body, but as organs, as micromolarities of the whole. Implicated in this schizophrenic logic of the cut, of biting off bits and reattaching them, is desire. Our missing tail that we lose in the womb becomes the fetish object that within the domain of the Internet becomes totemic. The Long Tail is also the long(ed for) tail, and this t@il can be very long: "What's truly amazing about the Long Tail is the sheer size of it. Again, if you combine enough of the non-hits, you've actually established a market that rivals the hits" (Anderson 22–23). So long, in fact, that it extends to infinity. As mentioned earlier, *Klammeraffe* derives from the German name for a spider monkey; its scientific genus, *ateles,* translates to "without end." Linking various social network sites, logos, email signatures, brands, etc. all add up and create a long tail(s) for the @v@t@r, which makes distributing that persona more efficient. To deliver one's @v@t@r, one assembles it in the form of a long t@il, consciously or not.

And toward this @v@t@r, the t@il becomes the primary means of circling around the user's unconscious desire and appears as a m@sk, an alt identity, forming a loop that i(con)ically resembles what it performs. Noting that one source of inspiration for Tomlinson's choice of the @ might have been an image of the title character in Alfred Jarry's play *Ubu Roi,* Daniel Soar writes,

> Père Ubu is fat, coarse, a tyrant, a greedy slob and would-be king of Poland ('that is to say, nowhere') who seeks instant gratification—not unlike the modern user of the internet—and, significantly, the play was written to be performed by actors pretending to be puppets. The spiral *gidouille,* engraved on Père Ubu's belly in Jarry's woodcut for the play-text's frontispiece, which also has him wearing a Klan-like mask, is meant to symbolise the tyrant's intestines. By linguistic association, it's felt to contain a gross combinationof *Gribouille, grenouille, andouille, couille, gargouille:* gargoyles, testicles, tripe, frogs, power-hungry fiends. The ubiquitous @, which had seemed so analytically secure, turns out to be engorged with potential meanings. That, presumably, is what people hope for when they sign up for Twit-

ter: that they can be anyone, and in 140 characters or fewer can produce a digested version of whatever personality they choose.

In this image of Père Ubu (figure 5) we see the anonymous @ user, shrouded in anonymity (even when one's name is exposed) with his "Klan-like mask," bulging from the gut, but bulging from what? A diarrhea relieved by tweets? An urge to spill one's guts, easier to do when one

Figure 5.5. Depiction of Père Ubu from Alfred Jarry; *Ubu Roi.* Trans. Beverly Keith and Gershon Legman. Mineola, NY: Dover, 2003. *Project Gutenberg.* Web. 20 Sept. 2011.

has taken an avatar and is not to be accountable for the mess? And of course, actors playing characters that are playing puppets provide an important correlate with the practice of playing a character that is disguised as a puppet (avatar) online. At *Ubu Roi*'s 1896 Parisian premiere, Jarry opened the play with a lengthy introduction in which he explained such puppeting: "Our actors have been willing to depersonalise themselves for two evenings, and to act behind masks, in order to express more perfectly the inner man, the soul of these overgrown puppets you are about to see" (1–2). Like Ulmer's description of the object @, the mark itself is not as important as the unconscious desires that seek to pass through it. The avatar becomes the online body (or in the case of Père Ubu, onstage) into which the soul may descend, protected by the m@sk that the spiraling @ affords.

Furthermore, Jarry's introduction details the *de-tails*, that is, the bits and pieces that he, for one reason or another, wasn't able to include (or purposely cut):

> The play having been put on prematurely, and with more enthusiasm than anything else, Ubu hasn't had time to get his real mask (which is very inconvenient to wear anyway), and the other characters will be fitted out, like him, somewhat approximately. It seemed very important if we were to be quite like puppets—Ubu Roi is a play that was never written for puppets, but for actors pretending to be puppets, which is not the same thing—for us to have carnival music, and the orchestral parts have been allotted to various brasses, gongs and speaking-trumpet horns that we haven't had time to collect . . . here you must accept doors that open out on plains covered with snow falling from a clear sky, chimneys adorned with clocks splitting to serve as doors, and palm-trees growing at the foot of bedsteads for little elephants sitting on shelves to munch on. As to our orchestra that isn't here, we'll miss only its brilliance and tone. The themes for *Ubu* will be performed offstage by various pianos and drums.

Jarry prefaces a play that appears not only absurd, but also stripped-down, reduced to the bare essentials that can stand-in for more extravagant sets, or more robust music. Yet, the description of the cuts (cuts which also include/exclude whole acts) provides a variety of rich images that, had they been included, would have seemed like Deleuze and Guattari's schizophrenic table rather than a traditional mise-en-scène.

If we were to read Jarry's introduction according to Soar's thoughts on the @, then we can see the same spontaneity and "enthusiasm" in this introduction as in the typical approach to Twitter. Every idea gets included and broadcast, but without much detail and explanation, spurred by desire and emotion rather than careful planning and reason, so that each tweet is a reactionary outburst rather than a thoughtful, full-fledged account. Beyond Twitter, instant and text messages in general make cuts by adopting short message system acronyms and shorthand. But one aspect of the play that Soar neglects to mention is *Ubu Roi* as a harbinger of the Theatre of the Absurd. If we accept a general definition that posits this movement has having "in common the basic belief that man's life is essentially without meaning or purpose . . . that human beings cannot communicate," which leads to "the futility of existence being conveyed by illogical and meaningless speeches and ultimately by complete silence" ("Absurd"), then communication in the Twitterverse, to Soar at least, seems to be the precursor to "silence." Thus, the @, which seemed like it served a logical function in accounting and email, has become @bsurd thanks to Twitter (at least according to Soar):

> Twitter, the social networking site that everyone is tweeting about, has been plotting the takeover of @ for a long time. When the site first launched, it called itself twttr, in evident homage to the first word of *Ubu Roi* ('Merdre!,' usually translated as 'Shittr!'), which caused a riot during the play's 1896 premiere. In email addresses, @ is all about precision and privacy: your message is routed to a particular individual at a particular domain, to a subset containing a single member. Twitter reverses the principle: it makes @ a tool for sending a message to an individual—@barackobama, @oprah, @therealdevil—that anyone who chooses to can overhear. The at sign used to indicate a whisper: now it's become a gargantuan shout. Since the most frenetic Twitterers are in the business of broadcasting their every daily doing to anyone who will listen, it's hardly surprising that when, earlier this month, Twitter's rock-star-like founders, @ev and @biz, tried to change this policy such that semi-private conversations could be semi-private once more, the Twitterverse shouted them down. Frankly, @ has got out of control.

The @ is @bsurd, but not because of the r@te at which it is used, but the holes that it opens for desire to link with. The @ isn't so much the signifier of all these potential meanings (although, of course, it could serve that function just as any symbol) but rather the link that makes such meanings and @ssemblages possible. The @ is the point of attachment. Like other tails, the t@il provides multiple uses, functionally and aesthetically, whether used for private messages via email, or broadcasts via other outlets. In either case, the @ provides this outlet, not just computationally, but psychically as well. The t@il provides the potential for rebirth into any desirous avatar one pleases, so that in cyberspace, we enter the world tail first, even in the simplest form of email, where the @ appears on the tail-end of our usernames, opening a wormhole for telepresence.[10] Through this hole—the @ referred to by Ulmer's theory of the object @—we are offered rebirth—several times over—and we are reborn through our tail. This tail of the @, the *Klammeraffe*, grasps the unconscious hole in the middle, providing a shield to hide the hole in the "a," but also to offer a secret point of entry, a cyclical maze or crypt-like structure that opens the possibility for discovery. Or, if a gr@y spot, a secret point of escape, once the tail has created the pathway. The process of attaching a prosthetic t@il does not involve starting at the hole, but with the t@il itself, working toward the unexpressible.

McLuhan's quote at the beginning of this piece is not meant to suggest a technological determinism regarding the t@il, but instead prompt questions of how the psychic and social complex responds to having a t@il, and what practices might develop around this posthuman feature of writing that integrates one with the machine at the symbolic (and perhaps other) level. Having a t@il can be good or bad, depending on how we use it. The conversation about this use has barely begun, regarding both the history of the @ itself, and how we have built practices around its use, transforming it from writing to print to screen. As Neil Verma observes:

> Notice that @ begins as a unit of denomination (*x* @'s of wine), then becomes an operator indicating a relationship *between* denominations (*x* casks of wine @ *y* euros). Then, notice that @ simulates the image of a person in a physical location (so-and-so@someplace), then it *conflates* place and person (@ so-and-so-*as*-someplace).
>
> While these two lines of etymological evolution seem separate, they obey a homologous principle. In both cases, the *aro-*

base gradually refuses to designate objects or to coordinate them between one another—instead, it wants to *transform* objects. Thus, the mystical character of the glyph lies less in its prodigiously engorged organ of meaning than in the promethean transformations undergone within its coil.

Verma—perhaps unwittingly—suggests that while we have transformed the @, it has a certain agency as well, one of transformation both of itself and of those who use it. Since such agency and transformation is undertheorized, perhaps we have not sufficiently considered the potential (dangers) of the @. If we have created a t@il for ourselves, or if that t@il has grafted itself onto our human posts, then we might further consider how this occurs, why we construct such t@ils, and what it offers our posthuman beings, in whichever way one considers such a being. For while the @ provides an aesthetic symbol that transcends its simple function as code, the birds in Klee's *Twittering Machine* have become ensnared with the machine's hand crank, and Père Ubu's bloated gut onto which the @ is inscribed suggests the symbol's nasty underside (which may, in fact, be our own). Aesop's fable about the Monkey and the Fishermen—also offered at the beginning of this writing—provides another caution, not only of taking on new technologies too quickly, but the dangers of blind imitation. Monkey see, monkey do. Monkey drown. The monkey has mastered its own tail, but not the net. We have mastered neither, and both t@il and (Inter)net may be mastering us.

Notes

1. As Cary Wolfe notes in *What Is Posthumanism?*, the term *posthuman* produces "different and even irreconcilable definitions" (xi). Rather than account for all of these definitions, this article begins with two. The first, a common perception of posthuman that occurs when the "natural" human body integrates with other machines, substances, and other "prosthetics" that lead to something other than human, either cyborg or more than human. The kind of posthuman I'm thinking of here permeates the work of Donna Haraway and the singularity theory of Ray Kurzweil, who offers that humans will reach an event horizon of machine integration where the two can no longer be pulled apart. While Kurzweil might be identified as a transhumanist, viewing technology as a means to improve the human toward a kind of liberal human transcendence (addressed by Hayles in *How We Became Posthuman*), my use of posthuman more aligns with Wolfe's: "posthumanism in my sense isn't posthuman at all—in the sense of being 'after' our embodiment has been transcended—but only

posthuman*ist*, in the sense that it opposes the fantasies of disembodiment and autonomy, inherited from humanism itself, that Hayles rightly criticizes" (xv, emphasis in original). However, although this article contends with the embodiment of the posthuman, rather than focusing on a techno-integration my concern is with the kind of thinking (from intellect to affect) that such integration makes possible or necessary for a posthuman organism to survive and thrive according to her own desires.

Another meaning of posthuman that I use here refers to the human that we have left behind, particularly the behind mentioned with the tail we no longer have, a tail that is post-human as it disappears. That is, what is the prehuman that the human posts, that eventually leads to the posthuman? Regarding tails, what is this post of the human, and what can it teach us about how to use and incorporate (literally) writing technologies that might require thinking with the post rather than the head? These two concepts of posthuman dominate much of this article, although the term could and should be read with other meanings in mind; I hope that the article will eventually lead to the need to consider other definitions of posthumanism—ones that might involve postspecies, postgender, postrace, postbody, and many others—by invoking the possibilities that a t@il might hold.

2. In the sense that "cybernetics" derives from the Greek word for "steersman," the tail provides a literal cybernetic function.

3. As of this writing, Google cannot find any results for it (nor can Yahoo!, AltaVista, Bing, nor image search results). While a search for "@" does not return any results, the @ is not totally invisible despite its ubiquity. Many foreign-language keyboards do not include the @ as a symbol, making the @ invisible in other ways.

4. The use of "t@il" is meant to show the connected nature of the "tail" with "tale," but also its connection with networked ways of tailing/telling. Any other words with @ embedded within are similarly meant to convey a networked sense of the word, as well as all the other senses of @ as theorized in this article. Similarly, while the usage of @ will at times refer to the "at-sign" properly, it should not always be "heard" as "at," but sometimes an unpronounceable symbol to be "seen" rather than "said."

5. Rui Coelho and Joana Fernandez de Carvalho, Portuguese ichthyologists formerly at the Florida Museum of Natural History, state that the term *arroba* now refers to the @ in Portuguese vernacular.

6. Also note the twitters that many celebrity Twitter users find themselves in after an ill-advised tweet. We must also consider the sn@res that one's t@il might get caught in.

7. "Black hole" is another one of @'s many epithets.

8. *Avatar*. Dir. James Cameron. Perf. Sam Worthington, Zoe Saldana, Sigourney Weaver, and Stephen Lang. Twentieth Century Fox, 2009. Film.

9. If we use the full Sanskrit version, avatara, then the tail letter becomes another t@il: @v@t@r@.

10. "Wormhole" is yet another one of @'s many epithets.

Works Cited

"Absurd, Theatre of the." *The Concise Oxford Companion to the Theatre*. Ed. Phyllis Hartnoll and Peter Found. *Oxford Reference Online*. Oxford: Oxford UP, 1996. Web. 29 September 2011.

Aesop. "The Monkey and the Fishermen." *Fables*. Ed. George Fyler Townsend. *Electronic Text Center, University of Virginia Library*. University of Virginia. July 1993. Web. 20 Sept. 2011.

Anderson, Chris. *The Long Tail: Why the Future of Business Is Selling Less of More*. New York: Hyperion, 2006. Print.

Chung, Karen S. "Summary: The @ Symbol." *The Linguist List*. Institute for Language Information and Technology and Indiana University. 2 Jul. 1996. Web. 20 Sept. 2011.

Deleuze, Gilles and Félix Guattari. *A Thousand Plateaus: Capitalism and Schizophrenia*. Tran. Brian Massumi. Minneapolis: U of Minnesota P, 1987. Print.

Dotov, Dobromir G., Lin Nie, and Anthony Chemero. "A Demonstration of the Transition from Ready-to-Hand to Unready-to-Hand." *PLoS ONE* 5.3 (2010): e9433. Web. 15 Mar. 2010.

Gibbons, Whit. "All Reptiles Have Tails with Many Uses for Them." *Aiken-Standard.com*. 6 Mar. 2010. Web. 10 Mar. 2010.

Hayles, N. Katherine. *My Mother Was a Computer: Digital Subjects and Literary Texts*. Chicago: U of Chicago P, 2005. Print.

Jarry, Alfred. *Ubu Roi*. Trans. Beverly Keith and Gershon Legman. Mineola, NY: Dover, 2003. *Project Gutenberg*. Web. 20 Sept. 2011.

Keim, Brandon. "Your Computer Really Is a Part of You." *Wired*. Wired Mag. 9 Mar. 2010. Web. 20 Sept. 2011.

Long, Tony. "May 4, 1536: C U @ the Piazza." *Wired*. Wired Mag. 4 May 2009. Web. 20 Sept. 2011.

McLuhan, Marshall. *Understanding Media: The Extensions of Man*. New York: McGraw Hill, 1964. Print.

Rawsthorn, Alice. "Why @ Is Held in Such High Design Esteem." *The New York Times on the Web*. New York Times, 21 Mar. 2010. Web. 20 Sept. 2011.

Soar, Daniel. "Short Cuts." *London Review of Books* 31.10 (2009): 18. Print.

Stabile, Giorgio. "L'icon@ dei mercanti." *Trecanni.it*. Istituto della Enciclopedia Italiana. 2005. Web. 20 Sept. 2011.

"Twitter." *The Oxford English Dictionary*. 2nd ed. 1989. *OED Online*. Oxford: Oxford UP. 1 Mar. 2009. Web. 20 Sept. 2011.

Ullman, Barthold Louis. *Ancient Writing and Its Influence*. Toronto: Medieval Academy of America, 1997. Print.

Ulmer, Gregory L. "Avatar." *Heuretics: Inventing Electracy.* n.p., 1 Dec. 2008. Web. 20 Feb. 2010.

—. "Corridor Window @ Shands Hospital." *Heuretics: Inventing Electracy.* n.p., 2 Jun. 2008. Web. 20 Feb. 2010.

—. "Letter l'etre." *Heuretics: Inventing Electracy.* n.p., 5 Mar. 2009. Web. 20 Feb. 2010.

Verma, Neil. "Glyphs Gone Wild." *Ducks and Drakes.* n.p., 21 May 2009. Web. 20 Sept. 2011.

Wolfe, Cary. *What Is Posthumanism?* Minneapolis: University of Minnesota Press, 2010. Print.

7 Inscriptions of the Possible; or, A Pedagogy of Posthumanist Style

J. A. Rice

Though the relationship between posthumanism and writing has a long history, perhaps nothing marks it more than a persistent struggle with the concept of *writing style*. In his "Thinking the Post-Human: Literature, Affect, and the Politics of Style," for instance, Lee Spinks argues that given a posthumanist horizon, writing "style becomes political, and in so doing, brings our concept of the 'political' into permanent crisis, when it creates new positions to register the multiplicities of lived experience that enable the subject to recognize itself as a subject at a particular moment in history" (43). As a political enterprise, a posthumanist writing style is more affective than supplementary. It disrupts and violates our taxonomic definitions—we can no longer really be sure what *political* signifies or how to categorize it—and forces us to reconsider how we approach the multiplicity of space, time, and historical particularity.

But this is not to say that a posthumanist style is without liability. Following Daniel W. Smith and Michael A. Greco, Spinks is quick to show that for all of its irreverent disruptions, a posthumanist style is still "a set of variations on language, a kind of modulation, and it is through style that language is pushed toward its own limit, but that which language alone makes possible' (such as the affects and percepts that have no existence apart from the words and syntax of the writer)" (43). There are a few things to notice here. The first is that while a posthumanist style might compel us to devise newer and more nuanced rhetorical positions, its disruptions never exceed the purview of rhetoric. We can write idiosyncratically, create new kinds of texts, and rethink sentence structure, but such stylistic variations cannot reconstitute what rhetoric itself makes possible. Style, in other words, is a reflection of rhetoric's capacity. The second, interrelated point is that a posthumanist style modulates the complexities of language. If a radical, disruptive style pushes language toward its own limit, style has to work concomitantly *with* language, and as a result, is held accountable *by* language. A posthumanist style's variations on language are therefore localized and cannot violate unequivocally or even systemically. Rather, its variations refigure rhetoric (and language), twists it in on itself and tries to develop new directions and positions, and, in that process, puts the relationship between posthumanism and style in a difficult position. Writing, and particularly writing style, is *supposed* to disrupt, it is supposed to violate rhetorical norms, but cannot do so because it is also supposed to be accountable to rhetoric. Consequently, style has to have meaning, its violations have to procure some sort of identity or, at the very least, modulate communicative practices. A writing style cannot violate in vain.

Of course, Spinks is not the first to point out the problematic relationship between the promises of a posthumanism politic and its stylistic realization. Lynn Worsham's "Writing Against Writing: The Predicament of *Ecriture Féminine* in Composition Studies" also warned those theorizing writing how writing (and language) would have to risk all to engender a posthumanist style. Style, she claims, is "the critical term—not just a style of writing but *writing as style,* style as a form of cultural critique . . . [that has to] resist the desire to give meaning" (Worsham 86, emphasis added). Like Spinks's conception, Worsham's style is a political act. But unlike Spinks, her politic of style understands that style's greatest danger is its propensity to encourage meaning. For writing to resist and create, style cannot reflect the latent possibilities of rhetoric. It rather has to disrupt—resist—without linguistic or conceptual recourse. As Worsham puts it, for style to disrupt, it cannot inscribe "specific content [because it is] an inscription of heterogeneity," and as such, should "only obliquely indicate a direction in which to think its operation" (88). Style is writing and writing is style. For style to critically resist, it should only inscribe. What a writing economy or formation "means," how it reflects content, is of little importance to what a posthumanism could call *style.* Perhaps more to the point: a posthumanist writing is always stylistically disruptive. Under the guidance of a posthumanist style, concepts will ever only find their horizon disjointed by communicative and even grammatical dissemblance. A posthumanist writing cannot express content or concepts because it only outlines a vague direction; it only marks difference. A posthumanist writing, then, acts almost like a series of random inscriptive events—it is an irreconcilable accident that connects a rhetor's choices and the nomadic moments of style's specific, iterable capacity. If "effective communication" endures, it is only because writing has not properly accomplished its task.

Yet it would be remiss to believe that our traditional conceptions of style are so easily dispelled. Though writing theorists might think style differently, it will take more than merely asserting a new theoretical program to enact such change. Writing theory history has shown that in the struggle between theoretically induced change and rhetorical habit, theory often loses. To be sure, in the 20-plus years since Worsham's warning, we have yet to refigure to a substantive degree how style and writing politically affect rhetoric, or to even realize what the fallout of such a pairing creates. This shortcoming is especially surprising given the revolutionary advances of contemporary writing technologies. It is no surprise that various internet technologies—from email and MOOs/MUDs to wikis and data clouds—have tested the connections between a posthumanist politic and style; however, they also end up recounting how style should account for meaning or even knowledge more often than not. Collin Brooke and Thomas Rickert's "Being Delicious: Materialities of Research in a Web 2.0 Application" perhaps best exemplifies how an accountable writing style should endure despite posthuman technological invention. As a Web 2.0 property, the *Delicious* website operates as a fluid network where users can reflexively create, name, link, and categorize information according to real-time changes in context. It is the fluidity of this network that Brooke and Rickert assert as a new opportunity for writing: "language and technology are constitutive and transformative, and *Delicious* concretely illustrates how this is so" (177). Unfortunately, illustrating change is as far as writing can go. "If all this suggests," Brooke and Rickert ask, is "a general loosening and lessening . . . of knowledge to go with new technologies, why would it be welcome? While it is risky to make predictions about something so new, we want to consider what might be seen as real benefits" (177). Though not exhaustive, these benefits include an increased awareness of audience, an alternative view of taxonomic methods, and a better understanding of education's dynamic processes (177–178). Brooke and Rickert's benefits are without a doubt welcome, yet they nevertheless sidestep how new writing technologies' networked logic complicate writing's function. Instead, a networked writing-as-style remains codified and generalized, and must be accountable for something in the end—in this case, knowledge.

If style is still liable in our technological, posthumanist context, what, then, are we to make of the possible links between a posthumanist politic and writing style? Can there be a posthumanist style, or will style's accountability always proscribe posthumanist disruptions? Moreover, if there can be a posthumanist style, how might it inform or challenge the ways we engage with writing and specifically its pedagogical lineage? These are certainly not new questions, but questions that I contend have not been answered as well as they could have been. Our tendency to accommodate posthumanism's disruptions is problematic, if for no other reason than because it suggests that the relationship between style and posthumanism has been settled, or worse, believed irrelevant. This is a dangerous view. For to simply dismiss questions about the relationship between posthumanism and style as anachronistic does little to reconcile more pressing contemporary concerns about discursive appropriation and rhetorical invention, to name just one. Accordingly, it would be worth our while to rethink posthumanism and style's enjoining logic so that it better reflects the possibilities of a disruptive grammar and the responsibility it sows.

A Genealogy of (Rhetorical) Style

A posthumanist style faces a few difficulties, not the least of which is the entrenched rhetorical belief that style is both a defining and a generative enterprise. Paul Butler, for instance, defines style as broadly involving "a series of both conscious and unconscious choices that writers make about everything from the words we use and their arrangement in sentences to the tone with which we express our point of view and the way we achieve emphasis in a sentence" (1). In this formulation, style is nothing if not conceptually inclusive (and somewhat overdetermined). It encompasses a variety of topics, from writerly choices—like how words are used and how they garner an effect—to the grammatical and rhetorical arrangement of any written text. Given such a wide berth, it should not be surprising that this definition of style is one of the more potent and recognizable commonplaces. Strunk & White's *The Elements of Style* describe this conceptually inclusive style as "an increment in writing" that both belies and exceeds rhetorical flourish (66). Style is a poetic, but one that we cannot "talk about [as] 'rhythm' and 'cadence'" because such definitions are "vague and unconvincing" (67). Rather, style signals a more grave and serious endeavor: it "*is* the writer, and therefore what you are, rather than what you know" (84). Joseph M. Williams's *Style: The Basics of Clarity and Grace* echoes Strunk & White's existential take on writing by arguing how frequently we forget that style is more than "the polish that makes a sentence go down smoothly" (124). Choosing subjects and verbs, he argues, offers us a unique view of how our choices of "subjects and verbs implies a philosophy of human action: do we freely choose to act, or do circumstances cause us to?" (Williams 124). Similarly, and perhaps to a lesser extent, Mignon Fogarty believes style (and grammar) entails "avoiding big annoyances [in language use]. It's a step on the way to style, which in the end, you must find for yourself, grasshopper" (167). In these conceptually inclusive definitions, style is never just about how a particular piece of writing happens and what that piece of writing looks like or does. It is instead a locus of thought and action that implicates everything from language use and word choice to how a writer and writing tarry with ontology. Writing's and the writer's contextual premises, their temporary considerations, and their mutually reflexive analytic, to name a few, are all issues of what we call *style*.

As the genealogical offspring of the rhetorical cannon, contemporary ideas of style should certainly do no less. Cicero's *Of Oratory* outlined long ago how style seizes the dialectic between rhetorical contingency and economy. Style, he writes, is "dignified and graceful and in conformity with the general modes of thought and judgment" (208), which means it is

> harmonious, graceful, and marked by a certain artistry and polish. Yet . . . if the underlying subject matter be not comprehended and mastered by the speaker, [it] must inevitably be of no account or even become the sport of universal derision. For what so effectually proclaims the madman as the hollow thundering of words—be they never so choice and resplendent—which have no thought or knowledge behind them? (207)

Style is not merely complimentary to rhetoric, but is in actuality a logic that conforms—and informs—general modes of thought and judgment. Just as the rhetor should study and imitate various writing styles, so too should they adjust their style to fit rhetoric's purposes. Like our more contemporary ideas of style, Cicero's advocates a philosophic endeavor where a rhetor's rhetorical choices reflexively interact and shape style.

But this does not mark style as a purely discursive affair. If, for example, style and substance are indubitably entwined, as Cicero believes, then style is the first premise of thought or knowledge. "[T]hat favorite assertion of Socrates," Cicero argues, "—that every man was eloquent enough upon a subject he knew—has in it some plausibility but no truth" because, even if a rhetor is knowledgeable about their subject, they still have to "know how to shape and polish [their] style [if they want to] speak fluently upon that which [they do] know" (209). Since style and thought are linked, their relationship is the way thought takes form. Simply speaking (or writing) without cause is therefore meaningless. Or, perhaps put a slightly different way: style has to forward an obvious logic. For beyond disclosing thought, it is supposed to be dignified and graceful, and above all should work *with* the general modes of knowledge. Style grounds thought, gives it form, but since one of its primary features is to work *with* knowledge, it risks that relationship every time it inscribes—it could, that is, ultimately choose the wrong or inappropriate words for the occasion ("the hollow thundering of words"). So, despite Cicero's assertions, style is in some sense defined by the inherent risk it takes when it tries to develop the appropriate links between thought and knowledge. Style is that which could precisely go awry, or more accurately, could always be different.

Foregrounding the contingency of style changes a few things. Style is, firstly, identified less by its relationship to knowledge than it is by how well it balances that relationship. This formulation, in contradistinction to contemporary views of style, is primarily a question of thinking style *as a logic*. Richard Lanham envisions this logic as a compressed or collapsed relationship between style and substance, where "both can be plotted on a common matrix . . . [as] an integral, and not simply metaphorical, way of relating" (448). If taken to the extreme, this renewed relationship is now a way to "relate judgments of the one sort to judgments of the other, [a way] to put style and substance into relationships that are as complex as human reality" (448). Style and substance—here, thought—still work concomitantly with general modes of knowledge, but the variables of that relationship have changed. Much like Cicero's formulation, Lanham's theory of style still reactively works with knowledge conventions. The judgments we make in one context can and will reflexively inform judgments we make in another context. However, this same style now additionally reflects its own inscribing or marking process. It becomes a kind of logical shorthand, as Paul Butler notes, for "[embracing] the cacophony of difference" (2). Making judgments is not enough; rather, thinking (and recording) how a judgment affects other judgments also constitutes what we can call *style*. By relating judgment to judgment, by thinking how one evaluative intervention into space and time ultimately changes an entire context, style better reflects difference and can more readily account for the act of writing and its rhetorical effects.

Style's contingency has a second, if not more subtle, implication. As a judgment in space and time, a style's logic highlights how pivotal a role chance plays in any and all contextual linkages. This means that developing a dialectic between style and substance (or thought) is less important than the temporality and arbitrariness of such encounters. Kenneth Burke discusses this temporally-sensitive dimension of style as a delicate balance between contingent and congruent logics. Using the analogy of a man dissuading another from drunken debauchery, Burke explains how style is a "hypnotic or suggestive process of 'saying the right thing'" (50). Once the audience is convinced to abstain from the prohibited act, we see how "style or ingratiation [is] successfully employed . . . to produce a desired state of mind in his audience," and moreover, how someone like Matthew Arnold "would have been too crude [to tackle this persuasive job]—his training would have been all incapacity" (50). Much like Cicero and Lanham, Burke's theory of style reveals a constitutive taxonomic connection between particular acts and our habitual understanding of those acts. What we determine, for example, to be rhetorically appropriate in a situation depends greatly on how well it resembles situations that came before it. If we are to navigate that situation successfully, we need to understand how a particular style works congruently with commonplaces and adapt them to the occasion. This stylistic logic, Burke believes, is why a man who is "schooled in the experiences of alcohol" knows what phrases and words carry rhetorical currency in the minds of drunken men (50).

But while what we call *style* might signify a successful rhetorical strategy, it is still a product of chance. Burke suggests that even when instance and commonplace form a coherent, particular logic,

> [c]hange, heterogeneity of occupation, and instability of expectation [still] have a radical bearing upon the range, quality, and duration of such linkages. Add geographical shifts, breakdown of former social stratifications, cultural mergers, introduction of 'new matter'—and you have so many further factors to affect the poetic medium adversely. (52)

Style persuades, but does so through an accordant economy that appropriates, aligns, and synchronizes iterations of place, purpose, and especially *kairos*. *Kairos* is particularly important in this context because it accentuates an alternative relationship between chance and style. For instance, in contrast to Cicero's and Lanham's stylistic contingency, Burke's introduction of *kairos* pinpoints not just how style is *informed* by contingency, but rather how contingency is a primary, if not constitutive *factor* in any stylistic logic. To be sure, as Cicero and Lanham point out, nothing guarantees style. A particular style could work without exception in one context and unequivocally fail in an almost identical context. Burke, however, enriches this conception by showing how style's contingency is not a wholesale concept—it is not made or broken by the successes of rhetorical application alone—but rather a logic that conceptually includes gradations of success. Here, style is certainly and reflexively affected by things like "change, heterogeneity of occupation, and instability of expectation," but trying to prepare for or protect itself from such changes is a moot point. Style, as Burke sees it, is ubiquitous and ultimately a product of time and circumstance; to pretend otherwise is to obscure writing. For this reason, Burke shows how style is less a question of how to account for potential change than it is an integration of it. To welcome and accept that unfettered change will indefinitely occur in any and all writing formations is indeed the mark of thinking style as a logic.

Given this brief rhetorical genealogy, we could say the concept of *style* chariots, among other things, a particular kind of rhetorical repetition as a way to ensure effective communication. This repetition, at its most basic, is "arrangements of formal features designed to produce a certain effect and project a certain vision of the world," and as such, is "finite and learnable" (Fish 134, 133). Learnability aside, Burke reminds us that this rhetorical repetition is ultimately style's contemporary politic. For if style is a balance between ubiquity and contingency, then its political significance lies in the degree to which it develops a relationship that respects both. From Strunk & White and Fogarty to Cicero and Lanham, *style* often does mean envisioning writing as a series of repeatable, logical relationships between combinations of words, contextual change, and rhetorical purpose. Our concept of *style* is therefore burdened with the difficult tasks of defining what can be written in a situation (arrangements of formal features) and of generating an amendable rhetorical logic that should strive to "say the right thing."

Such burdens are not without merit, however. As *style* negotiates the possibilities and proprieties of writing, it additionally highlights its relationship to several aspects of rhetoric, such as the rhetorical concept of genre. At its most advantageous, style's relationship to genre looks at "how and why texts . . . are produced" and ultimately defines "the rhetorical environments within which we recognize, enact, and consequently reproduce various situations, practices, relations, and identities" (Bawarshi, "The Genre Function" 336). Working in tandem with genre, style helps create and subsequently preserve writing's "finite and learnable" rhetorical and contextual formations, and thereby enables us to reproduce such formations for future purposes. On the one hand, this means that writing, say, a eulogy is merely a matter of balancing the conventions of a rhetorical environment with its contextual particularities. Yet, on the other hand, it means realizing style and genre's relationship as a precisely generative enterprise. As Anis Bawarshi notes, a genre and its stylistic conventions organize and generate their "own field" and, in turn, create a "constellation [that functions] to coordinate the dynamic relations that make up" its rhetorical contexts (*Genre & the Invention of the Writer* 38). If, then, *style* acts as a series of repeatable, logical relationships, it enjoins and emboldens genre by testifying to its analytic (and rhetorical) influence. Of course, this is another way of saying that genre and style work in a reflexive relationship: genre outlines environment—it engenders the "common" of rhetorical commonplace—and style attests to that environment's contingency. Writing in this formulation would therefore mean that less attention be given to how conventions and contextual particularities cooperate than to how they reflexively determine the ways in which they *can* relate. This, perhaps, is *style* at its most rhetorical and certainly at its most political. In its effort to preserve writing's "finite and learnable" rhetorical and contextual formations, *style* helps annotate and develop the evolution of rhetorical genres. Composing a eulogy in this scenario, for instance, would thereby entail both understanding the genre's rhetorical commonplaces *and* inventing new aspects of those commonplaces (such as broadening the eulogy's formal scope and purpose). Accordingly, we could say *style's* ability to determine—and in some senses amplify—its reflexive and dynamic relationship with genre is its greatest contribution to rhetoric.

At the same time, such a reflexive arrangement does little to promote *style* as anything but a handmaiden of rhetoric and rhetorical genres. To be sure, I do not mean to attack rhetoric or the rhetorical exigency of style per se, but rather to point out that as long as style supplements rhetoric, it will only ever be considered an analytic instrument of the former. For example, in Burke's comparison of style and labels, he argues that "the more homogenous a society's ways of living and doing and thinking are, the more homogenous will be the labels, hence the greater likelihood that [others] will use these labels to their purposes" (51). In this conception, *style* outlines the use of categories (labels) and the perceptible logic by which those same categories can be repeated and generalized. And while such an analytical dimension acknowledges a logic in its flirtation with the contingency of writing, it nonetheless subsumes this contingency for rhetorical purposes. Labels, and hence style, can and should be repeated—writing, that is, *can be* otherwise—but those repetitions have to create some sort of discernable rhetorical effect (in this case, a rhetorical commonplace). In Bawarshi's dynamic understanding of style and genre's relationship, for example, the concept of *style* allows writing to explore its contingency, while the concept of *genre* devises and develops the commonalities of that contingency. *Style* attests to inscriptive change, whereas *genre* attests to inscriptive repetition and, ultimately, rhetorical habits. Consequently, by defining what can be written in a given situation and generating the conditions in which that definition can be repeated, *style* might reflexively change the rhetorical landscape, but cannot change its function in that landscape.

What such an analytic burden suggests, then, is that if posthumanism and style are to forge any sort of productive relationship, that connection cannot be primarily rhetorical. As our genealogy demonstrates, thinking this relationship in terms of its rhetorical value risks proscribing it to only what has been already done. A posthumanist style's disruptions could, in that scenario, be bartered as just another rhetorical strategy, or more pointedly, as mere rhetorical alterity. Those accounts that solely wish to reevaluate or dismiss our stylistic genealogy most likely await a similar fate. While it might be easy to reevaluate or dismiss how style outlines and generates rhetorical effects, rethinking style's connection to rhetoric only isolates parts of that relationship while leaving its underlying logic untouched. In such a limited investigation, a posthumanist style would inevitably still create, still develop rhetorical generalities; it would, in the last analysis, still be accountable for something. Instead, our task seems to be not just one of reevaluation or dismissal, but rather a grammatical reenvisioning of how stylistic contingency interacts with rhetorical purpose, and more importantly, how that interaction can engender a more equitable rhetorical logic.

A Posthumanist Grammar of Style

In reenvisioning rhetoric and style, it might be helpful to consider how posthumanist disruptions share a common logic. Historically, posthumanism has been its most effective when making rhetorical familiarities unfamiliar, and the relationship between rhetoric and style is no exception. As Ian Barnard demonstrates, sometimes this unfamiliarity means disrupting our habitual understanding of writing's rhetorical effect and function. "Writing," he argues, "that gets demonized for its supposed lack of clarity may be 'unclear' out of necessity or accident. It might be working to create new or unconventional understandings and new or unconventional ways of making understandings" (447). Though conventionally a stylistic virtue, *clarity* or clear writing becomes suspect because it limits language to "the known, the old" (Barnard 447) and forego writing's capacity to create new ways of thinking. Raúl Sánchez seconds this perspective, adding that the relationship between rhetoric and writing should "not be an epistemic phenomenon" and should instead "theorize writing as an activity that produces sentences or statements, some of which come to be identified, after their production, as *knowledge*" (31). Similarly, Susan Miller points out how the most unfamiliar writing might be one that "is no longer usefully described as a container for [an agent's] thought" because it may be written for no other purpose than "*to have been written*" (79). There are a few things to note here, not the least of which is how posthumanism changes the status quo. Its disruptions pioneer new ways of thinking, create new grammatical units (sentences and statements), and, at their most radical, simply inscribe. However, a far more salient feature of a posthumanist disruption is how well it foregrounds writing and writing style as rhetoric's first premise. Much like Worsham's formative style, these posthumanist accounts consider style a primarily inscriptive technology. Writing can venture new ways of thinking and new grammatical formations because it can create and arrange words in infinitely new ways. If a sentence or a group of sentences mean something or seem familiar, it is only because they have been precisely written. Likewise, what a writer thinks or what style rhetorically evokes is less important than that it can first create a mark on the page (or screen or tablet or . . .). Style inscribes words and relationships between those words, and in the wake of a posthumanist disruption, asks rhetoric to make sense of them. The relationship between style and rhetoric is inverted.

Still, posthumanism's inversion of this relationship is less important than how it reimagines stylistic iteration. In style and rhetoric's conventional relationship, iteration—or more succinctly, writing's contingency—primarily *informs* the dialogue between rhetorical strategy and stylistic application. As Burke's description of congruent and contingent logics outlines, rhetoric is acutely aware that each writing situation requires some level of flexibility to be successful. If successful persuasion were simply a matter of applying a strategy wholesale, rhetoric would not be very successful. Instead, it has to conceptually account for contextual variances and then adjust its strategy and style accordingly. With posthumanism's inversion of style and rhetoric, however, iteration *grammatically coordinates* rhetorical strategies rather than just conceptually informing them. Here, Burke's discussion of contingent and congruent logics is again helpful. In his lamentation of science and technology's "homogenous mechanical language," he notes that it is a directive language "devoid of the tonalities, the mimetic reinforcements, the vaguely remembered human situations, which go to make up the full, complex appeal of the poetic medium. The very lack of pliancy helps to assist with [it] in avoiding the appeal of pliancy . . . [i]t is designed for machines" (58). To some degree, Burke's suspicions are warranted: scientific language (and style) does indeed use language for directive purposes, and in that process, loses some dialogic contingency. Yet, by the same token, the directive function of a mechanical language highlights not what words can *do*, but how they repeatedly *interact*. Indeed, as Burke points out "scientific terminology is conceptual, designed for *naming*, whereas the spontaneous symbols of communication are hortatory, suggestive, hypnotic. Its very muddle as regards the subtleties of mimetic and tonal ingratiation would force us to *name* things rather than *respond* to them (54). Language, and more importantly, style, directs (names) or coordinates explicit relationships between words and, as such, avoids the dialogically suggestive and mimetic.

In this situation, what words suggest, evoke, or mean in the wake of a posthumanist disruption require a rhetorical speculation that style cannot grammatically provide. Instead, style coordinates what *can be* explicitly written by considering what *has already been* explicitly written—it is a venture of how words interact. Consider, for example, Spinks's and

Worsham's ideas of posthumanist style. As an inscription of heterogeneity, a posthumanist style's unfamiliar forms of writing disrupt habitual understandings of what is stylistically possible. If a writing formation or series of words seems unclear or nonsensical, they may be intentionally violating our ideas of clarity and sensibility in an effort to write the new. But by using unfamiliar forms of writing, a posthumanist style focuses attention on how *writing*—words, formations of words, grammatical structures, and so on—could be different. This is a distinct and subtle point. In the horizon of a posthumanist style, what is important is *that* writing formations can be different and can be repeated, not *what* those unfamiliar forms of writing eventually produce. In outlining the repeatable relationships between words, a posthumanist style's iterability explicitly foregrounds a rhetorical grammar of both what is empirically available now *and* its capacity to be rewritten or reused in the future. Rhetoric and style are consequently no longer relegated to merely considering contingency as a composing principle; rather, they can work concomitantly with it.

But such a repetitious, inscriptive horizon means nothing if it only iterates the same stylistic formations and connections ad nauseam. To be sure, a posthumanist style is not a mechanistic repetition. Rather, its iterated, inverted relationship between style and rhetoric emphasizes how the disruptions of inscriptive repetition can engender a more equitable rhetorical logic. In this regard, previous theories of posthumanist style took a right step in the wrong direction. In Spinks's and Worsham's renditions of a posthumanist style, unfamiliar forms of writing violate, but they still accommodate some facet of rhetoric. For Spinks, a posthumanist style derives and reflects rhetorical idiosyncrasies, whereas for Worsham, style disrupts and then points to new or potential rhetorical meanings. In both accounts, a posthumanist style promises more than its grammar can guarantee, especially since nothing irrevocably links stylistic unfamiliarity to rhetorical progress. But such gestures signal significant rhetorical departures more than they do strategic shortcomings. If, for example, a posthumanist style inscribes the unfamiliar and disrupts our rhetorical commonplaces, then it can only really logically promise that other forms of writing *are precisely possible.*

Such a promise should not be taken lightly. As a defining characteristic of a posthumanist style, the promise of contingency and unfamiliarity means that style cannot logically guarantee anything—meaning, rhetorical concepts, certain writing formations, etc.—beyond its immediate inscriptive moment. Indeed, a posthumanist style's promises are analogous to what Jacques Derrida describes as a *spur*: a writing—a style of writing or a writing style—that in marking its particular history, it resists a prescribing any definitive future. For Derrida, *spurs* are best described by the hermeneutic and specifically inscriptive lacuna found in the nomadic aspects of Nietzsche's aphorisms. Citing a random and seemingly arbitrary note in Nietzsche's unpublished manuscripts, Derrida questions its meaning and points out how "we will never know [what it means]," and that "that powerlessness [of not knowing] must somehow be taken into account" because it "withdraw[s] it from any assured horizon of a hermeneutic question" (*Spurs: Nietzsche's Styles* 127). Derrida's point is twofold here: since writing, and specifically style, cannot explain its meaning to a reader or writer, its claims to meaning are at best hypothetical. Yet, it is not just that we cannot know meaning absolutely; rather, it is also that in marking its past, it offers a future open to a myriad of inscriptive possibilities. "The mark," Derrida explains, "which [writing] has left behind, irreducible though it may be, is just as irreducibly plural," and shows that "writing must be in the interval between several styles . . . if there is going to be style, there can only be more than one (*Spurs: Nietzsche's Styles* 105; 139). In the posthumanist juncture between unfamiliarity and disruption, there can only be indefinite writing styles. What a style looked like, what it rhetorically accomplished, how it formulated contexts and arrangements of words, etc. can certainly be repeated, but can never be absolutely replicated or guaranteed because such stylistic considerations could have been otherwise. In this sense, a posthumanist style marks a paradoxical moment in writing: its past opens up the possibility of future inscriptions while at the same time divorcing that possibility from any (rhetorical, conceptual, etc.) certainty. It marks, in other words, not a definitive style or even a preferred set of past styles, but rather the indefiniteness of style in general. Accordingly, by relinquishing rhetorical guarantees, a posthumanist style's disruptions effectively put style and rhetoric on the same footing, thereby making their relationship "not a gradual process but a repetitive movement, a movement of repeating the beginning, again and again" (Žižek, "How to Begin from the Beginning" 45). Every writing act, posthuman or not, belies its own possibility—it can, in fact, be repeated or be otherwise—but because a posthumanist style does not necessarily need to make sense, it primarily highlights inscriptive possibility. In other words, a posthumanist style is concerned *that* writing formations can change, *that* language can be used in various ways, and *that* the connection between style and rhetoric can be different.

This repetitious disruption, unlike Spinks's and Worsham's respective views, is not an rhetorical assertion but an stylistic investigation into the "hidden, non-realized potentials . . . not of the past as it was, but of those elements in the past which the past itself, in its reality, betrayed, stifled, failed to realize" (Žižek, *In Defense* 141). When a posthumanist style cannot guarantee anything beyond its own possible repetition, it becomes both the impetus of rhetoric and the force that violates it. A posthumanist logic of style thereby invents new rhetorical beginnings in each inscriptive moment—it "rethinks" each writing situation through writing's (and style's) very claim of contingency. For example, as philosopher Alain Badiou points out, the genius and politic of *The Communist Manifesto* derives not from its specific rhetorical message, but from its ability to rethink history through a writing style. As an act of writing, *The Communist Manifesto* taps into the hegemonic logics of the time (German Idealism, British political economy, and French socialism), and posits a counter-hypothesis that aims at the very immutability of these concepts' shared historical logic. As Badiou succinctly puts it, "The communist hypothesis is *that* a different collective organization is practicable, one that will eliminate the inequality of wealth and even the division of labor" (98, emphasis added). Since *The Communist Manifesto* could envision the logical relationships between these various intellectual contexts through the radical logic of political economy, it seizes and literally rewrites the possibilities of politics and sociality through its very inscriptive style, i.e. the manifesto form. For the relationship between style and rhetoric, such a conception illustrates that a posthumanist style is never *about* writing or even its rhetorical effects. It is rather the ubiquitous, permeable condition that exceeds, describes, and reflexively affects the relationship between rhetorical invention and stylistic logic: it is a contingent, inscriptive affair where time and knowledge are indubitably—and sometimes arbitrarily—entwined.

Departures of a Posthumanist Style: A Pedagogical Risk

With inscriptive contingency taking on such a pivotal role, style and rhetoric's relationship is in admittedly unfamiliar waters. A posthumanist style uses unfamiliar forms of writing to disrupt our rhetorical understandings, and in doing so, makes style's relationship to rhetoric one of a discrete possibility. Perhaps the most significant change here is that what a style rhetorically produces is of little or of no importance. In this way, style does not reflect a cacophony of rhetorical difference as much as it marks *that* difference is possible. Because the connection between style and rhetoric is a reflexively pervasive, equitable iteration, its logic is one that always repeats the possibility of that relationship. This configuration changes a few things. For one, it means that since style to some extent accentuates its ability to be rewritten, it "is never a natural exercise of a faculty" (Deleuze 108). Indeed, according to this grammar, the relationship between rhetoric and style "never thinks alone and by itself; moreover it is never simply disturbed by forces which remain external to it" (Deleuze 108). In the posthumanist relationship between style and rhetoric, writing's contingency acts as the very condition of rhetoric and, consequently, thought. Among other things, this suggests that style and thought are still linked, as, say, Cicero believes, but also shows how writing (and thinking) without cause is both permitted and encouraged. If a posthumanist style—a posthumanist writing—inscribes, if it disrupts, it does so for no other reason than because it can. Indeed, like Derrida's *spur*, a posthumanist style warrants no explanation and forwards no promise beyond its particular inscription because it effectively "*owes* [us] *nothing*" other than "*the fact that* [it] has something to write" (*The Post Card* 266). Consequently, how we write, what we write, and why we write will therefore always risk a real rhetorical uncertainty, and make writing (and writing style) "an extraordinary event *in* thought itself, *for* thought itself" (Deleuze 108). Given this situation, we could say a posthumanist style is an ubiquitous, contingent technology, or more simply, a logic of inscriptional conjecture.

At the same time, a posthumanist style's disruptions propose that we eventually return to their fallout, and specifically to how they explicitly rethink the ways writing happens. This is a pedagogical gesture, but not in the conventional sense of applied theories or classroom practices. Rather, a posthumanist style's pedagogy forwards disruption as an ethical and practical premise, and suggests that we reevaluate and reinvest in our relationship to writing in light of its speculative risks. Though such reevaluations advocate quite a few different directions, perhaps there is nothing more rudimentary and telling than their assertion that a posthumanist writing style, for all of its rhetorical uncertainty, should be the *horizon by which we think, and not the object* of our thought. This, of course, is much more than a call for a renewed (and radical) rhetorical approach; it is rather an unwarranted (and perhaps unwanted) assertion. For in this new horizon, the dynamic iterability that is posthumanist style can have no fidelity to ideology, to knowledge, or to even rhetorical goal. Our writing tasks, such as discussing the rhythm and cadence of a particular series of words (Strunk & White) or describing how to choose subjects and verbs (Williams), would therefore need to be rethought according to what writing—and not rhetorical strategy—gives us from moment to moment. As Sidney I. Dobrin suggests, this means conceiving a pedagogical relationship with writing that emphasizes "more possibles than actuals" that consequently help "step beyond the limits of thinking about writing . . . and tear down the boundaries" of writing's connections to convention, communication, or any sort of inscriptive guarantee (191; 190). Accordingly, the intervention of a posthumanist style could forward an unfamiliar rhythm and cadence not as a rhetorical strategy or guarantee—they are not the means to an end; in fact, they are not a *means* to anything—but to inscriptively conceive the novelty of rhetorical change. In this scenario, writing's pedagogical relationship to rhetorical knowledge and strategy switches from adjusting information for predetermined ends to celebrating its inscriptive moment and the multiple directions it could possibly take in the next. Yet, this is also to say that the relationship between style and rhetoric is one of anticipation, and that our approaches need to reflect such a dynamic. Certainly, viewing this relationship allows us to see not just what is possible in rhetoric and style's relationship, but also what is, broadly speaking, relationally possible. Since posthumanist style, like all styles, will persist, what it contributes to a particular situation is less important than *that* it inscribes; or, more precisely, *that* it articulates various possibilities in terms of what will have been, if for no other reason than because writing can have no friends.

However, to offer such speculations as a clear pedagogical direction misunderstands how the dynamic relationship between style and posthumanism alters our conceptions of writing, and ultimately rhetoric. A posthumanist style's disruptions use unfamiliar forms of writing to *assert*—a politic, a logic, a grammar—when it inscribes, and these assertions are all a posthumanist style can logically offer. To ask a posthumanist style to give more than an assertion of possibility asks a "very particular *style* of writing . . . to masquerade as *writing itself*" (Davis 6) and, more importantly, to make rhetorical promises it cannot keep. A style so pedagogically captured is hardly the model of a nomadic possibility, as Worsham so succinctly points out: "writing does not contain, possess, or appropriate but steals into language to make it fly, to make it move, to make *us* move without our ever knowing what worked or works on us and toward what end. [It] is a raid on the articulate" (93). Perhaps, then, in these contested and uncomfortable relationships between posthumanism, style, and rhetoric, we can only ask for a pedagogical pause. If we are to take a posthumanist writing seriously, our pedagogies must also maintain a fidelity to writing's contingency by pausing pedagogical (and rhetorical) prescriptions. On the surface, this pause respects the logical limits of a posthumanist style, especially since it "does not anticipate or desire answers. It is [rather] a nudge toward a much-needed tipping point" (Dobrin 188). But such a request has a second, if not more important, suggestion. By reflecting the disruptions of a posthumanist style, it forsakes rhetorical commonplaces and their contextual application for the very *possibility* of writing. In this view, asking for a pedagogical pause poses a precise ethical risk more than anything else. For if we are to ask for a pause, we must also forgo our "raids on the articulate" and categorically risk our relationship with writing. We must, that is, risk rhetorical certainty, strategy, and even pedagogical evocation when we reevaluate and reinvent our engagements with the advent of writing. We too must take pause and understand that our posthuman relationships to writing persist only because they promise a chance to write the new.

Works Cited

Badiou, Alain. *The Meaning of Sarkozy*. Trans. David Fernbach. London: Verso, 2008. Print.

Barnard, Ian. "The Ruse of Clarity." *College Composition and Communication* 61.3 (2010): 434-51. Print.

Bawarshi, Anis. "The Genre Function." *College English* 62.3 (2000): 335–60. Print.

—. *Genre & the Invention of the Writer: Reconsidering the Place of Invention in Composition*. Logan: Utah State UP, 2003. Print.

Brooke, Collin, and Thomas Rickert. "Being Delicious: Materialities of Research in a Web 2.0 Application." *Beyond Postprocess*. Ed. Sidney I. Dobrin, J. A. Rice, and Michael Vastola. Logan: Utah State UP, 2011. 163–79. Print.

Burke, Kenneth. *Permanence and Change: An Anatomy of Purpose*. 3rd ed. Berkeley: U of California P, 1984. Print.

Butler, Paul. "The Stylistic (Re)Turn in Rhetoric and Composition." *Style in Rhetoric and Composition*. Ed. Paul Butler. Boston: Bedford/St. Martin's, 2010. 1–9. Print.

Cicero. *Of Oratory*. Trans. E. W. Sutton and H. Rackham. *The Rhetorical Tradition: Readings from Classical Times to the Present*. Ed. Patricia Bizzell and Bruce Herzberg. Boston: Bedford, 1990. 200–250. Print.

Davis, D. Diane. *Breaking Up [at] Totality: A Rhetoric of Laughter*. Carbondale: Southern Illinois UP, 2000. Print.

Deleuze, Gilles. *Nietzsche & Philosophy*. Trans. Hugh Tomlinson. New York: Columbia UP, 2006. Print.

Derrida, Jacques. *Spurs: Nietzsche's Styles*. Trans. Barbara Harlow. Chicago: U of Chicago P, 1978. Print.

—. *The Post Card: From Socrates to Freud and Beyond*. Trans. Alan Bass. Chicago: U of Chicago P, 1987. Print.

Dobrin, Sidney I. *Postcomposition*. Carbondale: Southern Illinois UP, 2011. Print.

Fish, Stanley. *How to Write a Sentence and How to Read One*. New York: HarperCollins, 2011. Print.

Fogarty, Mignon. *Grammar Girl's Quick and Dirty Tips for Better Writing*. New York: Henry Holt and Company, 2008. Print.

Lanham, Richard. "Style/Substance Matrix." *Style in Rhetoric and Composition*. Ed. Paul Butler. Boston: Bedford/St. Martin's, 2010. 428–48. Print.

Miller, Susan. "Writing Theory : : Theory Writing." *Methods and Methodology in Composition Research*. Ed. Gesa Kirsch and Patricia A. Sullivan. Carbondale: Southern Illinois UP, 1992. 62–83. Print.

Sánchez, Raúl. *The Function of Theory in Composition Studies*. Albany: SUNY P, 2005. Print.

Spinks, Lee. "Thinking the Post-Human: Literature, Affect, and the Politics of Style." *Textual Practice* 15.1 (2001): 23–46. Print.

Strunk Jr., William, and E. B. White. *The Elements of Style*. 4th ed. New York: Longman, 2000. Print.

Williams, Joseph M., and Gregory G. Colomb. *Style: The Basics of Clarity and Grace*. 4th ed. Boston: Longman, 2012. Print.

Worsham, Lynn. "Writing Against Writing: The Predicament of *Ecriture Féminine* in Composition Studies." *Contending with Words: Composition and Rhetoric in a Postmodern Age*. Ed. Patricia Harkin and John Schilb. New York: MLA, 1991. 82–104. Print.

Žižek, Slavoj. "How to Begin from the Beginning." *New Left Review* 57 (2009): 43–55. Print.

—. *In Defense of Lost Causes*. London: Verso, 2008. Print.

8 Rethinking Human and Non-Human Actors as a Strategy for Rhetorical Delivery

Jim Ridolfo

> *It should not be surprising that it was professional actors who gave a special impetus to a study of delivery, for all the spellbinding orators in history (men like Demosthenes, Churchill, William Jennings Bryan, Bishop Sheen, Billy Graham) have all been, in a sense, great actors.*
>
> —Edward Corbett

Introduction

Oral. Print. Digital. For the last several decades these three terms have anchored field conversations on rhetorical delivery. In this chapter I argue that the next phase in delivery studies will not only need to encompass all three of these turns in delivery studies simultaneously, but will also need to frame these posthuman activities as "embedded in a material world of great complexity" (Hayles, 5). This moves the field well beyond Corbett's conception reflected in the quotation above, where the rhetorician is the only actor involved in a process of rhetorical delivery. As Latour reminds us, the production of meaning itself cannot be understood outside multiple human and non-human actors; however, rhetorical studies has rapidly moved through three turns related to the fifth canon: the revival of oral delivery, the reconsideration of print delivery, and the reinterpretation of delivery through the lens of the digital. In this essay, I explore delivery through the lens of multiple actors, arguing that the next turn in delivery will need to address the complexity of strategizing delivery beyond the localized speech act of classical oral delivery.

Three Turns: Oral, Print, Digital

In 1965 Edward Corbett published the first edition of *Classical Rhetoric for the Modern Student* (*CRMS*) and marked "a watershed in the revival of classical rhetoric" for many early scholars in the field of rhetoric and composition (Nelms and Goggin, 15). Corbett's delivery is imported directly from Aristotelian rhetoric, and in the opening section of the book Corbett states that he considers delivery to be mostly a matter of voice and style:

> There is no denying the importance of delivery in effecting the end that one sets for oneself. Many speeches and sermons, however well prepared and elegantly written, have fallen on deaf ears because of inept delivery. The writer lacks the advantage a speaker enjoys because of his face-to-face contact with an audience and because of his vocal delivery; the only way in which the writer can make up for this disadvantage is by the brilliance of his style (28)

This first turn in delivery studies posed a problem for writing, one that John Reynolds notes in the introduction to his 1993 collection *Rhetorical Memory and Delivery: Classical Concepts for Contemporary Composition and Communication*. Reynolds cites the forward to Winifred Horner's 1988 *Rhetoric in the Classical Tradition* where Corbett in his introduction to her book says that she "shows us the written equivalent of the oral delivery system for the ancient Greeks and Romans" (Horner, vi). Reynolds points out that Horner's conversation on delivery did not appear to have any influence on how Corbett discusses delivery in the third edition of *CRMS* published in 1990: "How puzzling it is, then, that his third edition did not acknowledge, include, challenge, or react in some way to these developments" (Reynolds, 5).

But Horner was not the first to mark the turn towards thinking about writing as the fifth canon. In his 1983 *Rhetoric Review* article "Actio: A Rhetoric of Manuscripts," Robert Connors argues that "composition studies have successfully adapted the first three of Cicero's canons to written discourse, but the status of the last two, memory and delivery, has always been problematical" (64). He contends that delivery and association with classical "elocutionary histrionics and gestures, seems . . . out of place among the writer's skill . . . the canon of delivery has to do simply with [sic] *the manner in which the material is delivered*" (64). In grounding delivery in the material, Connors opens up the door for a wide interpretation of delivery that is no longer centered exclusively around voice. Rather, Connors posits that another mode of "written *actio*" is largely synonymous with an *ethos* of document and material design, where the rhetorician presents "the reader with a legible, neat, pleasing manuscript, the writer is creating an image of herself for that reader, an image that she can support or sabotage" (64). While Connors made these conclusions about print delivery as early as 1983, they did not have as profound an impact on print theories of rhetorical delivery as have contemporary discussions on the digital and delivery.

This laconic gap lasted until 1993 when Reynolds published the first edited collection on the fourth and fifth canons. In the afterword of *Rhetorical Memory and Delivery,* Sheri Helsley's piece marks the first chapter in the fifth canon's digital turn when she argues that the canon will be "enormously important in an electronic age" because, she argues, of the new power to use "post-typewriter presentation technologies" and their potential for "new structures of consciousness in the electronic age" (158). From 1993 to 2009 over a dozen scholars focus on rhetorical delivery (see Dragga, 1993 & 1996; Kathleen Welch 1999; Skinner-Linnenberg 1999; Trimbur 2000 and 2004; Rude 2004; Sheridan, Ridolfo, Michel 2005 and 2012; McCorkle 2005 and 2012; Yancey 2006; DeVoss and Porter 2006; Lunsford 2006; Prior et all, 2007; Ridolfo and DeVoss 2009; Porter 2009; Ridolfo and Rife 2011; Ridolfo 2012) in their scholarship.

This digital turn in delivery could be understood as three phases of scholarship that largely correspond to the development and availability of technology such as desktop publishing software (early 1990s), increasing network access (mid 1990s), multimodal composing software (late 1990s) and broadband (late 1990s to early/mid 2000s). First, there's scholarship that discusses digital delivery in terms of electronic composing or desktop publishing abilities (Helsley; Dragga). These early conversations on digital delivery pick up many of the same concerns as Connors had in 1983 when he discussed the material (paper selection) and visual rhetoric (page layout/font size/margins) as a new *actio* of written delivery. The second stage in digital delivery focuses less on the composing abilities of computers, such as arrangement of text, and more on the potential to electronically transmit a message, such as e-mail and file sharing. This wave includes scholars such as Welch (1999), Trimbur (2000), and Carolyn Rude (2004). What these scholars have in common is a more explicit interest in thinking about the delivery and movement of texts, although for the most part they are still speaking about genres that have print counterparts.

The third stage of the turn in digital delivery is best described as the multimodal and broadband turn. Informed by new ideas about networks and a fresh revival of scholarship on delivery and orality (see Skinner-Linnenberg 1999; Mountford 2005; Buchanan 2005; Yancey 2006), the multimodal turn simultaneously blends oral, print/material, and digital concerns for delivery (Sheridan, Ridolfo, Michel 2005; Yancey 2006; Prior et all 2007; Ridolfo and DeVoss 2009), as well as copyright (DeVoss and Porter 2006; Ridolfo and Rife 2011) with the increased availability of broadband. As Porter (2009) correctly identifies, recent field conversations dealing with the role of the fifth canon and the body are now inseparable from a twenty-first century digital delivery that includes the body, audio, video, and text. For example, Dubisar and Palmeri's 2010 *Computers and Composition* article ""Palin/Pathos/Peter Griffin: Political Video Remix and Composition Pedagogy" seamlessly blends classical orality (Palin as a speaking subject/rhetorician) with case examples that demonstrate digital audio/video composing and access to broadband in order to explore how "political video remix assignments can potentially . . . offer opportunities for students and teachers to explore the delivery and circulation of digital texts" (77). Recent work on Twitter and Occupy Wall Street by Pennely and Dadas (2013) in "(Re) Tweeting in the service of protest: Digital composition and circulation in the Occupy Wall Street movement" includes a specific focus on how the widespread digital circulation of messages relates to widespread social movements.

THE FOURTH WAVE IN RHETORICAL DELIVERY: A POSTHUMAN TURN?

As the previous section shows, recent scholarship on digital delivery advances field conversations two ways. First, digital delivery now includes corporeal concerns specific to classical oral delivery. Whereas in the past delivery seemed limited to a discrete act and composition, now it may also encompass an ensemble of activities and texts. In this sense, digital delivery has come full circle to include the control and modulation of video and audio just as Aristotelian rhetoric was concerned with the modulation of the voice and gesture. Second, recent scholarship on digital delivery is increasingly concerned with the *movement* of texts from one location to another (see Trimbur; Rude; Sheridan, Ridolfo, Michel; DeVoss and Porter; Ridolfo and DeVoss; Ridolfo and Rife; Ridolfo; Dobrin).[1] Theorizing the movement of texts as rhetorical delivery has, for the most part, only been discussed in terms of a small number of print and digital technologies[2] and there has been little work done to theorize these technologies as extensions of the rhetorician.

To do this kind of theorizing would, I argue, bring us closer to Merleau-Ponty's notion in the *Visible and the Invisible* that a gesture into a world as flesh means that there is no clear boundary between subject/world: that we act into a world not as separate from our materiality but as an extension of our flesh. From a rhetorical p erspective, the transition in theory from the rhetorician and the rheorician's gesture to the rhetorician and the rhetorician's moving text may find affinity with what Hayles would call posthumanism, or a "(desired) loss of subjectivity that is based on bodies losing their boundaries" (Miah, 78). In a systemic sense, Latour's theory of "interrelated human and non-human actors who shape the way things are" may be useful for describing rhetorical gestures into systems of human and non-human actors (Mitev, 89). In this sense, these systems co-create with the rhetorician and help to shape the potentiality for various means of delivery. In the next section, I present two case examples involving a unique slice of non-human actor, twenty-first century pigeons and stencils, and theorize what these examples say to scholars about the combination of human and non-human actors.

Two Case Examples: Rhetorical Delivery and Non-Human Animal Actors

As one of the oldest domesticated animals in the world, pigeons have a long and distinguished history as non-human agents of delivery in Egypt, Rome, and Greece; however, in the nineteenth century these animals were combined with the latest form of photographic technology. During the Siege of Paris in 1871 "the departure of pigeons-post for Tours (where the letters were enlarged by photography and sent on to Paris) was regularly advertised by the British Post Office" as a service (Cornhill Magazine, 285). While this combination of a very old technology (pigeons) and a brand new technology (photography) may seem an anomaly particular to a transitional moment in the late nineteenth century, consider the following case example from an April 1 2009 *San Francisco Gate* story, "Pigeons fly cell phones into Brazilian prison":

> Inmates have devised an innovative way to smuggle in cell phones into a prison farm in Brazil: carrier pigeons. Guards at the Danilio Pinheiro prison near the southeastern city of Sorocaba noticed a pigeon resting on an electric wire with a small cloth bag tied to one of its legs last week. "The guards nabbed the bird after luring it down with some food and discovered components of a small cell phone inside the bag," police investigator Celso Soramiglio said Tuesday.
>
> One day later, another pigeon was spotted dragging a similar bag inside the prison's exercise yard. Inside the bag was the cell phone's charger, Soramiglio said.
>
> The birds were apparently bred and raised inside the prison, smuggled out, outfitted with the cell phone parts and then released to fly back.
>
> "Pigeons instinctively fly back home, always," the investigator said. (Lehman)

Similar to the British Post Office system in the late nineteenth century that combined pigeons and photographs, these inmates were strategically combining pigeons with a new technology, in this case the digital technology of cellular phones, in order to deliver a certain kind of message through a complex system of non-human actors. While the British combined the pigeon with photography to maximize the capacity of the message through photographic enlargement (an early form of message compression comparable in origin to the zip file of today), the prisoners combined the pigeon with the cell phone in order to open a means of unrestricted communication with the outside world. As classical delivery is concerned with the self-modulation of voice and gesture, these prisoners combine the two technologies to achieve self-modulation of their own communication. While the prison system undoubtedly shapes the form and modes of their communications, one can assume that the prisoners have greater autonomy to self-modulate through the cell phone. Beyond simply incorporating the pigeon as a non-human actor, this example provides a way to consider delivery as a confluence of technologies. Delivery in this instance is not simply an act of orality, analog delivery, or digital transmission. Rather, it's all of these parts together and, together, they add up to a delivery that in this context is strategic.

In another recent case example of pigeons and digital communication, a 2006 story in *Time Magazine* reported that at the height of the Sunni insurgency in Iraq, Coalition troops noticed that insurgents were using pigeons as a means of communication in the battlefield:

> Lately, troops say insurgents have been using a technique called pigeon flipping: while on patrol, the Marines have noticed flocks of pigeons circling above them, leading them to conclude that supporters of the insurgents have somehow trained the birds to signal when troops are in the area. "If it's a game of cat and mouse," says Corporal Richard Bass, "then who's the mouse?" (Donnelly)

Unlike the previous case example where pigeons were used in combination with digital communications devices, in this situation insurgents appear to be using a low-tech means of communication in order to subvert cell phone detection, monitoring, and jamming technologies. It's worth noting that the last known military pigeon service was maintained by India and decommissioned only as recently as 2002, less than a few years before some Iraqi insurgents appear to have adopted them as a means of communication with particular strategic advantages ("Indian"). At the same time that India opted to replace this signaling technology with newer forms of communication, insurgents engaged in asymmetrical conflict found that the pigeon was useful for circumventing the digital technology of State actors. How then might the insurgents' use of the pigeon be understood as rhetorical? While used to circumvent the US frequency scanners in Iraq, or the prison guards in Brazil, the pigeon in turn enables other forms of delivery and yet it cannot be viewed in these contexts as completely separate from the power dynamics implicit in these circumstances. These power dynamics call into question the human agency behind successful instances of delivery where the *telos* cannot be characterized as a single, completely intentional human act, but a combination of human and non-human actions and agencies working in tandem. Such an expanded perspective on the diversity of delivery may, in turn, benefit rhetoricians by broadening their rhetorical imagination to think beyond linear models of delivery such as the speaker-message-audience triad in classical rhetoric, or the famous 1948 Shannon Weaver model of communication. As the next two examples show, everyday acts of delivery may include strategies of rhetorical delivery (see Ridolfo 2012) that benefit from multiple human and non-human agents and infrastructure. I argue that these strategic combinations are especially important as they seem to offer a way to counter larger systems and regimes of power. As digital infrastructure now allows small groups or individuals to strategize delivery across media and networks, combining technologies of delivery becomes especially important for asymmetrical rhetorical situations and conflicts. The fourth wave of delivery theory will need to investigate how extremely small groups engage in asymmetical rhetorical conflicts with much larger regimes of power.

Rhetorical Delivery and Non-Human Analog and Digital Actors

In the fall of 2005 as part of a national campaign targeting Coca Cola, the national student organization United Students Against Sweatshops (USAS) worked with local student chapters to cut university beverage contracts. Called the Killer Coke campaign, USAS outlined its decision to target Coke in the "Why Target Coca Cola" section of its "Killer Coke Organizing Manual":

> Coca-Cola is one of the world's most powerful and profitable corporations. In 2004, Coca-Cola earned $4.85 billion in profits. Yet, despite repeated pleas for help, Coca-Cola has not found the time or resources to insure the most basic safety of the workers who bottle its products or prevent massive environmental devastation in the communities where it does business. Coca-Cola has responded by launching public relations campaigns and denying responsibility—it's time we show them that they need to actually change things on the ground—enough is enough![3]

In 2005–2006 USAS students at the University of Michigan were successful in pressuring the university to cut its beverage contract with Coca Cola. The effect of this act was a slew of stories about Coca Cola in the press, and in a January 26, 2006 article in *The Michigan Daily* an anonymous "financial analyst who monitors the beverage industry," argued that "even with the loss of revenue from the schools, the major victim of the suspensions will be the company's public image" ("Coca-Cola's image"). Following the victory at the University of Michigan, in the spring of 2006, the anti-Coca Cola campaign at Michigan State University was moving forward. Inspired by the events at the University of Michigan, students in MSU Students for Economic Justice and Moviemiento Estudiantil Xicano de Aztlan worked to pressure the MSU administration to cut their beverage contract. While the campaign was ultimately unsuccessful, what follows is a glimpse into how the students and Coke strategized against one another through the delivery, appropriation, and distribution of texts. What follows is a story of delivery, multiple human actors, and non-human technological actors from the MSU Killer Coke campaign—a story of the way one small group fought back against a much larger company in a highly local instance, which illustrates how multiple actors can work together to appropriate, modify, and deliver their arguments.

STU AND THE STENCIL

By the early spring of 2006, the Coca Cola Corporation was publically trying to counter the MSU Killer Coke campaign. Concerned that the press generated by the activists would have a negative impact on Coca-Cola or that the activists might succeed in pressuring Michigan State University to follow in the footsteps of the University of Michigan, Coca Cola had started to actively communicate with the MSU Administration. In addition, the company paid to publish full and half page responses to activist claims in student newspapers across the country.[4] According to SEJ member Triana Kazaleh-Sirdenis, the student activists had long-term goals to end the contract with Coke:

> The long term goal was definitely to end our contract with Coke. Some schools wait until the contract is up and for us that was four or five years until our contract was up, so it wasn't an option for us to wait for the contract to expire. So we're asking for the contract to be ended.

After several meetings with university advisors and a number of stories about the campaign in *The State News,* in February 2006 Coca Cola responded to the labor and environmental allegations with a full-page response in the student newspaper. As one activist remarked in a Facebook message to members of SEJ and MEXA on March 5, 2006, the purchase of the advertisement was a small victory for the activists because they had prompted a response from Coca Cola:

> I took the liberty of calling the [sic] state news, and found out that the advertisement cost $1524.6. This, of course is pennies to a corporation such as Coke, but we should see this as a small victory. This shows that the heat is on, and we are starting to make an impact to the extent that Coke recognizes it. In the near future with all the lies we [activists] should see this as a small victory.

Stuart "Stu" Niles-Kraft, one of the recipients of the message and an organizer of the MSU Killer Coke campaign, recalls the sequence of events that followed the advertisement. His account of gathering up the newspapers for strategic recomposition emphasizes the collective, dispersed nature of delivery:

> We used those advertisements which were a response to our Coke campaign from the company . . . [the day after the paper came out and] . . . a few people called each other and we all said we would get the paper from the news stands and so we collected newspapers after that day [the day after], mostly straight from news stands, some from recycling centers.

In choosing to wait a day after the newspaper came out, the activists learned from and avoided the issue of a censorship accusation. In March of 2001 when David Horowitz paid to publish his "Arguments Against Slave Reparations" in the *The Brown Daily Herald,* Brown activists stole approximately 4000 copies of the paper from distribution bins the morning it was published (Rosenbaum). The resulting controversy focused largely on the critique that the students censored the paper and "much of the campus and media turned against these students" (Sagrans). In the case of the 2006 MSU Killer Coke, activists set to work recycling two or three hundred copies of newspapers discarded or soon to be discarded. Stu describes what took place next as a "jamming sort of idea":

> So we got all these papers and then . . . I made sets of stencils just using . . . manila folders . . . like one was a Coke bottle with a scull and cross bones in it and . . . I found a font on my computer that looked a lot like the Coke font, had the same kind of curly Q design . . . So I tried to use Coca-Cola's trademark font or the closest thing we could get to it . . . kind of like . . . a jamming sort of idea using their own logo against them

Because the letter covered the full back page of *The State News,* the SEJ activists only needed to perform a single Exacto knife cut to fully detach the advertisement. In choosing to juxtapose the font and colors of Coca-Cola, the activists accomplished a visually powerful remix made possible by the ease with which they were able to appropriate Coca Cola's public relations materials. Stu describes this as a community activity, one with a group ethos in regards to the repurposing and appropriation of the materials:

> Everyone took turns spraying and drying and collecting . . . There were very few costs involved . . . The paper was free and . . . the paint was salvaged from somewhere . . . I thought it was pretty poetic in that we were using a piece of Coca Cola's propaganda which they bought and paid for, we used those materials to make posters . . . to use against them and that felt really cool to me. I'm not sure if everybody who saw them realized that it was a Coca-Cola ad that these posters were printed on . . . But that was the idea we went into it with.

Figure 7.1: Finished stencils. East Lansing, MI. March 2006.

Over the course of the next two months the newly created stencils were delivered across the campus landscape. Similar to the activist Kate's delivery in Nancy Welch's 2005 *CCC* piece "Living Room: Teaching Public Writing in a Post-Publicity Era" the SEJ and MEXA activists distributed the stenciled letters to student activists across campus and they were placed on walkways, bulletin boards and trash cans. For Stu, the repurposing of the letter and delivery of the finished product appealed to his creative sensibilities:

> the idea of making something like that that's kind of a piece of street art that's, you know, putting it on someone else's—on some other piece of public property, I thought placement was really important for like each piece. Especially like when I see stencils where [the place] it is put is almost as important as what the image is . . . I like to see stencils on campus where it's cleverly placed in accordance with you know whatever that message is . . . it [the stenciled Coke letter] was mostly specific I think for me anyways that it be on some kind of MSU or university property.

In our chapter "Rhetorical Velocity and Copyright: A Case Study on Strategies of Rhetorical Delivery" Martine Rife and I theorize potential of a text to be recomposed in ways that are positive or negative to the rhetorical goals and objectives of the authors with respect to copyright. In the case of Coca-Cola, Stu and others worked to circumvent their rhetorical goal, convincing the student body that the activist campaign was unfounded. Thus, the stenciled Coca Cola letter may have been a rhetorically damaging recomposition because of its negative appropriation. This is an example of theorizing for recomposition where the rhetorician, in this case Coca-Cola, theorizes how its rhetoric may be appropriated and used against its specific rhetorical campaign objectives.

In the example of the Coca Cola letter, it's not clear if the initial reach of the letter rhetorically outweighed its subsequent appropriation and recomposition and this would be difficult to quantify. In other words, it's difficult to judge who was more successful: Coca Cola because of the reach of the paper or the appropriators and remixers of Coke's letter. For while the MSU Killer Coke campaign was unsuccessful in meeting its long-term goals, Triana and Stu consider the appropriation of the letter to be successful in raising campus awareness about the campaign at that particular juncture. At the core of their story however is the idea that rhetorical delivery is increasingly dependent on the actions of other human actors and the force and potentiality of non-human actors, and this rhetorical situation over time poses an interesting research problem. The number of actors involved, the fact that this stencil was part of a national campaign spread across several years and university campuses makes it difficult to research the multiple roles of actors and activity in even a single instance of delivery. According to Stu, it's not even clear if Coca Cola ever knew about the stenciled letter:

> I'd like to think that they did. I'm not really aware of how closely they pay attention to our university campus but I imagine that it [the campaign] is a concern [for them]. The fact that they wanted to print the ads that were used in our papers makes me think that they are paying attention to our Coke campaign here and I know that the University of Michigan success in their Coke Campaign prior that year had been in the news so I do think they pay attention and I'd like to think that they at least did notice that composition. Maybe that's wishful thinking I'm not sure. I imagine they probably had someone here observing afterwards too.

Figure 7.2: A letter taped to the back door of a university building. East Lansing, MI. March 2006.

If we were to examine the technology alone utilized in this particular case example, there's paper, knives, word processors, network access to the Coca Cola font, Facebook and more. Each of these had a role in shaping the compositional process leading up to the letter on a window:. However, in both the pigeon and the Coke examples, there's also the issue of asymmetrical power relationships. In these instances, strategic delivery is used in an attempt to tip the balance in favor of one particular group. To do so, I argue, requires a combination of not only specific technologies, but also oral, print, digital, and non-human delivery and, as Sid Dobrin argues, to think about the flow of information as "noun *and* verb, the verb indicating movement . . . continuous increase or diminishment" (182, emphasis added). In doing so, asymmetrical groups are able to leverage strategic, unpredictable forms of delivery against their larger interlocutors.

Conclusion

As I show in the above case examples, taking into consideration how rhetoricians utilize a range and combination of human and non-human actors and infrastructures to deliver their messages highlights the strategic importance of these combinations in, especially, asymmetrical rhetorical situations. While previous approaches to rhetorical delivery focus primarily on a single mode of delivery—the orator delivers the speech (Skinner-Linnenberg), the writer pastes a flyer to a utility box (Kathleen Welch), the digital rhetorician uploads a file to LimeWire or YouTube (Sheridan, Michel, Ridolfo; DeVoss and Porter; Dubisar and Palmeri)— the print and digital combinations still represent relatively recent turns in the field of rhetoric and composition and one that is, as I've tried to show in the last hybrid example, complex. Complexity, however, also affords rhetoricians new strategic opportunities in how they approach the theory and practice of delivery. As I have worked to demonstrate in my scholarship on rhetorical velocity (see Ridolfo and DeVoss 2009; Ridolfo and Rife 2011; Sheridan, Ridolfo, Michel 2012), in some cases there's a strategic benefit to theorizing how certain kinds of writing and media may be recomposed or remixed by third parties. Theorizing the recomposition of a text, video, or audio file may mean theorizing the file's potential for future use and value to other audiences, including its individual audio, visual, textual components; however, theorizing rhetorical velocity may also include strategizing *how* the circulation of a text may lead to its future recomposition. This includes not only the delivery paths a text text may take, but also how it's packaged to traverse these paths. In the case of the Coca Cola stencil, if Coke had thought more carefully about the placement of the letter as a full back page of *The State News,* then they may have realized that it would only take one slice of the knife to turn the Coke letter into material for a future poster. If, however, the Coke letter were quarter page in size and in the middle of the newspaper, then the letter would not have been as valuable and tempting for the activists to recompose.

As we look to a future where the network of non-human actors is less flesh and more silicone, it may be difficult to see where one actor begins and another ends, or how combinations of non-human actors matter to a strategy of delivery. Perhaps the ubiquity of pigeons for so many centuries made them relatively invisible as a non-human actor, and perhaps the increasing ubiquity of digital forms of delivery will abate the field's focus on only digital delivery. What remains after a narrow focus on the digital, is a rich history of humans strategizing and relying on non-human actors for the delivery of messages (a multitude of aural and visual signaling technologies, horse messengers, epistles, and even messages in a bottle) and relatively little work in rhetoric examining how practitioners used combinations of these technologies to achieve specific rhetorical outcomes and objectives. While one might be tempted to look at the digital and consider this the pinnacle of rhetorical augmentation and extension of the self, in reality we have only started to pay attention to the means of delivery as print culture intersects with the digital.

Notes

1. It's beyond the scope of this chapter to discuss why scholars of digital delivery became so acutely interested in the movement and circulation of texts; however, one possible explanation is that the rise of the digital provided a backdrop against which print delivery is comparable. For example, the first two chapters of Adrian Johns's *The Nature of the Book: Print and Knowledge in the Making* and his discussion about the gradual introduction of "print culture" provide a useful backdrop for this question.

2. Digital: LimeWire (Sheridan, Ridolfo, Michel 2005), Napster (Porter & DeVoss) YouTube (Palmeri), e-mail (Rude), Web (Ridolfo and DeVoss), Twitter (Sheridan, Ridolfo, Michel 2012), Facebook, listservs (Ridolfo), to name a few.

3. The USAS activists cite specific allegations against Coca Cola and its bottling companies: the murder of eight Coca-Cola union organizers from

1989–2005 in addition to environmental crimes in Kala Dera, Rajasthan, Mehdiganj, Plachimada, Kerala, and Uttar Pradesh, India ("Unthinkable! Undrinkable!").

4. This case example is part of a larger project to learn about delivery from the stories of practitioner case examples. See my forthcoming article in *Rhetoric Review*, "Rhetorical Delivery as Strategy: Theory Building the Fifth Canon from Practitioner Stories."

Works Cited

Buchanan, Lindal. *Regendering Delivery: the Fifth Canon and Antebellum Women Rhetors*. Carbondale: Southern Illinois UP, 2005. Print.

"Coca-Cola's Image Main Casualty of Contract Cuts: University Only One of 19 Schools Who Have Suspended Coke Contracts." *The Michigan Daily* 26 Jan. 2006. University of Michigan. 1 Feb. 2009. Web.

Connors, Robert J. "Actio: A Rhetoric of Manuscripts." *Rhetoric Review* 2.1 (1983): 64–73. Print.

Corbett, Edward P. J. *Classical Rhetoric for the Modern Student*. 1st ed. New York: Oxford UP, 1965. Print.

Cornhill Magazine. "The Pigeon as a War Messenger." *The Living Age* Sept. 1887: 57–62. Print.

Davidson, Jeremy. "Coke to Return to Campus: University Reinstates Contracts with Soft-drink Giant after Coca-Cola Agrees to Third-Party Audits." *The Michigan Daily* 11 Apr. 2006. University of Michigan. Web. 1 Feb. 2009

DeVoss, Dànielle Nicole, and Porter, James E. "Why Napster Matters to Writing: Filesharing as a New Ethic of Digital Delivery". *Computers and Composition*, 23.1 (2006): 178–210. Print.

Dobrin, Sidney I. *Postcomposition*. Carbondale: Southern Illinois UP, 2011. Print.

Domsic, Melissa. "A Second Chance for Coke: Students Continue Campaign for Coca-Cola ban Despite End of U-M Boycott." *The State News* 12 Apr. 2006. Michigan State University.. Web. 11 Feb. 2009

Donnelly, Sally B. "Looking Out on Hostile Territory: Why the Iraqi City the Americans Conquered a Year Ago Is Still aTthreat." *Time Magazine* 6 Nov. 2005. *Time/CNN*. Web. 12 Jan. 2009.

Dragga, Sam. "The Ethics of Delivery." *Rhetorical Memory and Delivery: Classical Concepts for Contemporary Composition and Communication*. Ed. John Frederick Reynolds. Mahwah, NJ: Erlbaum, 1993. 79–95. Print.

Dubisar, Abby M., and Jason Palmeri. "Palin/Pathos/Peter Griffin: Political Video Remix and Composition Pedagogy." *Computers and Composition* 27.2 (2010): 77–93. Print.

Eyman, Douglas. *Digital, Rhetoric: Ecologies and Economies of Circulation*. Diss. Michigan State University, 2007. Print.

Fredal, James. "The Language of Delivery and the Presentation of Character: Rhetorical Action in Demosthenes' Against Meidias." *Rhetoric Review* 20.34 (2001): 251–67. Print.

Hayles, N. Katherine. *How We Became Posthuman: Virtual Bodies in Cybernetics, Literature, and Informatics*. Chicago, IL: U of Chicago P, 1999. Print.

Helsley, Sheri L. "A Special Afterword to Graduate Students in Rhetoric." *Rhetorical Memory and Delivery: Classical Concepts for Contemporary Composition and Communication*. Ed. John Fredrick Reynolds. Mahwah, NJ: Erlbaum, 1993. 157–59. Print.

"Indian Pigeons Lose Out to E-mail." *BBC News*. British Broadcasting Corporation, 26 Mar. 2002. Web. 12 Jan. 2009

Kazaleh-Sirdenis, Triana. Personal interview. October 14, 2007.

"Campaign to Stop Killer Coke." killercoke.org. 1 Feb. 2009. Web. 20 Feb. 2009.

Lehman, Stan. "Pigeons Fly Cell Phones Into Brazilian Prison." *SFGate*. 1 Apr. 2009. *San Francisco Chronicle*. 1 Apr. 2009. Web.

McCorkle, Ben. "Harbingers of the Printed Page: Nineteenth-Century Theories of Delivery as Remediation." *Rhetoric Society Quarterly* 35.4 (2005): 25–49. Print.

—. *Rhetorical Delivery as Technological Discourse: A Cross-Historical Study*. Carbondale: Southern Illinois UP, 2012. Print.

Miah, Andy. "A Critical History of Posthumanism" *Medical Enhancement and Posthumanity*. Ed. Bert Gordijn, Ruth Chadwick. Springer Science, 2008. Print.

Mountford, Roxanne. *The Gendered Pulpit: Preaching in American Protestant Spaces*. Carbondale: Southern Illinois UP, 2005. Print.

Merleau-Ponty, Maurice. *The Visible and the Invisible*. Trans. A. Lingus. Chicago, IL: Northwestern UP, 1964. Print.

Mitev, Nathalie. "Are Social Constructivist Approaches Critical?"*Handbook of Critical Information Systems Research: Theory and Application*. Eds Debra Howcroft, Eileen Moore Trauth. Northampton, MA: Edward Elgar Publishing, 2005. Print.

National Review. "Postal Communication, Past and Present." *The Living Age* (Sept. 1887): 284–92. Print.

Nelms, Gerald, and Maureen Goggin. "The Revival of Classical Rhetoric for Modern Composition Studies: A Survey." *Rhetoric Society Quarterly* 23 (1993): 11–26. Print.

Niles-Kraft, Stuart. Personal interview. November 20, 2007.

Penney, Joel and Caroline Dadas. "(Re)Tweeting in the Service of Protest: Digital Composition and Circulation in the Occupy Wall Street Movement." *New Media & Society* 15 (2013): 140-54. Print.

Porter, James E. "Recovering Delivery for Digital Rhetoric." *Computers and Composition* 26(4) (2009): 207–24. Print.
Reynolds, John Fredrick. *Rhetorical Memory and Delivery: Classical Concepts for Contemporary Composition and Communication.* Ed. John Fredrick Reynolds. Mahwah, NJ: Erlbaum, 1993. Print.
Rude, Carolyn. "Toward an Expanded Concept of Rhetorical Delivery: The Uses of Reports in Public Policy Debates." *Technical Communication Quarterly* 13.3 (Summer 2004): 271–88. Print.
Ridolfo, Jim. Rhetorical Delivery as Strategy: Researching the Fifth Canon Through Practitioner Stories." *Rhetoric Review* 31.2 (2012): 117–29. Print.
Ridolfo, Jim, and Dànielle Nicole DeVoss. "Composing for Recomposition: Rhetorical Velocity and Delivery." *Kairos: A Journal of Rhetoric, Technology, and Pedagogy* 13.2 (2009). Web. 2 Feb. 2015.
Ridolfo, Jim, and Martine Courant Rife. "Rhetorical Velocity and Copyright: A Case Study on the Strategies of Rhetorical Delivery." *Copy(write): Intellectual Property in the Writing Classroom.* Ed.: Martine Rife, Shaun Slattery, and Dànielle DeVoss. Anderson, SC: WAC Clearinghouse and Parlor Press, 2011: 223–44. Print.
Sagrans, Erica. "From Margin to Center: The Rise of Intellectual Diversity at Brown." *The Brown Daily Herald* 4 Apr. 2005. Brown University. Web. 1 Feb. 2009.
Sheridan, David, Jim Ridolfo, and Tony Michel. "Beyond Snap, Crackle, and Pop: Toward a Theory and Pedagogy of Multimodal Public Rhetoric." *JAC.* 25 (2005). Print.
—. *The Available Means of Persuasion: Mapping a Theory and Pedagogy of Multimodal Public Rhetoric.* Anderson, SC: Parlor Press, 2012. Print.
Skinner-Linnenberg, Virginia. *Dramatizing Writing: Reincorporating Delivery in the Classroom.* Mahwah, NJ: Erlbaum, 1997. Print.
Trimbur, John. "Composition and the Circulation of Writing." *College Composition and Communication* 52.2 (2000): 188–219. Print.
"Unthinkable! Undrinkable! A Campus Campaign Overview." *United Students Against Sweatshops:Campus Organizing Guide.* United Students Against Sweatshops. 2009. Print.
Weaver, Warren and Claude Elwood Shannon. *The Mathematical Theory of Communication.* Urbana-Champaign, IL: U of Illinois P, 1963. Print.
Welch, Kathleen E. *Electric Rhetoric: Classical Rhetoric, Oralism, and a New Literacy.* Cambridge: MIT, 1999. Print.
Welch, Nancy. "Living room: Teaching Public Writing in a Post-Publicity Era". *College Composition and Communication,* 56.3 (2005): 470–92. Print.
Yancey, Kathleen Blake. *Delivering College Composition: the Fifth Canon.* Portsmouth, NH: Boynton/Cook, 2006. Print.

9 Utopian Laptop Initiatives: From Technological Deism to Object-Oriented Rhetoric

Byron Hawk, Chris Lindgren, and Andrew Mara

When investigating a complex program like Nicholas Negroponte's One Laptop Per Child (OLPC) initiative, a rhetorician must consider how to align widely divergent interests into a singular, global endeavor. While traditional Aristotelian notions of rhetoric might focus on persuasion—a humanist frame for understanding how to compose a message to fit the predispositions of an audience and move constituencies into alignment—a posthuman rhetoric sees the human in relation to larger complex material ecologies and therefore has to also consider ways nonhuman agents, such as networks, nation-states, and even programming languages compose and are composed. Creating such complex technological movements requires a more nuanced notion of rhetoric that focuses on a diverse array of agents—everything from code to material objects, groups of actions to constellations of things. In his 2006 TED Talk, Negroponte's rhetorical strategy does foreground the laptop itself, but produces a rhetorical paradox from a posthuman perspective. On the one hand, it recognizes the laptop as an agent operating in complex configurations—from user interactions and technical infrastructures to government mandates and economic constraints. On the other hand, it covers over the complexities of human teaching and learning, neglecting the ways computers function in constellations of knowledge and practices to achieve pedagogical ends. Negroponte extols learning by experience rather than direct teaching, framing computers as a type of self-generating education machine. He claims that when kids were given laptops they "could swim like fish, play them like pianos." Simply letting students interact with a technology, according to Negroponte, will automatically revolutionize education. But these claims toggle too far toward effacing the human in favor of technology and covers over the complexities that are central to posthumanism.

Negroponte's foregrounding of the XO laptop developed for his OLPC organization as the only necessary element of an educational program creates what Bruno Latour calls a black box—a metaphor borrowed from cybernetics that denotes how a computer seems to run by itself. Users don't have to understand the inner complexity of a CPU in order to use it, so they draw a black box around those functions and only focus on the input and output. For Latour, science functions in a similar manner. Once theories, practices, methods, or models become accepted by a scientific community, a black box is drawn around them so future work can be built on that assumed foundation. Latour wants to examine these closed off complexities and processes, examining "science in action" or science in the process of building these black boxes (*Science in Action; Pandora's Hope*). Capturing the educational process within the laptop as a black box creates a type of technological deism, where learning is assumed and placed inside of a machine, only to unfurl from its mysterious processes. Negroponte's rhetoric simply frames the laptop as a proxy for this now-absent organizing presence, becoming a form of anti-humanist technological determinism that sets the stage for a later breakdown in the expressed goals of the OLPC project—a near-inevitability given Negroponte's choice of a black box rhetoric for an unpredictable and complex system. Looking at how Negroponte created this deist black box in his early rhetorical rollout, as described at prominent technology and TED conferences, allows us to better understand how particular notions of writing and learning contributed to the later difficulties with the eventual deployment of the laptops. Finally we consider how one might construct an open box rhetoric that more fully attends to code, discourse, and multi-object ecologies to better perceive limits and possibilities for co-producing arrangements of rhetorical actors, including humans.

In this rhetorical analysis we are extending Carolyn Miller's humanist approach to the rhetoric of technology into a particular model of posthumanism. In her essay "Opportunity, Opportunism, and Progress: *Kairos* in the Rhetoric of Technology," Miller uses the classical concept of *kairos* to analyze key themes or tropes within discourses of technology over the past few decades. Miller's reading of *kairos* comes down to the division between technological determinism and human agency.

Much of the rhetoric of technology frames the agency of technology as a deterministic threat, seeing rhetorical situations from a Bitzerian perspective where objects establish the exigencies that rhetors must then respond to. Other rhetorics of technology take up *kairos* not as this kind of material exigency, but as human opportunity, being able to identify the right moment for human intervention and the ability to produce rhetorical situations through discourse, not unlike Richard Vatz's linguistic turn response to Bitzer's positivism. This approach manifests itself most strongly in the genre of technological forecasting, which tries to imagine the emergent forces of technological change and capitalize on them. Through a set of rhetorical methods—trend extrapolation, analogy with the past, economic resource models, intuition, expert consensus building (Miller 89)—forecasters take and make advantage of the "realist-constructivist ambivalence in *kairos:* the forecaster can threaten the objectively inevitable future and simultaneously offer a way to reconstruct it" (Miller 90–91). Ultimately, however, human rhetors construct both threat and opportunity through discourses about technology, and then humans understand and respond to those discourses. In short, the use of classical rhetoric remains epistemological rather than ontological, human rather than posthuman.

Negroponte's rhetoric is a type of technological forecasting, but one that ultimately falls short. And traditional models of sophistic rhetoric or even contemporary models of epistemic rhetoric don't reveal its shortcomings. Instead of seeing forecasting as a human discursive construction in response to technological determinism, which produces Negroponte's technological deism, a posthuman perspective, particularly on the nature of objects and their co-productive agency, can provide an alternative way to understand how Negroponte's discursive forecasting neglects detailing objects in relation to human learning and ultimately forecloses on possible strategies for deploying and using the laptops. Because technological objects are more complicated types of agents, neither determining agents nor ultimately controllable by human agents, the rhetoric humans construct around these objects should reflect the level of complexity needed to invite a fuller range of agents for enacting multiple responses to a rhetorical forecast. Developing an object-oriented rhetoric to differentiate agents produced through rhetoric versus agents unfolding in material deployments might help close the gaps between Negroponte's deist or black box rhetoric and the posthuman possibilities of an open box rhetoric in the deployment of technological objects into the networks that objects and humans co-produce.

On Object-Oriented Rhetorics

Object-oriented rhetorics are still in the process of being defined and articulated. While they connect to and extend through various approaches to materialist and posthuman rhetorics, object-oriented rhetoric can be seen as extending the concept of object-oriented programming to issues in writing and rhetoric, from technical communication's work on writing as code, to Latour's rearticulation of object-oriented programming with public rhetorics, and John Law's decentering of objects in relation to writing. This version of object-oriented rhetoric extends beyond objects in programming, texts as objects, and the agency of single, isolated objects and into a shifting world of fragmented objects, relations, and actions. In this ontological view, humans are seen as material objects on an even plane with other objects, and collections of objects at various levels of scale are equally considered to be objects on such a plane of immanence (Latour, *We Have Never Been Modern;* Harman, *Tool-Being;* Deleuze, *Pure* 27). Writing and rhetoric, then, become centrally important to producing any material coherence that can be brought to objects from their smallest fragments to their largest networks of assemblages. This turn to object-oriented rhetoric extends the rhetoric of technology beyond an analysis of discourse and into the emergent co-production or composition of objects themselves. It would not only allow for an ulterior approach to rhetorical criticism, but a way to see how rhetoric functions as a key part of these complex processes of co-production.

Bill Hart-Davidson, in "Shaping Texts that Transform: Toward a Rhetoric of Objects, Relationships, and Views," takes the basic concept behind object-oriented programming and applies it to working with documents and their users. Object-oriented programming defines chunks or modules of code as "objects" that have certain features and functionalities connected to them. Different applications are built by combining the objects together. These relationships allow machines running the application to reuse the same chunk or object in multiple situations, applications, or interfaces. Generic "objects" such as windows can be drawn from one block of code without having to rewrite it for each iteration. The new window will inherit the generic qualities of a window, producing multiple views across different use-situations. Hart-Davidson argues that "we can apply many of these basic concepts behind object-oriented development to the design of documents, including the notion that a text is, itself, a collection of objects" (31). Following object-oriented modeling's position that objects have virtual or potential structures that vary from one set of relations to another, he extends rhetorical work beyond writing for multiple audiences to the more sophisticated task of constructing multiple relationships and effective views (39). In "From Wordsmith to Object-Oriented Composer," George Pullman connects this line of thinking to the dynamic multi-object screens that are now typical for most websites. These spaces extend the metaphor of multitasking to writing, making writing the ability to collect and arrange small bites of text, video, images, and sound bites (43). Since users are increasingly able to write or rewrite content, through everything from server or client side scripting to wiki, blog, or user contributions, Pullman argues that professional writing has to move away from uni-directional communication to object-oriented writing pedagogies (44). In short, technical communicators are no longer writing directly for human audiences but writing for an audience of databases and interfaces as much as human users. Audiences become rhetorical situations writ-large with all of their materiality and complexity.

Latour and Peter Weibel rearticulate object-oriented programming into a new model of public rhetoric with an eye toward an object-oriented democracy. In "From Realpolitik to Dingpolitik or How to Make Things Public," they outline their "object-oriented" politics through the multiple meanings of representation. To the two traditional meanings—the legitimate procedures for gathering the right people around an issue (politics), and the accurate portrayal of what is at issue (science)—they want to add a third—how to "represent" one and two through a particular medium (rhetoric). While the first signifies a sanctioned gathering, a council or congress, and the second creates a focus on the facts that are at issue, the third asks, how to articulate the body politik? Following the cover of Hobbes's *Leviathan*, the body politik is not only made of people: it is "thick with things: clothes, a huge sword, immense castles, large cultivated fields, crowns, ships, cities and an immensely complex technology of gathering, meeting, cohabitating, enlarging, reducing and focusing" (16). For them, this crowd of objects is "a whole new ecology loaded with things" that is never integrated into the definition of representation or politics (17). Their strategy is to pack things in the spaces that were once only imagined with people and issues. An object-oriented rhetoric would bring together things, people, and issues to express the material conditions that make politics possible. Rather than trying to establish WMDs as matters of fact with a few slides and the power of authority to force consensus and side-step debate, ala Colin Powell, a *dingpolitik* would bring together complex assemblages of concrete things, humans, and discourse around matters of concern, debate, and difference, with the willingness to conclude a dispute with disputable assertions. This new rhetoric does not revolve around policy—solutions to problems—but the articulation or assembling of the conditions for the emergence of solutions. It creates an "ecology of . . . interests" with more and more elements "taken into account, considered simultaneously, side by side (paratactic)" (40). Making things public is a function of this object-oriented rhetoric that makes things *open* to other assemblages.

Latour and Weibel connect this rhetoric to the assembly drawing of engineers, a turn toward writing taken up by others in Science and Technology Studies such as John Law. In *Aircraft Stories: Decentering the Object in Technoscience,* Law examines the British attempt to build the TSR2 military aircraft that started in 1950 but was finally cancelled in 1965 by a newly elected Labor government before it was ever built. Law argues that postmodernism's response to such large-scale modernist projects ultimately falls short. Postmodernism is skeptical of experts and authors as well as progressive, Enlightenment, or nationalist projects like the space program and responds by fragmenting these narratives and authorities. Law posits three ways to respond to this postmodern tactic: to dismiss the skepticism and continue to call on the authorities of experts and continue to develop grand narratives to support their projects (continue to be modernist); accept that knowledges are limited but continue to tell consistent stories and make rational arguments for things that are needed in particular situations (self-reflexive modernism); accept modernism's flaws but also recognize that the fragmentation of postmodernism is also a product of modernism and seek a third way to operate rhetorically in the world (fractional coherence). Law sees fractional coherence as "drawing things together without centering them" (2). The humanities tend to accept the claim that subjects are fragmented and multiple, but he argues that the same goes for objects. Institutional and discursive claims are made about objects as well, and their borders are often no more cleanly drawn. The TSR2, for example, is multiple— "wing shape, speed, military roles, and political attributes" (Law 2). Various collections of these fragmented attributes produce singularities, or "objects that cohere" (Law 3). These aren't separate fragments but relate and overlap in various constellations at various times in various situations to produce a singular object for those moments. Instead of thinking that objects are coherent and bounded, or fragmented and dispersed, fractional coherences follow the logic of fractals and occupy more than one dimension without existing separately in each of them.

The problem for Law, and for our analysis of Negroponte and the XO, becomes how to articulate these kinds of coherences—how to write multiplicity to produce singularity, or write singularity in a way that invokes multiplicity. How does a writer or rhetor compose an object through producing coherence rather than write *about* it? Like Latour, Law sees this problem as "an inquiry into ontology, into what is made, rather than what is represented" (5). What we write participates in the objects, co-produces their coherence. Law advocates writing a number of smaller stories and linking them together to build a performance of the object. This offsets the grand narratives of modernism but also the disconnected fragments of postmodernism. Writing multiple, overlapping stories produces "rhizomatic networks" that perform "elaborations and interactions that hold together, fractionally, like tissues of fibers" (5). This process may come at the cost of a single larger picture, but for him it produces something that wasn't there before, even if the effects of these co-productions can't be fully predicted (5). Law examines sales brochures, aerospace museums, journalists' accounts, policy narratives, technical documents, and visual accounts that overlap to produce a coherent object.

Combining the extension of audience into technologies, objects, and situations ala Hart-Davidson and Pullman, the gathering of things via rhetoric to produce conditions via Latour, and Law's analysis of how writing produces fractional coherence gives us a set of object-oriented rhetorical practices for thinking about what Negroponte does or doesn't do for the XO and its deployment. Rather than map this open, multiple, overlapping territory of possibility, Negroponte "black boxes" this complexity, leaving the audience to assume a technological determinism and educational deism. For Law, a writing performance stages and enacts reality. So when rhetors write from a modernist tree-logic or postmodernist fragment-logic, they are bringing those worlds into being. This seems to be the issue for Negroponte—a black box rhetoric brings the black box into being and produces the world and effects that come with it. In this case, those effects manifest as a problematic deployment and use of the technology for learning. Enacting the XO in a more open, rhizomatic articulation would produce a different object and a different set of possible deployments and responses. Opening up more possibilities, stories, potential connections, and ways to learn with and through the object would deploy more possibilities for connection and enactment. Even if they couldn't be predicted, it would at least open up those possibilities rather than foreclose them. Rather than deploy black box rhetorical appeals required to sell a program, Negroponte should perform more nuanced ontological topologies to better support the shifting exigencies that inevitably occur in any complex technology project.

Black Box vs. Open Box Rhetorics

In most of Negroponte's rhetoric, he produces a Latourian black box around the complexities of learning through bold claims about how the XO laptop will empower children to self-educate in impoverished learning and living conditions. He places such empowerment in the child-laptop relation, which he believes can overcome the lack of technological, institutional, and educational infrastructures. Accordingly, he argues that children in the regions he hopes to reach will thrive, despite lacking good teachers and schools, any adult or expert guidance, or even sources of electricity. In 2006, he likens children to a precious natural resource, arguing that the solution to a country's poverty, peace, and environment is education through his laptop, and he has expressed these bold claims on more than one occasion. In a 2007 interview posted on the OLPC YouTube channel, he states that "[The XO] is probably the only hope. I don't want to place too much on the OLPC, but if I really had to look at how to eliminate poverty, create peace, and work on the environment, I can't think of a better way to do it" (Vota). Although this trope posits children as a kind of knowable and quantifiable industrial material, Negroponte attempts to brush aside this position by declaring that teaching children through the model of the traditional classroom is an out-moded method of learning. Instead, he positions the XO, coupled with his "walk away" method, as a better-suited education solution to these larger systemic issues. Yet, where does Negroponte's confidence in the XO laptop come from?

In many of his talks, Negroponte discusses his personal experience working with Seymour Papert on the LOGO project in Senegal in 1982. Papert launched LOGO in 1967, naming it after the Greek word logos because it was one of the first programming languages that used words and sentences instead of the common emphasis on arithmetic computation (Harvey). Negroponte's passing references to Papert identify another critical object in the OLPC rollout—Papert's constructionist educational philosophy. Papert's influence on Negroponte's axiom, "give a kid a laptop and walk away," is rooted in Papert's vision for children and computers (Negroponte, OLPC 2006). Papert's vision derives from his research with Jean Piaget on the Epistemology in Geneva project, creating an educational model where "children appropriate to their own use of materials they find about them, most saliently the models and metaphors suggested by the surrounding culture" (Papert, *Mindstorms* 19). Papert contrasts the differences between traditional models of learning in educational institutions and constructionist environments, arguing that children who build and critique their own way of knowing learn far more than those who are delegated exercises and activities on a computer or in a classroom. To Papert (and Negroponte), the traditional classroom environment, where students use computer applications in the same way they use a worksheet, teaches children how to use the program to find the pre-determined set of answers, where the computer programs the child, what Papert would later come to call "instructionism" (*The Children's Machine* 137). Instead, Papert argues that the LOGO environment reverses this relationship, where, "The child, even at preschool ages, is in control: The child programs the computer" (19). LOGO, the language and the environment, created a field of relationships between the roles of student and teacher, allowing for Papert's central image of the "child as epistemologist."

Negroponte, however, takes Papert's central thesis and shrouds it in a rhetoric of the magical relationship between computers and children. In Negroponte's 2006 TED Talk, he discusses the ability for children to learn with computers by comparing it to the naturalness of how a child learns how to speak and walk. Again, in 2007, he alludes to Papert's epistemological claim that kids get the closest to learning about learning when they are producing and debugging programs, noting that the XO laptop will be "launched with three [programming] languages in it." Negroponte avoids explaining the nuances of his axiom, "give a kid a laptop and walk away," and how it is linked to Papert's vision for children and computers (Negroponte, OLPC 2006). Even though his educational paradigm may be influenced by Papert's vision for kids and computers, he sidesteps Papert's inclusion of the teacher-as-guide, or just another learner, by claiming that the XO-child relation does not necessitate any expert practitioner. Negroponte practices a strand of constructionism where learning happens spontaneously far from the boundaries of any well-outlined and measured curriculum, but also from much, if any, adult intervention. The XO, according to Negroponte, is designed to fill this role with its constructionist sandbox environment.

Papert and Negroponte both believe in the parallel construction between the production of programs and the production of knowledge, where learning happens spontaneously through engagement. In *Code/Space,* human geographers Rob Kitchin and Martin Dodge argue that software exercises agency in the world. Such agencies of things emerge through the various relations that coded objects like the XO laptop make in their environment. This code-driven, material-digital assemblage is "contingent and unstable—constantly on the verge of collapse as it deals with new data, scenarios, bugs, viruses, . . . and users intent on pushing it to its limits" (38). They add that "[a]s a result software is always open to new possibilities and gives rise to diverse realities" (38). Almost three decades before Kitchin and Dodge articulate software as an agent, Papert suggests that this "contingent and unstable" sense of software is what mimics the manifestation and aesthetics of learning with children, and it is this philosophy that sets the stage for Negroponte's claim that the XO is *the* teaching tool for children to learn how to learn. Unlike Negroponte's collapse of the philosophy of the code into the laptop, the ability for new users of the XO laptop to ascertain Papert's model separately from a particular manifestation demands that a rhetorician consider whether or not a particular code or hardware configuration allows children to not only adapt to a new code/space configuration, but also the host of non/human agencies sure to occur between users, code, hardware, and the surrounding environment. Coding bugs, glitches, and hardware breakdowns are inevitable and must be overcome, and the posthuman rhetorician has to consider the limits of the hardware, paradigms, and code environment even under ideal circumstances.

Yet, in his TED Talks, Negroponte neglects to detail Papert's influence on building constructionist environments. Negroponte's constructionist imperative seeks to create *ad hoc* learning-spaces if and when bug and breakdown events happen, but he makes students *the* responsible parties in resolving these issues. Side-stepping these complexities is due in part to time constraints, but also, more importantly, to allow for a broader appeal for his claims, which instead leaves a gap between

Papert's "children's machine" that helps children "learn how to learn" and the dominant GUI environments championed by Apple and Microsoft. This wide gap between the roles created by these contrasting environments—*constructionist, co-producer* in the XO versus *user* in Mac/PC—leaves everyone outside of the OLPC program with nothing but the dominant proprietary environments to align their epistemic definition of how we interact with a computer. Without accounting for the multiple ontologies of these objects, enacted by their situatedness in such a diverse set of material-discursive conditions, it becomes quite difficult to parse the XO laptop's environment to see how it differs from the dominant MAC/PC material-digital environments at work in the world. Most listeners of these TED speeches could be forgiven for thinking that Negroponte was simply driving down the cost of learning to $100 and a button-pushing smile. Still, the ubiquitous discussion of computers, or any object for that matter, as stabilized commodities dominates the unboxed possibilities of the XO for human-nonhuman learning practices situated across a diverse set of spaces.

On the one hand, Negroponte's image for the XO is as black boxed as traditional education. In *Tinkering Toward Utopia,* Larry Cuban and David Tyack argue in their archaeology of school reform in the U.S. that change in the public school systems "has remained remarkably stable over the decades" (85). The history of the relationship between the computer and the American educational system reveals a host of technological deists, who always claim that computer-assisted instruction produces a richer learning experience for students (Cuban, *Teachers and Machines*). Yet, the majority of educators have known little or nothing about how to implement new technologies entering their classrooms, creating a situation where such technology becomes *Oversold and Underused* in American educational contexts (Cuban). Classrooms are predominantly curriculum focused, and most of these these curriculums leave zero space for learning through debugging or hacking methods let alone about computer hardware and software itself. Kitchin and Dodge argue in *Code/Space* that code produces spatiality between user and machine, and that this space becomes hardened in the formulation of computer as a commodity. Negroponte's rhetoric around the XO creates such an anti-environment for both computing and education. In this blackboxed, stratified educational environment, proprietary computers (Mac, PC, and ultimately the XO) translate learners into the role of isolated user, learning the programs but never the architecture and its relation to its complex situatedness.

On the other hand, the XO's open sourced approach problematizes traditional education in ways that go beyond Negroponte's rhetoric and carries potential for an open box rhetoric. The XO laptop's open-source, constructionist environment contradicts traditional models of learning and proprietary environments in educational institutions by providing a way for children to build and critique their own knowledge pathways. This approach offers a radically different model than the delegated exercises and activities that teachers and programmers construct and then lock down on a computer or in a classroom exercise. The Sugar operating system developed for the XO creates an open box, rather than a black box, where students are supposed to grow with the software environment through what literacy scholar Annette Vee calls "proceduracy." According to Vee, proceduracy is "the ability to break down complex processes into smaller procedures and express them explicitly enough to be read by a computer" (8). Proceduracy becomes the Latourian translation between human and machine, where the computer demands that the user is turned into a co-producer of the structures built within the environment. By comparing Sugar (or even LOGO) to the dominant Mac and Windows environments, a posthuman analyst immediately reveals the prescriptive pedagogies and ontologies of the proprietary computer-user practices in most Western schools. This ontological condition signals to educators and students that modification of the code is neither wanted, nor warranted within their definition of how to utilize such learning materials and environments. Epistemic energy, instead, is best spent on understanding the affordances offered by the software interface—dropdown menus, templates, and forms to accomplish pre-scripted tasks that gesture away from the code and towards the professional and proprietary steps demanded by a particular social understanding. Educators in the West see software bugs, hardware issues, etc., as some of the common frustrations of technology, but for Negroponte debugging moments beget opportunities to learn and learn how to learn.

While this seems as though we are suggesting constructionist environments are better, we are instead trying to reveal the multiplicity of the computer as a thing. This gap between prescriptive and constructionist programming is only fully overcome when it is distributed across the ontological topology of a computer as space for code manipulation and a space for interfacing with and reassembling the very material environments that Negroponte's rhetoric relegates to the margins. Moving toward such an open box rhetoric more in line with the XO's potential disrupts the way that Negroponte pitched the relationship between the child and XO, as a natural flow of control toward proceduracy. The contradiction between the XO's proprietary marketing and its transformative potential as a procedural pedagogical environment gets reflected by the object-oriented programming that undergirds the operating system. In object-oriented programming, programmers understand relational meta-concepts called HAS-A and IS-A. The HAS-A relationship between objects indicates a relationship where one object is a part of another object, and behaves according to the rules of ownership, creating a possessive hierarchy. The IS-A relationship between objects indicates the inheritance of all of the traits from Object A to Object B. Negroponte's failure to disrupt relationships between the open or inventive versus black or prescriptive boxes within the topology of this rhetorical situation allows the XO to be prescribed, or subsumed, by a broader social ontological position where the XO is nothing more than a Mac/PC machine. The potential constructionism gets temporarily subsumed into the consumerist sales job used to push the XO into foreign markets through a rhetoric that remains bound by symbolic action alone.

Negroponte embedded a set of humanist assumptions about how the world works in his initial pitch for the XO initiative. His pitch foregrounded how a machine, and the grassroots network it would foster, would empower the children, and ultimately the communities that these children live in regardless of their specific circumstances. In other words, Negroponte went about building support for a machine in terms of the subjectivities it would foster. Ian Bogost, in his video presentation, "Seeing Things," described just how difficult it is for people to not frame objects in terms of how they serve the human-scape in which they are embedded. Negroponte's argumentative situation, in this view, is entirely understandable. However, the consequence of this technological forecasting creates a situation in which it becomes increasingly difficult to see the technology for what it affords as an object in a set of relations and practices that traverse new materials and spaces. To the posthuman analyst, the educational and rhetorical potential does not lie within the black box of the machine, nor in the subjectivities of the students but in the potential for open box rhetorics. Such potentialities unfold and emerge through the social assemblage between the actors, whether human or nonhuman.

Although the nesting of the open box computer in the black box rhetoric obscures the eventual difficulties that would emerge in the rollout and development of the XO initiative, the complications of XOs-in-the-making could not be avoided. Only in social and material interaction with Negroponte's black box would people be able to uncover the emergent properties of the open box. In his book on Latour, Graham Harman writes that in order to open the black box to see the multitude of networks, actants that make up this assemblage must be "born amidst strife and controversy" (*Prince* 34). Audiences in prescriptive technological forecasting may be dimly aware of the strife and controversy of technology deployments; however, they seldom bring this to their seats in the lecture hall. Despite the intensity of any potential controversies surrounding any black box, agents may eventually "congeal into a stable configuration" once again. Harman notes that for Latour users must reopen the black box to "reawaken the controversy, . . . and . . . see once more that the actant has no sleek unified essence. Call it legion, for it is many" (34). This controversy, dormant in the rhetorical rollout, re-awakens in the field and produces the conditions for any open box rhetoric.

Toward an Open Box Rhetoric

Negroponte's black box rhetoric is part of the assemblage that produces a particular deployment. A different rhetoric, perhaps an open box rhetoric, would contribute to a different constellation of objects and effects. The lesson of the rollout is the lesson of composing in posthuman environments—that is, recognize and acknowledge the complexity of agents, and prepare for the necessity of translation and reciprocity at intermittent points in the composition of the XO and OLPC program. In the initial rollout of the laptop, Negroponte did not develop extensive beta testing to provide a product as finished as the million-unit bluster seems to promise. The eventual deployments, which followed few of the early injunctions (the promise to not sell these in the developed world eventually subsided in "Buy One, Send One" programs), were often small. Kenya has only 400 laptops in the country, and Malaysia only hosts 100 ("OLPC: Map"). Despite this early black box rhetoric, Negroponte has always indicated that the XO is never finished. The small, more organic efforts to deploy these laptops has seeded the ground for the more than 2 million laptops that have been built and shipped to date. As the hardware has proved complicated, so too has the software development. Most programmers understand the complexity of software development, and the Sugar operating system is not a "finished" product, which conveys this sense of beta in its usability. This perpetual beta demands the attention of its users to not just use the programs, called Activities, available for download from the Sugar Labs wiki site, but also to eventually edit activities or produce and contribute their own programs to the community. On a smaller scale, Walter Bender created Turtle Blocks, which was inspired by Papert's LOGO environment ("Turtle Blocks"). In Turtle Blocks, students and educators can produce shapes, sounds, and even explore more complex procedures with Python scripts with its visual programming elements. While there are currently very few curriculums developed to implement these activities, Negroponte maintains that these activities provide the perfect constructionist, learning environment for kids to learn how to learn without any modules in place.

While Sugar developer, Bender, has similar ideas regarding constructionist learning, he suggests, as Mark Warshchauer cites, that there needs to be more of a teacher-as-guider infrastructure in place, and this is what some deployments, notably in Uruguay, provided. Typically, deployments often only include a 2-week XO camp for educators. After this camp, educators are (now) encouraged to share their successes on the OLPC Wiki, as well as stay in contact with the community via monthly educator workshops online (OLPC Team, "Deployment Guide 2011"). Despite this emerging network of organic growth, Negroponte should have planned for more robust documentation and pedagogical eventualities so users could plot the pathways for human-code and institution-discourse translations, and not just rely on Negroponte's leap with the hardware. According to Latour, "knowledge is a trajectory" that is made certain only through "retroactive" processes inherent of *"time, instrument, colleagues, and institutions"* ("A Textbook Case" 88). Negroponte's trajectory attempts to forecast the effects of the XO within the scope of this global educational reform project that, with great consequence, many in his audience did not fully grasp, jumping too far into unfamiliar territory and leaving the black box intact. Consequently, his re-composition of global education through the interpellating XO agent requires an explicit acknowledgement of potential emergent material-discursive networks—a laptop, a pedagogy, a global network of open-source documentation participants, a particular kind of educational institution in which the XO may or may not be deployed—to fill the ontological voids between himself, the OLPC project, and its various deployments, not to mention the void between the XO and a child.

These interruptions in the composition of the OLPC program and XO laptop reveal a new relationship between subject and object, which pushes away from the Kantian social epistemology, where "there is a mind facing an object above the abyss of words and world" (Latour, "A Textbook Case" 93). In the same mode that Latour criticizes three centuries of epistemology, the method to construct knowledge pathways is through a "continuous path," where subjects and objects are not the anchors holding up the "bridge thrown above the abyss of words and world . . . but rather they are *generated* as a byproduct" in the event of ontologically producing knowledge (89). The complex interplay between human and nonhuman throughout any of the OLPC deployments generates new "successive stations along the paths through which knowledge is rectified." Both human and nonhuman co-construct such stations, and Negroponte's negligence in tending to these stations highlights the ontological nature of cognition as quite literally the composition of knowledge pathways (89). Accordingly, the posthumanist sees knowledge acquisition not through a process of social epistemology, but rather foremost through social ontology.

As Negroponte jumped over the widening gap of his forecast, his re-composition would have profitably noted the hostility of multinational corporations like Intel and Microsoft (who famously joined, and then broke from the XO endeavor). Instead, he maintained and even negotiated a continuous connection between such material-digital environments, creating proverbial pitfalls between the ways subjects and objects co-produce knowledge. Perhaps, because Negroponte's rhetoric re-enacted the subject/object dichotomy, he failed to understand the multiple ontological conditions that would emerge from this global educational project. He failed to realize the agency of objects in this extremely diversified chain of material-discursive experiences with the XO laptop. Overall, his rhetorical rollout of the OLPC program indicates the improbability for what Latour calls the use of the "object/subject tool to grasp any *new* entity" ("Textbook" 90) without accounting for the ways non/humans both come to act upon and co-produce each other.

Kenya's XO projects—which could be considered quite small, as the entire country only has approximately 400 XO laptops—have proceeded through a recognition of the necessity for an open box rhetoric. From getting the laptops in-country (which must be two at a time to avoid the grey market that Negroponte believed he could overwhelm with million-laptop shipments), to storage, training, and even power, the Hands of Charity XO project in Kenya has opened up the box through the use of blogs, a Google group, and f2f meetings where each step of the deployment is negotiated. As one small example, Sandra Thaxter, in her December 2, 2011 blog post about evaluating rural XO programs, describes the kinds of educational programming that "open boxes" the classroom itself. Instead of trying to wedge the XO into standard classes, many of which are not attended by children in the target population, they create a type of open source educational happening: "These are called Youth Friendly Centers or Corners and are setup to attract kids who would be hanging out on unsafe corners and engaging in risky activities" (Thaxter). These Centers/Corners "advertise the opportunity to learn to use computers, make music and pictures. This is the draw" (Thaxter). There is inevitably an exploration of AIDS information, as well as other desired health and behavioral programming, but these flow out from the improvisational efforts on an open platform that respect the emergent situation rather than a scripted dance around a black box. These ad hoc open uses, however, are small compared to the overall rollout and the needs of various local or regional deployments.

In the largest deployment to date, at 510,000 laptops, Uruguay's rollout similarly reflects an open box rhetoric with the government initiative to implement technical programs such as Plan CEIBAL. In 2007, President Vasquez established CEIBAL, which is an acronym (*Conectividad Educativa de Informática Básica para el Aprendizaje en Línea*) that translates as "Basic educational connectivity for online learning" (Derndorfer, "OLPC in Uruguay"). He framed the program through a social justice lens to provide "equal access to information and communication tools for all our people," and, accordingly, Uruguay is the only deployment to provide one laptop per child in the public, primary school system. Yet, as of May 2011, just over 20% of the XO laptops in Uruguay are registered as either broken or being repaired by Plan CEIBAL, and roughly only 65% of the laptops in the poorest regions of the country are reported as functional (Vasquez qtd. in Derndorfer, "OLPC in Uruguay"; "Plan Ceibal Expands New Repair System"). This extensive XO deficiency reveals the crucial need for an established infrastructure reminiscent of Latour's *dingpolitik*, rather than Negroponte's claim that such maintenance can and should be done by the laptop owner, who in this case is the primary school child (TED 2006).

Uruguay's maintenance issues with the XO highlight how a laptop cannot, especially on such a large-scale, solely create a successful educational initiative without considering the sociopolitical climate and infrastructure in the network. Uruguay's effort to alleviate maintenance issues through new agencies and support systems reveal both the need and potential for emergent, open box rhetorics. More closely connected to the Sugar software, Uruguayan educators and volunteers published materials for the activity Etoys on a public Google Document, which provided more than just the usual lesson plans (Rabassa). This guide for the "real world" also included copies of former listserv discussions with Sugar developers and open letters that criticize and challenge the developer community to be more open and patient with the educator community (Rabassa, Section E075). One educator-volunteer expressed his opinion that the developer community created "artificial barriers" and launched programs not ready for the public to use. While the full context behind these issues cannot be examined here, (mainly the split between Negroponte's OLPC and Bender's formation of a fully separate Sugar Labs), it seems clear that Negroponte's black box rhetoric reinscribes the classic system-centered vs. user-centered divide.

Could a more nuanced social ontology, aggregates from the *dingpolitik*, produce the potential for even better systems than Uraguay's Plan CEIBAL? While Negroponte's black box rhetoric continues to oversimplify the process, even pushing to drop XO laptops from helicopters in more rural countries with no school systems at the United Nations Social Innovation Summit 2011, both OLPC Uruguay and Argentina have started their own open box forums to share what each deployment has learned throughout their respective rollouts (Vota, "XO Helicopter Deployments"; "Argentina y Uruguay Firman Acuerdo"). As Negroponte continues to curate the image of the OLPC model through his marketing of the "transformative" power of the XO-child power affair, other actors in this network seem to understand the vital nature of a more inclusive approach to negotiating the multifarious elements of the program and XO (qtd. in Vota). Here, the South American programs reveal the problem of seeing the OLPC and XO as static objects through a blackboxed infrastructure. Negroponte, the marketing head, and the team of programmers who build implicit barriers between themselves and the public, fail to see how the burgeoning open box forums analogous to Uruguay and Argentina could potentially co-produce the social ontology that currently finds itself trying to enact and re-compose these subjects and objects, human and nonhuman alike.

While the limits and core tenets of object-oriented rhetoric are still being defined, the broad outlines are there. A posthuman perspective can usefully combine the lessons learned from creating complex simulated environments with the complex rhetorics necessary for material deployments. Negroponte's hope that his constructionist approach to computers would not matter when talking about the black box business practices of scaling and selling millions of laptops proved naive. Instead, Negroponte needed to take his position at the center of the spotlight and use it to highlight exactly how his XO would change not only children, but must also change the machinery of an ecology built upon consumers who do not understand how their microcomputers create rigid processes. The iterative-reflective nature inherent in the systems Negroponte was seeking to install into the global landscape needed an open box rhetoric that invited national, organizational, and individual actors to participate in the formation of what the XO education would be. Instead of discussing things in aggregates of a million, a posthuman analysis indicates that the rhetoric should itself aggregate the actors into groups that would help grow the ecology into right-sized forwarders of the philosophy like those that drove the development of the XO in the first place. Now, in a similar chain of experience as Latour, the posthuman composer, can choose to highlight the traditional subject/object tools, much like Negroponte, and risk alienating the social, ontological, and epistemological forces within the network, or emphasize the translations or pathways required for the production of knowledge, creating potential stations along the path in the forecast to establish (re)generative relationships between both human and nonhuman actors.

In his introduction to *Aircraft Stories,* Law closes with a turn to what all of this means for criticism. Regardless of whether or not the TSR2 was ever made, it still "performed social distributions" such as racial and gendered articulations (7). But Law's position means that we could not critique such articulations from the outside. As soon as we write about them we become connected to them, part of their co-production. From this perspective, rhetorical criticism is always operating with one foot inside and one foot outside of the object-network it co-produces. This form of "collusion" means that politically we can alter the object and its effects (7). But this process is always partial, limited, and to certain extents unpredictable. What this means for extending Miller's rhetoric of technological forecasting is that our criticism of Negroponte's black box rhetoric both participates in reproducing it as well as rearticulating it. In suggesting possibilities for Negroponte to make a turn toward object-oriented rhetoric through an open box approach, we are also connecting our writing to the co-production of the XO. We are "interfering" with the practices of black box rhetoric in order to participate in the "erosion" of its assumptions and "exploring" what is involved with its "enactment" (8). This collusion problematizes any attempt to produce the XO as a singularly coherent object; instead we co-participate in its fractured coherence. These repeat performances are endemic to the kinds of object-oriented public rhetoric Latour espouses and the kinds of posthuman rhetorical criticism that would come from moving beyond the subject/object divide in traditional rhetorical criticism.

WORKS CITED

"Argentina y Uruguay Firman Acuerdo Para 'Un Computador Por Alumno.'" *Presna.com*. n.p., n.d. Web. 7 Dec. 2011

Bender, Walter. "Turtle Blocks." *Sugar Labs Wiki*. Sugar Labs, 28 Nov. 2011. Web. 5 Dec. 2011.

Bogost, Ian. "Seeing Things" OOOIII: The Third Object-Oriented Ontology Symposium, September 17, 2011. Web. 1 Oct. 2011

Cuban, Larry. *Teachers and Machines: The Classroom Use of Technology Since 1920*. New York: Teachers College Press, 1986. Print.

—. *Oversold and Underused: Computers in the Classroom*. Cambridge; Harvard UP, 2003. Print.

Cuban, Larry, and David Tyack. *Tinkering Toward Utopia*. Cambridge: Harvard UP, 1997. Print.

Deleuze, Gilles. *Pure Immanence: Essays on A Life*. Trans. Anne Boyman. New York: Zone Books, 2001. Print.

Derndorfer, Christoph. "OLPC in Uruguay: Impressions of Plan Ceibal's Primary School XO Laptop Saturation." *Edutechdebate.org*, n.p., Oct. 2010. Web. 7 Dec. 2011.

—. "Plan Ceibal Expands New Repair System to Address High XO Breakage Rates." *OLPCNews.com*. 7 Dec. 2011. Web. 7 Dec. 2011.

Hart-Davidson, Bill. "Shaping Texts that Transform: Toward a Rhetoric of Objects, Relationships, and Views." *Technical Communication and the World Wide Web*. Ed. Carol Lipson and Michael Day. New York: Routledge, 2005. 27–41. Print.Harman, Graham. *The Prince of Networks: Bruno Latour and Metaphysics*. Melbourne, Australia: re.press, 2009. Print.

—. *Tool-Being: Heidegger and the Metaphysics of Objects*. Chicago, IL: Open Court, 2002. Print.

Harvey, Brian. *Computer Science Logo Style 2/e, Vol. 1: Symbolic Computing.* Cambridge: MIT Press, 1997. Print.

Kitchin, Rob and Martin Dodge. *Code/Space: Software and Everyday Life.* Cambridge: MIT Press, 2010. Print.

Latour, Bruno. *Pandora's Hope: Essays on the Reality of Science Studies.* Cambridge: Harvard UP, 1999. Print.

—. *Science in Action: How to Follow Scientists and Engineers through Society.* Cambridge: Harvard UP, 1988. Print.

—. "A Textbook Case Revisited—Knowledge as a Mode of Existence." *The Handbook of Science and Technology Studies.* Ed. E.J. Hackett, et al. Cambridge: MIT Press, 2007: 83–112. Print.

Latour, Bruno, and Peter Weibel. "From Realpolitik to Dingpolitik or How to Make Things Public." *Making Things Public: Atmospheres of Democracy.* Ed. Bruno Latour and Peter Weibel. Cambridge: MIT, 2005. 14–41. Print.

Law, John. *Aircraft Stories: Decentering the Object in Technoscience.* Duke UP, 2002. Print.

Miller, Carolyn. "Opportunity, Opportunism, and Progress: *Kairos* in the Rhetoric of Technology." *Argumentation* 8 (1994): 81–96. Print.

Negroponte, Nicholas, "The Hundred Dollar Laptop—Computing for Developing." American Technologists Conference, Massachusetts Institute of Technology, Boston, 2005. Lecture

—. "Nicholas Negroponte on One Laptop Per Child." TED. Feb. 2006. Lecture. Web. 15 Feb. 2015.

—. "Nicholas Negroponte on One Laptop Per Child, Two Years on." TED. Dec. 2007. Lecture. Web. 15 Feb. 2015.

—. "One Laptop Per Child." *Social Innovation Summit 2011.* 6 Jun. 2011. United Nations Office for Partnerships. 7 Dec. 2011. Web. 1 Nov. 2014.

OLPC Team. "Deployment Guide." *One Laptop Per Child Wiki.* 25 Oct. 2011. Web. 20 Nov. 2011.

Papert, Seymour. *The Children's Machine: Rethinking School in the Age of the Computer.* New York: Basic Books, 1993. Print.

—. *Mindstorms: Children, Computers, and Powerful Ideas.* New York: Basic Books, 1993. Print.

Pullman, George. "From Wordsmith to Object-Oriented Composer." *Technical Communication and the World Wide Web.* Ed. Carol Lipson and Michael Day. New York: Routledge, 2005. 41–59. Print.

Rabassa, Carlos. *Real World Handbook.* Plan Ceibal. 1 Dec. 2011. Web. 10 Dec. 2011.

Thaxter, Sandra. "Evaluating Rural XO Laptop Programs." *Hands of Charity XO Project.* n.p., 2 Dec. 2011. Web. 2 Dec. 2011.

Vee, Annette. *Procuracy: Computer Code Writing in the Continuum of Literacy.* Diss. University of Wisconsin-Madison, 2010. PDF.

Vota, Wayan. "Is OLPC the only hope to eliminate poverty and create peace?" *OLPC News*. 30 Nov. 2007. Web. 2 Sept. 2013
—. "XO Helicopter Deployments? Nicholas Negroponte Must be Crazy!" *OLPC News*. 29 June 2011. Web. 7 December 2011.
Warschauer, Mark and Morgan Ames. "Can One Laptop Per Child Save the World's Poor?" *Journal of International Affairs* 64.1 (2010): 33–51. Print.

10 From Handwriting to 'Brain' Writing: Graphology and the Neuroscientific Turn

Melissa M. Littlefield

A 1921 *New York Times* article begins with this fascinating headline: "As a man breathes, so is he . . . French Physician Declares He Can Read Character Infallibly by 'Phrenoscopy'" (E4). The brief report focuses on this new science of reading one's *diaphragm* for clues about one's character. Dr. Maingot contends that "in the face, in the handwriting, in the shape of the head, one can see certain elements of character; but the radioscopic picture of the movement of the diaphragm is the surest method of all. The reason for that is that one breathes according to one's character, and no one can alter his method of breathing except as he alters his character" (E4). While contemporary readers are likely to scoff at Maingot's claims, we should recognize—if sheepishly—that his impulse to read information about the self from the body is not yet an outmoded inclination. We may have moved away from the diaphragm, but researchers continue to search the body and, in particular, the brain for neural correlates that could explain behavior, consciousness, and even subjectivity. In an era of increasingly pervasive medical imaging technologies, we are becoming what Nikolas Rose terms "neurochemical selves" (188) and what Pickersgill et al. have called "neurologic subjects" (348). However, as Joe Dumit aptly queries: "Why is it that when we find a reading correspondence in the brain we are satisfied that we are in the right place?"(20)

So, let's not leave Maingot behind too quickly. Notably, Maingot chooses to compare and contrast phrenoscopy with three other methods of modern character divination: physiognomy, graphology, and phrenology. Despite Maingot's assertion of phrenoscopy's difference and superiority, the phrenoscopic approach to the body, the self, and the personality shares much in common with the other three (pseudo)sciences. Each is focused on ascertaining the self by reading signs written on, in or by the body; each is also convinced that the ultimate source for the self is somewhere in the head: that so-called seat of identity, reason, and selfhood. For physiognomy, one's character is written on one's face; for phrenology, one's character is related to the shape of one's skull—and presumably the brain underneath. In a *Popular Science* essay published in October of 1921, we are told that Maingot's x-ray instrument images your torso, but "reveals your *mental* character, your temperament, how you rest, and how you work" (28). Likewise, early twentieth century graphologists claimed that handwriting was best described as brainwriting.

In this essay, I focus on that phrase, "handwriting is brainwriting," which has informed graphology over the past century. I am not interested in comparing the relative scientific merits of graphology and the neurosciences, determining whether graphology is a legitimate science, or even speculating about where graphology stands in terms of science and psuedosience. I take as a given that graphology is a contested field; in part, possibly because its sister discipline of forensic handwriting analysis is more widely accepted. The latter is used in forgery cases and for document authentication when officials seek to assign and identify a particular script with a particular person. Instead of worrying the status of graphology, I want to pose two questions: Why do neuroscience and graphology ostensibly share the brain as a common locus of self? How have both diagositic technologies constructed the self as stable and knowable via a transparent human body?

Not coincidentally, the selves we seek through a number of modern sciences—including graphology and neuroscience—are always already mediated by social, political, cultural, and technological constructs. In this sense, and in the context of this collection of essays, the so-called stable human self we seek to measure, codify, and 'know' through the body is and has always been posthuman. In other words, and although it seems paradoxical, the self presumed by both graphology and neuroscience reveals that humanism and posthumanism are not incompatible. If, as N. Katharine Hayles argues, "the human has traditionally been associated with consciousness, rationality, free will, autonomous agency, and the right of the subject to possess himself," and, "the posthuman sees human behavior as the result of a number of autonomous agents running their programs more or less independently of one another" (Interview 1999), then both graphology and the neurosciences could be said to "envision the human in terms that make it much more like an intelligent machine, which allows the human to be more easily spliced into distributed cognitive systems where part of the intelligence resides in the human, part in a variety of intelligent machines, and part in the interfaces through which they interact" (Interview). In the case of a concept such as "handwriting is brainwriting," the theoretical interface between mind and machine becomes the graphic record.

Here, I argue that graphology and neuroscience share several ideological assumptions: that the body *involuntarily* discloses information about the self; that interpretations of this data rely on discourses of transparency; and that underlying both technologies is what Fernando Vidal has termed an ideology of "brainhood." In what follows, I first explore several tenets and concepts of graphology before turning to an analysis of the phrase "handwriting is brainwriting." I conclude by returning to the posthuman as a means of reflecting on the self as it is constructed and assumed to exist in graphology and the neurosciences.

A Graphological Primer

In his 1939 volume *Analysis of Handwriting: An Introduction to Scientific Graphology*, H.J. Jacoby describes the basis of graphology as an equation between body and mind:

> we have to infer manifestations of the mind from the manifestations of the body. . . . Obvious as it may seem, it is necessary to emphasize this, for in it lies the foundation of the fact that the significance of handwriting as a characteristic of an individual personality is based on the general principle that every bodily movement is at the same time a movement expressing the mind. . . . When we proceed to examine the possibilities of correct graphological interpretation in a particular case, we are confronted by the following situation: on the one side there is a well measurable and comparable quantity, the handwriting, and on the other side an invisible quantity, the mind, and between them a theoretical equation has to be established. (38–39)

In this brief excerpt from Jacoby's text, we are introduced to the foundational concept and conundrums of graphology: the measureable body is an expression of the invisible mind; but how can we find a reading correspondence between body and mind? Modernist art, fiction, and science often sought to represent this correspondence via various waves and particles, or as a function of the ether (Clarke and Henderson 2004). Graphology finds its correspondence by matching handwritten inscriptions with involuntary self expression. The point of contact for the body, what Jacoby terms the "theoretical equation," has changed over time, and by the end of the nineteenth century, the hand was superseded by the brain (I will return to this point in a moment); however, what has remained relatively stable is the assumption that handwriting is expressive of not just linguistic knowledge of communicative intention, but of a mind—and by extension, an autonomous "self."

While space does not allow me to trace graphology's development before the modern era, it is worthwhile to note that the practice has long struggled with Jacoby's "theoretical equation," disagreeing about which signs count and how they should be interpreted. Graphologists trace the impulse to analyze handwriting to Biblical and Roman times. The first connections between personality and handwriting are often attributed to Camillo Baldi, a seventeenth century Italian physician; following Baldi is a long list of French, German, and American researchers who adopted and adapted graphology's various methods for character analysis. Abbé Jean-Hippolyte Michon coined the term "graphologie" and founded the Société Français de Graphologie in Paris in 1871; his work, including *Les Mystères de l'écriture* (1872), *System de graphologie* (1875), and *Méthode Practique de Graphologie* (1878), helped to establish graphology's taxonomical basis: it became a study of fixed signs and their relationship to one's character (Nickell 25). Michon's student, Crépieux-Jamin, transformed the field once again as he instituted a more holistic approach that attempted to read more broadly across individual signs. Crépieux-Jamin also brought graphology to the attention of Alfred Binet and Pierre Janet whose endorsements aided the esteem of the science (Roman 5). Conversely, German work on handwriting analysis relied on an older, intuitive approach—often associated with Ludwig Klages's expressivist movement. Klages argued that all gestures, from bodily movements to handwriting, reflected one's inner character.

Then, in the latter part of the nineteenth century, Wilhelm Preyer's research transformed German graphology once again; I will return to this important turning point in the next section. American work on graphology is often associated with M.N. Bunker and the founding, in 1929, of graphoanalysis.

> Graphoanalysis . . . has been called a protest against both the atomistic one-to-one sign graphology that typified the French school and the broad, sweeping, intuitive graphology of the German school. This middle-of-the-road compromise position drew heavily from the then new Gestalt school of psychology, which insisted that people must be studied as dynamic wholes and that those wholes are more than the sum of their individual parts. (Crumbaugh 109).

This passage illuminates and settles the debate about which signs are worthy of interpretation, at least for an American, graphological audience.

As a method and a system of analysis in the contemporary U.S, graphology catalogues and interprets various aspects of handwriting, including but not limited to, such features of handwritten script as letter direction, consistency of production, stylus pressure, stroke length, and overall layout of the handwritten text. Volume after volume on the topic from the early twentieth century to the twenty-first century includes specific directions for collecting and analyzing handwriting data and offers a catalogue of possible interpretations. In his essay "Graphoanalytic Cues" (1992) James Crumbaugh presents several handwriting samples that he glosses with possible interpretations: "the low t-bar in Figure 4a reveals a lack of self-confidence, while the high t-bar of 4b indicates strong will power. Figure 5a shows simplicity or modesty in the small *a* of *Ann*, while 5b reveals ostentation in the large *a*" (112). Even though he takes the time to work through individual signs, Crumbaugh is invested in a more holistic analysis. He also argues that the system is only as good as the analyst: "the validity of a projective technique is in the clinician and not in the instrument" (115). This gatekeeping maneuver reminds us of graphology's contested status and graphologists' desire to legitimate their field.

The question of legitimacy is important for the American reception of graphology. As Thornton points out, American scientists were skeptical of German claims about graphology (136). Take, for example, Klara Roman's 550 page volume. *The Encyclopedia of the Written Word: A Lexicon for Graphology and Other Aspects of Writing* (1968). Roman was a Hungarian graphologist and psychologist who lectured across the U.S. and instituted a course on graphology at the New School for Social Research in New York. In the Preface to her posthumously published *Encyclopedia*, Maurice Edwards tells readers that "here the clinical psychologist can find the different types of language disorders conveniently cross-referenced to related entries that may give him new insights in his field. Similarly, the graphologist can find his own terminology correlated with other disciplines, and thereby broaden his background and understanding" (vi). Edwards goes on to reassure readers—presumably those scientifically minded ones—that "certainly the author did not see this work as yet another easy handbook or glossary to 'armchair' graphology. The reader will find no pat, easy answers to handwriting analysis here" (vi). Beyond offering a prescriptive list of uses for the *Encyclopedia*, Edwards's explanation of the volume attempts to bring established scientists (and fields), including clinical psychologists, into conversation with graphologists; at the same time, Edwards's prefatory remarks separate scientific graphology from popular or "armchair" graphology, and thereby legitimate the field. The remainder of the book contains hundreds of handwriting samples alongside information about possible interpretations.

Defining Concepts in Graphology

At each historical and cultural turn, graphology has adapted and survived, despite its contested status. In recent memory, graphology—and specifically graphoanalysis—has been used for employment, educational, and mental health screenings. A *Washington Law Journal* report from 1997 claims that "about six thousand American companies report using graphology" ("Legal Implications of Graphology" 1). Often times, businesses do not disclose their use of graphology, but a 1980s *New York Times* article reveals some of the logic behind the use of the technique for the purpose of hiring. According to an interview with Sheila Kurtz concerning her Manhattan-based graphoanalysis business, "The analysis is used in conjunction with the job interview and it is evaluated along with the applicant's experience and skills" ("Judging a Job Seeker by the Cross of His 'T'" C16). However, in a more glib moment, we learn that "'Our slogan is "handwriting is brainwriting,"' says Sheila Kurtz, who has a background in psychology, 'We believe that the pen is mightier than the personal interview'" (C16). Here, the equation between body and mind, self and script, is foreclosed with reference to the graphologist's slogan: "handwriting is brainwriting." I will return to a more detailed analysis of this type of reference in a moment; first, allow me to say a bit more about the basic tenets of graphology.

Graphology is premised on the idea that the body ostensibly (and helpfully) reveals the self, even as it remains separate from the self. Indeed, and as we shall see in a moment, the self is often figured as leaking out of the body through various involuntary gestures. In her analysis of penmanship manuals in America from the eighteenth to the twentieth century, Tamara Plakins Thornton notes that graphology provided an outlet for the self to escape the body. She refers, for example, to Louise Rice, a popular graphologist of the early twentieth century, who was convinced that "there is no instinct so strong in the human heart as that one which yearns to get outside the envelope of flesh, and there, for the first time, really see what self looks like" (qtd. in Thornton 129). At the same time, the graphological 'self' is a construct, one that was created, in part, to address the destabilizing effects of modern life. As Thornton argues, "Given the close identification of script with self, graphology was uniquely poised to redefine and soothe the troubled selves of early twentieth-century America," which would include soothing apprehension about the shift from character (core) to personality (mask), trepidation that the revealed self might simply be "plain and colorless, consigned to a drab fate," and fear that there may be no self at all (132).

In this vein, June Downey's book *Graphology and the Psychology of Handwriting* (1919) serves as a kind of litmus test for graphological analysis. Downey, who was a psychologist at the University of Wyoming and published academic papers on topics such as disguised handwriting in *The Journal of Applied Psychology* (1917), attempts a taxonomic investigation of graphology, providing a wealth of tabular information concerning what she terms "The Graphological Elements": "(I) Size, or dimension; (II) Pressure and line-quality; (III) Direction, including slant and alignment; (IV) Continuity; (V) Proportion" (39). In addition to meting out the various elements, Downey also concerns herself with a mixed expressivist and Gestalt approach that defines the "Basal Concepts in Graphology" (6). Threaded throughout these elements are two foundational assumptions: handwriting is said to be involuntary and individual.

On the first count, handwriting is characterized by its level of control. Indeed, during graphology's formative development, another "discipline" was also extending its reach: penmanship. In *Handwriting in America: A Cultural History*, Thornton notes that penmanship manuals underwent a fundamental shift from the eighteenth to the nineteenth century; by the Victorian era, manuals intimated that "Victorians were to form their letters as they formed themselves, through moral self-elevation and physical self-control" (47). The trouble for graphologists is the charge that handwriting is disciplined by copybooks and penmanship lessons and that, as a result, handwriting is both a self-conscious act and one that is shaped by muscular control, not the inner character. June Downey responds to these claims by noting a difference between artificial handwriting (calligraphy, forgery, copying, copy book writing) and "natural" handwriting (free writing informal letters): the latter is said to be "a more involuntary type of writing" (11).

Assumptions concerning handwritings' involuntary nature are crucial to conceptualizations of graphology as part of a continuum both in early twentieth century science and in neuroscience. Sister sciences, including polygraphy and human electroencephalography (EEG), depend on similar assumptions concerning other parts of the body: the autonomic nervous system (which controls activities such as breathing and heart rate) and the electrical activity of the brain (which is understood as involuntary, but revelatory).[1] As I explain in a moment, assumptions of non-volition are also central to ideologies of transparency and neuroscience itself. For now, it is enough to note that graphologists assume that in both artificial and natural handwriting, the character eventually and ultimately betrays itself: "the most careful disguise let's light through at some point" or "some trick in making a comma, or crossing the 't' may give away the secret" (Downey, 11).

Downey's second "basal concept" involves her discussions of individuality in which she acknowledges some disagreement among practitioners: from a "practical" standpoint, "graphic individuality is acquired; its origin is to be sought in the system learned in school, in acquired habits of the arm, wrist and finger movement, in the kind of writing apparatus that is utilized, in the amount of practice, in professional requirements, social imitation and the like" (7). Here, Downey foregrounds factors in the social construction of handwriting and its analysis. However, she also recognizes—if skeptically—that graphologists "assume that the individual stamp of penmanship is largely of central origin, 'Handscript' is, essentially 'Hirnschrift'" (8). Here, one possible German word for "brain" (Hirn) turns "handscript" into "brainscript." This latter point is absolutely instrumental to graphology's connections with neuroscience. The hand serves and reveals a more centralized master: the brain, through which an amorphous entity, the self, finds expression. It is this organ, the brain—common to both graphology and neuroscience—that will serve as the focus for the rest of this essay. Downey is not the first—or the last—to make reference to this nervous resolution to the "theoretical equation" of body to mind.

Handwriting Is Brainwriting

Graphology's intersections with neuroscience are both historical and contemporary. Historically, the link between writing and the brain is most often attributed to the late nineteenth century work of English/German physiologist Wilhelm Preyer who experimented with various ways of writing: with the hand, the mouth and the foot. Preyer's research sought ["the morphological substrate of the writing movement in the brain"] (*Zur Psychologie des Schreibens [The Psychology of Writing]* 38); [2] his results led him to believe that writing originates in the brain. Preyer's work, which is rarely if ever referenced in the original German by graphologists, has been transformed into the catchphrase, "handwriting is brain writing." The popularized phrase could be more directly linked to another German, neurologist Rudolf Pophal. Working on what has been termed "motor-physiological graphology" (Roman 1952, 10), Pophal eventually published *Die Handschrift als Gehirnschrift* after the second World War (1949). His title, which translates as "Handwriting as Brainwriting" may be one of the missing links between Preyer and more contemporary instantiations of the phrase "handwriting is brainwriting."[3]

Over the past century, the phrase "handwriting is brainwriting" has been taken up by scientists, graphologists, and the lay public to mean a variety of things. In its most literal incarnations—that at least reference the spirit of the original—graphologists have simply stated, "It is not the hand that writes, but the brain" (*New York Times*, 2); such phrases imply that biomechanical movements are controlled by the central nervous system, a claim that Wilhelm Preyer would support. However, I should note that this particular example, taken from a 1923 story in the *New York Times*, concerns the work of Rafael Shermann, a graphologist psychic who predicted future behavior by examining handwriting. So, even in cases that sound closest to Wilhelm Preyer, the catchphrase loses sight of its potential referent.

In contemporary graphological circles, and as Barry L. Beyerstein has argued, the phrase "handwriting is brainwriting" has also become a rhetorical device used to link graphology to neuroscience. This is at once an authorizing and disempowering move allying the field to an authorized field, such as the neurosciences, grants graphology status; at the same time, this linkage does the profession of graphology a disservice. On the one hand, graphology is simply doing what many undervalued fields have done and continue to do: ally themselves to the harder, physical sciences. In today's academy, emergent neurodisciplines (including neuroeconomics, neurohistory, and neuroaesthetics) have linked philosophical questions concerning subjectivity to neuroscientific methods, ushering in what Jenell Johnson and I have termed a "neuroscientific turn" (Littlefield and Johnson 2012).[4] As with graphology, these transdisciplines [5] have both invested neuroscience with cultural capital and drawn from the already invested scientific capital of the neurosciences.

On the other hand, Beyerstein contends that the phrase "handwriting is brainwriting" does graphology a disservice: it highlights graphology's hierarchically lower status in relation to neuroscience by irreverently joining two fields that are incompatible. He concludes his argument by suggesting that:

> in order to accept graphology as a valid method of discerning human strengths and weaknesses, one would have to consign a century if well-documented data in psychology and the neurosciences to the rubbish heap. The fact that so much of what we have learned about the neurological underpinnings of must be wrong if graphology is right does not automatically rule out graphology's claims. But surely, it makes the gravity of accepting them such that a prudent observer would demand an especially high standard of proof before concluding that graphology is valid and that the whole edifice of psychobiological research, which serves us so well in so many areas, is in need of drastic revision. (Beyerstein 415)

What is interesting about Beyerstein's arguments in this 1992 essay "Handwriting is Brainwriting, So What?" is his rhetorical strategy: he does not dismiss graphology outright, but by comparison, thereby displaying his bias toward the social and physical sciences, including neuroscience. Beyerstein's dismissal of graphology depends on the presumption that neuroscience is superior to handwriting analysis via graphology; for graphology to be unseated—for graphology's claims to be validated—the field would have to meet an especially high standard of proof.

However, if we flip the hierarchy and the paradigm, we might see some important reversals of fortune: that fields such as graphology—and even phrenology and physiognomy with which I opened this essay—paved the way for the neurosciences because of their focus on the brain, and as a result, graphology and neuroscience share common ideologies than reinforce an understanding of the relation between body and mind. In short, the shift from handwriting to brainwriting is a discursive one; it does not represent a fundamental, physical change, but a discursive reallocation of agency through which the brain, instead of the amorphous mind, becomes the seat of the self. Before Wilhelm Pryer's research, the mind held precedence over the hand (body). However, with the advent of the neurosciences, the mind has been positioned within the brain (Beaulieu 2000, 2002; Littlefield 2009, 2011). It is, as Elizabeth Wilson has argued, perpetuating a "Cartisianism that has been repositioned but not resolved" (124). Likewise, and depending on who you ask, the debate about where the *self* resides has been momentarily resolved or forever complicated by the neurosciences. In scientific journals and media outlets, neural correlates for various emotions, behaviors, and actions abound and the implicit or explicit implication that "you are your brain" (Gazzaniga, *The Ethical Brain* 31) resonates loud and clear. It is little wonder then that neuroethicists have recently cautioned us about a new kind of essentialism: *neuroessentialism*, "the concept that the brain becomes short hand for other concepts (e.g. the person, the self) that may serve to express features of the individual not ordinarily found in the concept of the brain" (Racine, et al. 728).

All of these discursive shifts gloss over an important and ideological *consistency*: as Fenando Vidal has aptly argued, neuroscience is not simply the catalyst for brain-centered research, but is, instead, a product of the Western world's longstanding philosophical obsession with the brain. In other words, the drive to find the secrets of the self—and now the warrant for various disciplines—in the brain has a history that precedes neuroscience. Foregrounding theorization of what he terms *brainhood*, "the property or quality of *being*, rather than simply *having*, a brain" (6), Vidal argues that

> a good number of 20th and 21st century neuroscientists seem to think that their convictions about the self are based on neuroscientific data. In fact, things happened the other way around: brainhood *predated* reliable neuroscientific discoveries, and constituted a motivating factor of the research that, in turn, legitimized it. (Vidal 14, emphasis added)

Vidal's essay, which is extremely wide-ranging, traces brainhood throughout modernity. In particular, Vidal is attentive to the shifting signifier of the body and its relation to brainhood and the self. "The notion of the *self* or *I* that concerns us here crystallized in systems that distanced self and body in such a way that the body is existentially or experientially significant, yet ontologically derivative. Correlatively, being an *I* or having a *self* has been equated with consciousness and self-awareness" (11). The body is phenomenologically relevant to these discussions, "but its relationship to the self is nonetheless open to interpretation and historical transformation" (11). The discursive shift from handwriting to brain-writing capitalizes on both a larger and longer ideology of *brainhood*, one that requires a dismissal of the body (the hand writing) in favor of the self of consciousness, which modernity situated in the brain.

That the body is a (mere) medium of transference for the self informs discourses of transparency in both graphology and neuroscience. Here I am thinking of work by Lisa Cartwright (1995), Jose van Dijk (2005), and Kelly Joyce (2008), among others. Transparency implies that what we see when we look at and into the body is unmediated data, images, and truths. The trouble with transparency, and this is similar to the trouble with objectivity (Lorainne Daston and Peter Galiston 1992, 2007), is one of erasure, black boxing, and agnotology: we do not see, are not allowed to see, or simply ignore many of the cultural and mechanical choices that influence the construction of seemingly transparent images. Both graphology and neuroscience assume that the normal brain is a leaky brain; the brain readily discloses information that seems self-evident. More specifically, and in certain circumstances, this normal, leaky brain exposes the self via mechanical mediums (handwriting or brain activity).

As I discuss elsewhere in relation to lie detection—and as we saw earlier in the writings of June Downey—scientists in search of some truth about the self often assume that the best and easiest method is to measure bodily systems and organs that are under less conscious control (Littlefield 2011). Monitoring the blood pressure or blood oxygenation levels in the brain is purported to reveal inner truths that may be inaccessible to the person being measured. As Joe Dumit aptly notes in *Picturing Personhood*, "ironically, the 'normal' brain-type is the one that is, so to speak, passive and lets the real self talk through it" (163). In addition, I would note that graphology came of age during the same era as Hans Berger's experiments on human electroencephalography (EEG), the same era as William Marston's experiments on lie detection, and the same era as Étienne Jules Marey's cardiograph. These and other emotional inscription technologies illustrate that one basic assumption of the decades between 1910 and 1940 was that writing—by pen or by stylus—

was the best means of making the character, the mind, and the emotions transparent (Dror 1999, Littlefield 2011).

The ideal of the transparency is evident in graphological texts throughout the twentieth —and now the twenty-first century. Transparency works quite literally in Jerome Meyer's popular book, *Mind Your P's and Q's* (1927), which provides the reader with transparent pages and instructions for analyzing friends' writing: "simply put anyone's handwriting under the transparent pages—and out comes his real character!" explains an advertisement for the volume ("The Newest Rage" BR20). The book, which also includes samples of handwriting from famous people (Isaac Newton, Benjamin Franklin, and Benjamin Disraeli among others), constructs graphology as a hobby, a pastime, and something that can be undertaken by non-experts. It is "the handwriting analysis book with the transparent pages *that see through you*" ("The Newest Rage" BR20, emphasis mine). Here, the transparency of self and the transparency of graphology are made apparent: the practice (as well as the self) is simplified, mechanized, and made accessible to a lay audience.

Beyond popular graphology, experts, too, rely on discourses of transparency. In a 1934 letter to the editor of the *New York Times*, Gladys Almy argues that "handwriting is primarily a mental gesture" (E5). A graphologist by training, Almy goes on to suggest that "when we consider the cerebral functions and the sensitive nerve mechanism back of the pen, the art of fine penmanship is soon lost as the fundamental traits of character creep out" (E5). Almy's definition of handwriting condenses and encapsulates many aspects of graphology, perhaps most notably that handwriting is a betrayal of the self: no matter your education, social status, or even your own conscious efforts (all of which should be evident in your 'fine penmanship'), 'fundamental traits of character creep out.' Implicitly and explicitly, Almy's letter speaks to the links between handwriting and brainwriting that are also links between graphology and the neurosciences. Importantly, this ideal of transparency continues to influence the field nearly a century later and as emergent neurodisciplines litter the academy and the media.

In her 2004 self-help book, *Brainwriting: See Inside Your Own Mind and Others' with Handwriting Analysis,* Irene B. Levitt explains that "Handwriting is really BRAINWRITING. . . . Your hand is merely a tool that holds a pen, while handwriting is the pen of the brain—a sort of x-ray that enables us to see what goes on in the body, mind, and emotions of human beings" (11). While it would be easy to dismiss Levitt's argument and her prose (mixed metaphors and all) as part of the oft-parodied self-help genre, it is far more interesting and revelatory to follow her points to their logical conclusions. That handwriting is an imaging technology—an x-ray—that reveals the internal workings of the body (and implied here: the brain and the mind), is also an oft-used metaphor in graphology; the ideals of transparency that underwrite this metaphor are shared by the neurosciences as well. Levitt's claim that "handwriting is the pen of the brain." presumes that the body metonymically represents transparent, mechanical access to the intangible self through one organ (the brain) via an appendage (here, the hand).

For psychology and the neurosciences, the brain's connections to and involvement in writing has resulted in a century of research. Much of the work has centered on the ways that handwriting can be indicative of mental illness (for a recent study, see Fontana et al. 2008). From early lesion studies (Exner 1881) on agraphia to recent studies of neuro correlates (Sugishita et al. 1996, Katonoda et al 2001), writing has been situated in the brain. The tricky thing about handwriting—for fMRI at least—is the difficulty of capturing a hand writing while the subject is in the scanner. Movements of any kind, including movements of the head, hand, and even the eyes can cause artifacts or distortions in the data. Much of the neuroscience related to writing has been conducted outside of scanners in lesion studies. However, there has been at least one study using fMRI in which subjects "wrote" while in the machine; it was conducted in Japan by Kota Katonoda and associates. In their study, they use subtraction to separate out several variables, including simple hand movements (tapping) and silent naming, from writing. They found that activity in "two cerebral regions, the anterior part of the left superior parietal lobule and the posterior part of the left middle and superior frontal gyri, are engaged in the process of writing as compared to naming and finger tapping" (Katonoda, Yoshikawa, and Sugishita 40). While this study is far from conclusive, it succeeded in its goals; as the authors explain, "these analyses are expected to reveal candidate brain regions for the writing centers'" (35).

In the Katonoda study, discourses of transparency play a role in both the design of the experiment and the analysis of extant data. First, the goal of finding "the writing centers" in the brain presumes the existence of the very thing they seek: a neural correlate that can be located by subtracting out other activities, including finger tapping and naming. Here, the brain becomes an input/output machine whose variability can be controlled in an experimental setting. What we "see" in the data and images after subtraction takes place, is activation that can ostensibly be tied to the activity in question: writing. Importantly, the researchers do note that what they call writing is not actual writing: "strictly speaking, this writing task is different from writing in the common usage of the word in that the former does not require a writing tool (e.g., a pen or a pencil), and therefore the subtle movements of the wrist and digits required for using these tools are not engaged in the task" (Katonoda, Yoshikawa, and Sugishita 35). Handwriting has been reduced to a process of index-finger tracing of—in this case—Japanese kana (phonemes). In the analysis of data, the authors go so far as to claim that "this result [quoted above] successfully confirmed the classical notion that these two regions are important as the writing centers" (40); they back up their analysis with both numerical and pictorial data. We know from the research of Anne Beaulieu, Joe Dumit and Kelly Joyce that these images are problematic *translations* of information; however, and as the authors of this study illustrate, brain-imaging data is understood not in terms of translation, but in terms of revelation—of transparency. The authors note that their study "revealed activation" (41) even as they note that there are myriad processes involved in writing that their study cannot account for: finger movement, visual processing, picture naming, etc (41). While neuroscientists would not yoke themselves or their work to a field such as graphology, their research methods, ideologies, and assumptions reveal similarities to character divination in their reliance both on discourses of transparency and brainhood.

Writing Posthuman Handwriting

In her discussion concerning anxieties associated with the posthuman, N. Katharine Hayles reminds us that the posthuman seems threatening because it may lead to the undoing of cherished assumptions:

> when the self is envisioned as grounded in presence, identified with originary guarantees and teleological trajectories, associated with solid foundations and logical coherence, the posthuman is likely to be seen as antihuman because it envisions the conscious mind as a small subsystem running its program of self-construction and self-assurance while remaining ignorant of the actual dynamics of complex systems. (Hayles 286)

If we can, first and foremost, question our construct of the *human*, then the *posthuman* will seem less terrifying. As Cary Wolfe explains, "far from surpassing or rejecting the human [the posthuman] actually enables us to describe the human and its characteristic modes of communication, interaction, meaning, social significations, and affective investments with *greater* specificity once we have removed meaning from the ontologically closed domain of consciousness, reason, reflection, and so on" (Wolfe xxv).

If we extend this posthumanist analysis, the difference between voluntary and involuntary physiological events—and their correlation with intangible concepts, such as the self—is also revealed to be a productive construction of humanism. Hayles explores the deconstruction of this binary in *How We Became Posthuman,* noting that "mastery through the exercise of autonomous will is merely the story consciousness tells itself to explain results that actually come about through chaotic dynamics and emergent structures" (Hayles 288). Over and over, Hayles returns to the conscious mind and/or consciousness as an accident, a side effect of our humanistsic construct. This paradigm collapses the key difference (for graphology and the neurosciences) between conscious and unconscious control, illustrating Hayle's point that the conscious mind may simply be a side effect and/or an accident. If this is the case, then technologies aimed at recording the battle between conscious and unconscious *mind* or between voluntary and involuntary bodily events do not reveal a/the self, but our own constructs concerning the human. Perhaps they reveal the "chaos," but they certainly don't reveal the core.

In this sense, and in the scope of this essay, the posthuman should not be seen as coming after (post) the human, but being developed in tandem with it. As Wolfe conceptualizes it, the posthuman

> comes before and after humanism: before in the sense that it names the embodiment and embeddedness of the human being in not just its biological but also its technological world . . . But it comes after in the sense that posthumanism names a historical moment in which the decentering of the human by its imbrications in technical, medical, informatics, and economic networks is increasingly impossible to ignore, a historical development that points toward the necessity of new theoretical paradigms. (Wolfe xv-xvi)

We might well read the phrase "handwriting is brainwriting" as an extension, both historically and theoretically, of the human's embeddedness in the biological and the technological. Read through this lens, handwriting and brainwriting reveal the remains of humanism—the constructs that could be decentered by the posthuman, that could reveal the imbrications of the human in multiple, historical and contemporary networks.

By way of conclusion, I would like to return very briefly to Joe Dumit's question: "Why is it that when we find a reading correspondence in the brain we are satisfied that we are in the right place?"(Dumit 20). Perhaps it is because *brainhood* infiltrated our cultural understandings of the self long before neuroscience. Perhaps it is because the body has always already been a site for selfhood. Perhaps it is because the remains of humanism haunt current constructions of diagnostic technologies. So, the phrase "handwriting is brainwriting" is always already a construction of brain-centrism. Yet, as Beyerstein argues, "no educated person seriously doubts that handwriting is controlled by the brain, but so are coughing, yawning, spitting and vomiting. Why, then, should writing deserve special status as a putative window on character and talent?" (Beyerstein 401). The answer may simply be: if not writing, then what? . . . the diaphragm is always an option.

Notes

1. I discuss both the autonomic nervous system and EEG at length in *The Lying Brain* (2011); of particular interest concerning EEGs is its inventor's hopes for the technique: in measuring electrical activity in the brain, Hans Berger sought to create a "Hirnschpiel" or brain mirror. For further discussion of Berger and his experiments, see David Millet, 2001; Cornelius Borck, 2001; and Pierre Gloor, 1994.

2. The original German sentence in its entirety is "Nichtsdestoweniger läfst sich vom Schriebcentrum, als des morphologischen Substrats der Schreibbewegung im Gehirn, zweierlei mit der hochsten Wahrscheinlichkeit aussagen" (Preyer 1895, 38).

3. The purpose of this paper is not to trace the genealogy of the phrase "handwriting is brainwriting," but, instead, to trace the implications of this phrase for graphology. I take up the question of genealogy in a longer project.

4. Theorizing the emergent neurodisciplines has taken several forms thus far. Alongside our collection (Littlefield and Johnson 2012) is the work of *Critical Neuroscience* (by Suparna Choudhury, Max Stadler and Jan Slaby among others); individual disciplines have also self-reflexively begun work in this area:

the best examples include neuroeconomics and sociology (especially Pickersgill and van Kleuen *Sociological Reflections on the Neurosciences*, 2011).

5. We consider these new (sub)disciplines to be "transdisciplinary" because each is creating new knowledge at the site of the merger. As in the case of "team science," theorized by Daniel Stokal et al., each neurodiscipline "synthesizes and extends discipline-specific theories, concepts, methods, or all three to create new models and language to address a common research problem" (Stokals et al. S79).

Works Cited

Anonymous. "Your Character Is Indicated by Every Breath." *Popular Science* 99 (Oct. 1921): 28 Print.
Almy, Gladys. "Graphology Held Well Accredited." *New York Times* 23 Sept. 1934: E5. Print.
"As a Man Breathes, So He Is" *New York Times* 13 July 1921: E4. Print.
Beaulieu, Anne. *The Space Inside the Skull: Digital Representations, Brain mapping, and Cognitive Neuroscience in the Decade of the Brain*. Diss. University of Amsterdam, 2000. The Netherlands. Print.
—. "Images Are Not the (Only) Truth: Brain Mapping, Visual Imaging, and Iconoclasm." *Science, Technology and Human Values* 27.1 (2002): 53–86. Print.
Beyerstein, Barry. "Handwriting is Brainwriting, So What?" *The Write Stuff: Evaluations of Graphology—The Study of Handwriting Analysis*. Ed. Barry Beyerstein and Dale Beyerstein. Buffalo: Prometheus Books, 1992. Print.
Burwood, Stephen. "Are We Our Brains?" *Philosophical Investigations* 32.2 (2009): 113–33. Print.
Cartwright, Lisa. *Screening the Body: Tracing Medicine's Visual Culture*. Minneapolis: U of Minnesota P, 1995. Print.
Clarke, Bruce and Linda Henderson, eds. *From Energy to Information: Representation in Science and Art, Technology and Literature*. Palo Alto: Stanford UP, 2004. Print.
Crumbaugh, James. "Graphoanalytic Cues." *The Write Stuff: Evaluations of Graphology—The Study of Handwriting Analysis*. Ed. Barry Beyerstein and Dale Beyerstein. Buffalo: Prometheus Books, 1992. Print.
Dastin, Lorraine and Peter Galison. "The Image of Objectivity." *Representations* 40 (1992): 81–128. Print.
—. *Objectivity*. Newton: Zone Books, 2007. Print.
Downey, June. "Handwriting Disguise." *Journal of Applied Psychology* 1.4 (1917): 368–79. Print.
—. *Graphology and the Psychology of Handwriting*. Baltimore: Warwick & York, Inc., 1919.

Dror, Otniel. "The Scientific Image of Emotion: Experience and Technologies of Inscription." *Configurations* 7.3 (1999): 355–401. Print.

Dumit, Joseph. *Picturing Personhood: Brainscans and Biomedical Identity*. Princeton: Princeton UP, 2003. Print.

Exner, Sigmund. *Untersuchungen uber die Lokalisation der Funktionen in der Grosshirnrinde des Menschen*. Vienna: Wilhelm Braumuller, 1881. Print.

Fontana, P et al. "Handwriting as a Gauge of Cognitive Status: A Novel Forensic Tool for Posthumous Evaluation of Testamentary Capacity." *Neuological Science* 29.4 (2008): 257–61. Print.

Fukuyama, Francis. *Our Posthuman Future: Consequences of the Biotechnology Revolution*. New York: Picador, 2002. Print.

Gazzaniga, Michael. *The Ethical Brain*. Chicago: U of Chicago P, 2003.

"Graphologist Says Brain Does Writing." *New York Times* 20 Nov 1923: 2. Print.

Halyes, Katherine. *How We Became Posthuman: Virtual Bodies in Cybernetics, Literature, and Informatics*. Chicago: U of Chicago P, 1999. Print.

Haraway, Donna. "Cyborg Manifesto: Science, Technology, and Socialist-Feminism in the Late Twentieth Century." *Simians, Cyborgs and Women: The Reinvention of Nature*. New York: Routledge, 1991. 149–81. Print.

"Interview/Dialogue with Albert Brgnamm and N. Katharine Hayles on Humans and Machines" University of Chicago Press, 1999. Web. 1 Nov. 2014.

Johnson, Jenell, and Melissa M. Littlefield. "Lost in Translation: Popular Neuroscience and the Emergent Neurodisciplines." *Advances in Medical Sociology: Sociological Reflections on the Neurosciences* 13 (2011): 279–97. Print.

Joyce, Kelly. *Magnetic Appeal: MRI and the Myth of Transparency*. Ithaca: Cornell UP, 2008. Print.

"Judging a Job Seeker by the Cross of His 'T.'" *New York Times* 30 Jan 1980: C16. Print.

Katanoda, Kota, Kohki Yoshikawa, and Morihiro Sugishita. "A Functional MRI Study on the Neural Substrates for Writing." *Human Brain Mapping* 13 (2001): 34–42. Print.

Levitt, Irene. *Brainwriting: See Inside Your Own Mind and Others' with Handwriting Analysis*. Richmond: The Oaklea Press, 2004. Print.

Littlefield, Melissa M. "Constructing the Organ of Deceit: The Rhetoric of fMRI Lie Detection and Brain Fingerprinting in Post-9/11 America." *Science, Technology and Human Values* 34.3 (2009): 365–392. print.

—. *The Lying Brain: Lie Detection in Science and Science Fiction*. Ann Arbor: University of Michigan Press, 2011. Print.

Littlefield, Melissa M., and Jenell Johnson. *The Neuroscientific Turn: Transdisciplinarity in the Age of the Brain*. Ann Arbor: U of Michigan P, 2012. Print.

Lynch, Zack and Byron Larson. *The Neurorevolution: How Brain Science is Changing Our World*. New York: St Martin's, 2009. print.

Meyer, Jerome. *Mind Your Ps and Qs*. New York: Simon and Schuster, 1927. Print.
Nikell, Joe. "A Brief history of Graphology." *The Write Stuff: Evaluations of Graphology—The Study of Handwriting Analysis*. Ed. Barry Beyerstein and Dale Beyerstein. Buffalo: Prometheus Books, 1992. Print.
Pickersgill, Martyn, Sarah Cunningham-Burley, and Paul Martin. "Constituting Neurologic Subjects: Neuroscience, Subjectivity and the Mundane Significance of the Brain" *Subjectivity* 4 (2011): 346–65. Print.
Pophal, Rudolf. *Die Handschrift als Gehirnschrift*. Rudolstadt, Greifenverlag, 1949. Print.
Preyer, Wilhelm. *Zur Psychologie des Schreibens [The Psychology of Writing]*. 1895. Print.
"Radioscopic Examination of Mind as Well as Body." *Popular Mechanics* Aug 1921: 165. Print.
Racine, Eric, Sarah Waldman, Jarett Rosenburg, and Judy Illes. "Contemporary Neuroscience in the Media." *Social Science and Medicine* 71.4 (2010): 725–33. Print.
Roman, Klara, G. *Encyclopedia of the Written Word: A Lexicon for Graphology and Other Aspects of Writing*. New York: Frederick Ungar, 1968. Print.
—. *Handwriting: A Key to Personality*. New York: Pantheon Books, 1952. Print.
Rose, Nikolas. *The Politics of Life Itself: Biomedicine, Power and Subjectivity in the Twenty-first Century*. Princeton: Princeton UP, 2006. Print.
Spohn, Julie L. "Legal Implications of Graphology" *Washington University Law Review* 75.3 (1997): 1307–1333. Print.
"The Newest Rage." *New York Times* 18 Sept. 1927: BR20. Print.
Thornton, Tamara Plakins. *Handwriting in America: A Cultural History*. New Haven: Yale UP, 1996. Print.
Van Dijk, Jose. *The Transparent Body: A Cultural Analysis of Medical Imaging*. Seattle: U of Washington P, 2005. Print.
Vidal, Fernando. "Brainhood: Anthropological Figure of Modernity." *History of the Human Sciences* 22.1 (2009): 5–36. Print.
Wilson, Elizabeth. *Neural Geographies: feminism and the Microstructure of Cognition*. London and New York: Routledge, 1998. Print.
Wolfe, Cary. *What is Posthumanism?* Minneapolis: University of Minnesota Press, 2010. Print.

11 I Am Spam; A Posthuman Approach to Writer's Block

Kyle Jensen

> *The task is to focus on the noise, the interference, not just as an engineering element to be reduced but as a key trait within the network societies of digital culture, a trace to be followed, a tendency to be thought with.*
>
> —Jussi Parikka

One would be hard pressed to find a concept in writing studies that is more humanistically oriented than *writer's block*. With few exceptions, the concept is defined as a "psychophysical obstacle to progress within the writing process" that human writers must overcome if they hope to produce meaningful compositions (Hjortshoj 36).[1] Given these definitional parameters, it is not surprising that the prevailing purpose of writer's block research is to theorize its symptoms in order to cure them "in the interest of current writing theory and pedagogy" (Worsham 95). As rigid rules and inflexible plans give way to more pliant heuristics, instructors may take comfort in the fact that even the most pernicious writing maladies can be treated with the proper pedagogical method.[2]

Although compelling in their narrative presentations, writer's block research has offered little to writing studies as a whole. Perhaps the reason for this scant offering is that psychophysical blocking is so intimately tied to individual circumstance that it resists general abstraction. However, a closer look reveals that this research struggles in the context of contemporary writing research because it fails to imagine the operations of writing outside of human subjects. By assuming that only humans can write and thereby assuming that only human writers can become blocked, this research consigns the concept of writer's block to an unnecessarily limited set of possible inquiries. Consequently, it forecloses opportunities to explore how the concept might be reimagined in the context of a posthuman theoretical program that understands writing in more expansive terms.[3]

Reimagining writer's block from a posthuman perspective will involve more than decentering the current focus on human subjects. As Cary Wolfe explains, this work must also confront "what thought has to become" in the face of humanism's limitations (xvi). Crucial to this process is demonstrating how humanism's "aspirations are undercut by the philosophical and ethical frameworks used to conceptualize them" (xvi). Once established, scholars may then begin to envision writer's block in terms that confront the complexities of both human and non-human writing.

To approach these complexities, I define writer's block as an effect of overlapping psychic and social systems focused on helping human writers produce meaningful discourse in the face of impending information overload.[4] By treating human subjects as elements within these overlapping systems, this definition emphasizes their relation to non-human elements such as algorithms that not only constitute human writers through their respective writing practices, but maintain the systems in which each element functions. The concept of systems maintenance should be understood in the terms of Niklas Luhmann's second-order systems theory, which emphasizes self-referential closure as a condition of differentiation. According to Luhmann, self-referential closure involves a selective reduction of complexity that distinguishes a system from its environment so that the system may adapt to changing environmental pressures through self-observation. Insofar as this systems/environment distinction holds, systems can create openness from closure as their increased selectivity (instigated by a perceived environmental threat) broadens environmental contacts and thereby produces more complex differentiations.[5]

Describing the operational logics of second-order systems is accomplished through the method of functional analysis. As Luhmann explains, this observational approach "regulates and specifies the conditions under which differences make a difference" (53). Consequently, functional analysis is concerned with the identification of problems because problems disclose how systems subject "everything that normally happens in the processing of information (namely, the scanning of differences) to specific conditions and thereby gives it determinate form" (52). Locating the presence of causal explanations is crucial to this process because they establish the basis for comparing how a system's responses to difference "open up what lies at hand for a sidelong glance at other possibilities" (54). By broadening and limiting the system's possible responses to difference, scholars may "ascertain relations among relations" by "relat[ing] this [specific solution] to other problem solutions" (54). The identification of functional equivalence subsequently allows scholars to describe the underpinning logics of systems evolution with more precision.[6]

While it is tempting to analyze writer's block as an ongoing threat to the systemic closure of post-secondary writing instruction, I focus instead on the junk of email systems correspondence: spam. At first glance, this focus will seem odd given that spam typically manifests as bulk advertisements for pornography, prescription medication, and penis enlargement devices. However, spam serves as a representative anecdote because it brings into high tension the complexities of non-human writing that may expand both writer's block research and writing studies. In facilitating this research, spam ceases to be the abject filth that populates our virtual dustbins by becoming "the prime agent of conjunction, of joining together" that exposes writing studies to a new posthuman terrain (Bardini 13).

Before launching into this argument it is important to recognize that the concept of *posthumanism* may be defined in a variety of ways. Whatever those definitions may be, Rosi Braidotti crystallizes their starting point when she claims "Posthumanism is the historical moment that marks the end of the opposition between Humanism and anti-humanism and traces a different discursive framework, looking more affirmatively towards new alternatives" (37). The stress in this passage should fall on *affirmatively* because it punctuates what I believe to be one of posthumanism's principal advantages. Rather than abandon or directly oppose the conceptual terminologies that define the humanist project, a posthumanist approach affirms the value of such concepts by repeating them in alternative theoretical contexts. These contexts focus, most notably, on the non-human actors who expose the limits of humanism's anthropocentric tendencies and spur revision. Of course, these revisions emanate from the vibrancy of non-human actors whose existence inspires broad leaps of the imagination.

Everyday Abjects

Although researchers routinely note the difficulty of assigning definitional parameters to spam, it is generally characterized as an unsolicited form of electronic messaging sent in bulk for commercial purposes (Cormack 8). But as the Controlling the Assault of Non-Solicited Pornography and Marketing Act (CAN-SPAM Act) explains, the distinction between spam and 'legitimate' commercial bulk advertising is a tenuous one. The hard line that many would use to separate these practices is compromised by spam's ability to boost consumer purchasing. In a 2003 editorial for *Wired* magazine, for example, Brian McWilliams reports that an "order log left exposed at *one* [spam company's] websites revealed that, over a four-week period, some 6,000 people responded to e-mail ads and placed orders for the company's [penis enlargement] herbal supplement. Most customers ordered two bottles of the pills at a price of $50 per bottle" (1).[7] If, as conservative estimates suggest, "40% of e-mail traffic is spam," then "some 12.4 billion spam mails are being sent daily" (Parrika and Sampson 3).[8] Even if a fraction of these advertisements are persuasive to consumers, spammers stand to make a considerable profit.[9]

The cost of spam is rarely figured in terms of consumer purchasing, however. Much more prevalent are studies that calculate the economic harm resulting from spam's overwhelming capacities. In many cases, researchers divide this damage into two categories: direct and indirect (Schryen 24). Direct economic harm refers to the staffing costs, network infrastructure costs, downloading costs, and losses of productivity that result from the threat of spam overload (both on the company and user-side). By contrast, indirect costs refer to the company's loss of reputation, the cost of legal fees, the collateral effects of fraud, and the development of anti-spam marketing programs. Whether the emphasis falls on direct or indirect economic harm, the resounding conclusion is that researchers must eradicate or at least reduce the payload of spam advertisements in order to protect companies and users from being overwhelmed to the point of incapacity.[10]

In the process of advancing this conclusion, researchers routinely note that the infrastructure of e-mail systems was not "designed to tackle security issues like authentication, integrity, secrecy, and a mass of unsolicited emails" (Schryen 29). Spammers are therefore cast as exploitative opportunists who have destroyed a "trustworthy" public resource in a manner analogous to "air pollution, overfishing, and roadside litter" (McWilliams xii). Because initial interventions fostered an increase in the complexity of spamming methods, researchers have been forced to develop a series of "laws and regulations, organizational approaches implementing different kinds of cooperation, behavioral measures, economic measures, and technological measures" (Schryen 43). Consequently, anti-spam measures have forged an increasingly intricate social system whose writing practices place our field's researchers on the threshold of a posthuman theoretical terrain.

Observing the complexity of these writing practices requires that a distinction be drawn between spammers and spam. Spammers are humans who commission or produce programs that streamline the process of bulk e-mail messaging. By contrast, spam is an email message that has been designated as such by an authentication-based filtering mechanism. In early spam research, emphasis was placed on identifying spammers because exposing their identity was commensurate with shutting down their operation. As an anti-spam measure, this approach was moderately successful because the spamming process hinged on the distribution of email addresses via CD-ROM. In current research, however, anti-spam measures focus on spam detection because spammers no longer constitute the greatest threat to the email system's closure. Instead, spam-bots have become the greatest threat because, through their writing practices, they can work independently of humans to increase the payload of spam messaging.

A relatively new invention, spam-bots are algorithmic programs that overtake the operations of a computer in order to increase the payload of spam emails. They are often disseminated through email messages that invite users to click on a "malicious" link or attachment. Once downloaded, the spam-bot "changes the system registry and system files, and makes a series of system/library calls which create network connections or disable antivirus programs" (Jeong et. al 10). By establishing this network connection, spam-bots may transfer information to and receive commands from a human user (spammer) through Internet Chat Relay (IRC) servers. Of course, the ability to send user information through IRC servers requires that spam-bots first collect it. In many instances, they will do so by studying the user's Internet browsing history or keystroke patterns.

After collecting and sending this information, spam-bots may receive alternative commands from human users to collect more information, send more spam emails, or change their tendencies to prevent detection. What distinguishes spam-bots from past approaches, then, is their ability to decentralize the distribution of spam email and thereby make it difficult for anti-spam measures to shut down the operation. Whereas early spamming practices were easier to track down because the email distribution could be traced to a central location, spam-bots make detection difficult because they create and participate in a much larger network whose operations can be reverse engineered only after the network has been firmly established.

While the common impulse has been to treat spam-bots as a parasitic threat to the longstanding health of email systems, this impulse misses an opportunity to explore how they function as writers. Similar to human writers, spam-bots appropriate the trajectory of existing discourses in a manner that may challenge prevailing assumptions about how such discourses should be used. They do so by rewriting a computer system's registry and files so that they may identify and collect inscripted patterns valuable to its project. Once collected, these patterns enable spam-bots to initiate more efficient and inventive applications of their logic. The identification of these patterns is guided by an observational search for relevant information. Insofar as spam-bots have the capacity to filter information according to relevance, they have the capacity to interpret discourses according to specific goals. In the process of identifying relevant patterns, spam-bots tag and redistribute such discourses in a manner that is functionally distinct from its previous iteration. A set of alphanumeric keystrokes that connect users on a social networking website, for example, may be appropriated to provide a threshold for extending the spam-bot network. The extension of such networks relies on the spam-bot's capacity to inscribe new directions in a computer's system that enables functionally different forms of networked communication. Thus, similar to human writers, spam-bots cannot write in isolation.

A spam-bot's inability to write in isolation is punctuated by its reliance on established grammars that enable it to carry out intelligible actions. To operate within email systems, for example, spam bots must contain an IP address in their hard code that locates them in relation to other computer systems (Jeong et. al 10). In the email message proper, spam-bots must construct and distribute grammatically complex and topically dense messages in order to avoid detection from current filtering mechanisms (Lopes et. al). A spam-bot's reliance on established grammars should not, however, be construed as an inability to catalyze grammatical evolution. In order to avoid detection, spam-bots have modified IRC protocols by becoming capable of receiving voiced instructions. Thus, a spammer may now speak directly to the spam-bot network and thereby reduce the amount of traces that would make it easier to identify the network's architecture. With respect to the spam email's content, these messages have manipulated grammatical language to the point where they may not only be treated as linguistically distinct, but theorized as "the heirs of the poetry of Tristan Tzara or Hugo Ball" (Galloway and Thacker 147; see also Parikka and Sampson 2).

Therefore, just as human inscriptions defer meaning through the play of differences, the traces initiated by a spam-bot cannot totalize the meaning of the patterns it identifies and repeats.[11] But, spam-bots can revise the prior inscription in a manner that increases the internal complexity of email systems. Most commonly, these traces help email security specialists track down the operations of the spam-bot network with the goal of shutting it down. However, they can also help legislators develop a more precise definition of spam so that anti-spam measures may be more effective in preventing the development of spam-bot networks. At the very least, they help computer scientists generate increasingly sophisticated machine learning technologies and insofar as they accomplish that task, they fuel economic development centered on email systems security.

Perhaps less predictably, spam creates the conditions for initiating a searching revaluation of writer's block that exposes the field to the possibility that writers can be otherwise than human. A key component to this argument is that just as spam-bot algorithms may observe inscribed patterns, revise them for alternative purposes, and network with human and non-human programs, so too may spam filtering mechanisms for the purposes of blocking spam messages. Following the logics of genetic algorithms, many spam-filtering mechanisms "'evolve' solutions to complex problems by generating 'populations' of possible solutions" (Helmreich 138; see also Mohammed and Zitar). They approach this work by extracting word frequencies from the subject and body of all email messages and encoding them into a vector that measures the number of occurrences of specified variables (Lopes et. al 9366). These filter outputs can then be used "as the inputs of another (meta-level) learner" which is dynamically trained to assign different weights to the filters over time. Others mechanisms approach this work by reviewing sender reputation (blacklists) and engaging a context-specific analysis of the email. Either way, the filtering mechanisms have set a path toward human-independent algorithms that learn from experience, share information with other filtering mechanisms, evolve according to that networked sharing, build thesauruses that account for the complexity of language variation, and generate approaches that respond to the evolutionary threats of spambots to construct an increasingly complex email system.

When studying the writing practices of algorithms one must remember that although they "can deal with contingencies . . . they must be finite and articulated in the grammar of the processor so that they may be parsed effectively" (Thacker and Galloway 113). Recognizing this point is tantamount to accounting for the algorithm's "mise-en-écriture," whether it appears on "punch cards used to parse U.S. census data" or on the semiconductor memory chips of digital computers (113). By focusing on the materialization of algorithm-based anti-spam measures and spam technologies, one may "learn from them what the collective existence has become in their hands, which methods they have elaborated to make it fit together, which accounts could best define the new associations that they have been forced to establish" in their effort to respond to system-specific problems (Latour 12). Accordingly, they may begin to serve not "as a stable object or a set of mathematically determined, prescribed routines, but as the emergent field of critical software studies is proposing . . . a process that reaches outside the computer and folds as part of the digital architectures, networks, social, and political agendas" (Parrika and Sampson 8).

THE AUTHENTICITY FUNCTION

Undertaking this form of research requires one to trace the limits of the prevailing emphasis on email authentication. Although this emphasis has enabled email systems to remain closed to environmental threats and has thereby facilitated an increase in the system's complexity vis á vis self-reference, it obfuscates the complexity of the "inauthentic" artifact's operations by characterizing it as abject. Foucault outlines the stakes of this logic when he explains how differentiating "the false (the simulators, the 'so-called') from the authentic (the unadulterated and pure)" leads to the production of "a model that exists so forcefully that in its presence the sham vanity of the false copy is immediately reduced to nonexistence" ("Theatricum" 167). Once reduced to nonexistence, the false copy can be ushered quickly off stage.

One needn't venture far into anti-spam research to discover that the emphasis on gauging an email's authenticity is, in fact, a way of differentiating the human from the non-human. Traces of this humanistic imperative can be found in nearly every anti-spam artifact, but is perhaps most bluntly encountered in Clive Thompson's essay "Slaves to Our Machines" in which he reports that when "*Yahoo!* wanted to block porn spambots from obtaining free email accounts. It created a brilliant but simple reverse Turing test: To get an account, you have to identify a randomly generated word that's been slightly stretched and distorted. This proves you're a human, not a robot." Tracing the limits of this human/nonhuman binary, or, at minimum, acknowledging its instability in the context of anti-spam filtering mechanisms should complicate the will to abjection and motivate more in-depth studies of spam-bot technologies. After all, many anti-spam filtering mechanisms are modeled on the "cognitive capabilities of the immune system" and therefore punctuate the symbiotic relationship between human and machine (Guzella 215). However, the unproblematized will to differentiate "*self* from *non-self* and ultimately suppress the threshold point of a viral epidemic" suggests this blurring between human and machine is not a self-conscious irony, but an anthropomorphic tendency that has become naturalized to the point of mystification (Parikka and Sampson 13).

While the human/non-human mystification requires critical attention, the work of disarticulation must begin with the authentic/inauthentic binary. Beginning here allows one to confront the limits of humanistic imperatives while simultaneously exposing the complexity of filter-based algorithmic writing that facilitates writer's block. To facilitate this work, I advance the concept *the authenticity function*. The root source for this concept is, of course, Michel Foucault's essay "What is an Author"; however, the authenticity function shares with this essay more than a source inspiration. A close reading of Foucault's argument indicates that his landmark concept *the author function* is an effect of the authenticity function insofar as the former is established through the evaluative conditions established by the latter. K.K. Ruthven makes this point compellingly when he argues, "To install authenticity as a foundational value is to legitimise [sic] 'authentication' as a disciplinary practice, particularly as it relates to questions of authorial attribution and the establishment of 'correct' texts" (160). Thus, "to construct the rational entity we can an author" and in so doing "characterize the existence, circulation, and operation of certain discourses within society" one must first develop a set of procedures that attest "to the 'reliability' of the evidence" (Foucault, "What" 127, 124, 126).

Within the context of Foucault's essay, this point becomes evident by studying how the concept of *authenticity* iterates in his discussion of the author function. For example, when explaining how names establish particular relationships among texts, Foucault argues, "Neither Hermes nor Hippocrates existed in the sense that we can say Balzac existed, but the fact that a number of texts were attached to a single name implies that relationships of homogeneity, filiation, reciprocal explanation, authentification, or of common utilization were established among them" (123). Later, when explaining that the author function is not a universal phenomenon, he argues that when "those texts which we now call 'literary' . . . were accepted, circulated, and valorized without any question about the identity of their author. Their anonymity was ignored because their real or supposed age was a sufficient guarantee of their authenticity" (125). Further on, when explaining that scientific texts dispensed with the name of the author yet remained committed to the process of establishing authenticity, Foucault writes, "Authentification no longer required reference to the individual who had produced them" (126). Finally, noting the congruities between Christian exegesis and modern criticism, Foucault writes, "even while Saint Jerome's four principles of authenticity might seem largely inadequate to modern critics, they, nevertheless, define the critical modalities now used to display the function of the author" (129).

The concept of *the authenticity function*, then, highlights the procedures by which researchers gauge the provenance of a textual artifact for the purposes of securing the system in question. Keeping Foucault's historical focus, this concept emphasizes that such procedures are implemented to determine the artifact's authorship while noting that the concept of *authorship* may or may not be attributed to a single name such as Shakespeare or Melville. This point is crucial once the question of authentication navigates outside of disciplines such as literary studies. Irrespective of the definition of authorship in place, these procedures operate according to the claim that authenticity is an immanent condition of textuality. Insofar as these procedures scientifically measure (or produce) the authenticity of the textual artifact, they help researchers "avoid confronting the specific event that makes [the work] possible and, in subtle ways, continues to preserve the existence of the author" (119). Therefore, the purpose of the authenticity function is to help researchers confront how a preoccupation with authenticity "sustains the privileges of the author through the safeguard of the a priori" (120). By confronting how this authentication process is accomplished procedurally for the purposes of sustaining the system in question, scholars may reorient their study of non-human writing by focusing on the functional conditions that allow systems to differentiate the self from non-self.

Because authentication procedures maintain the social systems that give them form, they necessarily identify environmental threats that increase their internal complexity. In literary studies, the environmental threat to systemic closure is literary forgery; however, as Foucault notes in his discussion of the author function, threats may also include marginalia such as "a reminder of an appointment, an address, or a laundry bill" (118). In some instances, these traces may prove indispensible for the authentication of a creative work, in which case they would be marked as a part of the stemma of the work's revision history. If these traces fail to coach a new appreciation for the complexity of the artistic work, however, they will be "disparaged as [the artistic work's] bogus Other" (Ruthven 3). On the basis of the distinction made available by the authenticity function, the system of literary studies may therefore practice a "cultural eugenics designed to eliminate the dreck" (3).

The process of "eliminating the dreck" is not unique to literary studies, of course. As Guido Schryen discusses in *Anti-Spam Measures,* email systems implement the authenticity function to determine legitimate email messages from spam through an increasingly sophisticated set of scientific procedures. Although these filtering mechanisms are hardly unified in their approach, they are all designed to differentiate legitimate email from spam. While any number of them may prove helpful for examining the limits of the *a priori* definition of authenticity that sustains this approach, the naïve Bayesian model proves to be most instructive.

As Guzella and Caminhas explain, the Bayesian model implements an algorithm that determines the probability of an email's authenticity on the basis of common phrases appearing in previously identified spam messages. For example, Bayesian filters measure terminological pairings such as "selected medication" and "buy online" by comparing them to an established and, in some cases, evolving data set. To arrive at such pairings, these filters extend a complex apparatus for preparing the content for analysis. First, the filters undertake a process of tokenization, which involves extracting the words from the body of the email message. Next, the filters initiate the process of lemmatization, which reduces extracted words to their root form. After this reduction, the filters engage in stop-word removal to eliminate common words that appear in all email messages. Finally, the filters extend a process of representation, which involves the conversion of the remaining word sets to a specific format that the algorithm can process.

The process of representation is crucial not only for filtering mechanisms, but also for the purposes of confronting the authenticity function of email systems. The absence of representation would prevent filters from responding to the ongoing threat of spam because there would be no data set to measure the occurrence and/or frequency of selected terms. From a second-order systems standpoint, then, representation constitutes the threshold upon which email systems can remain closed to evolving environmental threats because it serves as the principle apparatus of differentiation. Accordingly, representation is more accurately characterized as the *problem* of representation as the ongoing problem of representing complex data sets creates the conditions for self-referential closure.

Once characterized as a self-referential problem of systems maintenance, representation can be treated as an integral component in the ongoing development of the email system's authenticity function. Insofar as an email's authenticity is evaluated according to the evolutionary patterns of spam messaging, it may become increasingly selective in how it differentiates the authentic from inauthentic. For example, in their review of machine learning approaches to spam filtering, Guzella and Caminhas discuss targeted revisions to the Bayesian filtering model, noting how researchers have begun to apply "a naïve Bayes classifier based on word n-grams, using only some of the first words to reduce the classification time" (10212). By reducing classification time, researchers increased the filter's speed while more effectively differentiating spam from legitimate email. Although this model proved to be more accurate, it was not cost effective because of its computational demands. Thus, researchers began developing hardware servers that enabled filters to be more accurate without bogging down the overall computational speed of email systems.

In this example, the problem of determining an email's authenticity led to an increasingly selective form of filtering that self-referentially produced more complex differentiations within the email system. Whereas traditional naïve Bayesian filtering models examine the entire term and measure it according to a much larger data set, this revision measured pieces of key terms to develop a probabilistic determination of the email's authenticity on a singular basis. Although this approach led to an overall increase in spam detection, it simultaneously created a problem of computational efficiency for email systems performance. Insofar as this problem led to an even more selective approach to optimizing the efficiency of email systems (producing new server technologies that can handle more selective forms of filtering), it constitutes an instance of self-referentiatlity that led to an even more complex email system.

In the context of the authenticity function, these procedures demonstrate that authenticity is not immanent to textuality, but manufactured through increasingly selective filtering practices designed to self-referentially maintain system/environment distinctions. By implication, the email's authorship is installed retroactively as the email content accords with or deviates from the representational standards established through prior analysis. Crucial to the ongoing evolution of email systems is the misidentification of legitimate email because it presents elements with the problem of increasing selectivity and differentiation. In this context, adequate emphasis should be placed on the term *elements* because it underscores the importance of algorithmic writing practices in maintaining email systems. While human subjects play a role in such maintenance (hence, the definition of writer's block as an effect of overlapping social and psychic systems), overemphasizing their value risks capitulation to *a priori* distinctions that diminish the writing capacities of filtering mechanisms. If the current trajectory of email systems filtering holds, this risk will consign the study of writer's block to its current status, as it will be unable to imagine how algorithms search out and evaluate the practices of other algorithms and thereby create the conditions for human writers to produce meaningful compositions according to the familiar practices of computer-based writing.

Rather than dismiss email authentication as unnecessarily hampered by the humanistic imperatives for systems control, the authenticity function emphasizes how selective differentiation evolves new procedures for differentiating the authentic from the inauthentic. Consequently, it pays close attention to the invention of alternative procedures that allow email systems to become even more selective in their self-referentiatlity. In emphasizing the production of belief in the distinction between authenticity and inauthenticity, the authenticity function complicates *a priori* distinctions that understand authenticity and authorship only in terms of what is *human*. Accordingly, it emphasizes how the human writing within email systems is an effect of the authenticating procedures that characterize systems maintenance.

In advancing these emphases, the authenticity function therefore creates a new terrain for writer's block research. Following its lead, writer's block research may attend to authentication practices that evolve solutions to the problems of systems maintenance. In contrast to previous approaches, this research can be characterized by its orientation to functional analysis rather than resolving the problem of writer's block through instructional intervention. Despite this key difference, this posthuman approach to writer's block will not abandon the problems that are associated with it, but rather treat identified problems as an opportunity to examine how a system's complexity emerges through writing from a self-referential closure to environmental threats.

Once Freed from Representation

To extend the implications of this approach to writer's block and, in the process, further develop a posthuman approach to Writing Studies, scholars should consider three potential trajectories for research. First, Writing Studies should develop a more rigorous engagement with writing practices characterized as abject, as these sites consistently complicate prevailing humanistic assumptions about writing in general. This approach to abject writing practices has a longstanding history in rhetoric and composition studies as scholars such as Rebecca Moore Howard have theorized plagiarism and scholars such as Amy Robillard and Ron Fortune have examined the complexities of literary forgery. However, these studies are often justified by their pedagogical focus. While a posthuman approach to Writing Studies has and should continue to involve pedagogical considerations, the field's longstanding investment in validating research on the basis of its pedagogical application will consign it to a future characterized by humanistic imperatives.

By complicating these imperatives, the algorithmic writing practices of spam-bots and spam-filtering mechanisms will encourage scholars to expand their study of abject writing practices to other abject forms of writing, whether such writing involves other forms of algorithmic filtering or writing diseases such as hypergraphia and hypographia. Perhaps, as Matthew Fuller and Andrew Goffey suggest, this will also involve the development of an "evil media studies" designed to "create a problem of a different order to that of representation and then follow through practically what it entails" (141).[12] Thus, by way of examining how writing "becomes object, in a number of senses: objectified by a range of practices that submit communication processes to the quantificational procedures of programming" or as "an element in the purely objective order of things in themselves, escaping from the complementarity of subject and object and the range of processes we normally think of as mediating between the two," Writing Studies may begin to simulate malignant writing practices or develop an "inattention economy" that exploits the elemental inefficiencies of our current writing economies (142, 143, 152). In undertaking this work, scholars should expand the definitions of prevailing concepts in Writing Studies so as to punctuate what thought has to become in the face posthuman theory's intellectual challenges.

Second, Writing Studies should become more transdisciplinary in its orientation. Speaking to this point in the context of rhetorical studies, Debra Hawhee advocates a form of transdisciplinarity that "simultaneously respects disciplinary knowledge and acknowledges the limitations of working within a single discipline" (3). Although this definition seems like interdisciplinarity writ new, "what distinguishes transdisciplinarity from interdisciplinarity is its effort to suspend—however, temporarily—one's own disciplinary terms in favor of a broad, open, multilevel inquiry" (3). Insofar as it seeks "the limits of knowledge itself," a trandisciplinary approach is more radical in its orientation and serves as a better model for posthuman research. Thus, by suspending one's disciplinary terms in the context of posthuman writing research, our field will be better able to measure what thought has to become in the face of humanism's theoretical and ethical limitations.

Within the context of writer's block research, writing scholars may follow this lead by undertaking a more historically robust engagement with the relationship between authentication and information overload. This pairing places scholars on the cusp of a theoretical terrain where the questions of literary art, human psychology, materialist economics, and cryptography intersect to form new ways of thinking about the complexities of writing (see Ellison). Read in the context of this study, such approaches would network with Sociology, Continental Philosophy, Computer Science, Rhetoric and Composition Studies, and Critical Software Studies (among others), thereby raising new questions and avenues for research.

In advancing this recommendation, I am mindful of claims that Writing Studies needs to develop "a recognizable disciplinary knowledge base" before interdisciplinary or trandisciplinary connections can foster mutual recognition between current disciplines (Johnson 683). While this is a relevant concern, framing the construction of knowledge for the purposes of developing a discernible discipline works against the theoretical reorientation that posthuman theoretical research sponsors. To be clear, I am not suggesting the field abandon its concern with disciplinarity any more than I have encouraged writer's block research to dispense with concerns over human writers, causal explanations, or the identification of problems. What I am suggesting is that if Writing Studies wishes to respond to the challenges of posthuman theoretical research, the question of building a base knowledge for the purposes of securing disciplinary boundaries is a subsidiary concern.

Finally, Writing Studies should more fully examine the writing practices of algorithms. The constraints of this forum have prevented a more comprehensive engagement with the algorithmic writing practices that challenge and maintain email systems; thus, scholars may begin by exploring how emerging spam and anti-spam technologies enrich the study of writer's block. However, a study of writer's block may also include the search-filtering algorithms of google and robot.txt. Speaking to the possibilities of the former example, Eli Pariser notes how google's filtering algorithms are becoming personalized to the point where "Now you get the result that Google's algorithm suggests is best for you in particular—and someone else may see something entirely different" (2). Thus, the study of writer's block may confront how algorithms prevent human subjects from encountering content in its project to become "a tool for soliciting and analyzing our personal data" (6). For Pariser, this form of filtering must be theorized because, unchecked, "it could prevent us from coming into contact with the mind-blowing, preconception-shattering experiences and ideas that change how we think about the world and ourselves" (15). With regard to the latter recommendation, Greg Elmer explains that robot.txt is "a short script inserted into Web code that informs automated search robots not to archive specific information/files from a site" (Elmer 218). Although an informal protocol, this script was used in the Bush White House protocol in 2003 to "confuse and defuse accusations of information control and censorship" in the context of public records on the war in Iraq. According to Elmer, "[a]pproximately half of all White House Web files excluded from search engine indexing included the term 'Iraq,' assuring the story extra attention" (221). Of course, blocking public access to such material has serious implications for studies concerning "technology, publicity, and the writing of history" (221).

Taken together, these recommendations direct Writing Studies toward a broader set of questions that further test the limits of our field's humanistic underpinnings: "'What are the modes of existence of this discourse?' 'Where does it come from; how is it circulated; who controls it?' 'What placements are determined for possible subjects?' and 'Who can fulfill these diverse functions of the subject?'" ("What" 138). In raising these questions, scholars necessarily confront how "writing and printing enforce an experience of the difference that constitutes communication . . . [and] therefore require a more specific reaction by communication to communication than is possible orally" (Luhmann 163). This reaction, as Cary Wolfe argues, is characterized by a commitment to the view that "the trace structure of writing/communication is not limited to the domain of the human and the linguistic alone" (24). In this way, it proceeds as Foucault would have it, with little more than a murmur of indifference asking, "what does it matter who is writing?"

NOTES

1. One recent exception to this rule is Geoffrey V. Carter's "Everything is in Everything," in which he focuses on the transformative role that blank pages can have on Writing Studies research and instruction. As Carter explains, however, his essay undertakes a "lateral" study of writer's block and, consequently, continues to focus on human writers despite its interest in blank pages and backlit monitors.

2. For a comprehensive account of historical approaches to writer's block, see Boice and Leader.

3. For more on this, see Wolfe (3–30).

4. Although writer's block as I define it involves machinic and organismic systems, I emphasize it as a psychic and social system because "unlike machines and organisms . . . [they] can be characterized by their use of meaning" (Luhmann 3). The importance of emphasizing meaning should be apparent in the third section of this essay.

5. Systems create the conditions for differentiation by strategically attributing change to environment. Thus, the notion of environment is always filtered through the system's attributions. This does not mean, however, that systems theory understands environment only in terms of systems attribution. For more on this, see Luhmann 17ff.

6. For more on this, see Bednarz.

7. In a recent *Wired* article, Julie Rehmeyer reports that a hacked spambot network grossed 7,000 dollars per day.

8. In a 2011 article promoting new semantics-aware spam filtering, Igor Santos et. al report that "more than 85% of received emails are spam" (1).

9. For more on the sociopolitical costs of spam, see Moberly.

10. For more on spam's cost to worker productivity, see Chabrow; Roberts; Schryen.

11. For more on this, particularly as it relates to memory, see Chun (137–73).

12. Although he does not cast it as a form of "evil media studies," Stuart Selber discusses the importance of having students create Internet filters, demonstrating that rhetoric and composition studies is already poised to engage is these forms of writing. For more on this, see Selber 66.

Works Cited

Bardinni, Thierry. *Junkware*. Minneapolis: U of Minnesota P, 2011. Print

Bednarz Jr., John. "Functional Method and Phenomenology: The View of Niklas Luhmann." *Human Studies* 7 (1984): 343–362. Print.

Boice, Robert. "Writing Blocks and Tacit Knowledge." *Journal of Higher Education* 64.1 (1993): 19–54. Print.

Braidotti, Rosi. *The Posthuman*. Malden: Polity P, 2013. Print.

Carter, Geoffrey V. "Everything is in Everything: Why Writer's Block Still Matters *for Donald M. Murray*." *Pre/Text* 20.1–4 (1999, printed 2010): 45–73. Print.

Chabrow, Eric. "Spam Costs Keep Rising for Business." *Information Week*. n.p., 8 June 2004. Web. 21 Oct. 2011

Chun, Wendy Hui Kyong. *Programmed Visions: Software and Memory*. Cambridge: MIT P, 2011. Print.

Cormack, Gordon V. *Email Spam Filtering: A Systematic Review*. Hanover: Now Publishers, 2008. Print.

Ellison, Katherine. *Fatal News: Reading and Information Overload in Early Eighteenth-Century Literature*. New York: Routledge, 2006. Print.

Elmer, Greg. "Robots.txt: The Politics of Search Engine Exclusion." *The Spam Book: On Viruses, Porn, and Other Anomalies from the Dark Side of Digital Culture*. Ed. Jussi Parikka, and Toni D. Sampson. Creskill: Hampton P, 2009. 217–27. Print.

Foucault, Michel. "Theatricum Philosophicum." *Language, Counter-Memory, Practice: Selected Essays and Interviews by Michel Foucault*. Ed. Donald F. Bouchard. Ithaca: Cornell UP, 1977. 165–96. Print.

—. "What is an Author?" *Language, Counter-Memory, Practice: Selected Essays and Interviews by Michel Foucault*. Ed. Donald F. Bouchard. Ithaca: Cornell UP, 1977. 113–38. Print.

Fuller, Matthew, and Andrew Goffey. "Toward an Evil Media Studies." *The Spam Book: On Viruses, Porn, and Other Anomalies from the Dark Side of*

Digital Culture. Ed. Jussi Parikka, and Toni D. Sampson. Creskill: Hampton P, 2009. 141–59. Print.

Galloway, Alexander R., and Eugene Thacker. *The Exploit: A Theory of Networks.* Minneapolis: U of Minnesota P, 2007. Print.

Guzella, Thiago S., and Walmir M. Caminhas. " A Review of Machine Learning Approaches to Spam Filtering." *Expert Systems with Applications* 36 (2009): 10206–222. Print.

Hawhee, Debra. *Moving Bodies: Kenneth Burke at the Edges of Language.* Columbia: U of South Carolina P, 2009. Print.

Helmreich, Stefan. *Silicon Second-Nature: Culturing Artificial Life in a Digital World.* Berkeley: U of California P, 1998. Print.

Howard, Rebecca Moore. "Plagiarisms, Authorship, and the Academic Death Penalty." *College English* 57.7 (1995): 788–806. Print.

Hjortshoj, Keith. *Understanding Writing Blocks.* New York: Oxford UP, 2001. Print.

Jeong Ok-Ran, Culyun Kim, Won Kim, and Jungmin So. "Botnets: Threats and Responses." *International Journal of Web Information Systems* 7.1 (2001): 6–17. Print.

Johnson, Robert. "Craft Knowledge: Of Disciplinarity in Writing Studies." *College Composition and Communication* 61.4 (2010): 673–690. Print.

Latour, Bruno. *Reassembling the Social: An Introduction to Actor-Network-Theory.* Oxford: Oxford UP, 2005. Print.

Leader, Zachary. *Writer's Block.* Baltimore: Johns Hopkins UP, 1990. Print.

Lopes, Clotilde, Paulo Cortez, Pedro Sousa, Miguel Rocha, and Miguel Rio. "Symbiotic Filtering for Spam Email Detection." *Expert Systems with Applicaions* 38 (2011): 9385–72. Print.

Luhmann, Niklas. *Social Systems.* Trans. John Bednarz, Jr. Stanford: Stanford UP, 1995. Print.

McWilliams, Brian. *Spam Kings: The Real Story Behind the High-roling Hucksters Pushing Porn, Pills, and @*#?% Enlargements.* Sebastopol, CA: O'Reilly, 2005. Print.

—. "Swollen Orders Show Spam's Allure." *Wired.* 6 Aug. 2003 Web. 19 Oct. 2011.

Moberly, Kevin. "SPAM Wars: The Sooper Sekrit Rhetoric of Frea Speech." *Kairos: A Journal of Rhetoric, Technology, and Pedagogy* 9.2 (2005). Web. 21 Oct. 2011.

Mohammed, Adel Hamdan, and Raed Abu Zitar. "Application of Genetic Optimized Artificial Immune System and Neural Network in Spam Detection." *Applied Soft Computing* 11 (2011): 3827–45. Print.

Parikka, Jussi. *Digital Contagions: A Media Archaeology of Computer Viruses.* New York: Peter Lang, 2007. Print.

Parikka, Jussi, and Toni D. Sampson. "On Anomalous Objects of Digital Culture: An Introduction." *The Spam Book: On Viruses, Porn, and Other Anom-*

alies from the Dark Side of Digital Culture. Ed. Jussi Parikka, and Toni D. Sampson. Creskill: Hampton P, 2009. 1–18. Print.

Pariser, Eli. *The Filter Bubble: What the Internet is Hiding from You.* New York: Penguin P, 2011. Print.

Rehmeyer, Julie. "Equation: How Much Money Do Spammers Rake In?" *Wired* 28 Feb. 2011 Web. 21 Oct. 2011.

Roberts, Paul. "Report: Spam Costs $874 Per Employee Per Year." *InfoWorld.* 1 July 2003. Web. 21 Oct 2011.

Robillard, Amy E., and Ron Fortune. "Toward a New Content for Writing Courses: Literary Forgery, Plagiarism, and the Production of Belief." *JAC* 27.1–2 (2007): 185–210. Print.

Ruthven, K.K. *Faking Literature.* Cambridge: Cambridge UP, 2001. Print

Santos, Igor, Carlos Laorden, Borja Sanz, and Pablo G. Bringhas. "Enhanced Topic-based Vector Space Model for Semantics-aware Spam Filtering." *Expert Systems with Applications* (2011): 1–8. Print.

Schryen, Guido. *Anti-Spam Measures: Analysis and Design.* New York: Springer, 2007. Print.

Selber, Stuart A. *Multiliteracies for a Digital Age.* Carbondale: Southern Illinois UP, 2004. Print.

Thompson, Clay. "Slaves to Our Machines: Welcome to Your Future as a PC Plug-in." *Wired.* 1 Oct. 2002. Web. 19 Oct. 2011.

Wolfe, Cary. *What Is Posthumanism?* Minneapolis: U of Minnesota P, 2009. Print.

"Writing against Writing: The Predicament of *Ecriture Féminine* in Composition Studies." *Contending With Words: Composition and Rhetoric in a Postmodern Age.* Ed. Patricia Harkin and John Schilb. New York: MLA, 1991. 82–104. Print.

12 Cyborg Vision for Cyborg Writing

Kristie S. Fleckenstien

> *I am making an argument for the cyborg as a fiction mapping our social and bodily reality and as an imaginative resource suggesting some very fruitful coupling"*
>
> —Donna J. Haraway, "A Cyborg Manifesto" 153

Donna J. Haraway in "A Cyborg Manifesto" asserts the importance of feminist "cyborg writing" as a key strategy in changing inequitable realities and creating earth-friendly projects and policies. "Writing is pre-eminently the technology of cyborgs," she claims (176), and a central aim of feminist cyborg writing consists of subverting the cold war computer culture where realities and identities are construed out of the paradigm of C^3I: command, control, communications, and information.[1] This framework rests on the illusion of "perfect communication," a common language or the "one code that translates all meaning perfectly" (176), which in turn essentializes and then hierarchalizes identities.[2] Rather than the dangerous dream of a seamless match between code and reality, Haraway defines feminist cyborg writing as "recoding communication and intelligence to subvert command and control" (175) through "playing" on the cusp of the three boundaries: human and animal, organism and machine, physical and non-physical. Cyborg writing moves across boundaries in a transactional flow, creating relationships that challenge the concept of boundaries. This advocacy of cyborg writing is no small matter because, as Haraway explains, "contests for the meaning of writing are a major form of contemporary political struggle," a struggle of special significance for all colonized groups who perceive in writing access to "the power to signify" (175).

But writing in and of itself, even a feminist cyborg writing, constitutes only one strategy for contravening C^3I and the illusion of perfect coding. For Haraway, as crucial as redefining the meaning of writing is redefining the meaning of seeing. "Single vision produces worse illusions than double vision or many-headed monsters," Haraway notes in "A Cyborg Manifesto," underscoring the cyborg's commitment to seeing from the multiple perspectives within which it is embedded (154). She expands on this key point in "Situated Knowledges." Her goal in that essay is to develop both a "critical practice for recognizing our own 'semiotic technologies' for making meanings, *and* a no-nonsense commitment to faithful accounts of the 'real' world" (187, emphasis original). She seeks to effect the emergence of this new epistemology through the reclamation of vision, "the sensory system that has been used to signify a leap out of the marked body and into a conquering gaze from nowhere" (188). Vision, Haraway argues, "can be good for avoiding binary oppositions" (188), but only if that vision is embodied and situated within the materiality of specific positions. By changing how we understand vision—from the "god-trick of seeing everything from nowhere," a kind of seeing that endows "Man and White" with the power to represent others while escaping representation themselves, to an embodied vision that insists on the positionality of any perspective—we gain a "usable, but not an innocent, doctrine of objectivity," Haraway claims (189). However, while privileging a transactive cyborg writing and embodied-embedded seeing, Haraway leaves unexplored the interdependencies between the two, the degree to which writing like a cyborg intersects with seeing like a cyborg and the degree to which change, on whatever level, requires the transactive, embodied, and embedded performances of both.[3]

In this essay, I examine the reciprocity between discourses on vision and writing, particularly the ways in which the epistemology undergirding a theory of vision reinforces the epistemology undergirding a theory of writing. I illustrate that reciprocity in two ways: first, through an examination of the historical intersection between Renaissance perspectivalism and Ramist rhetoric, a union of vision and writing central to the Enlightenment agenda that Haraway seeks to dismantle; and, second, through an examination of the intersection between ecological approaches to vision and composing. I contend that the qualities of embodiment, embeddedness, and transactivity that characterize discourses on vision and writing as ecologies support Haraway's cyborgian agenda by privileging the dynamic relationship among individual bodies, material-social environments, and coding systems as a strategy and site for change. When we see and write ecologically, we see and write through the partiality and particularity of sited bodies, in-corporating the cyborg writing and vision that Haraway advocates.

The value of such an exploration is three-fold, particularly as the reciprocity of vision and writing supports the emergence of posthuman subjectivities and realities. Although cautious of the term *posthuman* (Braidotti 197), Haraway constitutes the cyborg as its doppelganger, implicitly characterizing the posthuman through a "network ideological image" replete with the profusion as well as the permeability of spaces and iden tities (Haraway, "Cyborg" 170). The posthuman for Haraway arises out of the blurring of ecological, techno-corporeal, and geopolitical boundaries, embracing at the same time the ethical and political accountability of the networked subject (Braidotti 197). Therefore, if, as Haraway argues, effecting "liminal transformations" (177) in stories, words, and worlds rests on the dual goals of rescuing vision from disembodiment and giving birth to feminist cyborg writing, then we need to better understand the contiguity of vision and writing especially as informed by cutting edge theories of both, a goal this chapter addresses.[4] In addition, if, as Haraway implies, embodied seeing and cyborg writing conspire to shape a shared posthuman epistemology important to the overthrow of the C^3I paradigm, then transitioning into the posthuman requires determining the ways in which theories of vision and writing, normally perceived as operating on separate disciplinary trajectories, complement each other. Finally, by emphasizing the discursive nature of this understanding—we know vision and writing through our discourses[5] on these phenomena—this project maintains an important tension between the materiality of seeing and writing and its necessarily discursive expression, thus allowing space for the continued critique of vision and writing as they operate jointly and separately. Theories of the embodied nature of seeing and writing thereby remain semiotically as well as materially positioned, a point crucial to Haraway's cyborgian agenda.

I begin this project with an exploration of the complementarities between the way of seeing and writing intrinsic to Haraway's point of resistance: Renaissance perspectivalism and Ramist rhetoric, a union that reifies the separations between mind/body, human/nature, and human/technology. Tied to both modern spaces and selves, Renaissance perspectivalism and Ramist rhetoric constitute a way of seeing and writing that, by separating self and other, invites actions that threaten the survival of bodies, environments, and cultures. Then, I turn to a union that potentially forwards Haraway's posthuman agenda: an ecological approach to vision and writing. Drawing particularly on the work of Gerald Edelman, 1972 Nobel prize winner for his work in immunology, I explore his theory of vision as a process involving perceiver and environment in a complex transactive dance. Drawing on a group of scholars in composition studies who advocate an ecological approach to writing, I describe writing as a fusion of composer and physical-social systems. Each approach highlights the importance of embodiment, embeddedness, and transactivity, a shared similarity that holds implications for Haraway's commitment to social change through a cyborgian posthuman.

DISEMBODIED VISION, DISEMBODIED WRITING: A HISTORICALLY SITUATED MARRIAGE

> *The promises of progress, control, reason, instrumental rationality—all the promises seem to have been broken in the children.*
>
> —Donna J. Haraway, *Modest_Witness* 121

While teacher-scholars in writing studies have begun to address the importance of the visual in composing, rarely is the act of perceiving considered in conjunction with the act of writing; more rarely is a theory of vision considered in conjunction with a theory of writing, as a force either supporting or eroding a particular approach to writing. My goal in this section is to highlight the important, if seldom acknowledged, nexus between the two. I do this through a historical analysis of Renaissance perspectivalism and Ramist rhetoric, and I choose this moment because these discourses on seeing and rhetoric serve as Haraway's point of resistance. I begin with Haraway's rationale for rejecting perspectivalism, then describe the theory of vision intrinsic to Renaissance perspectivalism, and finally relate that to the precepts of Ramist rhetoric, the dominant rhetoric during the late Renaissance. This analysis reveals the degree to which a theory of seeing and a theory of rhetoric conspire to reinforce a particular epistemology, one that Haraway considers a threat to both life and knowledge making in the West.

Haraway's advocacy of a new way of seeing and writing stems in part from her rejection of perspectivalism, an epistemology that undergirds not only science studies but also everyday beliefs about vision. In *Modest_Witness* Haraway addresses the dangers of perspectivalism, the "power of the technology of perspective to discipline vision to produce a new kind of knowledge of form" (180). Her aim in *Modest_Witness* is to read and disrupt the historical moment her modest witness inhabits: late twentieth century secularized Christian realism in which the story of salvation has become inextricably mixed with the story of technoscience. Simultaneously real and constructed, secularized Christian realism constitutes what Haraway calls a *figuration:* "performative images that can be inhabited" (11, 179). Performative images are figures, both in the sense of tropes—figures of speech—and in the sense of perceived objects. Thus, figurations involve both interpretative practices (speech) and that which is interpreted (a reality figured by speech). "Verbal or visual, figurations can be condensed maps of contestable worlds" (11, 179), Haraway suggests, guiding people to experience reality, study reality, and write about reality in particular ways. As a result, "challenging the material-semiotic practices of technoscience" for the "deeper, broader, and more scientific literacy" of situated knowledges requires grappling with the figuration constituting technoscience (179). Key to that struggle is disrupting perspectivalism, an amalgamation of the Renaissance and the Scientific Revolution.

As Haraway argues, the Western sense of what is real and natural arises out of a set of visual innovations dating from the Renaissance. "Twentieth-century scientists call on this earlier visual technology for insisting on a specific kind of reality, which readily makes today's observers forget the conditions, apparatuses, and histories of its production" (*Modest_Witness* 182). Beginning with the fifteenth-century rediscovery and codification of perspective in art—a seismic cultural shift that reorganized both space and subjectivities (Ivins; Panofsky)—and reaching critical mass during the eighteenth century with its fascination with optical technologies, industry, and scientific methods, perspectivalism consists of a knowing/seeing from which the human observer is separated from the object of the gaze. Leon Battista Alberti's *On Painting* underscores this essential separation in two ways. First, he divides the mathematic properties of vision from the physiological: he does not *"think it necessary to speak of all the functions of the eye in relation to vision"* (41, emphasis original), highlighting the importance of geometry, not body, in vision.

Second, he separates the painter from the object, manifested physically by his advocacy of the veil: a finely woven cloth, criss-crossed by thick threads which run in parallel vertical and horizontal lines, producing a pattern of squares. This veil is stretched on a frame and positioned between the painter and the object of the painterly gaze as a means to fix the object's outlines (65—66). The result institutionalizes the separation between artist and object, vision and eye. Haraway explains the impact of this perspectivalism: "In Renaissance visual technology, form and narrative implode, and both seem merely to reveal what was already there, waiting for unveiling or discovery" (182). Circulating through Haraway's interpretation of perspectivalism are the double influences of Cartesian rationalism and empiricism.[6]

Martin Jay provides insight into the influence of Descartes's systematic doubt on what he calls "Cartesian perspectivalism," a way of seeing and knowing that, like Haraway's perspectivalism, privileges a disembodied unitary subject and a binary gaze that divides reality into the empowered seer and the disempowered seen. Freed from the limitations of embodiment, this rational subject acquires the "infinite vision" that Haraway excoriates as a "god-trick" ("Situated" 189). Again like Haraway, Jay believes that Cartesian perspectivalism serves, "as a shorthand way to characterize the dominant scopic regime of the modern era" (Jay 69–70) with direct links to science and technology.[7] William M. Ivins concurs, pointing out that, without the homogeneity and uniformity of space promulgated by perspective in art, "science and technology as now conceived would necessarily cease to exist" (9), a point that Karsten Harries reinforces: "our science and technology, even our common sense with its faith in reason and reason's power to grasp and manipulate reality owe much to Descartes" (28). In addition, Haraway integrates empiricist elements in her take on perspectivalism, especially the reinforcing beliefs in a quantifiable and measurable reality that operates according to linear causality. To underscore this union, she couples perspective with the rise of scientific methodology emerging from Robert Boyle's experiments with the air pump in the mid-seventeenth century. These early efforts to craft an experimental science founded the protocols for both the doing and the reporting of science. As Haraway notes, "This epistemology [perspectivalism] underlies the European-indebted sense of what counts as reality in the culture, believed by many of its practitioners to transcend all culture, called modern science" (*Modest_Witness* 180).[8] Even on the cusp of the twenty-first century, the existence of science in the West and the sway it has over the popular imagination owe much to perspectivalism: "Reality, as Westerners have know it in story and image for several hundred years, is an effect but cannot be recognized as such without great moral and epistemological angst" (182). It is this way of seeing, with its complex amalgamation of Renaissance perspective, Cartesian rationalism, and empiricism, that Haraway seeks to disrupt. However, important to my argument is the degree to which perspectivalism as a visual technology with epistemological implications embraces vision *and* writing.

Haraway consistently emphasizes the importance of writing throughout her critical work, citing the role of "writing technologies" or "writing machines" in the creation and disruption of "laboratory inscription practices" (*Modest_Witness* 120). She emphasizes as well, albeit more implicitly, the mutuality between scientific witnessing and the documentation of that witnessing. What she does not address, however, is writing as rhetoric and thus is unable to account for the ways in which emergent visual technologies and dominant rhetorical theory—a theory of writing—historically intersect to reinforce one another and the epistemology that circulates through both.[9] So, when Haraway speaks of "gestat[ing] together in the manly and natural time machines of modernity and enlightenment" (119), she is unable to make a key connection to what Miriam Brody calls the "manly writing" of late Renaissance and Enlightenment rhetorics. What remains invisible in Haraway's account of perspectivalism is the degree to which the cultural milieu that gave rise to perspectivalism is also the cultural milieu that gave rise to a complementary rhetoric.[10] As a result, Haraway's agenda of dismantling perspectivalism is undercut by the failure to acknowledge the ways in which that visual technology is supported by a particular set of rhetorical practices operating outside of as well as within science. The reciprocity between Ramist rhetoric and perspectivalism, especially its Cartesian face, offers a compelling example of this complementarity.[11]

As Brody notes in *Manly Writing*, the "changing ways of seeing the material world encouraged a new understanding of the relationship between language and things" (41). She accords a central role in this "new understanding" to sixteenth-century French professor of eloquence and philosophy Peter Ramus, whose work was widely read in the seventeenth century. Walter J. Ong in *Ramus, Method, and the Decay of Dialectic* expands on the impact Ramism had on rhetoric and method. Ramism, Ong writes, was like "nerve ganglion": it connected to obvious "end organs," such as specific theories or doctrines, but it also connected more implicitly to the rise of modern physics and the relationship between rhetoric and the scientific method as it evolved in its initial form in the sixteenth century (ix). It was a "huge movement," Ong claims, holding at its center the belief in a "cluster of mental habits" that conceived of thought "in terms of spatial models apprehended by sight," which means that a specific embodied individual who perceives and speaks "will be eclipsed insofar as the world is thought of as an assemblage of the sort of things that vision apprehends—objects or surfaces" (8–9). Considered both a forerunner of Cartesian rationalism and a participant in controversies concerning teaching, the scientific method, logic, and rhetoric (Ong 198; Sharratt 172), Ramist precepts reached subsequent generations through textbooks to such an extent that his theories of logic and rhetoric became less and less "Ramist" and more and more simply logic and rhetoric (Ong 9). Thus, Ong concludes, the thinking "pounded into the minds of whole generations of schoolboys" about logic, rhetoric, and method became part of the "sinews and bones of civilization" (10).

Essential to my argument concerning the reciprocity between perspectivalism and rhetoric is the Ramist separation of dialectic and rhetoric in theory if not always in practice, a separation that severed the world from the word. In the medieval *trivium*, the basic course of study for school boys consisted of grammar, dialectic, and rhetoric (although not always in that order). Grammar taught the building block of language and literature; dialectic trained the student in logic, or understanding; and rhetoric, the queen of the arts, combined them both into the creation of arguments appropriate for communication in specific situations (Baldwin 90–91). Within the *trivium* tradition, instruction in rhetoric consisted of training in the five offices or canons: invention, arrangement, style, memory, and delivery, the combination of which assigned key importance to rhetoric not only as a means of expressing arguments but also as a means of creating arguments, thus creating knowledge of the world. However, Ramus radically reconfigures rhetoric by integrating the canons of invention, arrangement, and memory into dialectic. Within this theory of logic, invention—or the discovery of single arguments—becomes the first step of dialectic, whereas joining arguments the second, which Ramus variously called arrangement, judgment or discretion. Rhetoric, then, becomes solely the realm of "striking expression" (style) and delivery (273), establishing a sharp division between knowledge of the world and language used to express that knowledge.

Rather than a vital process in the creation of knowledge, rhetoric merely served as the means by which the conclusions of cognition, produced via the mathematically oriented spatialized logic of Ramist dialectic, were dressed in language. Thus subordinated, rhetoric, through delivery and style, became associated with the discredited body, and dialectic, as the source of truth, became associated with disembodied mind. The mental representations—the results of cognition—were primary, the expression secondary, a situation heralding a similar division in Descartes.[12]

By emphasizing rhetoric as a process that occurs only after dialectic—that is, rhetoric as the art of operating on the results of a mathematically spatialized dialectic—Ramist rhetoric reinforces perspectivalism, supporting not only a specific way of "doing" language but also a specific way of "seeing" the world that renders invisible that which Haraway wishes to expose: the contingencies of its production (*Modest Witness* 182). Here, then, is my central position: the integration of seeing and writing constitute an epistemology, a way of knowing resistant to change unless that change includes not just an alternative way of writing *or* seeing, but an alternative way of doing both. My goal in the next two sections is to explore an ecological approach to vision and writing, the combination of which offer just such an alternative. Combined, ecological vision and writing provide a matrix for the emergence of Haraway's cyborgian epistemology. I begin with the work of neuroscientist Gerald Edelman, who addresses the complex phenomenon of perception within the context of his larger effort to return the mind to the brain. I then derive a reciprocal theory of writing from the work of a cohort of teacher-scholars in writing studies who advocate an ecological approach to writing, a proto-theory that privileges the materiality of the writing agent and that agent's embeddedness within a labyrinthine array of physical and socio-cultural systems. Remaining sensitive to the threat of reductiveness, I isolate three key themes that characterize both cyborgian epistemology and the two ecological approaches: *embodiment*, *embeddedness*, and *transactivity*.

SEEING AS A CYBORG

> *A scientific analysis of consciousness must answer the question: How can the firing of neurons give rise to subjective sensations, thought, and emotions?*
>
> —Gerald Edelman, Wider Than the Sky

Called a "biologically based epistemology" (*Second Nature* 2), Edelman's theory of consciousness, from which his theory of vision derives, seeks to heal the Cartesian divide between mental and physical events and, in the process, re-embody vision. Edelman articulates the challenge that confronts him as follows: "The key task of a scientific description of consciousness is to give a causal account of the relationship between these domains [neurons and sensory experiences] so that properties in one domain may be understood in terms of events in the other" (*Wider* 12). Such a task is necessary because Western traditions, especially since Descartes, have conceptualized mind as a "thinking substance" separate from the biology of the brain, thus reifying the separation of mind from body, or mental events from physical events. This separation has resulted in the rise of computation models of human intelligence and consciousness in the twentieth century wherein the mind is treated as a software program with executable functions that run according to machine logic and clock time regardless of their material instantiation in digital circuitry or brain anatomy. By theorizing the neural correlates of consciousness, Edelman seeks to dispel the illusion that human consciousness can be equated with or downloadable to a digital platform, an illusion intrinsic to C^3I thinking predicated on the belief in a one-to-one match between reality and code.

Rather than a software program, Edelman contends that consciousness (and subsequently vision) emerges from the complex "organization and operation of the brain" (*Wider* 5). It is an outgrowth of the dynamic transaction of the more than 30 billion nerve cells with their more than 100 billion connections. As Edelman points out, the combination of neurons and connections yields more potential active pathways in the brain than the number of elementary particles in the universe (*Second* 18). All of this immense complexity is organized into functioning patterns whereby sensory sheets and neuronal maps connect to one another (*Bright Air* 21–22; 25). Instead of operating as a set of individual modules, each tidily executing a specific function, the brain accomplishes its tasks through a distributed network. Populations of neurons in many different areas of the brain act in concert with one another (*Wider* 6–7). In addition, this process unfolds as a kind of evolution, what Edelman calls *neural darwinism,* or the theory of neuronal group selection (TNGS).

Edelman borrows Darwin's concept of *population thinking* to explain the logic by which brains produce perception and consciousness. Simply put, evolution operates within a population group (such as fruit flies) wherein a specific quality (red eyes) among a set of variant traits (red and black eyes) eventually dominates, with the other traits disappearing. Like human evolution, the brain operates through the process of selection. TNGS purports that diverse groups of neurons comprised of variant networks or pathways are either expressed (selected) or silent (not selected) as a result of an organism's transactions with the environment and its resultant behavior (*Neural* 64). This evolutionary process begins during fetal development and continues after birth.[13] The immense complexity of brain anatomy operating through selection results in what Edelman characterizes as a self-organizing system, and the phenomenon of consciousness emerges from that self-organization as a process, not a thing. Thus, unlike computer programs, human consciousness (both the experience of sensations and its awareness of its own experiences) is dynamic, organized via neuronal group selection. So, too, is vision, which Edelman frequently uses as an illustration of the brain in action. As with consciousness, vision is "quite sensitively dependent on place (which others cells are around), time (when one event occurs in relation to another), and correlated activity (whether cells fire together or change together chemically over a period of time)" (*Bright Air* 22). Key to Edelman's theory are the three qualities of *embodiment*, *embeddedness*, and *transactivity*.

First, Edelman re-embodies consciousness and thereby re-embodies vision. This commitment to the body *in* the mind impels his work, which Edelman refers to as his "brain-based epistemology" (*Second* 2). All mental activities, including vision, "depend on signals to the brain from the body" (24) to the extent that neural connections are themselves affected by "how you sense and how you move" (24). Thus, "if we include the brain as your favorite organ, you *are* your body" (24), and vision is no exception. For Edelman visual perception emerges from the hyperdense neural connections across various sites of the brain, and those hyperdense connections are unique to the individual neural anatomy. Unlike Alberti's effort to disengage the physiological eye from geometric perspective, Edelman returns the visual experience—the percept itself—to its dependency on the physical strata of cells, organs, and appendages (such as the eye itself, optical nerve, and so forth). In addition, while the visual experience of all organisms emerges from the brain's anatomy, the variations in that anatomy render each individual's perceptual experiences unique. Embodied vision is partial and situated because each animal's neural make up is configured in conjunction with its environment, disordering the "god trick" of perspectivalism.

Second, the quality of embeddedness emphasizes vision's positionality, for each individual's embeddedness within an environment results in different brain anatomy. "The brain is embodied and the body is embedded," Edelman says, highlighting what he calls a critical triad of brain, body, and eco-niche (*Second* 24, 25). The body does not exist in a vacuum; rather, it operates within an environment which it shapes and which, in turn, shapes it (24). Beginning in fetal development, the individual body responds to its amniotic sea by forming axonal connections between neurons and extending dendrites in branch-like formations to create a unique brain anatomy for each organism. "The brain is enormously variable at the finest levels" (24), Edelman points out, even among identical twins because of their presence in and responses to their prenatal environments. Then, after birth, the environment that a baby (of whatever species) confronts constitutes an "inherently ambiguous" eco-niche (*Neural* 3, 24) which can be sorted into an almost infinite array of objects or events. How the baby partitions or punctuates that environment is an outcome of a kind of co-evolution in which changes in the baby's brain prompted by environmental factors result in actions that consequently change the environment, a dialectical process that renders porous the separation between what is inside the bonehouse and what is outside. A quality highlighting the connections between inner and outer is *degeneracy*, or overlapping pathways. Responding to "diverse inputs from the body, the world, and the brain itself," the brain creates multiple and coinciding neural circuits which can each perform the same function but in different combinations (*Second* 34). Through such degeneracy an organism can construct a unified percept and maintain the stability of that percept. In other words, degeneracy constructs a visual image by selecting overlapping circuits, allowing an animal, human and otherwise, to "create a scene . . . with which the animal could lay plans" (36). Stemming from an organism's embeddedness within an eco-niche, the evolution of different circuits consequently endows the visual system with responsiveness to that embeddedness.

Finally, the third theme of Edelman's ecological theory of vision concerns transactivity, a trait gestured to in the preceding descriptions of embodiment and embeddedness. Transactivity consists of the co-constitutive movement among components, such as neurons, neuronal groups, and so forth. In addition, transactivity occurs inside and outside the organism's bonehouse, preventing embodiment from becoming biological determinism, or what Edelman calls "strict biological chauvinism" (*Bright Air* 29). We might be inextricable from our bodies, but all mental processes, including consciousness and vision, emerge not from the substance of the cortical sheet but from the dynamic arrangement of neural pathways (30). For example, vision cannot be reduced to a single "module" of the brain, a single neuronal map or synaptic connection no matter how strong. It exists as a constellation operating across regions of the brain and in conjunction with the environment. As Edelman explains, at least 33 different cortical areas are involved in some way with the experience of vision (*Second* 20), connected through a process he calls *reentry* whereby electro-chemical changes move back and forth between areas along various circuits. In addition, while different portions of the brain contribute to vision—V_1 orients objects, V_4 contributes color, and V_5 factors in motion—no single area orchestrates or controls the transaction among the various areas. Instead, the experience of vision emerges from the transactivity of areas working together (32). Rather than parsing the visible world into color, to which is added shape and or motion, we perceive a cohesive pattern. This cohesion emerges from transactivity.

The combination of embodiment, embeddedness, and transactivity in Edelman's powerful theory of consciousness and seeing rescues vision, as Haraway demands, from its leap from the body. Ecological seeing emphasizes partiality, individual variability, and situatedness within an eco-niche. Thus, Edelman provides a necessary component to Haraway's cyborg agenda. But, while ecological vision is necessary, it is not sufficient. To complete that agenda, we need an ecological theory of writing, which I address next.

Writing as a Cyborg

We cannot escape materiality. We can only better define it, better critique it, and better engage it.
—Krista Ratcliffe

Less a systematic articulation of a theory and more an informal aggregation of scholarship revolving around the concept and metaphor of ecology, an ecological theory (or, more accurately, a proto-theory) of writing encompasses a wide array of agendas, orientations, and self-selected identifiers. Perhaps the earliest twentieth-century expression of an ecological orientation to meaning-making occurs in 1936 with Louise Rosenblatt's *Literature as Exploration* in which she describes the imaginative experience as emerging from "the live circuit set up between reader and text," a circuit by which reader and text mutually construct the other (25). Focusing on reading, especially reading literature, Rosenblatt explicitly aligns her approach with "current ecological views" ("Reading" 120), offering its fullest description in *The Reader the Text the Poem*. Published in 1972, this systematic articulation of reading asserts that reader and text gain meaningfulness only in conjunction with the other, the product of a co-constitutive transaction rather than interaction. In a similar spirit, Sidney I. Dobrin and Christian R. Weisser define a movement in composition studies that they call *ecocomposition* as a "holistic, encompassing framework for studies of the relationship between discourse and environment" (6). They trace the roots of an ecological approach to the 70s and map interconnections among different fields: literary criticism, literary nonfiction, especially nature writing, and composition studies. As Dobrin and Weisser point out, the rubric *ecocomposition* embraces a range of approaches and orientations: writing and ecological sustainability; the inextricability of physical place with the act of composing, including both bodies and natural or manmade environments; writing about/in nature; writing as embedded with a network of complex systems, including the socio-cultural as well as the material. In sum, it includes anyone in writing studies using ecology "conceptually, methodologically, metaphorically, and pedagogically" (3). Regardless of their differences, scholars operating within this broad ecological niche, even those who do not specifically use the term, hold in common (to varying degrees) the three themes of embodiment, embeddedness, and transactivity.

First, harmonizing with both Edelman and Haraway, an ecological theory of writing emphasizes the importance of writing bodies. For compositionists, an important move in twentieth and twenty-first century writing studies has been "complicating the idea of materiality as well as its relationship with bodies and discourse" (Ratcliffe 615), an agenda that many scholars have addressed from a variety of perspectives. Perhaps the most explicit statement about embodiment among those embracing an ecological orientation emerges from Margaret Syverson's work.[14] In *The Wealth of Reality*, Syverson seeks to develop a "richer, more comprehensive theory of composing," one that will answer an array of questions concerning the nature of collaborative authorship and writing pedagogy. Her mechanism for developing that comprehensive theory involves conceiving an "ecology of composition" as the "unit of analysis" (2). Based on complex systems theory wherein an array of agents "act and interact in parallel," an ecology of composition envisions components of the writing act as co-constructing each other and their environments (3). Pertinent to that unit of analysis is embodiment, which she defines as the physical experience of being in, using, and relying on one's body (12): "Embodiment grounds our conceptual structures, our interactions with each other and with the environment, our perceptions, and our actions" (13). She contends that embodiment operates across a range of dimensions—physical-material, social, psychological, spatial, and temporal—illustrating throughout separate chapters the way in which texts, writers, and readers are embodied within and as complex systems. To illustrate, Syverson analyzes a long autobiographical poem by Charles Reznikoff, highlighting the way in which any text "has a body, is part of a larger body, and is produced by a body," including potential distribution across a range of bodies (48). For Syverson, embodiment embraces the physical scenes of Reznikoff's upbringing as well as the material act of holding the pages of various family memoirs; it includes time, too, manifested in the materiality of an aging grandfather or one's own changing body. Her point is that embodiment spreads out from the neuron to the eco-niche, leaving us with a text that exists as an activity, a physical as well as social ensemble (74).

Second, embeddedness is as intrinsic to an ecological approach to writing as it is to Edelman's theory of vision and Haraway's commitment to situated knowledges. Syverson points unambiguously to the importance of embeddedness: "we are embedded in and co-evolving with our environments, which include other people as well as social and physical structures" (xv). In fact, embeddedness, or immersion within a web of material-discursive relationships, serves as the heart of an ecological theory of writing, a point that Dobrin and Weisser make clear in *Natural Discourse*. Writing studies in its post-process guise is "a study of relationships," and those relationships encompass environments (from political to natural), texts, cultures, ideologies, and languages (9). By privileging an organism's embeddedness within relationships, both physical and discursive, Dobrin and Weisser seek to resist the "dualistic splits" that concern Haraway and Edelman: the artificial separations between nature/culture and human/nature (10). Motivated by a similar resistance to such dichotomies, Derrick Owens offers multiple examples of embeddedness, particularly in terms of the intersection of place and identity: "who we are," he points out, "and what we have to say is in so many ways interwoven, directly and indirectly, consciously and unconsciously, with our local environs" (37). He illustrates the potentially pernicious result of ignoring embeddedness by turning to his students' writing. Particularly evocative is Mike's account of a typical weekend in an area that lacks pedestrian-centered affordances, such as parks and open spaces, as well as affordable housing and a healthy mixture of retail and entertainment. What results, Mike reveals, is boredom, an emotion that leads to vandalism and violence (67). Identity and behavior are inextricable from one's embeddedness in a specific place. Thus, Owens can wonder "to what extent do poorly designed neighborhoods become catalysts for self-hatred" (67). Given the irrevocability of embeddedness, he concludes, "we need to pay more attention to how external or 'outside' conditions are never really outside us at all" (8). Without such a sea change in attitudes, he fears, we will be unable to secure a livable world for our children and grandchildren

The third trait of writing, one important to Edelman's theory of vision and to Haraway's cyborg, is transactivity: the dynamism of the elements in a system co-creating themselves. Embeddedness is about relationships; transactivity is about forming those relationships through an ongoing reciprocal process. Both perspectives are important. Ecologically oriented scholars embrace transactivity without always using the specific term. For instance, Syverson employs *enaction*, or the principle that knowledge (identity, reality, and so forth) emerges from "*activities and experiences*" (13), a term that aligns with the spirit of transactivity.[15] Like Syverson, Marilyn M. Cooper does not use the term *transactivity* per se, but she emphasizes its importance to an ecological theory of writing, as her foreword to Weisser and Dobrin's edited collection *Ecocomposition* reveals. An ecological approach to composition aligns itself with the major paradigm shift in the twentieth century, Cooper explains, from a focus on substances or structures to a focus on systems thinking, or seeing relationships as dynamic patterns (xi-xii). Important in this shift is not just a respect for relationships but a respect for the *making*—the transactivity—of relationships. To illustrate this significant difference in thinking, Cooper turns to her seminal and highly influential1986 *College English* article. She points out that, although she used the term relationships in that essay, she described only the "structures and contents" of those relationships. Thus, she ended up reifying relationships into static patterns instead of emphasizing the necessary dynamism in those patterns. Crucial to an ecological approach to writing, she asserts, is not relationships per se but the activity of relating. Thus, without using the term *transactivity*, Cooper in her foreword emphasizes the importance of the concept of *transactivity* where "writing and writers are not just *like* ecological systems but are precisely ecological systems" because through the making and remaking of relationships the boundaries between writing, writer, and world evanesce (xiv). She concludes that a focus on *relating* mitigates the temptation still circulating in the discipline to treat relationships mechanistically, a focus that helps open up systems thinking to compositionists.

Resonating to Haraway's cyborg, an ecological approach to writing identifies the writer as a self-conscious hybrid who—embodied, embedded, and transactive—abides on (and sees from) both sides of a divide; again like the cyborg, writing as an ecology "splices" itself together from elements of the multiple lived milieus of which it is a part ("Cyborg" 175). It "both represents and forges webs of relationships," an "ordinary bit of the material-discursive apparatus for the production of technoscience culture" (*Modest_Witness* 125), thereby potentially contributing to the erosion of perspectivalism and the emergence of a cyborg epistemology.

LIVING AS A CYBORG

The great divide between Man and Nature, and its gendered corollary and colonial racial melodrama, that founded the story of modernity has been breached.

—Donna J. Haraway, *Modest_Witness*

"There is no way out of stories," Haraway writes. But we are not limited to the story narrated by the "One-Eyed Father." Rather, "changing the stories, in both material and semiotic senses, is a modest intervention worth making" (*Modest_Witness* 45). This essay, then, constitutes my modest intervention, my effort to re-write the story told by One-Eyed Father by highlighting the important intersection between discourses on vision and discourses on writing. By deliberately intertwining vision and meaning-making as mutually reinforcing processes that emerge from embodiment, embeddedness, and transactivity, I hope to move toward an epistemology that releases the One-Eyed Father into the play of writing, "committed to partiality, irony, intimacy, and perversity" ("Cyborg" 151). Told from a double perspective, the ecological story of vision and writing challenges the hegemony of perspectivalism because it enables us—perhaps even requires us—to re-see and re-write the spaces within which we live, thereby re-seeing and re-writing ourselves.

Furthermore, because of the salutary potential posed by this ecological story, I do not want to end with the implication that all stories are equal. Rather, I want to conclude by privileging this tale told from a double perspective, pointing to the crucial advantages it offers for social and environmental health. I believe, as Haraway suggests, that "our hopes for accountability, for politics, for ecofeminism, turn on revisioning the world as coding trickster with whom we must learn to converse" (*Modest_Witness* 201), and the ecological story helps us begin that conversation. I also concede that this narrative, no matter how persuasive, only constitutes the conversational opener, the salutation, if you will. To work toward a cyborgian agenda, what Cooper might call a "postmodern morality realized in the responsibility for others" (xii), we need to do more than see and write as a cyborg. We also need to live like one. Thus, while an acknowledgment of the similarities between theories of vision and writing is necessary, I also realize that acknowledgment by itself is not sufficient for effecting the kind of substantive social and environmental change Haraway envisions. So I end with what I see as the next challenge: the call to write another chapter in this ecological story told from double perspectives, one that narrates for us different versions—maybe double versions—of what it means to live like a cyborg, in and out of the classroom, in and out of a public sphere, and in and out of a discipline's scholarship. When we write that chapter, perhaps we have a better chance of ensuring that posthuman is "tuned to resonance, not to dichotomy" (Haraway "Situated,"195).

Notes

1. Although Haraway shifts her focus away from cyborgs to dogs in *When Species Meet*, she notes that she does not abandon the cyborg. Rather, "the cyborg and dog come together," (12) finding her "siblings" in the "queer kin group that finds lapdogs and laptops in the same commodious laps" (10).

2. Haraway acknowledges the potential of the cyborg metaphor to serve American Cold War politics; thus, she advocates the reclamation, as well as the use, of the cyborg metaphor for purposes of subversion.

3. While writing and social change have been frequently joined in the same discourse, especially when writing is used synonymously with rhetoric, vision and change as well as vision and writing have been less typically linked. For

efforts to bring vision and writing together as reciprocal agencies of change, see Fleckenstein, *Vision, Rhetoric, and Social Action in the Composition Classroom*.

4. Twenty-first century scholarship on vision, arising particularly from the disciplines of neuropsychology and cognitive science, seems initially disconnected from scholarship on writing; however, the two processes have loose connections historically. For instance, Aristotle was one of the first philosophers in the West to write extensively on both the art of rhetoric (*Rhetoric*) and the science of vision (Book II of *De Anima*). In addition, vision circulated throughout the rhetorical canon in intriguing ways, from the use of topics in invention to the use of Method of Loci in *ars memoria* (see Cicero, *De Oratore*, Book II). Finally, the way in which one prepared to speak in either the Athenian *Ekklesia* or the Roman Forum was intertwined with a theory concerning the impact of one's physical appearance as well as one's words.

5. I define *discourse* as the juncture between speaking and practicing. A discourse implicates a way of knowledge with a capacious set of assumptions about and interpretations of reality framed by an identifiable set of conventions embodied in particular social practices.

6. See Merleau-Ponty, Part I, for a critique of the empirical and the Cartesian theories of perception, especially vision.

7. See Fleckenstein, "A Matter of Perspective," for a description of Cartesian perspectivalism and its circulation throughout The Spellings Commission's *Report on the Future of Higher Education*.

8. See Law for an account of the complementarities between theories of vision and theories of language, including rhetoric, among various British empiricists.

9. A similar elision is evident in writing studies as well.

10. Significantly, Descartes had nothing positive to say about the use of rhetoric. See Carr, *Descartes and the Resilience of Rhetoric: Varieties of Cartesian Rhetoric Theory*, for an effort to uncover a "hidden" fondness for rhetoric in Descartes's writings.

11. Ramus also contributed to scholarship on optics, but it is beyond the scope of this essay to examine the potential linkages between his theory of vision and his theories of dialectic and rhetoric.

12. While Ramus is perceived as a precursor to Descartes, he and Francis Bacon, considered the father of modern science, also shared a like emphasis on the importance of method, or thinking systematically (see Walton).

13. Evolution for Edelman operates on multiple levels, both within the brain—through the selection, or de-selection, of certain neural pathways in conjunction with environmental influences—and within the population at large. Consciousness, he contends, is itself an evolutionary development. See, especially, *Neural Darwinism* for a summation of TNGS and its refutations of information processing models of consciousness (64–69).

14. Syverson identifies four qualities particularly pertinent to a complex systems approach: distribution, emergence, embodiment, and enaction.

15. It is worth noting that Syverson uses the phenomenon of vision as her example of enaction, emphasizing the incredible degree of coordination required for the experience of seeing. Vision requires the coordination of physiological mechanisms with cognitive and cultural training (14–16). Focusing on pathways across the brain required by vision, Edelman also refers to his theory of consciousness as an enactive theory, a similarity that underscores the complementarities between ecological approaches to writing and to vision.

WORKS CITED

Alberti, Leon Battista. *On Painting*. Trans. Cecil Grayson. London: Penguin, 1991. Print.

Aristotle. *On Rhetoric*. Trans. George A. Kennedy. New York: Oxford UP, 1991. Print.

—. *De Anima*. Trans. Hugh Lawson-Tancred. London: Penguin, 1986. Print.

Baldwin, Charles Sears. *Medieval Rhetoric and Poetic*. Gloucester, MA: Peter Smith, 1959. Print.

Braidotti, Rosi. "Posthuman, All Too Human: Towards a New Process Ontology." *Theory, Culture & Society* 23 (2006): 197–208. *SAGE Premier*. Sage, 2012. Web. 5 Sept. 2011.

Brody, Miriam. *Manly Writing: Gender, Rhetoric, and the Rise of Composition*. Carbondale: Southern Illinois UP, 1993. Print.

Carr, Thomas M., Jr. *Descartes and the Resilience of Rhetoric: Varieties of Cartesian Rhetorical Theory*. Carbondale: Southern Illinois UP, 1989. Print.

Cicero. *On the Ideal Orator*. Trans. James M. May and Jakob Wisse. New York: Oxford UP, 2001. Print.

Cooper, Marilyn M. "Foreword: The Truth Is Out There." *Ecocomposition: Theoretical and Pedagogical Approaches*. Ed. Christian R. Weisser and Sidney I. Dobrin. Albany, NY: SUNY P, 2001. xi-xviii. Print.

Dobrin, Sidney I., and Christian R. Weisser. *Natural Discourse: Toward Ecocomposition*. Albany, NY: SUNY P, 2002. Print.

Edelman, Gerald M. *Bright Air, Brilliant Fire: On the Matter of the Mind*. New York: HarperCollins, 1992. Print.

—. *Neural Darwinism: The Theory of Neuronal Group Selection*. New York: Basic Books, 1987. Print.

—. *Second Nature: Brain Science and Human Knowledge*. New Haven: Yale UP, 2006. Print.

—. *Wider than the Sky: The Phenomenal Gift of Consciousness*. New Haven: Yale UP, 2004. Print.

Fleckenstein, Kristie S. *Vision, Rhetoric, and Action in the Social Classroom*. Carbondale: Southern Illinois UP, 2009. Print.

—. "A Matter of Perspective: Cartesian Perspectivalism and the Testing of English Studies." *JAC: Rhetoric, Writing, Culture, Politics* 28 (2008): 85–121. Print.

Haraway, Donna J. "A Cyborg Manifesto: Science, Technology, and Socialist-Feminism in the Late Twentieth Century." *Siminans, Cyborgs, and Women: The Reinvention of Nature.* New York: Routledge, 1991. 149–82. Print.

—. *Modest_Witness@Second_Millennium.FemaleMan©_Meets_OncoMouse™: Feminism and Technoscience.* New York: Routledge, 1997. Print.

—. "Situated Knowledges: The Science Question in Feminism and the Privilege of Partial Perspectives." *Simians, Cyborgs, and Women: The Reinvention of Nature.* New York: Routledge, 1991. 183–201. Print.

—. *When Species Meet.* Minneapolis, MN: U of Minnesota P, 2008. Print.

Harries, Karsten. "Descartes, Perspective, and the Angelic Eye." *Yale French Studies* 49 (1973): 28–42. *JSTOR.* Web. 6 Sept. 2011.

Ivins, William M. *On the Rationalization of Sight.* New York: De Capo, 1973. Print.

Jay, Martin. *Downcast Eyes: The Denigration of Vision in Twentieth-Century French Thought.* Berkeley: U of California P, 1994. Print.

Law, Jules David. *The Rhetoric of Empiricism: Language and Perception from Locke to I. A. Richards.* Ithaca, NY: Cornell UP, 1993. Print.

Merleau-Ponty, Maurice. *Phenomenology of Perception.* Trans. Colin Smith. London: Routledge, 1958. Print.

Ong, Walter J. *Ramist, Method, and the Decay of Dialogue.* Cambridge, MA: Harvard UP, 1983. Print.

Owens, Derrick. *Composition and Sustainability: Teaching for a Threatened Generation.* Urbana, IL: NCTE, 1998. Print.

Panofsky, Erwin. *Studies in Iconology: Humanistic Themes in the Art of the Renaissance.* New York: Harper & Row, 1972. Print.

Ratcliffe, Krista. "Material Matters: Bodies and Rhetoric." *College English* 64.5 (2002): 613–23. Print.

Rosenblatt, Louise M. *Literature as Exploration.* 4th ed. New York: MLA, 1983. Print.

—. *The Reader the Text, the Poem: The Transactional Theory of the Literary Work.* Carbondale: Southern Illinois UP, 1998. Print.

—. "The Reading Transaction: What For?" *Developing Literacy: Young Children's Use of Language.* Ed. Robert P. Parker and Frances A. Davis. Newark, DE: International Reading Association, 1983. 118–35. Print.

Sharratt, Peter. "Peter Ramus, Walter Ong, and the Tradition of Humanistic Learning." *Oral Tradition* 2.1 (1987): 172–87. Print.

Syverson, Margaret A. *The Wealth of Reality: An Ecology of Composition.* Carbondale: Southern Illinois UP, 1999. Print.

Walton, Craig. "Ramus and Bacon on Method." *Journal of the History of Philosophy* 6.3 (1971): 289–302). *ProjectMuse.* Web. 6 Sept. 2011.

13 Evolutionary Equality: Neocybernetic Posthumanism and Margulis and Sagan's Writing Practice

Bruce Clarke

Beginning with *Microcosmos: Four Billion Years of Evolution from Our Microbial Ancestors* (1986), microbiologist Lynn Margulis and science writer Dorion Sagan have authored a series of expositions on life, sex, evolution, and the biosphere.[1] Briefly stated, these volumes do not purvey the anthropocentric, hence "selfish," gene-centered neo-Darwinist biology one gets from an author such as Richard Dawkins. Rather, they present cell-centered, microcosmic and Gaia-connected autopoietic-systems biology. As I will discuss, Margulis and Sagan's longstanding investment in the concept of autopoiesis for a discourse on evolutionary biology is particularly crucial: it consolidates the identification of their discourse as a dialect of neocybernetic posthumanism. Margulis and Sagan do not introduce either term of this latter phrase into their self-descriptions. Nonetheless, their pervasive displacement of the human from a central role in a biosphere returned to Gaia's true inside players, the microbes, yields a form of posthumanism worthy of serious contemplation. This article starts with definitions of the posthuman and of two varieties of posthumanism, followed by a brief excursus on systems theory and deconstruction in relation to writing. It then pays particular attention to Margulis and Sagan's *Microcosmos* for its development of scriptive and rhetorical strategies, and for its accretion, in the paperback edition, of a self-reflective preface that works out a resolution of their own writing practice in relation to their posthumanist constructions. I conclude with a consideration of Gaia theory as a dialect of neocybernetic posthumanism, and assess Margulis and Sagan's adherence to the discourse of autopoiesis in this context.

* * *

Posthumanism is to be distinguished from the posthuman. The posthuman is an image, of desire or dread, the image of some entity or state coming after the time or the state of the human. For instance, a fictional character that begins as a human being but ends up as something other than human would then be posthuman, what I term a posthuman metamorph. In this sense the notion of the posthuman is as old as metamorphic mythopoiesis. At the moment, drawing especially on the cybernetic technosciences, the posthuman imaginary is going stronger than ever, vigorously developed in narrative fictions. For instance, at the end of the movie *Avatar*, once the human protagonist Jake Sully passes permanently into an alien, Na'vi body, he too is officially posthuman, a posthuman metamorph. In contrast, posthumanism is not an image but a discourse, a contested set of philosophical statements or doctrines concerning ways of thinking that stand apart from and may conceivably replace or surpass those philosophies gathered under the name of humanism. This distinction clarifies the circumstance that there's nothing necessarily posthumanist about any given image of the posthuman. The propriety of the philosophical designation will depend on what that posthuman image does, on how it is constructed. So, for example, while the story of *Avatar* drives toward a sort of posthuman climax, one could contest whether the film communicates a posthumanist message, and if so, of what sort. Once again, posthumanism is a contested set of doctrines, a heterogeneous discourse.[2]

It is heterogeneous in that different versions of posthumanism may be distinguished, depending, for instance, upon the particular form of the cybernetics with which they are coordinated. By *neocybernetic posthumanism* I mean to mark for that discourse a crucial distinction between first-order and second-order cybernetics. There are first-order modes of posthumanism that are cybernetic per se. Cybernetic posthumanisms partake of the first-order cybernetic synthesis of information theory with the technosciences of communication and control systems. This earlier cybernetics of signal, noise, and feedback control still remains the primary frame around popular images of the posthuman. The obvious example here is, of course, the cyborg. Elaborated from early cybernetic analogies connecting the homeostatic processes of bodily organs and technological devices, linking organic control systems with communications technologies, the cyborg image transgressed humanist essentialisms. Donna Haraway's ironic treatments of the cyborg's liberatory potential put it to work doing feminist philosophy, debunking gendered dualisms and other myths of pristine origins by challenging the classical ontological boundaries around sexual difference and the absolute separations of the human, the animal, and the machine (149). As a posthuman image the cyborg has been more than suggestive; however, as a posthumanist concept it has been less than rigorous, and its purchase has shown diminishing returns. Like the *Terminator* franchise, it is running out of creative juice. Cybernetic posthumanism continues in earnest in the movement called transhumanism, which has shown itself to be a retrohumanist fantasy preserving Cartesian priorities, instrumentalizing the body by digitalizing the mind.

What, then, is neocybernetic posthumanism? To begin with, it is a way of doing cybernetics otherwise than as prosthetic variations on the mingling of the mechanical and the organic. In the early 1970s the cyberneticist Heinz von Foerster generalized the concept of computation for a turn toward cognitive systems. This demanded a cybernetics *of* cybernetics, the self-referential turn von Foerster called "second-order cybernetics." Neocybernetics started here, as a discourse pointed toward the "observation of observation," the point being that a cognitive system in the non-trivial sense has to refer its cognitions to itself, first of all, as the self-constructed ground of possibility of its ability to refer them, when appropriate, to its world.[3] The main line of this second-order systems theory began to form through von Foerster's close working relations with the biologists Humberto Maturana and Francisco Varela as they developed the concept of autopoiesis. In an autopoietic system, cognitive self-reference takes the form of operational self-production maintained by an organizational closure, not of the system *tout court*, but of the autopoietic process internal to it. Maturana and Varela's material instance of an autopoietic system is the living cell. In their formulation, living processes—selecting and transforming the elements in its environmental medium so as to produce its own continuing production of selective transformations—are coterminous with a basal sense of cognition, what Margulis and Sagan will come to term *sentience*. Sociological systems theorist Niklas Luhmann lifted autopoiesis out of its biological instance for a general theory of self-referential, self-producing systems encompassing but also enclosing psychic and social levels of operation, the autopoiesis of consciousness and the autopoiesis of communication.

Neocybernetic posthumanism, then, is the view of posthumanism one gets when framing it through this neocybernetic line of second-order systems theory.[4] In this view, the unity of the humanist subject is operationally disarticulated and redistributed within a worldly nexus with a complex inter-embedding of semi-autonomous systems and their environments. Notions of intersubjectivity are dissolved because psychic and social systems do not merge, even as they co-evolve by taking each other as their immediate environments. The self-construction of psychic systems is possible only in ongoing corporeal coupling with living systems, while the self-construction of social systems is possible only in ongoing mediatic relation to psychic systems. One has a situation of complex co-dependencies or co-observances among co-evolutionary partners. The different kinds of autopoietic systems possess operational concurrence—in that living, psychic, and social systems all exhibit the autopoietic, self-referential and self-producing form—but without overriding operational unity, in that each kind of autopoietic system produces only its particular mode of cognition—life, consciousness, or communication, as the case may be. Life is cognition but not yet consciousness, consciousness is not yet communication, and vice versa. Moreover, at right angles to its environmental openness as a cognitive system, any autopoietic system maintains the operational closure of its own processes within its particular medium. Operational closure in the midst of environmental interaction—this is the minimal condition of the viability of organic bodies, as well as of the psychic and social systems that emerge from them. This is also the form of their capacity both to observe and to couple with other systems.

* * *

In the tradition of Western metaphysics, the privileging of speech over writing has also privileged—over and above mind over body—mind over society, consciousness over communication. In second-order systems theory, or neocybernetics, Luhmann's contention that "humans can't communicate" is a deliberate provocation, disarming this high-humanist presumption of subjective prerogative with the posthumanist dictum that "only communication can communicate." In other words, once social systems are observed as constituted by the recursive re-production of communicative events, human beings properly reside in their environments.[5] It is social systems that succeed, when they do so, of producing and reproducing communications. To avail themselves of that operation, to "participate in communication," individuals must couple themselves by means of material media to ahuman, supra-individual systems.[6] With regard to the relation between systems theory and deconstruction—two prime dialects of posthumanist discourse—Cary Wolfe notes that Luhmann

> makes essentially the same point about the difference between "consciousness" and "communication" that we have quite readily accepted for decades now as gospel from Derrida—namely, his deconstruction of the "auto-affection" of the voice-as-presence and of the valorizing of speech (as an index of the self-presence of consciousness to itself) over writing (a recursive domain of iterative communication that is, properly understood, fundamentally ahuman or even antihuman).

Wolfe is an important thinker at this crucial intersection, particularly due to his illumination of the resonance between the systems theories of Luhmann and the deconstructive axioms of Derrida. As we see in the passage just given from "Meaning as Event-Machine," Wolfe's seminal insight is that Derrida's disarticulation of speech and writing closely maps onto Luhmann's disarticulation of consciousness and communication.

Moreover, in a manner that deepens Derrida's scheme, Luhmann's operational template disarticulating consciousness and communication also lifts the interrelation of language and meaning out of the specifically human linguistic moment. Derrida's deconstruction of the speech/writing opposition is a conceptual insight carried out at the level of the linguistic signifier; Luhmann's disarticulation of consciousness and communication is a functional distinction carried out at the level of systemic operations. Speech per se is not a modality of consciousness, but it produces clamorous psychic effects due to the self-affection of a speaking subject. And unlike writing, which can wait for its moment to have social effects, spoken traces must be registered by a co-present consciousness in all of *its* extra-conscious materiality and systemic capacity. After all, the point of producing speech is usually its social, not just its conscious, effect. In other words, both speech and writing are properly taken as different modes of *communication*. From the social point of view (typically elided by metaphysical and linguistic discourse), speech is just as external to the "self" as writing is. But due to the auto-affection of the speaking subject, it doesn't *feel* at first that ahuman externalities are always already in play the moment one speaks.

Wolfe underlines how for Derridean posthumanism the written trace—the logic of the grammè—marks the contingency of the self-production of events of consciousness upon "exteriority in general." But Wolfe also systems-theorizes Derrida by unfolding his notion of general exteriority—"The trace is the intimate relation of the living present to its outside, the opening to exteriority in general" (from Derrida's *Speech and Phenomena*)—with a specification of some particular modes of exteriority. That is, Wolfe observes the kinds of environments to be coordinated with the systems for which writing is one kind of operation: "Herein lies the radically posthumanist dimension of writing-as-difference: the subject . . . only comes to be by conforming to a strictly diacritical system of differences. . . . Moreover, those effects and relations are at once material, bodily, external, institutional, technological, and historical" (227).

In the introduction to *What is Posthumanism?*, Wolfe notes that "Luhmann's handling of systems theory accomplishes just the sort of 'conservation' of the logic of the grammè that Derrida calls for, a conservation that is crucial to any posthumanism whatsoever," by referring Derrida's evocation in *Of Grammatology* of the cybernetic program as a machine-writing to Luhmann's neocybernetic operationalization of concurrent and coevolutionary systems. In Luhmann's coordinated disarticulations of self-referential autopoiesis in biological, psychic, and social systems, their simultaneous semi-autonomies explode and replace the notional unity of the human subject. Derrida's writing-in-general then provides an ahuman infrastructure germane to any and all of them: "once the notion of the program is invoked, one no longer has 'recourse to the concepts that habitually serve to distinguish man from other living beings (instinct and intelligence, absence or presence of speech, of society, of economy, etc. etc.)'" (8).

In sum, systemic posthumanism in Derrida and Luhmann immerses the human once more into the multiplicity of environments constituted by the multiplicity of biotic and metabiotic systems for which the human has always been implicated. Writing itself is immersed into a sea of operational sentience, a welter of autopoietic cognitions, whether these are consciously immediate or socially delayed. Communication itself may be rethought as an emergent evolutionary process shared out wherever social autopoiesis has chanced to happen. It is this neocybernetic form of posthumanist observation that will characterize the micro- and macrocosmic posthumanism of Margulis and Sagan.

* * *

Let us back up and review some of Margulis and Sagan's biographical and collegial contexts. The literary chemistry of this family team may be unprecedented. Over and above its transmission of a singular synthesis of scientific ideas, the literary quality of its science writings is certainly unrivalled. A social and scholarly prodigy born in 1938, Margulis matriculated at the University of Chicago at fifteen. She dated graduate student Carl Sagan at sixteen and married him at nineteen, the year she received Chicago's multidisciplinary undergraduate degree. She then became a scientific prodigy who persevered against academic and disciplinary headwinds through two marriages and four children to establish herself professionally by the turn of the 1970s. Born in 1959 of uncommonly literate world-class scientists, Dorion Sagan took a literature and philosophy major and established himself as a polymath wordsmith with a well-tempered and timely exposure to poststructuralism as well as a cosmopolitan knowledge of scientific matters. Both Margulis and Sagan now have extensive separate publications, but their twenty-five-year-long span of collaborative writing stands out for its unique blend of hard scientific erudition, speculative and theoretical audacity, pugnacious candor, and literary style.

How, then, does one write science for non-scientists in a way that challenges and ultimately subverts the verities of scientific humanism? How does one present what amounts to a posthumanist scientific discourse to a general audience largely unconscious of its inherited humanist assumptions? Margulis and Sagan carry this off by working from a suitably paradigm-shifting scientific vision, conveyed through an astute selection of expository and rhetorical techniques. I begin an analysis of their writing practice with some close readings of a pivotal source and literary model. In *Microcosmos* Margulis and Sagan borrow several techniques at work in the signature text of a biological popularizer who preceded them, *The Lives of a Cell* by Lewis Thomas. In this collection of short articles first published in the *New England Journal of Medicine* in the early 1970s, Thomas was popularizing the new bioscience of, among others, Lynn Margulis, as her seminal work on "serial endosymbiosis theory" (SET) was then coming forward.[7] Her confirmation and reconfiguration of earlier suggestions about the origins of cellular organelles and cytoplasmic (non-nuclear) genes has now rewritten the textbooks on the evolution of the eukaryotic or nucleated cell. In SET, the cilia of eukaryotes originate as spirochetes, mitochondria as purple bacteria, and chloroplasts as cyanobacteria, before being absorbed, one at a time ("serially" over many hundreds of millions of years), into organellar status within evolving iterations of the eukaryotic cell.[8] For his part, Lewis's writings modeled the vivacity possible in popular science writing, and concocted some proto-posthumanist templates for the contemplation of this evolutionary scenario at the microbial level.

For instance, Thomas figures this new understanding of the hybrid nature of the nucleated cell as the dispossession of a prior presumption of human—more precisely, modern Western bourgeois—proprieties: "I was raised in the belief that [organelles] were obscure little engines inside my cells, owned and operated by me or my cellular delegates, private, submicroscopic bits of my intelligent flesh. Now, it appears, some of them, and the most important ones at that, are total strangers. . . . I only hope I can retain title to my nuclei" (82–83). One could call this the "trading places" scenario—here, the owner becomes the owned, the operator the operated. A page later Thomas offers another variation of this tactic of narrative peripeteia or reversal of perspective: "The usual way of looking at [organelles] is as enslaved creatures. . . . This master-slave arrangement is the common view of full-grown biologists, eukaryotes all. But there is the other side. From their own viewpoint . . . I could be taken for a very large, motile colony of respiring bacteria" (84). Margulis and Sagan will develop this shot-countershot technique in their own writings, for the good reason that it yields another way to envision the relinquishing of nominal humanist unity for the posthumanist appreciation of coordinated systemic multiplicities. Not only are we humans (and most other postbacterial organisms) multicellular in composition, but each eukaryotic cell therein is itself multi-genomic, a consortium of differential genomes retaining operational semi-autonomy, as Thomas notes in a particular, "respiring" instance—the oxygen-processing mitochondria that endow the eukaryotic cells of protoctists (e.g., algae), animals, fungi, and plants with their aerobic capacities: "The mitochondria do not arise *de novo* in [eukaryotic] cells; they are always there, replicating on their own, independently of the replication of the cell" (82–83).

Thomas wrote the foreword for *Microcosmos*. In it he revisited these place-trading scenarios. Not so long ago, he writes there, the "general sense was that Nature is a piece of property, an inheritance, owned and operated by mankind. . . . But there is another way to look at us, and this book is the guide for that look" (10). From this unfolds another technique, also worthy of retrospective labeling as a posthumanist trope—pronominal manipulation, a destabilizing of the humanist "we":

"*We* used to believe that *we* arrived *de novo*, set in place by the Management" (11); but then came Darwin, and then came the newer, microbial revelations of Margulis and company: "In evolutionary terms, *we* have only just arrived. . . . The first of *us*, the very first of our line, appeared sometime around 3.5 billion years ago, a single bacterial cell. . . . *We* go back to *it*, of all things. . . . Our microbial forebears . . . are still with *us*, part of *us*. Or, put it another way, *we* are part of *them*" (11; emphasis added). This way of insinuating hereditary continuities through subverting the stability of separate biological identities shows up on occasion in Margulis and Sagan, for instance, in their follow-up volume to *Microcosmos*, What is Life?: "As sheer persistence of biochemistry, '*we*' have never died during the passage of 3,000 million years. . . . *We* have, of course, had to 'up the stakes' at various junctures to stay alive" (81; emphasis added). Here, the insertion and then removal of scare quotes around a first-person plural pronoun whose antecedent is all the life forms that have ever lived, as an evolutionary whole, these pronouns communicate *our*—Life's—communality, the communal status of all past and present living beings.

* * *

Margulis and Sagan's *Microcosmos* carries out a critique of anthropocentric arrogance. It pursues a posthumanistic writing practice, for one instance, in its broad relinquishing of the pretense of scientific certainty as an index of humanity's overcoming of its humble natural origins. Riffing on this refreshing sensibility, Thomas concluded his foreword with the etymology that links *human* and *humble* by way of the Earth deposited in their roots: "It is there like a linguistic fossil, buried in the ancient root from which we take our species' name. The word for earth . . . was *dhghem*. From this word . . . came our word *humus*, the handiwork of soil bacteria. Also, to teach us the lesson, *humble, human*, and *humane*" (12).[9] Note the relative humility with which Margulis and Sagan, at the outset of their narrative, underscore the provisional status of scientific knowledge, especially of matters relating to the eons before life on Earth began. Concerning the origin of the Earth, the representation they give is, in all modesty, "the best picture we have": As with "any other look into what Shakespeare called 'the dim backward and abysm of time,' we must not mistake our best guesses or relatively straight-line extrapolations of present conditions into the past for the literal truth. . . . Nevertheless, such extrapolations yield the best picture we have of the cosmos which preceded the evolution of life in the microcosm" (39–40).[10] Similarly, when they broach the Gaia hypothesis—of which Margulis is the second author, after James Lovelock—they render it in its proper uncertainty.[11] Even before the evolution of the eukaryotic cell, "Microbes by themselves *are thought* to have maintained the mean temperature of the early Earth so that it was hospitable for life. . . . Barring divine intervention and luck, only life itself *seems* powerful enough to have promoted the conditions favoring its own prolonged survival in the face of environmental adversity" (66–67; my italics).

The paperback edition of *Microcosmos* adds to the earlier volume a remarkable preface. It foregrounds, directly after the republication of Thomas's foreword, a self-critique of the rhetorical strategy they likely borrowed from Thomas, role reversal between humanity and the microbes. While that aspect of the main text is left intact—only the notes are revised and updated, the new preface nevertheless indicates as a philosophical desideratum a movement beyond the hierarchical binaries in which either human or nonhuman nature is placed on top of the other. However, audaciously, this self-critique is itself framed by a second self-critique, with a different "we," directed outward toward their fellow humans, launching a straightforward mockery of human pretentions to planetary dominion. Rhetorical indirection now gives way to a blunt rebuttal directly to arguments, scientific and otherwise, that inflate humanity's planetary ego. The bracing opening paragraph of the preface they add to *Microcosmos* reads:

> What is the relationship between humans and Nature? The Linnaean, or scientific, name of our own species in *Homo sapiens sapiens*—"Man, the wise, the wise." But, as a humble proposal or wisecrack, we suggest that humanity be rechristened *Homo insapiens*—"Man, the unwise, the tasteless." We love to think we are Nature's rulers . . . but we are less regal than we imagine. *Microcosmos: Four Billion years of Evolution from Our Microbial Ancestors* (first published in 1986) strips away the gilded clothing that serves as humanity's self-image to reveal that our self-aggrandizing view of ourselves is no more than that of a planetary fool. (13)

This is posthumanist indiscretion of the highest order, a most superb humility. What immediately follows is equally remarkable and, I would wager, unprecedented in a book of popular scientific exposition. Surely coming from Dorion Sagan's side of the collaboration, it is a suggestion regarding the indiscretion of *writing* altogether, with reference to Plato and Socrates, and, although unstated, to the dialogue *Phaedrus*. Margulis and Sagan invoke Socrates for another reason. He was no planetary fool, but had the wisdom to confess his own ignorance: "Through Plato, Socrates speaks of the folly of inscribing one's opinions: although your views may change, your words as committed to paper remain. Socrates at least did not write, and what he knew, first and foremost, was that he did not know. We, however, did write" (14). In the *Phaedrus*, you will recall, Socrates relates the myth of Thoth and the King. The inventor of writing, Thoth offers it as a gift to the King, praising it as a *pharmakon*, a potion with a remedy for forgetfulness. Regarding this drug, the King replies, just say no; while it supplements, it also anesthetizes the memory, and it substitutes for the changeable life of the spoken word a static tissue of dead traces:

> Reversing the usual inflated view of humanity, we wrote of *Homo sapiens* as a kind of latter-day permutation in the ancient and ongoing evolution of the smallest, most ancient, and most chemically versatile inhabitants of the Earth, namely bacteria. . . . Unlike spoken words floating off noncommittally into the fickle winds of opinion, our words as hard symbols on paper sat, as here they sit—obstinately confronting us with dogma and didacticism instead of what otherwise might have been merely a provisional opinion. Happily, though, the occasion of the paperback reprinting of *Microcosmos* offers us an opportunity, if not to rewrite and revise, at least to reflect on the book and its main concerns. (14–15)

Writing is addictive: the only cure for it is more writing. Systems-theoretically, this is just to say that social autopoiesis demands that one communication lead to another, ad infinitum. The parallel to biological autopoiesis is clear: life cannot correct what it has been, it must just keep going and, if it can, as a result, over time, it becomes, not something better, but something else. In Margulis and Sagan's writing practice, what we witness in the preface to *Microcosmos* is a sophisticated self-referential moment, a brief discourse upon their own discourse. It is not a moment of self-correction, since the prior text still stands. It is rather a moment of self-adjustment, announcing a change of strategy. Having taken some initial cues from Lewis Thomas, they applied the trope of reversal at book length to the human/microbe opposition. The process was certainly productive: the book is vibrant, bristling with information and attitude, with certainly no more, likely rather less "dogma and didacticism" than one finds in any comparable popular evolutionary text. However, this rhetorical strategy did tend to squeeze out consideration of the biological middle ground, most every living thing lying between microbes and humanoids. The chapter "Late Bloomers: Animals and Plants" is only one out of thirteen. *What is Life?* adjusts this balance to brilliant effect. The imbalance of *Microcosmos*, relative to the breadth of life altogether, would be, I think, the sole evidence justifying their self-indictment of "overcompensation": "*Microcosmos* approaches . . . large questions from the particular perspective of a planet whose evolution has been largely a bacterial phenomenon. We believe this formerly slighted perspective is a highly useful, even essential compensation required to balance the traditional anthropocentric view which flatters humanity in an unthinking, inappropriate way. Ultimately we may have overcompensated" (18). Perhaps, but in any event, "dogma and didacticism" are what one does *not* want to purvey if the point of the exposition is to reformat a general reader's most basic ideas about humanity's place in the larger scheme of life.

Their self-critique immediately continues with an appearance from Jacques Derrida. One wonders whether "Plato's Pharmacy" is lurking behind the appearance of Socrates and the ironic demotion of writing a few pages earlier. Be that as it may, one just does not expect to encounter Derrida in a trade paperback edition of popular science writing: "In the philosophical practice known as deconstruction, powerful hierarchical oppositions are dismantled in a dual process Jacques Derrida caricatures or characterizes as 'reversal and displacement.' This process is at work in *Microcosmos*: humanity is deconstructed as the traditional hierarchy—recently evolved humans on top, evolutionarily older 'lower' organisms below—is reversed" (18). That a discussion of Derrida and deconstruction occurs here at all brings us back to the considerations of posthumanism with which we began. Is posthumanism to be nothing more than the reversal of a hierarchical opposition starting with the human installed on top, whether it be human/microbe, human/animal, or human/machine? Images of the posthuman often take this more simplistic form. Just as often they evacuate their posthumanist credentials when such narratives climax with restorative reversals of the initial reversal, as the evil machines, or the nefarious aliens, or the mindless killer viruses are vanquished in some spectacular fashion. Nor does mere reversal, the defeat or utter humbling of the human, amount to a robust posthumanism. This is the crux of the deconstructive component of Margulis and Sagan's self-critique: "from the view of deconstructive practice, *Microcosmos*, which reverses the hierarchical opposition, does not take the next step of displacement: man is taken off the top of nature only to be put on the bottom. What ultimately must be called into question is not the position assumed by humans in the opposition Man/Nature but the oppositional distortions imposed by hierarchy itself" (18).

Here, in the movement beyond binary hierarchy, is the crucial adjustment that fully releases Margulis and Sagan's discourse into the second-order posthumanism of *What is Life?* and their other subsequent writings. Philosophically, humanism is contaminated with the hierarchical assumptions that tether it back to the theological mindsets of which *it* is the oppositional reversal. One sees this all too often in (pseudo-)secular science writings, especially of an evolutionary cast, when the qualifiers "higher" and "lower" are applied to life forms. For instance, in her early days, Margulis herself purveyed a humanist rhetoric, presumably absorbed from her standard biological training. Note the hierarchical formulations in this passage from her 1971 *Scientific American* article listed in the references of *The Lives of a Cell*, "Symbiosis and Evolution," compounded by progressivist notions of evolutionary "advance" and "perfection":

> Mitotic cell division was the crucial genetic step toward further evolutionary *advance*. One would not expect it to have developed in a straight-line manner, starting with no mitosis and concluding with *perfect* mitosis. There must have been numerous dead ends, variations and byways. Evidence of just such uncertain gradualism is found today among the *lower* eukaryotes, for example the slime molds, the yellow-green and golden-yellow algae, the euglenids, the slime-net amoebas and others. Many of their mitotic arrangements are unconventional. The *perfection* of mitosis must have occupied as much as a billion years of Precambrian time. (10; emphasis added)

By the time she co-writes *Microcosmos* fifteen years later, Lynn Margulis has sloughed off this sort of conventional science prose and surpassed the evolutionary attitudes it implies. But it remained for the composition of their supplementary preface, and Dorion Sagan's transfusion of philosophical self-awareness into it, to bring out an explicit articulation of the new, virtually posthumanist orientation of their current evolutionary discourse. Let's return to the preface. Margulis and Sagan continue: "Nearly all our predecessors assumed that humans have some immense importance, either material or transcendental. We picture humanity as one among other microbial phenomena, employing *Homo insapiens* as a nickname to remind ourselves to stave off the recurring fantasy that people master (or can master) Gaia. The microbial view is ultimately provisional; there is no absolute dichotomy between humans and bacteria" (18–19).

I want to claim this superb proposition for neocybernetic posthumanism. Just as "there is no absolute dichotomy between humans and bacteria," there is no absolute dichotomy, period. All dichotomies are provisional. This can be restated in the language of systems theory by saying that all dichotomies are self-referential cognitive constructions produced on the inside of observing systems. Thought is not possible without them, without making distinctions from moment to moment, but dichotomies are all relative; they relate to the contingencies of their systemic production. They refer in the first instance to the dichotomizing system, and only then, it may be, to the dichotomized environment. For instance, Margulis and Sagan have just distinguished between a hierarchical and a post-hierarchical philosophy of living things. This meta-dichotomy has the great virtue of rendering fine-grained information about the doctrinal self-awareness as well as the specific doctrines of the writers of this popular science text. On that basis we may grant them epistemological authority on a matter that must appear to many readers as utterly counter-intuitive—the notion that the long unfolding of biological evolution has *not* entailed any "advancement" or "perfection" of species. I know the resistance to this rethinking for a fact from my experience teaching Margulis and Sagan texts in my literature and science classes. Inculcated as they are in conventional humanist attitudes, if not also in theological notions of a creationist and/or moral-perfectionist stripe, many of my students are at first taken aback particularly by those passages in which Margulis and Sagan put into discursive practice what they have just preached in the preface to *Microcosmos* about the surpassing of absolute hierarchical dichotomies. Passages like these:

> From the paramecium to the human race, all life forms are meticulously organized, sophisticated aggregates of evolving microbial life. Far from leaving microorganisms behind on an evolutionary "ladder," we are both surrounded by them and

composed of them. Having survived in an unbroken line from the beginnings of life, all organisms today are equally evolved. (*Microcosmos* 28)

All extant species are equally evolved. All living beings, from bacterial speck to congressional committee member, evolved from the ancient common ancestor which evolved autopoiesis and thus became the first living cell. (*What is Life?* 48)

All beings alive today are equally evolved. All have survived over three thousand million years of evolution from common bacterial ancestors. There are no "higher" beings, no "lower animals," no angels, and no gods. The devil, like Santa Claus, is a useful myth (3). [12]

Each of these radical affirmations of evolutionary equality stresses contemporaneity, the temporal simultaneity of the material biosphere. Cell by cell, from moment to moment, each autopoietic unit of life does or does not maintain itself as a living system. It is not a mere tautology to insist that, as a composite result of each separate but interdependent evolutionary history having brought it to this moment, all life is equally living at that moment. Currently coexisting life is an ongoing self-maintaining achievement in itself. This Gaian vista evacuates any vestiges of a teleological approach to evolutionary processes. By whatever means necessary, "all beings alive today" have managed to continue their lines to this moment: the continued self-maintenance of one's species *is* the measure of an equality of evolutionary outcome. This is the gist of the statement cited from Margulis and Sagan earlier, that "we"—the collective phenomenon of life in the profusion of its evolutionary history—have "had to 'up the stakes' at various junctures to stay alive. This continuous 'upping of the stakes' . . . is on the species level described as evolution. Beings . . . often . . . have to evolve, to change into new forms, simply to self-maintain. . . . Evolution, no less than the nucleic acid replication of autopoiesis and reproduction, is a 'stumbling forward' to stave off the threat of thermodynamic dissolution" (*What is Life?* 81). In other words, regarding evolution, it is not that the *forms* of life get "higher," it is that the *stakes* that life must wager against entropy do. It is this cosmic dynamic that drives the evolution of Gaia altogether into *more complex* individual forms and more complex co-evolutionary arrangements with their environments.

We note here as well Margulis and Sagan's coupling together the logic of evolution with the logic of autopoiesis. This bio-logic must give autopoiesis priority: "To be alive, an entity must first be *autopoietic*—that is, it must actively maintain itself against the mischief of the world. . . . This modulating, 'holistic' phenomenon of autopoiesis, of active self-maintenance, is the basis of all known life" (*Microcosmos* 56). Life must first exist and then maintain its existence in order for there to be something to evolve. When Maturana and Varela, the inventors of the concept of autopoiesis, approach the matter of biological evolution, they develop a relatively passive model of "natural drift" in the structural coupling of organisms and environments over geological time.[13] In contrast, with a boost from the work of Erich Jantsch, Margulis and Sagan inscribe autopoietic self-maintenance into the abiotic dynamics of far-from-equilibrium thermodynamics and the metabiotic cycles of geobiological processes.[14] Theirs is a more compelling description of an autopoietic "impatience" impelling Gaia altogether to "stumble forward" through incessant testings of hereditary variations and recursive inventions of favorable niches, maintaining geobiological momentum against physical inertia.[15] Autopoiesis is rounded out here as the necessary conservation of the self-referential form of metabolic self-production achieved through evolutionary time by structural compensations for the continuous recursive tweakings of life forms by environmental contingencies. Margulis and Sagan encapsulate their fusion of autopoiesis and evolution this way: "Changing to stay the same is the essence of autopoiesis. It applies to the biosphere as well as the cell. Applied to species, it leads to evolution" (*What is Life?* 31).[16]

* * *

I will conclude by inscribing Gaia theory explicitly into the discourse of neocybernetic posthumanism. As we have seen, Margulis and Sagan not only extend an autopoietic approach to evolutionary theory, they also initiate an autopoietic approach to Gaia theory: "The biosphere as a whole is autopoietic in the sense that it maintains itself" (*What is Life?* 20). Insofar as the form of autopoiesis may be generalized to psychic and social systems, this connection suggests a second-order posthumanism addressed to the formal and operational (systems-theoretical) rather than genetic and reproductive (neo-Darwinist, sociobiological) interrelations between geobiology on the one hand and minds and societies on the other. Here is a strong recent comment from Myra Hird's *The Origins of Sociable Life* approaching this theoretical terrain from within feminist science studies: "Gaia theory emphasizes lively biotic/abiotic co-productions that sustain the biosphere. In so doing, it collapses the traditional social scientific distinction between living and nonliving matter. Second, Gaia theory shifts the focus from animals to bacteria. . . . For Gaia theory, studying animals is essentially another way of studying ourselves: humanocentric business-as-usual" (130).

Despite the evident posthumanism of such a statement, however, Hird does not evoke that description for her treatment of relations between the bacterial microcosm and the Gaian macrocosm. So let me briefly summarize the implicit case this article has also been making for Margulis and Sagan's revision of Gaia theory as a form of neocybernetic posthumanism. Gaian science altogether is bound up with Margulis's work, especially as, from the early 1970s onward, she collaborated with Lovelock to infuse her microbiology into his framework of geochemical ideas on planetary self-regulation. As we have also seen, persistently ushering the human off center-stage in the evolutionary drama in order to give the microbes starring roles, Margulis and Sagan's expositions of the microcosmos constitute a posthumanist discourse. They inform us that all bacteria living today, as well as the algae, the fungi, the plants, and the other animals, are equally evolved—as thoroughly honed and culled through eons of natural selection. Gaia theory in its adequate construction confirms this radical evolutionary leveling and couples it to the global environment.

Lovelock has recently redescribed the theory like so: "organisms and their environment form a coupled system . . . *what evolved was this system, the one that we call Gaia.* Organisms and their environment do not evolve separately" (22, emphasis added).[17] Lovelock's reformulation of Gaia's metasystemic coupling in this fashion, whether or not this was his intention, helps to undo the superorganicism that has plagued popular notions of this discourse, as well as a number of Lovelock's own statements. In fact, the Earth is not alive. Gaia is not a living superorganism. These organic metaphors have sidetracked the theory for many observers, and rightly so. It is better systems theory to turn the observation around in order to see that life in any of its forms or in its entirety is also on the same plane as the evolving Earth within which those forms unfold. Ever since the bacteria took over the planet, there has been *a Gaian evolution of the biosphere altogether.* All living and nonliving things within the biosphere—human beings and their vaunted technologies included—are interconnected, and no Earthly system, Gaia included, has any more ultimate control than any other. Moreover, in its neocybernetic redescription, Gaia need assume neither the form of a living system, nor the agency or *anima* of a conscious system, to comprise an *autopoietic* phenomenon—to be a self-referential cognitive system producing self-maintaining regulatory dynamics.

Neocybernetics is the form of systems theory adequate to the thought of an autopoietic planet in which Gaia emerges not as a living being but as an operationally closed, hence autonomous and cognitive, meta-biotic geobiological phenomenon. Margulis and Sagan's adaptations of autopoiesis to Gaia theory bring it to the threshold of such a neocybernetic consideration: "The simplest, smallest known autopoietic entity is a single bacterial cell. The largest is probably Gaia—life and its environment-regulating behavior at the Earth's surface. Cells and Gaia display a general property of autopoietic entities: as their surroundings change unpredictably, they maintain their structural integrity and internal organization, at the expense of solar energy, by remaking and interchanging their parts" (267, 269). In order to develop further, both as a scientific discourse and as a form of posthumanist philosophy, autopoietic Gaia theory could be developed beyond the point to which Lovelock and Margulis have brought it and further reformulated along neocybernetic or second-order systems-theoretical lines.

A common misunderstanding must first be overcome: an autopoietic description of living systems does not undermine the functions of symbiosis and symbiogenesis for Gaian dynamics. In an article drawn from *The Origins of Sociable Life*, as well as in that book, Myra Hird gets tangled in a misapprehension about the "autonomy" produced by autopoietic closure. While she states correctly that "Gaia, for Margulis, is autopoietic insofar as it is a system that produces the components that produce its own organization," her continuation is based on a second-hand grasp of the detail of second-order systems theory drawn from flawed sources: "insofar as autopoiesis stresses the individuated self that creates its own environment, it undermines symbiosis and symbiogenesis, which operate through assemblages proliferated more through contamination and contagion than the interaction of autonomous entities" (61). However, the autopoietic system/environment distinction is not an absolute dichotomy. Autopoiesis produces semi-autonomy in the same sense that a biological membrane is semi-permeable. Autopoietic cognition concerns the capacity of that system, within viable limits, to select what crosses its boundaries. The operational boundedness of autopoietic processes in no way precludes the structural coupling, nor even the operational merger, nor any other environmental interactions of autopoietic systems—as long as autopoiesis is preserved in the host system. To the contrary, as William Irwin Thompson has remarked, striking the right note of cosmic bemusement: "Paradoxically, Varela's thesis that 'Every autonomous system is operationally closed' results, rather whimsically, in a universe of openness. Small disturbances can accumulate, and the cumulative effect is to unfold a world" (119–120).

Precisely as second-order systems theory, autopoietic Gaia theory poses crucial epistemological challenges within and without science proper and offers much-needed reorientations of thinking altogether. The cultural returns one can anticipate from its successful accession to paradigmatic status are profound. Moreover, the lines that connect Gaia theory to neocybernetic discourse can go both ways. It may be that the metabiotic resolution that generalized autopoiesis and so moved it beyond the limitation to biotic specificity can now go back in the biotic direction in order to reconceptualize the forms of life's linkages with its abiotic, non-autopoietic milieu. This implication is also folded up in Margulis and Sagan's insistence on Gaia's autopoietic status. Let me try to unfold it.

Psychic and social systems in the autopoietic description given by Luhmann are metabiotic in that they emerge but also depart from living systems. While they process incommensurably different kinds of elements—events of consciousness on the one hand, events of communication on the other—and are thus operationally autonomous, nevertheless, they couple their autonomous operations together. In other words, the extent of their autonomy is strictly internal to their own operations. Externally, their existence is absolutely contingent upon environments that contain other kinds of systems. Moreover, in humans, both psychic and social systems occupy a shared medium of *meaning* introduced by linguistic functions.[18] Luhmann applies the phrase "meaning systems" to both psychic and social systems with regard to their common material and virtual media. Derrida might add that meaning systems are themselves contingent upon the ahuman exteriority of arche-writing.

Could one adapt to the Gaian instance of this second-order schema of a coupled metabiotic emergence dependent upon an environmental stratum? What that would entail is a confirmation that the biotic realm, as coupled to the abiotic, non-autopoietic world, yields a view of Gaia as a metabiotic autopoietic system that, as Myra Hird nicely puts it, "emphasizes lively biotic/abiotic co-productions that sustain the biosphere."

In which case, the metabiotic emergence of the autopoietic and non-autopoietic (technological) systems specific to minds and societies can then be seen as more recent epiphenomena and recursions of the Archean event some 3.5 billion years ago by which life and its planetary environment gave rise to the metabiotic system called Gaia. In this moment, within the geological environment a quantum mass of abiotic and biogenic elements coupled together with the sum of the bacterial biota to lock in an emergent level of metabiotic self-production, autopoietic Gaia—not as a living system, not as a superorganism, in no way as a spirit of the Earth, but nonetheless as a self-referential system of planetary cognition operating to produce globally regulative processes binding together geological and biological evolution into a whole system. Margulis and Sagan expressed this feedback scheme of biotic/abiotic reciprocation in a Gaian chiasmus given at the end of *Microcosmos*: "On Earth the environment has been made and monitored by life as much as life has been made and influenced by the environment" (265).

Now, is there a medium that binds together the non-autopoietic processes of the physical world—with its atomic valences, chemical bonds, radiant and electromagnetic fields, and dynamical and thermodynamical systems—and of the geological world—with its hydrological processes and oceanic, atmospheric, and meteorological systems—with the autopoietic processes that emerged when life began within the non-autopoietic cosmos? If so, this would be the counterpart to the medium of meaning that provides a formal milieu allowing psychic and social systems to coordinate their respective operations. I think that there is a straightforward answer to this. It names a substance that is, akin to the curiously virtual thing we call meaning, infinitely transformative. You will have anticipated the answer—it is *matter*. The metabiotic autopoiesis of Gaia couples together the material-energetic processes of abiotic systems and the autonomous operations of biotic systems within the physicochemical medium of matter. Just as meaning in incessant motion might be called the spirit of autopoiesis at the human level, matter bound up in the coevolutionary forms of Earthly and living transformations is the spirit of Gaia, when its theory is rendered as a dialect of neocybernetic posthumanism.

Notes

1. A selection of key texts co-authored by Lynn Margulis and Dorion Sagan: *Microcosmos: Four Billion Years of Microbial Evolution* (New York: Summit Books, 1986; Berkeley: University of California Press, 1997); *Origins of Sex: Three Billion Years of Genetic Recombination* (New Haven: Yale UP, 1986); *What Is Life?* (1996; Berkeley: University of California Press, 2000); *Acquiring Genomes: A Theory of the Origins of Species* (New York: Basic Books, 2002); *Dazzle Gradually: Reflections on the Nature of Nature* (White River Junction, VT: Chelsea Green, 2007).

2. See my *Posthuman Metamorphosis: Narrative and Systems* (New York: Fordham UP, 2008); and "Embodied Mediation: Avatar and its Systems," in *ZMK—Zeitschrift für Medien-* under Kulturforschung (2012).

3. For details, see Bruce Clarke and Mark B. N. Hansen, eds., *Emergence and Embodiment: New Essays in Second-Order Systems Theory* (Durham: Duke UP, 2009).

4. See my "The Neocybernetic Posthuman," Posthuman Metamorphosis, pp. 193–96; and Bruce Clarke and Mark B. N. Hansen, "Neocybernetic Emergence: Retuning the Posthuman," *Cybernetics and Human Knowing* 16:1–2 (2009): 83–99.

5. An advanced introduction to the cultural implications of Luhmann's systems theory is Hans-Georg Moeller, *The Radical Luhmann* (New York: Columbia UP, 2012).

6. See Niklas Luhmann, "How Can the Mind Participate in Communication?" in *Theories of Distinction: Redescribing the Descriptions of Modernity*, ed. William Rasch (Stanford: Stanford UP, 2002), pp. 169–84.

7. Thomas's references in The Lives of a Cell list two texts by Margulis, *The Origin of Eukaryotic Cells* (New Haven: Yale UP, 1970), and "Symbiosis and Evolution," *Scientific American* 225:2 (1971): 48–57.

8. Margulis continues to explore vectors of symbiogenesis—the evolutionary merger of separately evolved genomes into viable cellular consortia lifting their instructions for various metabolic capacities into higher-order syntheses. See in particular Margulis and Sagan, *Acquiring Genomes*; and Lynn Margulis, Celeste A. Asikainen, and Wolfgang E. Krumbein, eds., *Chimeras and Consciousness: Evolution of the Sensory Self* (Cambridge: MIT Press, 2011).

9. Late in life Lewis published *Et Cetera, Et Cetera: Notes of a Word-Watcher* (New York: Little, Brown, 1990). Despite the charm of his philological investigations, as an old-school archeologist of linguistic fossils trying on some new-fangled sociobiology, on the topic of language Lewis reverts to a classical humanist outlook. While registering unease at the thought that this is the "single" differentiating feature left in the arsenal of humanist separatism, led astray by Noam Chomsky's biologized linguistics, Lewis writes in *The Lives of a Cell*: "It begins to look, more and more disturbingly, as if the gift of language

is the single human trait that marks us all genetically, setting us apart from all the rest of life" (105). This notion runs counter to the proto-posthumanism otherwise abroad in his properly biological musings, where the key concepts of "society" and "communication" allow Thomas to connect human matters to other living things and their other ways of life. Cary Wolfe provides a formidable philosophical and systems-theoretical critique of the "language makes humans unique" myth in "In the Shadow of Wittgenstein's Lion: Language, Ethics, and the Question of the Animal," *Animal Rites: American Culture, the Discourse of Species, and Posthumanist Theory* (Chicago: University of Chicago Press, 2003), pp. 44–94.

10. This and all subsequent quotations from *Microcosmos* are taken from the revised edition: Lynn Margulis and Dorion Sagan, *Microcosmos: Four Billion Years of Microbial Evolution* (Berkeley: University of California Press, 1997).

11. See for instance Lynn Margulis and James E. Lovelock, "The Atmosphere as Circulatory System of the Biosphere—The Gaia Hypothesis," *CoEvolution Quarterly* 6 (Summer 1975): 31–40; republished in Margulis and Sagan, *Dazzle Gradually*, pp. 157–71.

12. This quote indicates how Margulis, when doing general or "philosophical" writing on her own, as a memoirist without Dorion Sagan as co-author, is rather more blunt and digressive.

13. See "The Natural Drift of Living Beings," in Humberto Maturana and Francisco Varela.

14. See Jantsch, especially the section "Gaia," pp. 115–20.

15. Margulis and Sagan write autopoiesis into their origin-of-life scenario: "Autopoiesis is what happens when a self-bounded chemical system . . . reaches a crucial point and never stops metabolizing. . . . Autopoiesis [is] the chemical basis for the impatience of living beings" (*What Is Life?* 77–78).

16. A good overview of autopoiesis in light of contemporary bioscience is Pier Luigi Luisi, "Autopoiesis: The Logic of Cellular Life," in *The Emergence of Life: From Chemical Origins to Synthetic Biology* (Cambridge: Cambridge UP, 2006), pp.155–81.

17. See also my "Neocybernetics of Gaia: The Emergence of Second-Order Gaia Theory," in Gaia in Turmoil, eds. Crist and Rinker, pp. 293–314.

18. See the chapter "Meaning" in *Luhmann, Social Systems*, trans. John Bednarz, Jr. with Dirk Baecker (Stanford: Stanford UP, 1995), pp. 59–102.

Works Cited

Dawkins, Richard. *The Selfish Gene*. Oxford: Oxford UP, 1976. Print.

Derrida, Jacques. "Plato's Pharmacy." *Dissemination*. Trans. Barbara Johnson. Chicago: U of Chicago P, 1981. 63–169. Print.

Haraway, Donna J. "A Cyborg Manifesto: Science, Technology, and Socialist-Feminism in the Late Twentieth Century." *Simians, Cyborgs, and Women: The Reinvention of Nature*. New York: Routledge, 1991. 149–81. Print.
Hird, Myra J. "Microontologies of Environment." *The Origins of Sociable Life: Evolution After Science Studies*. Houndmills, Basingstoke: Palgrave Macmillan, 2009. 130. Print.
—. "Indifferent Globality: Gaia, Symbiosis and 'Other Worldliness.'" *Theory, Culture & Society* 27.2–3 (2010): 54–72. Print.
Jantsch, Erich. *The Self-Organizing Universe: Scientific and Human Implications of the Emerging Paradigm of Evolution*. New York: Pergamon P, 1980. Print.
Lovelock, James. "Our Sustainable Retreat." *Gaia in Turmoil: Climate Change, Biodepletion, and Earth Ethics in an Age of Crisis*. Ed. Eileen Crist and H. Bruce Rinker. Cambridge: MIT P, 2009. 21–24. Print.
Margulis, Lynn and Dorion Sagan. *Microcosmos: Four Billion Years of Microbial Evolution*. Berkeley: U of California P, 1997. Print.
—. *What Is Life?* Berkeley: U of California P, 2000. Print.
Margulis, Lynn. *Symbiotic Planet: A New Look at Evolution*. New York: Basic Books, 1998. Print.
—. "Big Trouble in Biology: Physiological Autopoiesis versus Mechanistic Neo-Darwinism." Margulis and Sagan, *Slanted*. 265–82. Print.
Margulis, Lynn, and Dorion Sagan, eds. *Slanted Truths: Essays on Gaia, Symbiosis, and Evolution*. New York: Springer-Verlag, 1997. Print.
—. *Microcosmos: Four Billion Years of Evolution from Our Microbial Ancestors*. Berkeley: U of California P, 1986.
Maturana, Humberto, and Francisco Varela. "The Natural Drift of Living Beings." *The Tree of Knowledge: The Biological Roots of Human Understanding*. 2nd ed. Boston: Shambhala, 1992. 93–117. Print.
Thomas, Lewis. *The Lives of a Cell: Notes of a Biology Watcher*. New York: Bantam, 1974. Print.
—. "Foreword." Margulis and Sagan, *Microcosmos*. 1986. Print.
Thompson, William Irwin. *Imaginary Landscape: Making Worlds of Myth and Science*. New York: St. Martin's P, 1989. Print
Wolfe, Cary. *What Is Posthumanism?* Minneapolis: U of Minnesota P, 2010. Print.
—."Meaning as Event-Machine, or, Systems Theory and 'The Reconstruction of Deconstruction': Derrida and Luhmann." *Emergence and Embodiment: New Essays on Second-Order Systems*. Ed. Bruce Clarke and Mark B. Hansen. Durham: Duke UP. 2009. 220-45. Print.

Contributors

Michelle Ballif is Associate Professor of English at the University of Georgia, where she teaches courses in rhetoric, composition, and contemporary literary and cultural theory. Her current research focuses on the intersections between classical rhetoric and continental theory and its implications for historiography. She is the author of *Seduction, Sophistry, and the Woman with the Rhetorical Figure* and co-author of *Women's Ways of Making It in Rhetoric and Composition*. She has edited several volumes on the history and historiography of rhetoric, including *Theorizing Histories of Rhetoric*.

Kate Birdsall is Assistant Professor of Rhetoric, Writing, & American Cultures at Michigan State University. Her research centers on discourses of race, class, gender, sexuality, and health, and on how those things are defined in popular media. Her most recent work investigates the precarious balance, as it is represented in popular culture, between hero and villain, crimefighter and criminal. Her second in a series of detective novels is also in the works.

Bruce Clarke is the Paul Whitfield Horn Professor of Literature and Science and chair of the Department of English at Texas Tech University. His research focuses on nineteenth and twentieth century literature and science, with special interests in systems theory, narrative theory, and ecology. He edits the book series *Meaning Systems*, published by Fordham University Press. In 2010–2011 he was Senior Fellow at the International Research Institute for Cultural Technologies and Media Philosophy, Bauhaus-University Weimar. His latest book is *Neocybernetics and Narrative* (Minnesota, 2014). His current book project is *Systems Countercultures*, a cultural history of the American locations and transnational authors of the systems discourses gathered in the *Whole Earth Catalog* and *CoEvolution Quarterly*.

Diane Davis is Professor of Rhetoric & Writing and English at the University of Texas at Austin, and she holds the Kenneth Burke Chair at the European Graduate School in Saas-Fee, Switzerland. Davis is the author of *Breaking Up [at] Totality: A Rhetoric of Laughter* (2000) and *Inessential Solidarity: Rhetoric and Foreigner Relations* (2010), coauthor of *Women's Ways of Making It in Rhetoric and Composition* (2008), and editor of *Reading Ronell* (2009) and *The UberReader: Selected Works of Avital Ronell* (2008).

Sid Dobrin is Professor of English and Director/Editor of the TRACE Innovation Initiative at the University of Florida. He is author and editor of many books and articles, including *Gone. Fishing. Recreational Saltwater Sportfishing and the Future of the World's Oceans* (forthcoming, Texas A&M University Press).

Julie Drew is Professor of English at The University of Akron, where she teaches writing, cultural studies, and film. Her recent publications include *Sound-bite Saboteurs: Public Discourse, Education, and the State of Democratic Deliberation* (2010 from SUNY Press), and *Daughter of Providence* (2011, a novel from Overlook Press). Drew's research interests include discourse analysis, narrative theory, argumentation, feminisms and identity theory, and the politics of education.

Kristie S. Fleckenstein is Professor of English at Florida State University where she teaches graduate and undergraduate courses in rhetoric and composition. Her research interests include feminism and race, especially as both intersect with material and visual rhetorics. She has published in a variety of venues, including *College English, College Composition and Communication, Rhetoric Review, Computers and Composition*, and *JAC*. She is the recipient of the 2005 CCCC Outstanding Book of the Year Award for *Embodied Literacies: Imageword and a Poetics of Teaching* (SIUP, 2003), and the 2009 W. Ross Winterowd Award for Best Book in Composition Theory for *Vision, Rhetoric, and Social Action in the Composition Classroom* (SIUP, 2009). Her current project explores photography as a resource for visual rhetoric in nineteenth-century debates about racial identities.

Kyle Jensen is an assistant professor of English at the University of North Texas. His book *Reimagining Process: Online Writing Archives and the Future of Writing Studies* is forthcoming with Southern Illinois

University Press. He has also published essays in *JAC* and *Rhetoric Review*.

Melissa M. Littlefield is an associate professor at the University of Illinois, Urbana-Champaign where she has appointments in the Department of English and the Department of Kinesiology and Community Health. She is affiliated with the Writing Studies Program and the Beckman Institute for Advanced Science and Technology. Her work can be found in *Science, Technology & Human Values*; *Advances in Medical Sociology*; *Frontiers in Human Neuroscience*; *Social Studies of Science*; and *Crime, Media Culture*. Her book, *The Lying Brain: Lie Detection in Science and Science Fiction* (University of Michigan Press, 2011) is a socio-cultural history of mechanical lie detection and its relationship to the emergent, neuroscientific research on the neural correlates of deception. She is also the co-editor (with Jenell Johnson) of *The Neuroscientific Turn: Transdisciplinarity in the Age of the Brain* (University of Michigan Press, 2012).

Andrew Mara is currently an Associate Professor and the Director of Upper-Division Writing at North Dakota State University. He specializes in Rhetoric, New Media and Writing Studies, and takes a community-centered approach to all aspects of his university career. Dr. Mara's teaching and research focuses upon innovation, and investigates the convergence of writing and institutional design. Dr. Mara has co-edited a special issue on posthumanism for *Technical Communications Quarterly*, and has published in *Technical Communications Quarterly*, the *Journal of Business and Technical Communication*, *IEEE Transactions in Professional Communication*, *Academe*, *Innovative Higher Education* as well as several essays for collections. He has founded and co-founded a number of organizations, including the Communication Technology Think Tank (CT3), ND State UX, and the Art Marathon.

Sean Morey is an Assistant Professor of Rhetoric and Professional Communication at Clemson University, where he teaches writing and digital media in the Department of English. His research focuses on developing theories of writing at the intersections of rhetoric, new media, and technology, primarily through the lens of electracy. He is the author of *The New Media Writer* (Fountainhead Press, 2014) and co-edited the collection *Ecosee: Image, Rhetoric, Nature* (SUNY Press, 2009).

J. A. Rice is an assistant professor of English at Western Kentucky University. His research focuses on writing and pedagogical theory, and has appeared in numerous scholarly journals, including *Composition Forum*, *IEEE Transactions on Professional Communication*, and *Educational Theory and Philosophy*. With Sidney I. Dobrin and Michael Vastola , he is editor of *Beyond Postprocess* (USUP, 2011)."

Jim Ridolfo (Ph.D 2009, Michigan State University) is assistant professor of writing, rhetoric, and digital studies at the University of Kentucky and associate researcher at Matrix, the Center for Digital Humanities and Social Sciences at Michigan State University. His work focuses on the intersection of rhetorical theory and digital technology, and his work has appeared in *College English, Ariadne, Journal of Community Informatics, JAC, Enculturation, Journal of Community Literacy Studies, Pedagogy, Kairos, Rhetoric Review*, and edited collections. He also maintains http://rhetmap.org.

Lynn Worsham is now an independent scholar living and working in Buffalo, New York. After three decades of successful teaching at several public universities, she decided in 2013 to devote herself full-time to writing and research. Her research has focused on the relationship been emotion, violence, and representation. She views her more recent interest in the human-animal relation as a natural and necessary outgrowth of this enduring interest in the way violence shapes our affective lives. She is also editor of *JAC*, a journal publishing interdisciplinary scholarship on rhetoric, culture, and politics.

Index

Adorno, Theodor, 103
Aesop, 133, 151, 153
AIDS, 208
Alberti, Leon Battista, 258, 264, 273
Allman, William, 42, 51
Almy, Gladys, 226, 231
Anderson, Chris, 54, 144–146, 153, 191
Angerer, Marie-Luise, 99, 129
animal, 3, 9,–11, 19, 23, 24, 51–52, 53–54, 56, 64–68, 75, 77, 78, 86–87, 96, 101, 117, 128, 130, 178, 296
animal studies, 9, 19–21, 23, 35, 39, 42–43
Appadurai, Arjun, 38, 48, 51
Argentina, 209, 211
Aristotle, 89, 96, 120, 272, 273
Arnold, Matthew, 132, 161
artificial intelligence, 110, 127
authenticity, 16, 108, 241–247
Avatar, 143, 152, 154, 276, 295

Badiou, Alain, 169, 172
Baldi, Camillo, 217
Ball, Hugo, 240
Ballif, Michele, 11, 74, 79, 80, 95–96
Barash, David, 34, 51
Barnard, Ian, 165, 172
Barthes, Roland, 135
Battista, Leon, 258, 273
Bawarshi, Anis, 163–164, 172

Bayesian filtering, 245
Beaulieu, Anne, 224, 228, 231
Bender, Walter, 206, 209, 211
Bennett, Jane, 99, 100, 129
Bentham, Jeremy, 39
Benveniste, Émile, 102, 119, 129
Beyerstein, Barry L., 222–223, 230–231, 233
Binet, Alfred, 217
biotechnology, 4
Birnbaum, Daniel, 92– 93, 96
Blanchot, Maurice, 80, 88, 90, 96– 97
Bogost, Ian, 204, 211
Boyle, Robert, 259
Brooke, Collin, 6, 18, 157, 172
Brooke, Colling Gifford, 6, 18, 157, 172
Brown Daily Herald, 183, 191
Brown University, 191
Bunker, M.N., 217
Burke, Kenneth, 30–31, 46, 51, 95–96, 108, 130, 161–162, 164, 166, 172, 252
Burke, Timothy, 107
Bush, George W., 63, 249
Butler, Judith, 12, 46, 52, 100, 102, 106, 108, 117, 126, 128, 130
Butler, Paul, 158, 160, 173

Caminhas, Walmir M., 244, 245, 252
Caprica, 110, 116, 127, 130

303

Cartwright, Lisa, 225, 231
Cascio, Jamais, 85
Cavell, Stanley, 28, 52
Chemero, Anthony, 136, 153
Cicero, 159, 160, 161, 162, 170, 173, 175, 272, 273
Clark, Andy, 3, 18, 128, 130
Clarke, Bruce, 17, 217, 231, 275, 295, 297
Coca Cola, 181, 182, 184, 185, 187, 188
Coetzee, J.M., 27–30, 36, 41, 47, 48, 52, 54
Colbert Report, The, 56
Colbert, Stephen, 56, 57, 68, 74
Cole, Thomas, 82, 96
complexity, 3, 8, 13, 16, 68, 83, 108, 174, 193, 194, 196, 198, 205, 235, 238, 240–242, 244, 247, 263, 264
Connors, Robert, 175, 176, 189
Continental Philosophy, 96, 248
Controlling the Assault of Non-Solicited Pornography and Marketing Act (CAN-SPAM Act), 237
Cooper, Marilyn M., 269, 271, 273
Corbett, Edward, 174, 175, 189
Costello, Elizabeth, 27–30, 35, 41, 48
Couric, Katie, 107, 130
Crépieux-Jamin, 217
Critchley, Simon, 94, 96
Critical Software Studies, 248
Crumbaugh, James, 218, 231
Cuban, Larry, 202, 211
cybernetics, 3, 11, 100, 105, 118, 125, 128, 152, 193, 276–277
cyborg, 6, 11, 16, 115, 116, 128, 136, 151, 254–256, 266, 269, 270, 271, 276

Dadas, Caroline, 177, 190
Darwin, Charles, 263, 283

Dawkins, Richard, 275, 296
de Waal, Frans, 56, 57, 61, 68, 74
deflection, 10, 28, 29, 30, 31, 32, 33, 35, 36, 40, 41, 44, 45, 49, 50
Deleuze, Gilles, 7, 18, 106, 109–112, 124, 130, 140, 142, 143, 146, 149, 153, 170, 173, 195, 211
Delicious, 157, 172
Democratic Republic of Congo, 70
Derrida, Jacues, 11, 12, 19, 23, 26, 35, 36, 40, 41, 46, 47, 49, 52, 64–68, 75, 77, 79, 80, 81, 86, 87, 89, 91, 93–98, 101, 102, 117, 118, 125, 128, 130, 168, 170, 173, 279, 280, 286, 293, 296, 297
Descartes, René, 57, 66, 259, 262, 263, 272–274
Dewdny, Christopher, 4
Diamond, Cora, 26–30, 39, 41, 46, 49, 52
Dickey, Jack, 107, 108, 130
Didur, Jill, 5, 18
Dobrin, Sidney I., 3, 82, 83, 95, 97, 171–173, 178, 187, 189, 267–269, 273
Dodge, Martin, 201, 202, 212
Dotov, Dobromir G., 136, 153
Downey, June, 220, 221, 225, 231
Drew, Julie, 11, 99
Drezner, Daniel W., 79, 97
Dubisar, Abby M., 177, 187, 189
Dumit, Joe, 214, 225, 228, 230, 232

ecocomposition, 267
ecology, 143, 196, 210, 266, 268, 270
Edelman, Gerald, 257, 262–269, 272, 273
Edwards, Maurice, 218
Ehrenreich, Barbara, 37, 38, 40, 48, 52

Einstein, Albert, 115, 120, 122
Elmer, Gregg, 249, 251
embeddedness, 16, 229, 230, 255, 257, 262, 264–268, 270
embodiment, 11, 16, 21, 42, 44, 100, 103, 118, 151, 229, 255, 257, 259, 262–267, 270, 273
Embry, Karen, 81, 82, 95, 98

false witness, 32–35, 37, 38, 40, 41, 43, 46
Fleckenstien, Kristie S., 16, 254
Fogarty, Mignon, 159, 162, 173
Fortune, Ron, 247, 253
Foucault, Michel, 12, 16, 108, 111, 114, 125, 126, 128, 130, 241–244, 250, 251
French, Norman, 137, 169, 214, 217, 218, 260, 274
Freud, Sigmund, 77, 84, 85, 91, 97, 102, 173
Fukuyama, Francis, 4, 18, 232
Fuller, Matthew, 247, 251
Fynsk, Christopher, 57, 77

Gaia, 275, 284, 288–294, 296, 297
General Theory of Relativity, 120, 122
Georgia State University Language Research Center, 69
Gilligan, James, 34, 52
Girard, René, 33, 43, 46, 53
Goffey, Andrew, 247, 251
Google, 104, 106, 107, 126, 145, 152, 208, 209, 249
Google Glasses, 104
graphology, 14, 214–223, 225–230
Great Ape Trust, 68–70, 76, 77
Greco, Michael A., 155
Greene, Richard, 79, 97
Greystone, Zoe, 110

Guattari, Félix, 7, 18, 106, 109–112, 124, 130, 140, 142, 143, 146, 149, 153
Gunkle, David J., 7
Gunn, Joshua, 82, 95, 97
Guzella, Thiago S., 242, 244, 245, 252

Hall, Stuart, 53, 100, 101, 131
Haraway,, 53, 130, 232, 274, 297
Harman, Graham, 195, 205, 211
Harold, Christina L., 7, 18, 97
Harries, Karsten, 259, 274
Hart-Davidson, Bill, 195, 198, 211
Hawhee, Debra, 6, 18, 248, 252
Hawk, Byron, 7, 8, 14, 18, 192
Hawking, Stephen, 120–122, 129–131
Hayles, N. Katherine, 4, 8, 11, 18, 44, 53, 83, 97, 101, 102, 104, 108, 111, 112, 118, 119, 122, 127, 131, 133, 151, 153, 174, 178, 190, 215, 228, 229, 232
Hegel, Georg Wilhelm Friedrich, 91
Heidegger, Martin, 57, 61–62, 65–66, 75, 77, 136, 211
Heisenberg Uncertainty Principle, 121
Helsley, Sheri, 176, 190
Herman, Judith, 10, 32, 40–42, 46, 49, 53
Hird, Myra, 290–293, 297
Hobbes, Thomas, 196
Horkheimer, Max, 103
Horner, Winifred, 175
Horowitz, David, 183
Howard, Rebecca Moore, 247, 252
Hutcheon, Linda, 109, 131
Huyssen, Andreas, 105

Ika, 72, 73
informatics, 3, 4, 229

Ingmanson, Ellen J., 70–74, 76–77
Internet Chat Relay (IRC), 238
Ivins, William M., 258, 259, 274

JAC: A Journal of Rhetoric and Culture, 6, 18, 51, 55, 78, 191, 253, 274
Jacoby, H.J., 216, 217
Jameson, Fredric, 112–115, 123, 124–125, 128, 131
Janet, Pierre, 217
Jantsch, Erich, 290, 296, 297
Jarry, Alfred, 146–149, 153
Jay, Martin, 10, 22, 52, 53, 259, 274
Jensen, Kyle, 15, 234
Johnson, Jennel, 14, 68, 77, 96, 97, 223, 230, 232, 248, 252, 296
Journal of Applied Psychology, 220
Joyce, Kelly, 225, 228, 232

kairos, 7, 162, 193
Kant, Immanuel, 57, 66
Kanzi, 69, 75, 76, 78
Katonoda, Kota, 227
Kazaleh-Sirdenis, Triana, 182, 190
Kearney, Richard, 85, 87, 97
Kekua, Lennay, 106–108
Kenya, 205, 207
Kitchin, Rob, 201, 202, 212
Klee, Paul, 140, 141, 143, 151
Krell, David Farrell, 93, 98
Kristeva, Julia, 31, 49, 53, 83, 85, 98
Kurtz, Sheila, 219

Lacan, Jacques, 57, 63–66, 70, 76, 77, 91, 101, 102, 105, 142, 143
Lanham, Richard, 160, 161, 162, 173
Lapi, Francesco, 137

Latour, Bruno, 174, 178, 193, 195–198, 205– 208, 210–212, 241, 252
Lauro, Sarah Juliet, 79, 81, 82, 95, 98
Law, John, 54, 195, 197, 198, 210, 212, 233, 272, 274
Levinas, Emmanuel, 57, 66, 74, 77
Levitt, Irene B., 226, 232
Lifton, Robert Jay, 10, 22, 32–34, 39, 41, 44, 46, 52, 53
LimeWire, 187, 188
Lindgren, Chris, 14, 192
Lipton, Judith, 34, 51
Littlefield, Melissa M., 14, 214, 223– 225, 230, 232
LOGO, 199, 203, 206
Lovelock, James, 284, 291, 292, 296, 297
Luhmann, Niklas, 235, 250–252, 277–280, 293, 295–297
Lyotard, Jean-François, 80, 98, 105, 125

Maingot, Dr., 214
Malaysia, 205
Mara, Andrew, 14, 192
Marey, Étienne Jules, 225
Margulis, Lynn, 17, 275, 277, 280–283, 285, 287, 288–297
Matada, 69
Matrix, The, 12, 134, 173
maturana, Humberto, 277, 290, 296, 297
McLuhan, Marshall, 133, 150, 153
McWilliams, Brian, 237
Melville, Herman, 243
Merleau-Ponty, Maurice, 178, 190, 272, 274
Meyer, Jerome, 226, 233
Michigan Daily, The, 181, 189
Michigan State University, 182, 189, 190
Michon, Abbé Jean-Hippolyte, 217

Microsoft, 202, 207
Miller, Carolyn, 165, 173, 193, 210, 212
Miller, Susan, 165, 173, 193, 210, 212
Modern Language Association, 173, 253, 274
Mohammad, K. Silem, 79, 97
Mon, 71–73
Moret, Sean, 12, 13, 133
Mori, Masahiro, 84
Morton, Timothy, 100, 131
Muckelbauer, John, 6, 18

Nancy, Jean-Luc, 57–61, 67, 70, 74, 77, 130, 185, 191
Negroponte, 14, 104, 192–194, 198–213
Negroponte, Nicholas, 14, 104, 192–194, 198–213
neocybernetics, 278
neuroscience, 14, 215, 216, 221–225, 227, 230
New School for Social Research, 218
New York Times, 19, 23, 40, 53, 54, 77, 107, 127, 153, 214, 219, 222, 226, 231–233
Newton, Isaac, 120, 226, 231
Nie, Lin, 136, 153
Nietzsche, Friedrich, 7, 18, 80, 90, 98, 126, 132, 168, 173
Niles-Kraft, Stuart, 183, 190
non-human, 3, 5, 13, 15, 174, 178–180, 182, 186–188, 235, 236, 240, 242, 244
Notre Dame, 106, 107
Nussbaum, Martha, 25, 46, 54

Olsson, Anders, 92, 93, 96
One Laptop Per Child (OLPC), 14, 192
Ong, Walter J., 260, 274

Palmeri, Jason, 177, 187–189
Panbanisha, 69, 70, 76
Papert, Seymour, 199–201, 206, 212
Parikka, Jussi, 234, 240, 242, 251, 252
Pariser, Eli, 249, 253
Pennely, Joel, 177
physiognomy, 214, 223
Piaget, Jean, 200
Pickersgill, Martyn, 214, 231, 233
pigeons, 178–180, 188
Pinker, Steven, 22, 44, 54
Plato, 11, 88, 89, 98, 285, 286, 296
Pophal, Rudolf, 222, 233
Popular Science, 215, 231
Porter, James, 176–178, 187–189, 191
Powell, Colin, 197
Preyer, Wilhelm, 217, 222, 230, 233
Prometheus, 89, 231, 233
Pullman, George, 196, 198, 212
Python script, 206

Ramist rhetoric, 16, 255–257, 260, 262
Ramus, Peter, 260, 261, 272, 274
Rawsthorn, Alice, 138, 139, 153
Renaissance perspectivalism, 16, 255–257
Reynolds, John, 175, 176, 189–191
Reznikoff, Charles, 268
Rhetoric and Composition Studies, 248
rhetorical velocity, 187
Rice, J.A., 13, 155, 172, 220
Rice, Louise, 13, 155, 172, 220
Rickert, Thomas, 157, 172
Ridolfo, Jim, 13, 174, 176–178, 181, 187, 188, 191

308 *Index*

Rife, Martine, 176–178, 185, 187, 191
Robillard, Amy, 247, 253
Ronell, Avital, 60, 75, 78
Rose, Nikolas, 214, 233
Rosenblatt, Louise, 267, 274
Rude, Carolyn, 176–178, 188, 191
Ruthven, K.K., 242, 244, 253

Sagan, Dorion, 17, 275, 277, 280–297
San Francisco Gate, 179
Sanskrit, 143, 153
Sartre, Jean-Paul, 62
Savage-Rumbaugh, Sue, 69, 70, 72, 75, 76, 78
Schiavo, Terry, 82
Schryen, Guido, 237, 244, 251, 253
Schulman, Nev, 107, 130
Second Life, 144
Segerdahl, Pär, 69, 78
Sehgal, Tino, 140
sentience, 277, 280
Shakespeare, William, 243, 283
Shermann, Rafael, 222
Simon, Bart, 4, 5, 18, 51, 52, 94, 96, 132, 233
Singer, Peter, 28, 47
Smith, Daniel W., 155
Smith, Sidonie, 100
Soar, Daniel, 146, 149, 153
Sociology, 232, 248
Socrates, 160, 173, 285, 286
SPAM, 15, 252
Spinks, Lee, 155, 156, 166, 167, 169, 173
Stabile, Giorgio, 137, 153
State News, The, 182, 184, 188, 189
Sterelny, Kim, 37, 48, 54
Style, 13, 155, 156, 158–165, 169, 173, 212
Sully, Jake, 276

Syverson, Margaret, 267–269, 273, 274
techné, 89

TED Talks, 14, 70, 78, 192, 193, 200, 201, 208, 212
Terminator, 277
Thaxter, Sandra, 208, 212
Thomas, Lewis, 77, 82, 96, 130, 157, 172, 273, 281–285, 295–297
Thompson, Clive, 242
Thompson, William Irwin, 293
Thornton, Tamara Plakins, 218, 220, 233
Time Magazine, 180, 189
Tomlinson, Raymond, 138, 139, 146, 173
transactivity, 16, 255, 257, 262, 264–270
transhuman, 6, 17, 80, 85
trauma, 10, 23, 32–34, 37–42, 46, 48, 49
Treat, Shaun, 82, 97
Trimbur, John, 176–178, 191
trivium, 261
Tuiasosopo, Ronaiah, 107
Turing test, 242
Turkle, Sherry, 99, 132
Turtle Blocks, 206, 211
Twitter, 107, 138, 140, 142, 144, 149, 152, 153, 177, 188
Tyack, David, 202, 211
Tzara, Tristan, 240

Ullman, Berthold Louis, 137, 153
Ulmer, Gregory, 8, 18, 142, 143, 148, 150, 154
Uncanny Valley, 84–86, 88
United Nations Social Innovation Summit, 209
United Students Against Sweatshops (USAS), 181

University of Chicago, 232, 281, 296
University of Michigan, 181, 182, 186, 189, 232
University of Wyoming, 220
Uruguay, 206, 208, 209, 211

Vampire, 81
van Dijk, Jose, 225
Varela, Francisco, 277, 290, 293, 296, 297
Vasquez, President Tabaré, 208
Vee, Anette, 203, 212
Verma, Neil, 150, 151, 154
victimage, 30, 32, 43, 46
Vidal, Fernando, 216, 224, 233
von Foerster, Heinz, 277

Waldby, Catherine, 5
Warshcauer, Mark, 206
Washington Law Journal, 219
Watson, Julia, 100
Waugh, Patricia, 109, 132
Weibel, Peter, 196, 197, 212
Weisser, Christian R., 267–269, 273
Welch, Nancy, 176, 177, 185, 187, 191

White House, the, 249
Whitlock, Gillian, 100, 132
Whitman, Walt, 99, 132
Williams, Joseph M., 159
Williams, Raymond, 100
Wilson, Elizabeth, 44, 52, 224, 233
Wired, 153, 237, 250, 252, 253
Wittig, Monique, 100, 106, 126, 128, 132
Wolfe, Cary, 20, 21, 25, 42, 44, 47, 54, 151, 154, 229, 233, 235, 250, 253, 279, 280, 296, 297
Wood, David, 23–26, 36, 42, 46–49, 54
Worsham, Lynn, 9, 10, 19, 21, 55, 156, 157, 165, 167, 169, 172, 173, 234
Writing Studies, 9, 15, 17, 247, 248, 249, 250, 252
Wyschogrod, Edith, 8, 18
Yahoo!, 152, 242
YouTube, 76, 77, 187, 188, 199
Zombie, 11, 79–93, 95–98

www.ingramcontent.com/pod-product-compliance
Lightning Source LLC
Chambersburg PA
CBHW030523230426
43665CB00010B/747